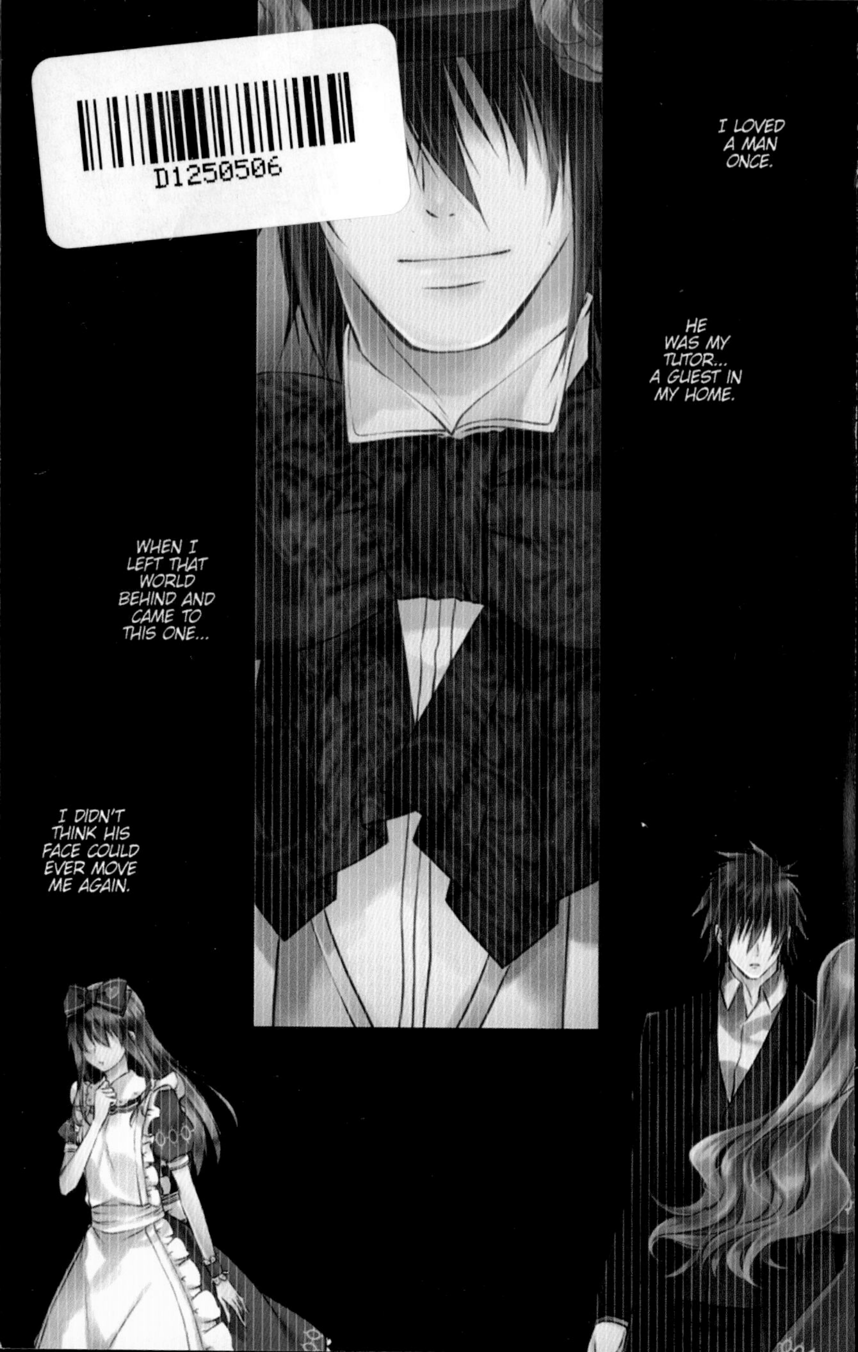
I LOVED A MAN ONCE.
HE WAS MY TUTOR... A GUEST IN MY HOME.
WHEN I LEFT THAT WORLD BEHIND AND CAME TO THIS ONE...
I DIDN'T THINK HIS FACE COULD EVER MOVE ME AGAIN.

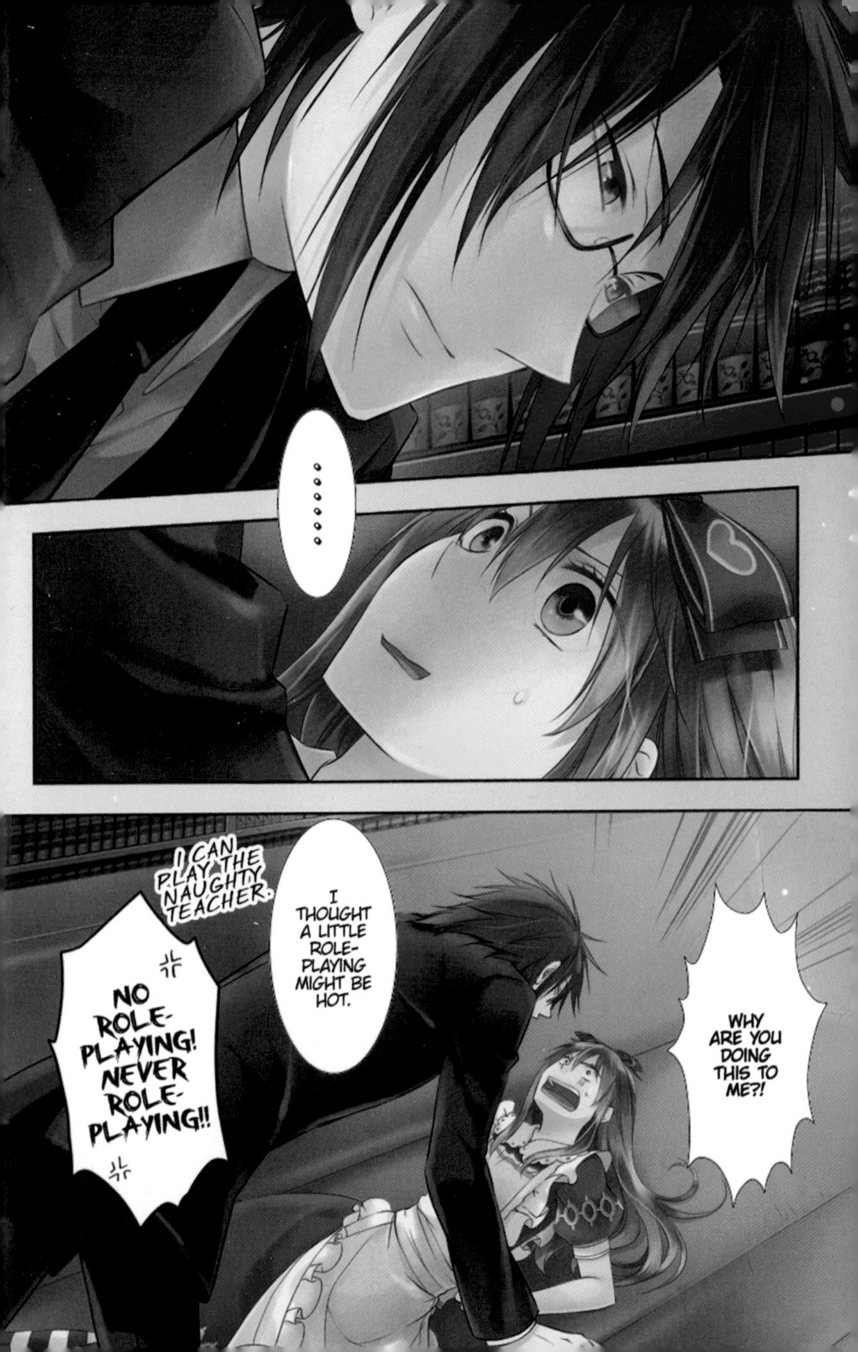
......
WHY ARE YOU DOING THIS TO ME?!
I THOUGHT A LITTLE ROLE-PLAYING MIGHT BE HOT.
I CAN PLAY THE NAUGHTY TEACHER.
NO ROLE-PLAYING! NEVER ROLE-PLAYING!!

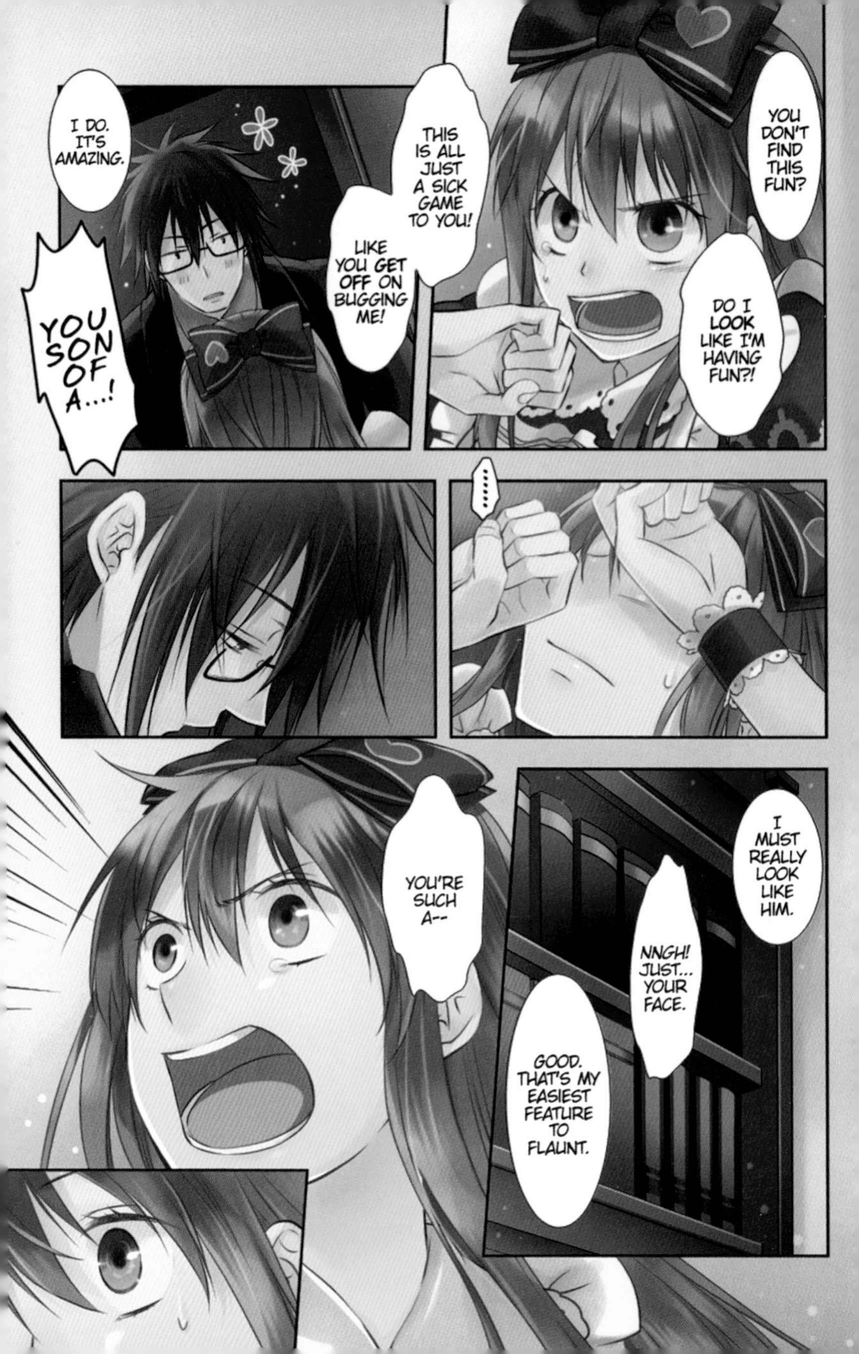
YOU DON'T FIND THIS FUN?
DO I LOOK LIKE I'M HAVING FUN?!
THIS IS ALL JUST A SICK GAME TO YOU!
LIKE YOU GET OFF ON BUGGING ME!
I DO. IT'S AMAZING.
YOU SON OF A...!
......
YOU'RE SUCH A--
I MUST REALLY LOOK LIKE HIM.
NNGH! JUST... YOUR FACE.
GOOD. THAT'S MY EASIEST FEATURE TO FLAUNT.

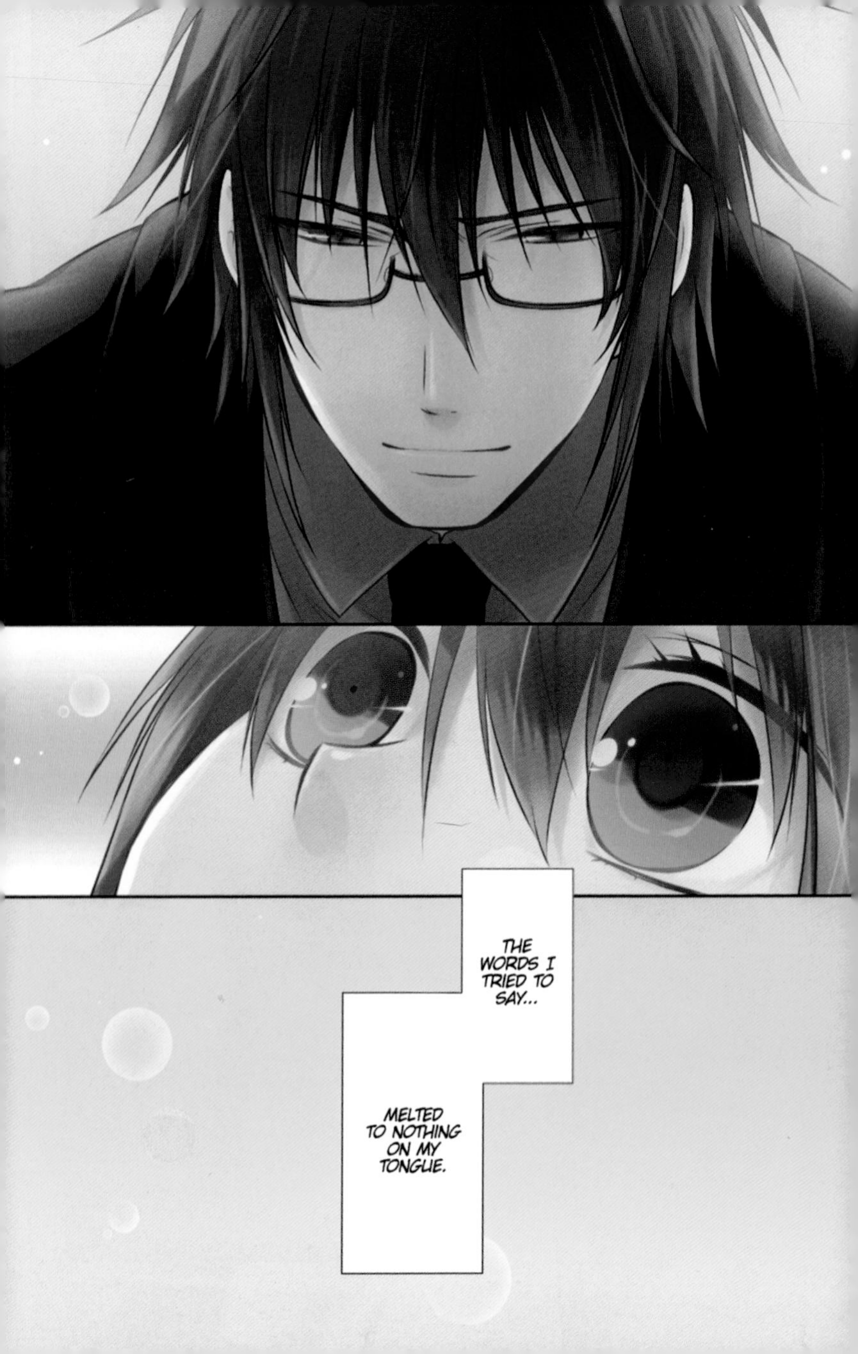
THE WORDS I TRIED TO SAY...
MELTED TO NOTHING ON MY TONGUE.

Alice in the Country of Joker

~Circus and Liar's Game~

- STORY -

This is a love adventure game based on Lewis Carroll's *Alice in Wonderland* that develops into a completely different storyline. This Wonderland is a fairy tale gone very wrong—or very *right,* if you like a land of gunfights where the "Hatters" are a mafia syndicate.

The main character is far from a romantic. In fact, she's especially sick of love relationships.

In *Alice in the Country of Joker,* Alice can experience the changing seasons that were absent in the other storylines. The Circus comes along with April Season, the season of lies. The Circus's dazzle and glitter hides its terrible purpose, and as Alice tries to wrap her head around the shifting world, she falls deeper and deeper into a nefarious trap.

When this story begins, Alice is already close to the inhabitants of Wonderland but hasn't fallen in love. Each role-holder treasures Alice differently with their own bizarre love—those who want to *protect* Alice from the Joker are competing with those who would rather be jailers. In the Country of Joker, there's more at stake than Alice's romantic affections...

Alice
IN THE COUNTRY OF
Joker

VOLUME 3

story by QuinRose

art by Mamenosuke Fujimaru

STAFF CREDITS

translation	Angela Liu
adaptation	Lianne Sentar
lettering	Laura Scoville
logo design	Courtney Williams
cover design	Nicky Lim
proofreader	Shanti Whitesides
editor	Adam Arnold
publisher	Jason DeAngelis
	Seven Seas Entertainment

ALICE IN THE COUNTRY OF JOKER: CIRCUS AND LIAR'S GAME VOL. 3
Copyright © Mamenosuke Fujimaru / QuinRose 2012
First published in Japan in 2012 by ICHIJINSHA Inc., Tokyo.
English translation rights arranged with ICHIJINSHA Inc., Tokyo, Japan.

ISBN: 978-1-937867-68-3

Printed in Canada

First Printing: October 2013

10 9 8 7 6 5 4 3 2 1

Seven Seas

FOLLOW US ONLINE: www.gomanga.com

READING DIRECTIONS

This book reads from *right to left*, Japanese style.
If this is your first time reading manga, you start
reading from the top right panel on each page and
take it from there. If you get lost, just follow the
numbered diagram here. It may seem backwards
at first, but you'll get the hang of it! Have fun!!

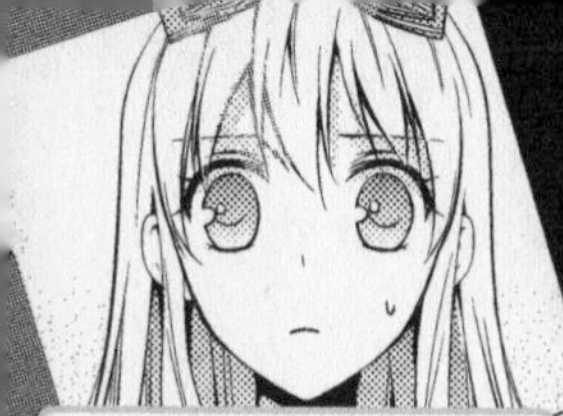

Alice Liddell

An average teenage girl...with a heavy complex. After being dragged to Wonderland by the White Rabbit, she's managed to adapt and even enjoy her bizarre surroundings.

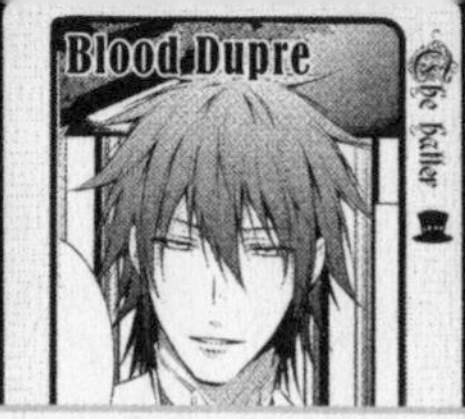
Blood Dupre
The Hatter

The dangerous, shadowy leader of the mafia group known as the Hatter Family. He's incredibly smart, but due to his temperamental moods and his desire to keep things "interesting," he often digs his own grave—and the graves of many others.

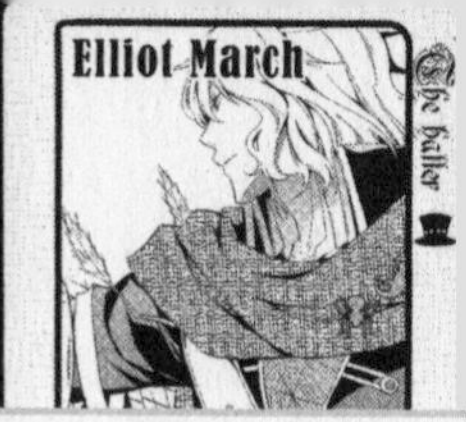
Elliot March
The Hatter

The No. 2 of the Hatter Family and Blood's right-hand man, Elliot is an ex-criminal and an escaped convict. After partnering with Blood, he improved his violent nature and thinks for several seconds before shooting. In his mind, this is a vast improvement.

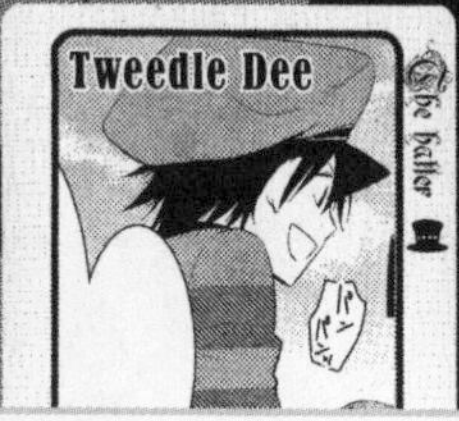
Tweedle Dee
The Hatter

Gatekeeper of the Hatter territory, Dee loves days off. He and his brother can be innocent at times, but their (frequent) malice and unsavory activities earned them the nickname "Bloody Twins." He can shifts his body between a child and an adult version of itself.

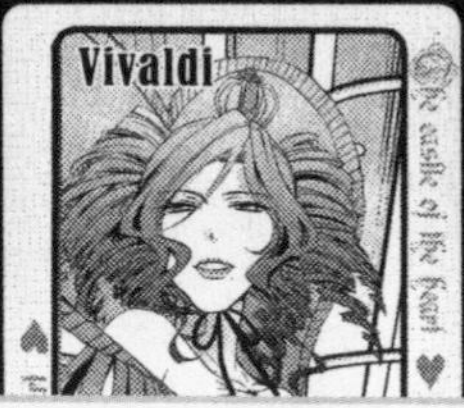
Vivaldi
The castle of the Heart

Ruthless and cruel, Vivaldi is an arrogant beauty with a wild temper. She takes her fury out on everyone around her, including her poor subordinates. Although a picture-perfect Mad Queen, she cares for Alice as if Alice were her little sister... or a very interesting plaything.

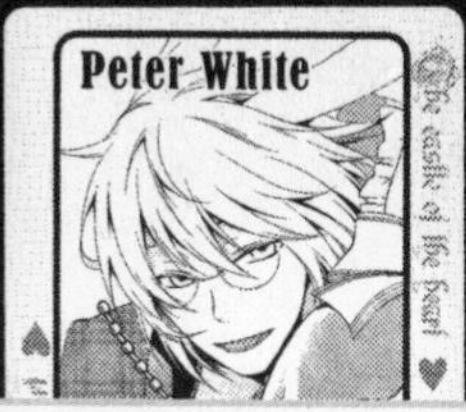
Peter White
The castle of the Heart

Prime Minister of Heart Castle who has rabbit ears growing out of his head. He loves Alice and hates everything else. His cruel, irrational actions are disturbing, but he acts like a completely different person—er, rabbit?—when in the throes of his love for Alice.

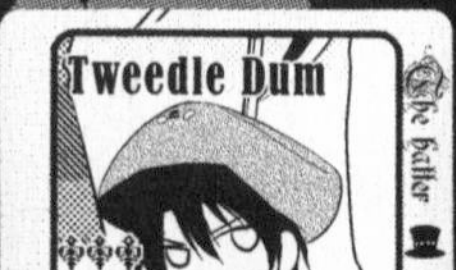
Tweedle Dum
The Hatter

The other Bloody Twin, Dum loves money. He can also become an adult when he feels like it.

Alice IN THE COUNTRY OF Joker

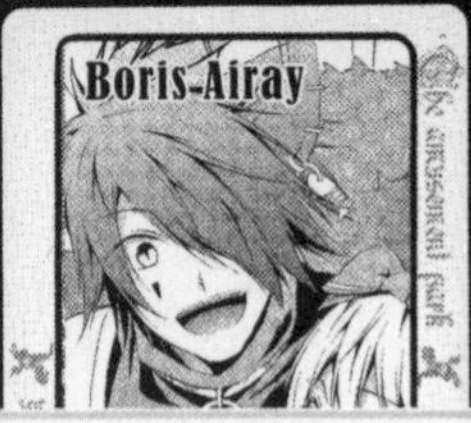
Boris Airay
The amusement park

A riddle-loving cat with a signature smirk, he has a tendency to pose questions and never answer them. Since seeing the Sleepy Mouse whets his appetite, he carries a fork and knife at all times.

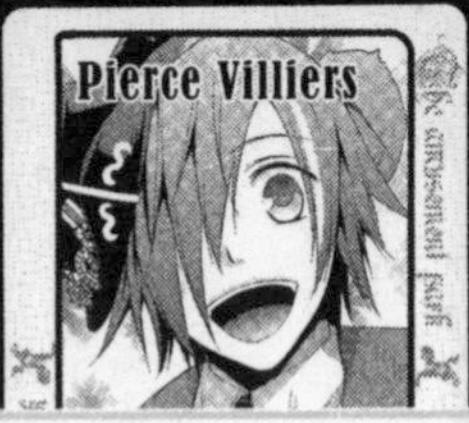
Pierce Villiers
The amusement park

An insomniac mouse who drinks too much coffee. He's terrified of Boris but loves Nightmare, who brings precious sleep. He used to be a part of the Hatter family, but after relentless bullying from the cat and twins, he's become a runaway.

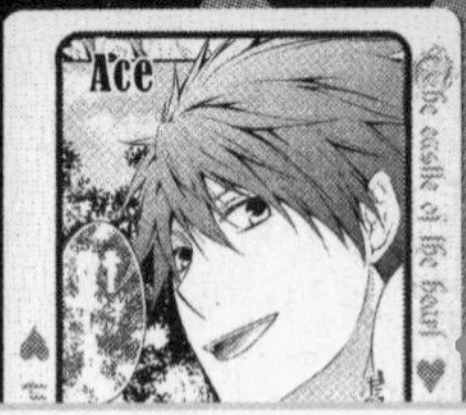
Ace
The castle of the heart

The Knight of Hearts and subordinate of Vivaldi. He's a very unlucky (yet strangely positive) man...who tends to plow forward and only worsen his situation. Ace is one of the Clockmaker's few friends and visits Julius frequently—usually getting lost on the way.

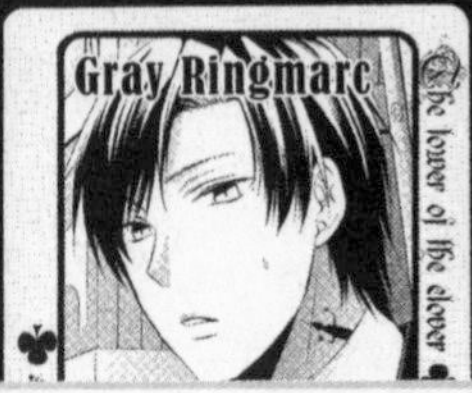
Gray Ringmarc
The tower of the clover

Nightmare's subordinate. This sound thinker with a strong work ethic is surprisingly good with a blade. Elliot considers Gray a comrade, since they share a strong dedication to their bosses...which annoys Gray.

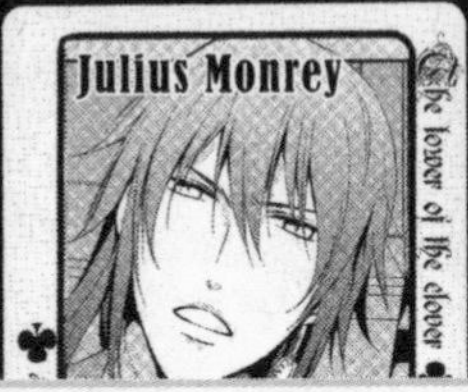
Julius Monrey
The tower of the clover

This gloomy Clockmaker is also known as the Undertaker. Despite being a sarcastic workaholic, he gets along with Ace. He had some part in the imprisonment of Elliot, the March Hare, and is thus the target for hatred.

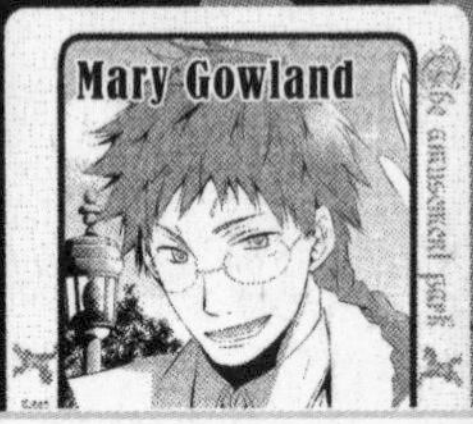
Mary Gowland
The amusement park

The owner of the Amusement Park. He hides his hated first name, Mary, but pretty much everyone already knows it. His full name is a play on words that sounds like "Merry Go Round" when said quickly. He's a terrible, terrible musician.

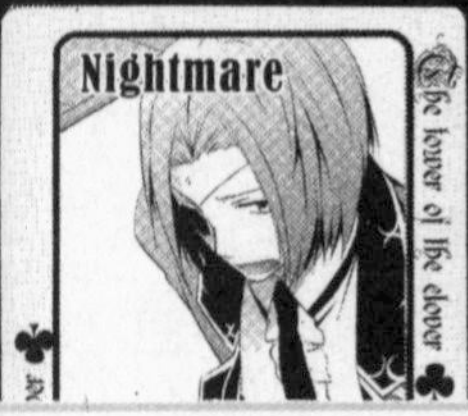
Nightmare
The tower of the clover

A sickly nightmare who often coughs up blood. He has the power to read people's thoughts and enter dreams. He technically holds a high position and has many subordinates, but since he can't even take care of his own health, he leaves most things to Gray.

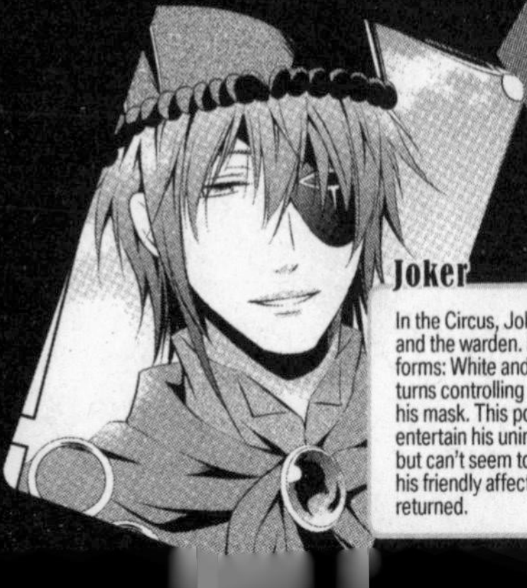
Joker

In the Circus, Joker is the leader... and the warden. He exists in two forms: White and Black, which take turns controlling either his body or his mask. This poor card loves to entertain his uninterested peers, but can't seem tounderstand why his friendly affections are rarely returned.

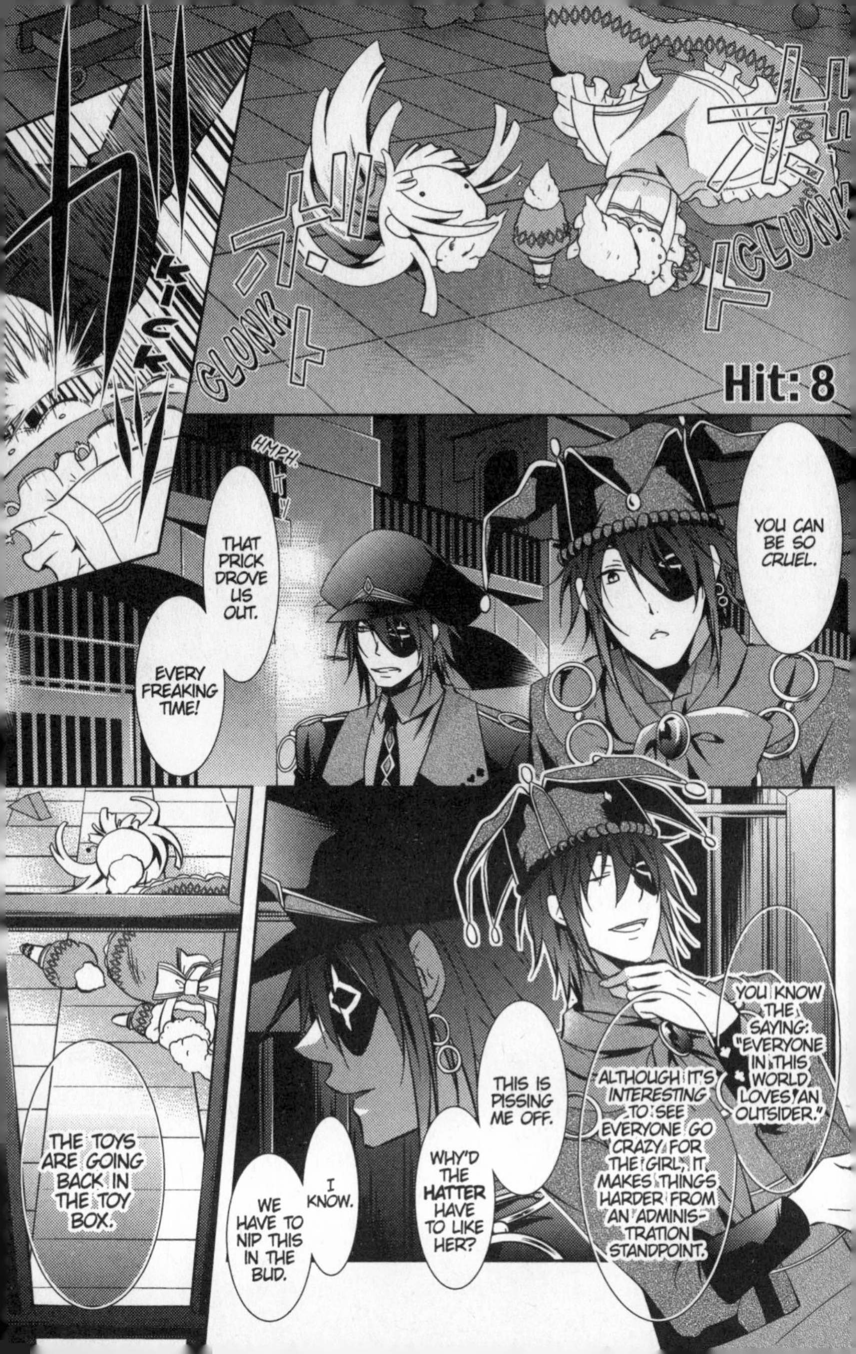
CLUNK
CLUNK
Hit: 8
KICK
YOU CAN BE SO CRUEL.
HMPH.
THAT PRICK DROVE US OUT.
EVERY FREAKING TIME!
YOU KNOW THE SAYING: "EVERYONE IN THIS WORLD LOVES AN OUTSIDER."
ALTHOUGH IT'S INTERESTING TO SEE EVERYONE GO CRAZY FOR THE GIRL, IT MAKES THINGS HARDER FROM AN ADMINISTRATION STANDPOINT.
THIS IS PISSING ME OFF.
WHY'D THE HATTER HAVE TO LIKE HER?
I KNOW.
WE HAVE TO NIP THIS IN THE BUD.
THE TOYS ARE GOING BACK IN THE TOY BOX.

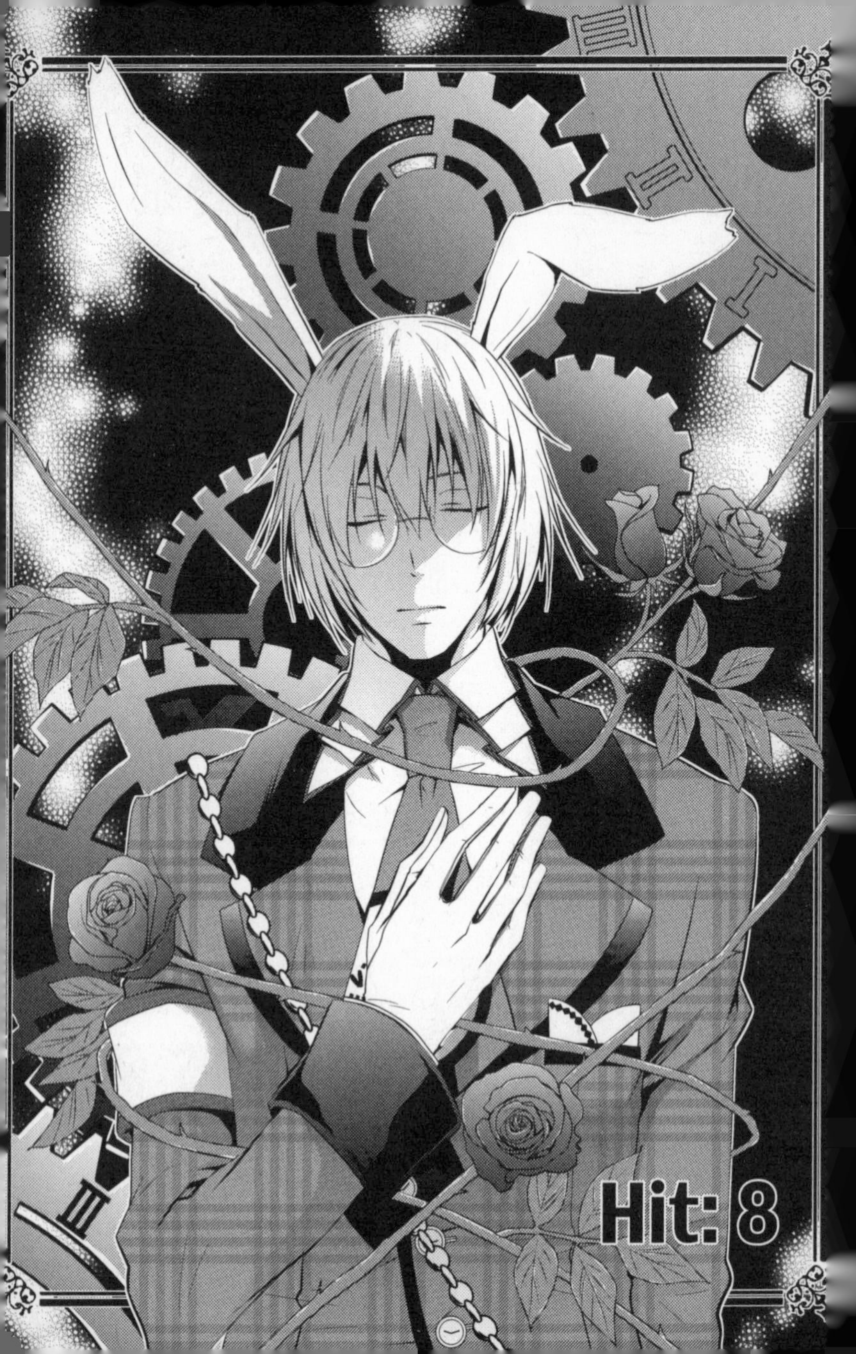
Hit: 8

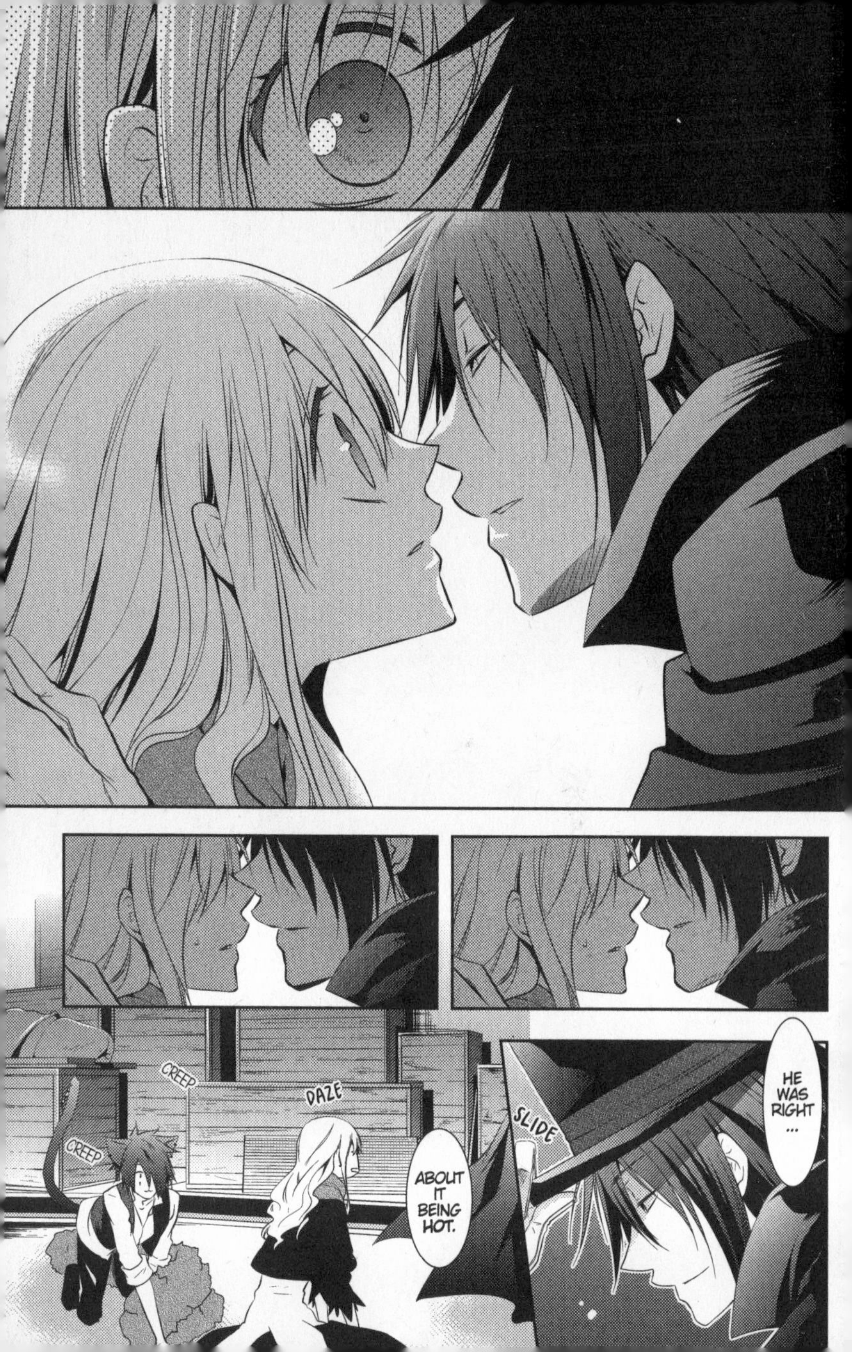
HE WAS RIGHT ...
SLIDE
ABOUT IT BEING HOT.
DAZE
CREEP
CREEP

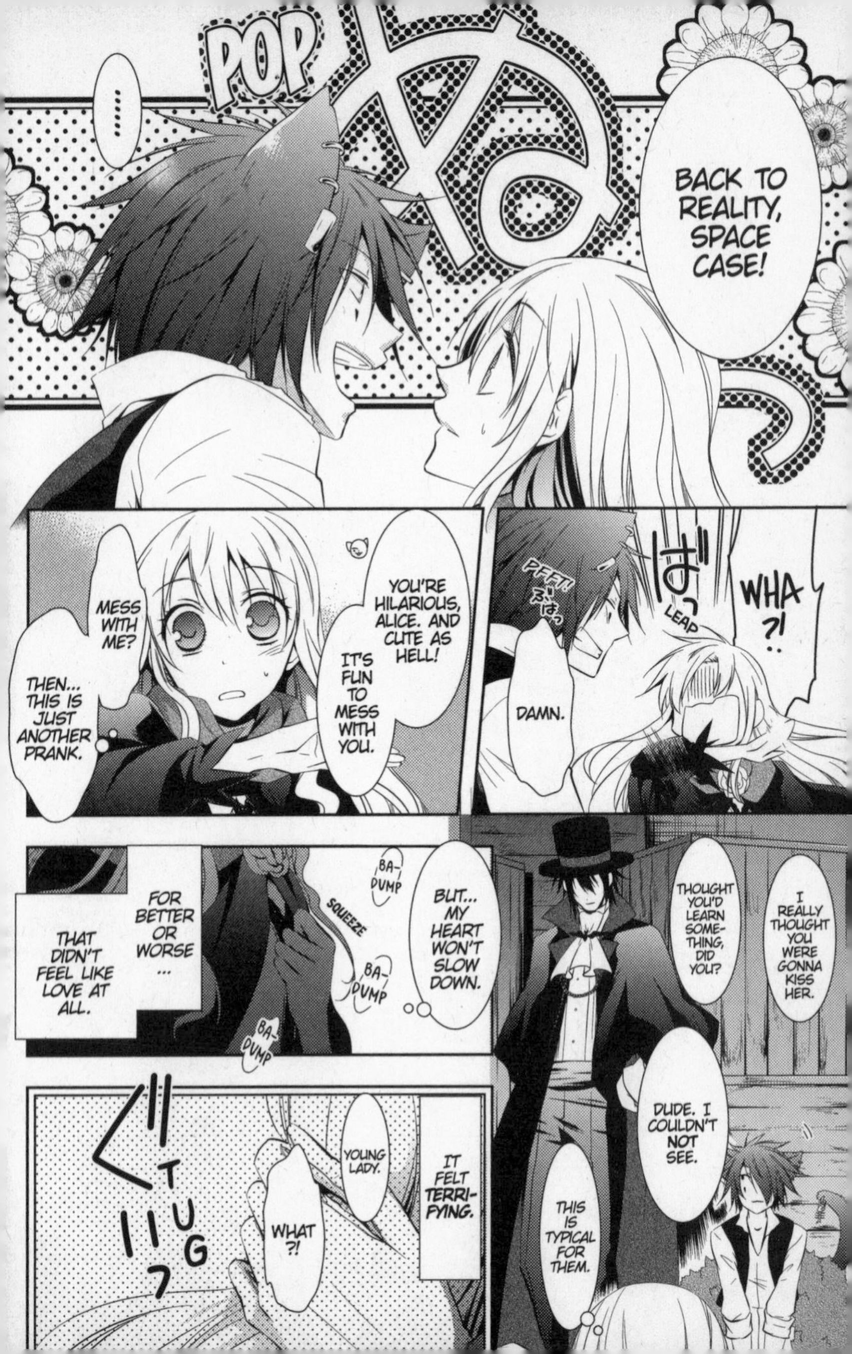
BACK TO REALITY, SPACE CASE!
POP
......
WHA ?!
ばっ LEAP
PFFT! ぶはっ
DAMN.
YOU'RE HILARIOUS, ALICE. AND CUTE AS HELL!
IT'S FUN TO MESS WITH YOU.
MESS WITH ME?
THEN... THIS IS JUST ANOTHER PRANK.
I REALLY THOUGHT YOU WERE GONNA KISS HER.
THOUGHT YOU'D LEARN SOME-THING, DID YOU?
DUDE. I COULDN'T NOT SEE.
THIS IS TYPICAL FOR THEM.
BUT... MY HEART WON'T SLOW DOWN.
BA-DUMP
SQUEEZE
BA-DUMP
FOR BETTER OR WORSE ...
THAT DIDN'T FEEL LIKE LOVE AT ALL.
BA-DUMP
IT FELT TERRI-FYING.
YOUNG LADY.
WHAT ?!
TUG

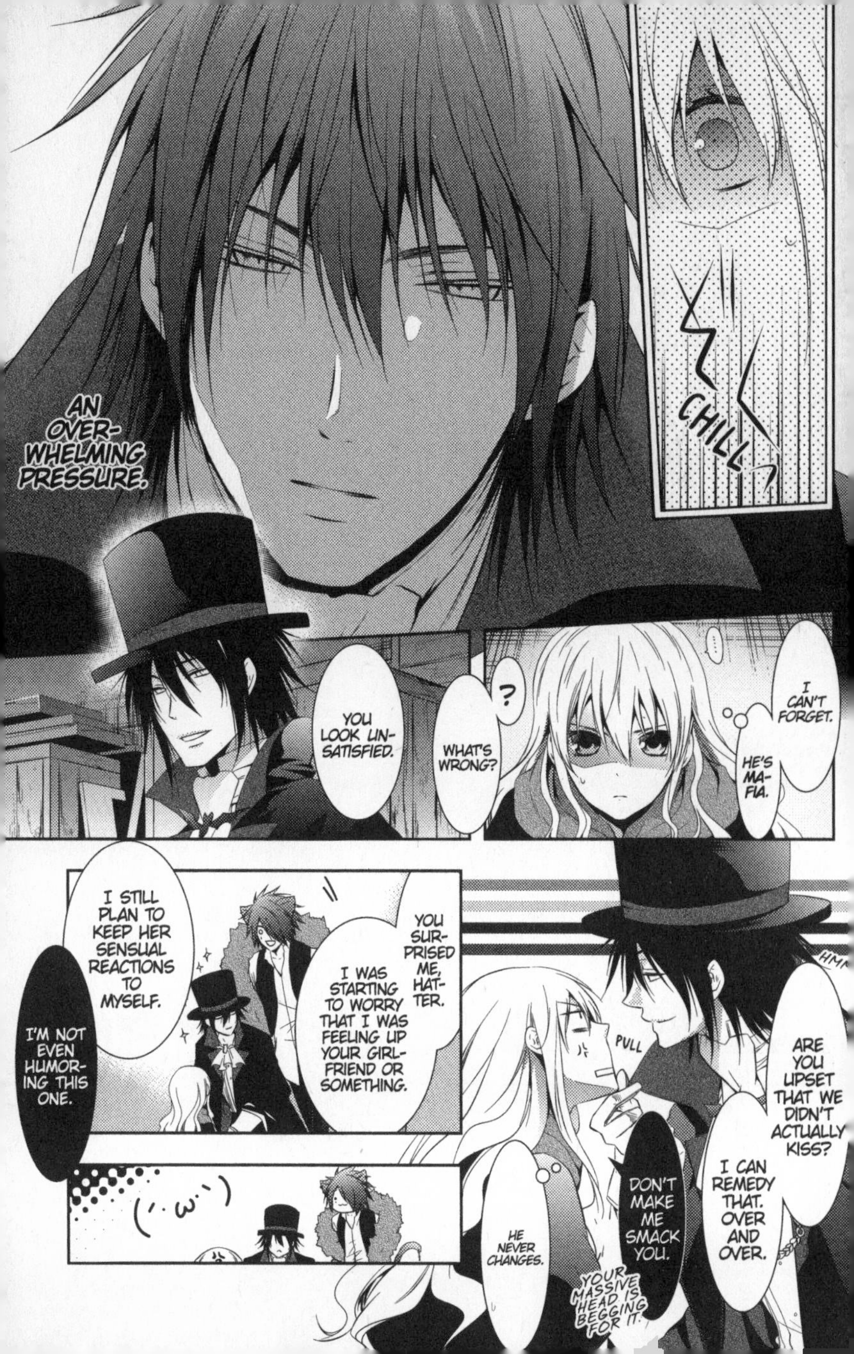

CHILL
AN OVER-WHELMING PRESSURE.
...
I CAN'T FORGET.
HE'S MA-FIA.
?
YOU LOOK UN-SATISFIED.
WHAT'S WRONG?
HMM
ARE YOU UPSET THAT WE DIDN'T ACTUALLY KISS?
PULL
I CAN REMEDY THAT. OVER AND OVER.
DON'T MAKE ME SMACK YOU.
HE NEVER CHANGES.
YOUR MASSIVE HEAD IS BEGGING FOR IT.
YOU SUR-PRISED ME, HAT-TER.
I WAS STARTING TO WORRY THAT I WAS FEELING UP YOUR GIRL-FRIEND OR SOMETHING.
I STILL PLAN TO KEEP HER SENSUAL REACTIONS TO MYSELF.
I'M NOT EVEN HUMOR-ING THIS ONE.
(´・ω・`)

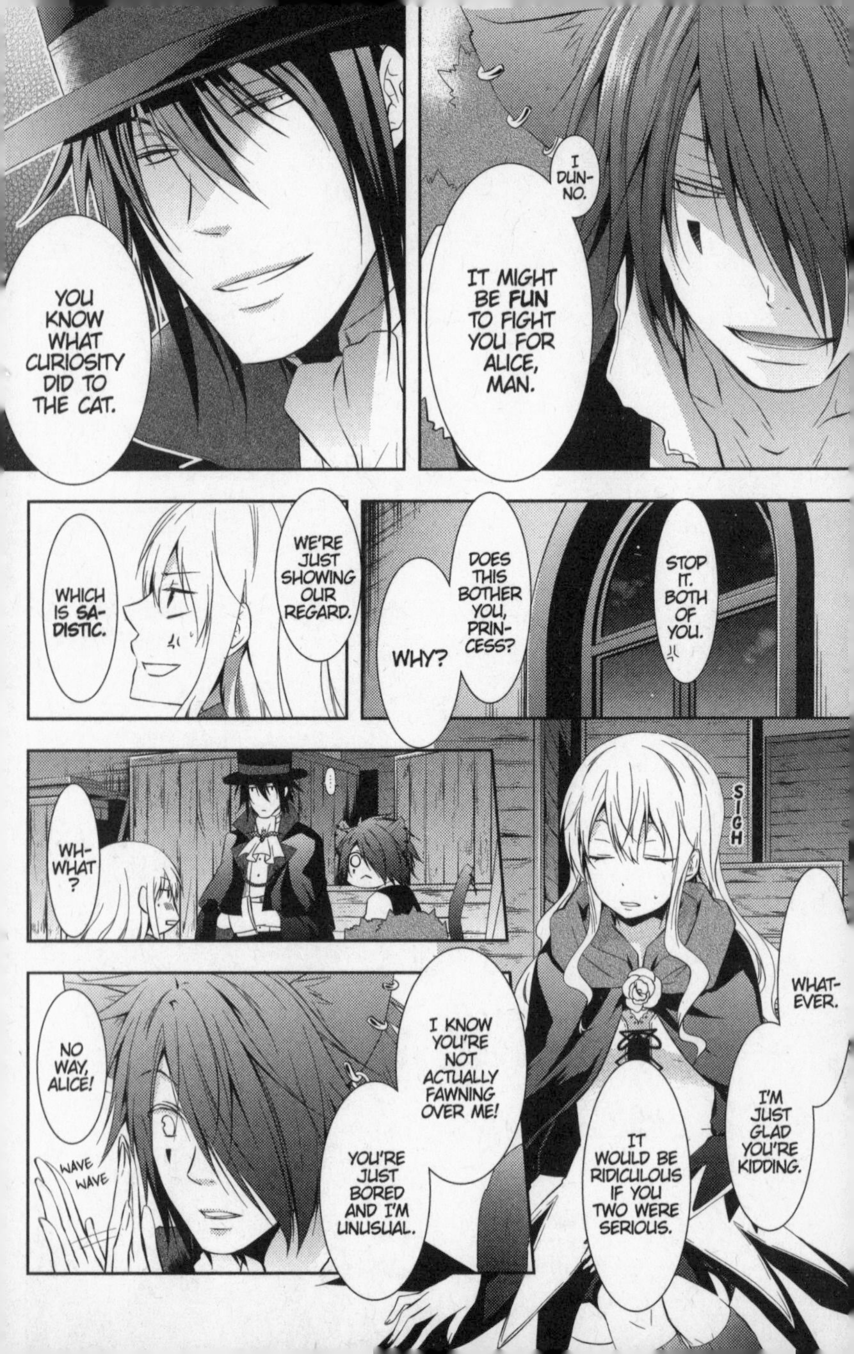

I DUN-NO.
IT MIGHT BE FUN TO FIGHT YOU FOR ALICE, MAN.
YOU KNOW WHAT CURIOSITY DID TO THE CAT.
STOP IT. BOTH OF YOU.
DOES THIS BOTHER YOU, PRINCESS?
WHY?
WE'RE JUST SHOWING OUR REGARD.
WHICH IS SA-DISTIC.
SIGH
WHAT-EVER.
I'M JUST GLAD YOU'RE KIDDING.
IT WOULD BE RIDICULOUS IF YOU TWO WERE SERIOUS.
...
WH-WHAT?
I KNOW YOU'RE NOT ACTUALLY FAWNING OVER ME!
YOU'RE JUST BORED AND I'M UNUSUAL.
NO WAY, ALICE!
WAVE WAVE

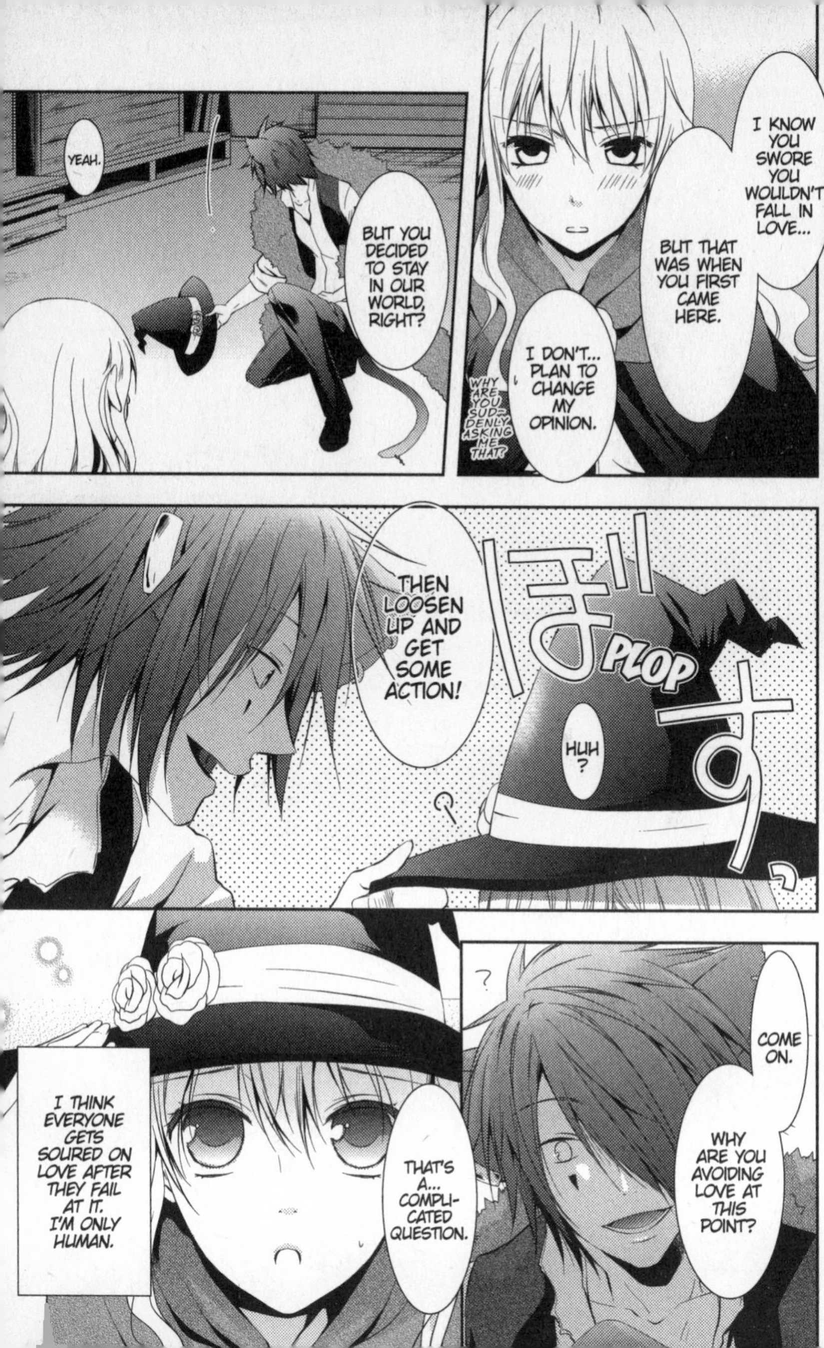
I KNOW YOU SWORE YOU WOULDN'T FALL IN LOVE...
BUT THAT WAS WHEN YOU FIRST CAME HERE.
I DON'T... PLAN TO CHANGE MY OPINION.
WHY ARE YOU SUDDENLY ASKING ME THAT?
BUT YOU DECIDED TO STAY IN OUR WORLD, RIGHT?
YEAH.
THEN LOOSEN UP AND GET SOME ACTION!
PLOP
HUH?
COME ON.
WHY ARE YOU AVOIDING LOVE AT THIS POINT?
THAT'S A... COMPLICATED QUESTION.
I THINK EVERYONE GETS SOURED ON LOVE AFTER THEY FAIL AT IT. I'M ONLY HUMAN.

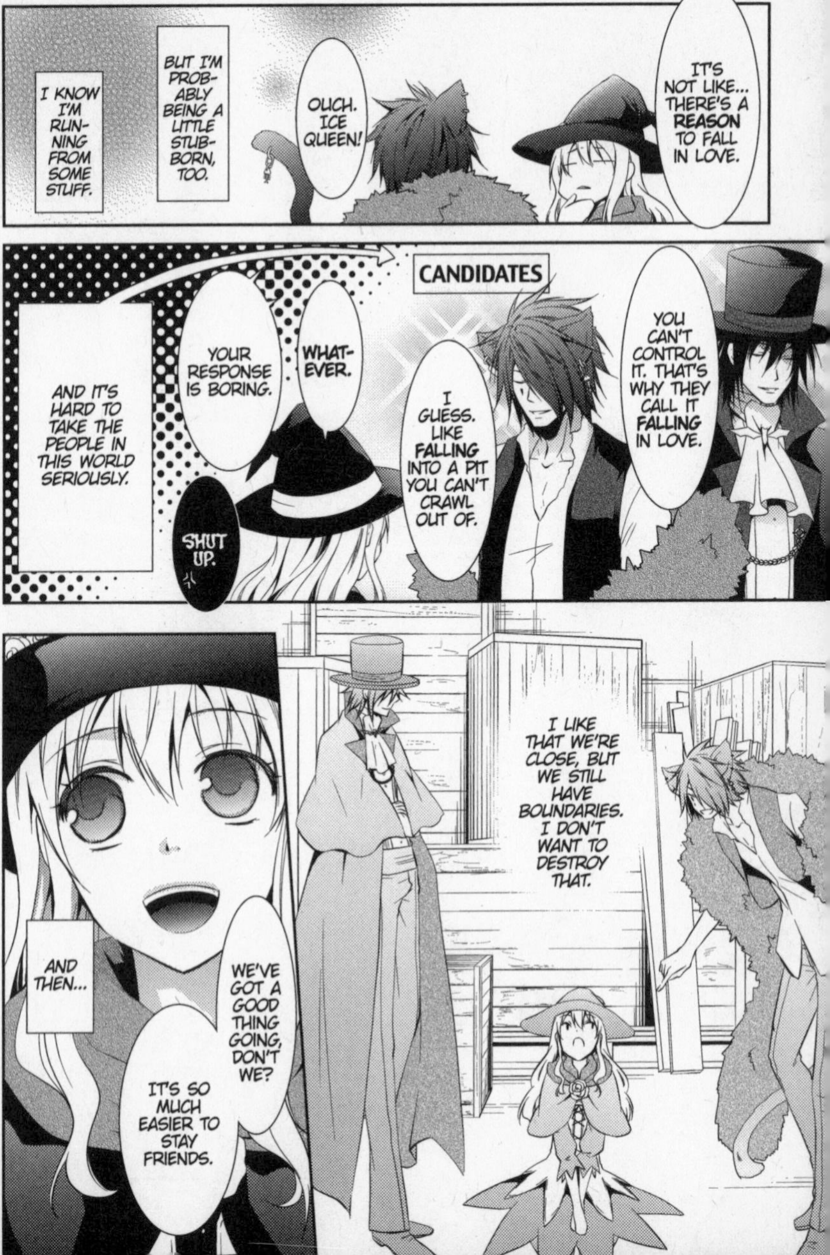
IT'S NOT LIKE... THERE'S A **REASON** TO FALL IN LOVE.
OUCH. ICE QUEEN!
BUT I'M PROBABLY BEING A LITTLE STUBBORN, TOO.
I KNOW I'M RUNNING FROM SOME STUFF.
YOU CAN'T CONTROL IT. THAT'S WHY THEY CALL IT **FALLING** IN LOVE.
CANDIDATES
I GUESS. LIKE **FALLING** INTO A PIT YOU CAN'T CRAWL OUT OF.
WHATEVER.
YOUR RESPONSE IS BORING.
SHUT UP.
AND IT'S HARD TO TAKE THE PEOPLE IN THIS WORLD SERIOUSLY.
I LIKE THAT WE'RE CLOSE, BUT WE STILL HAVE BOUNDARIES. I DON'T WANT TO DESTROY THAT.
WE'VE GOT A GOOD THING GOING, DON'T WE?
AND THEN...
IT'S SO MUCH EASIER TO STAY FRIENDS.

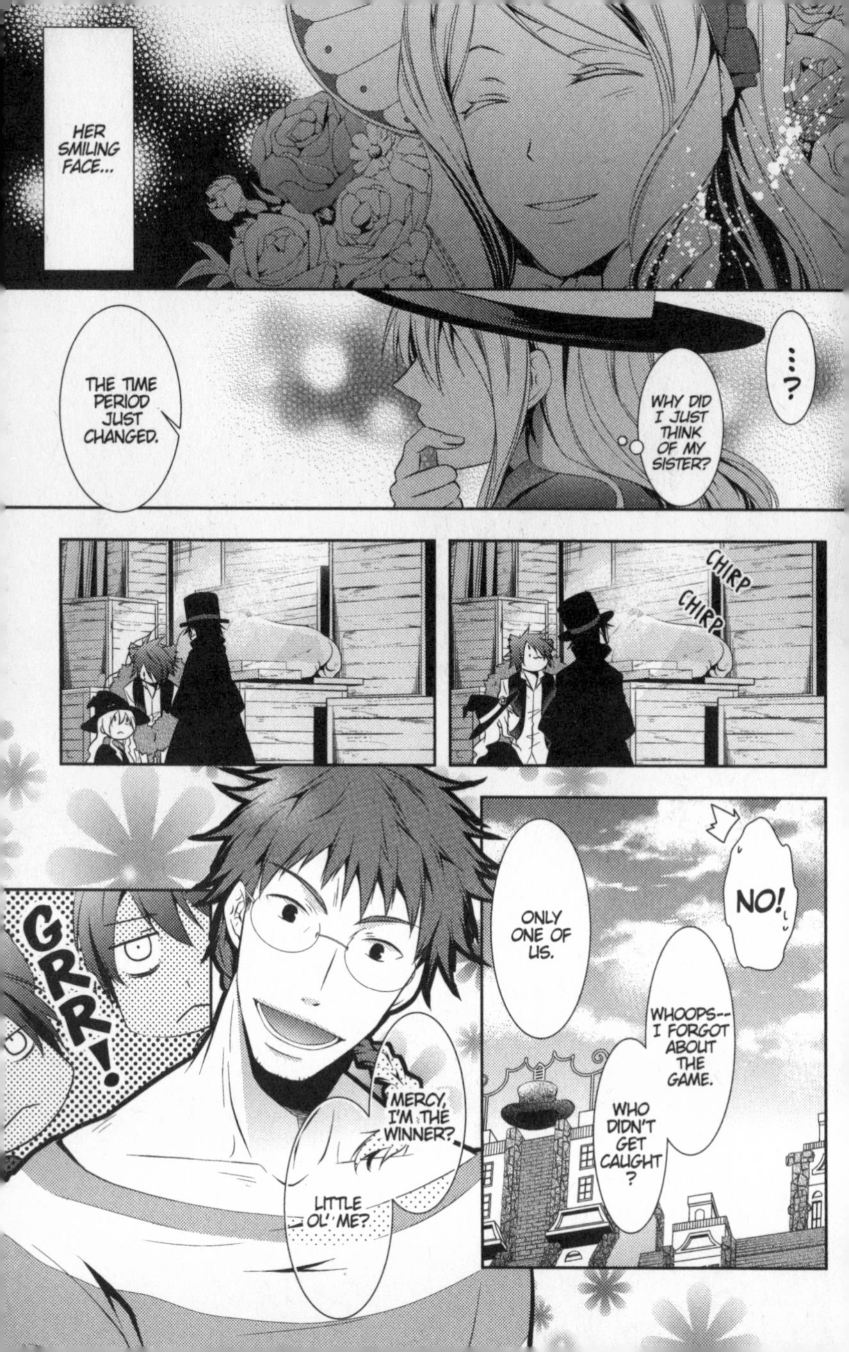
HER SMILING FACE...
...?
WHY DID I JUST THINK OF MY SISTER?
THE TIME PERIOD JUST CHANGED.
CHIRP
CHIRP
NO!
ONLY ONE OF US.
WHOOPS-- I FORGOT ABOUT THE GAME.
WHO DIDN'T GET CAUGHT?
MERCY, I'M THE WINNER?
LITTLE OL' ME?
GRR!

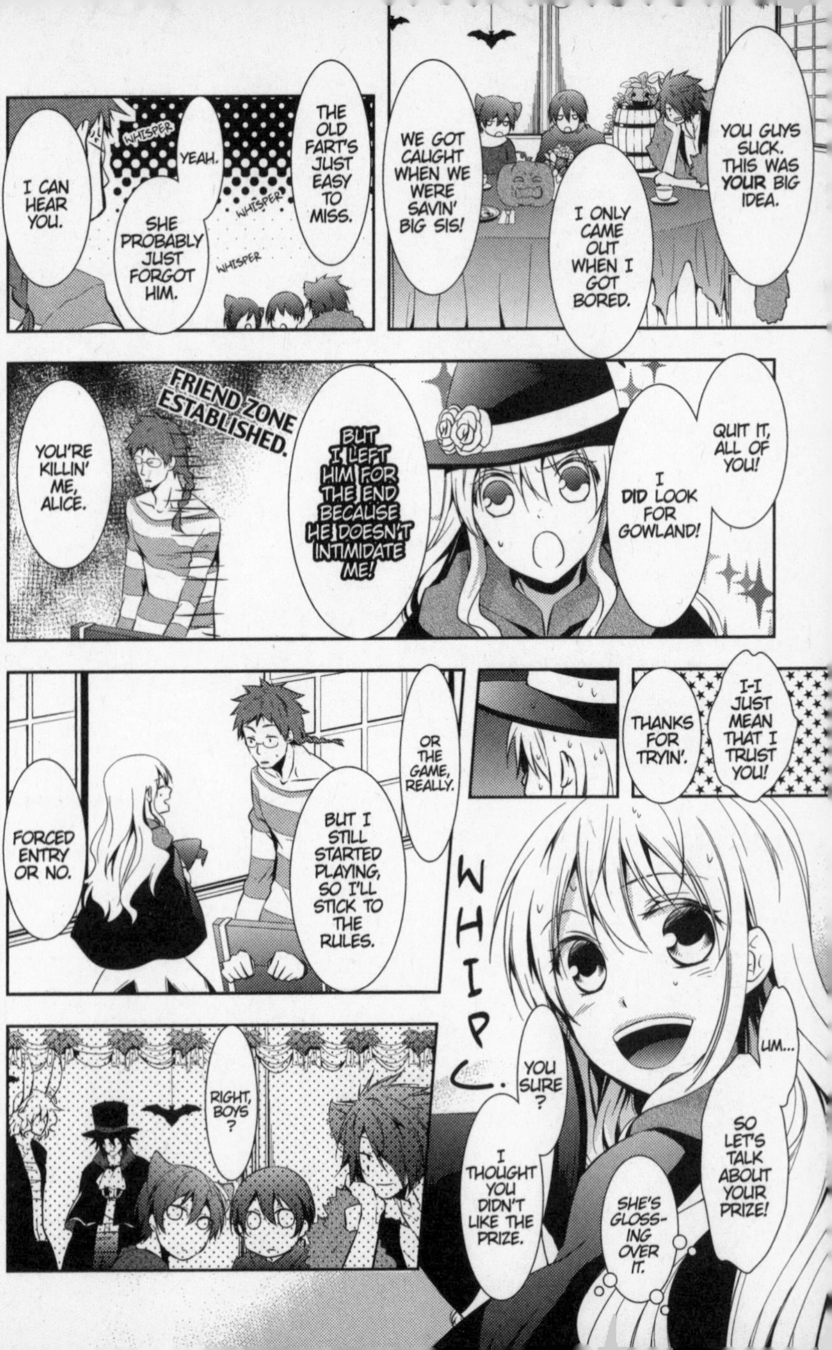
YOU GUYS SUCK. THIS WAS YOUR BIG IDEA.
I ONLY CAME OUT WHEN I GOT BORED.
WE GOT CAUGHT WHEN WE WERE SAVIN' BIG SIS!
THE OLD FART'S JUST EASY TO MISS.
WHISPER
SHE PROBABLY JUST FORGOT HIM.
WHISPER
YEAH.
WHISPER
I CAN HEAR YOU.
QUIT IT, ALL OF YOU!
I DID LOOK FOR GOWLAND!
BUT I LEFT HIM FOR THE END BECAUSE HE DOESN'T INTIMIDATE ME!
FRIEND ZONE ESTABLISHED.
YOU'RE KILLIN' ME, ALICE.
I-I JUST MEAN THAT I TRUST YOU!
THANKS FOR TRYIN'.
OR THE GAME, REALLY.
BUT I STILL STARTED PLAYING, SO I'LL STICK TO THE RULES.
FORCED ENTRY OR NO.
UM...
SO LET'S TALK ABOUT YOUR PRIZE!
WHIP
YOU SURE?
I THOUGHT YOU DIDN'T LIKE THE PRIZE.
SHE'S GLOSSING OVER IT.
RIGHT, BOYS?

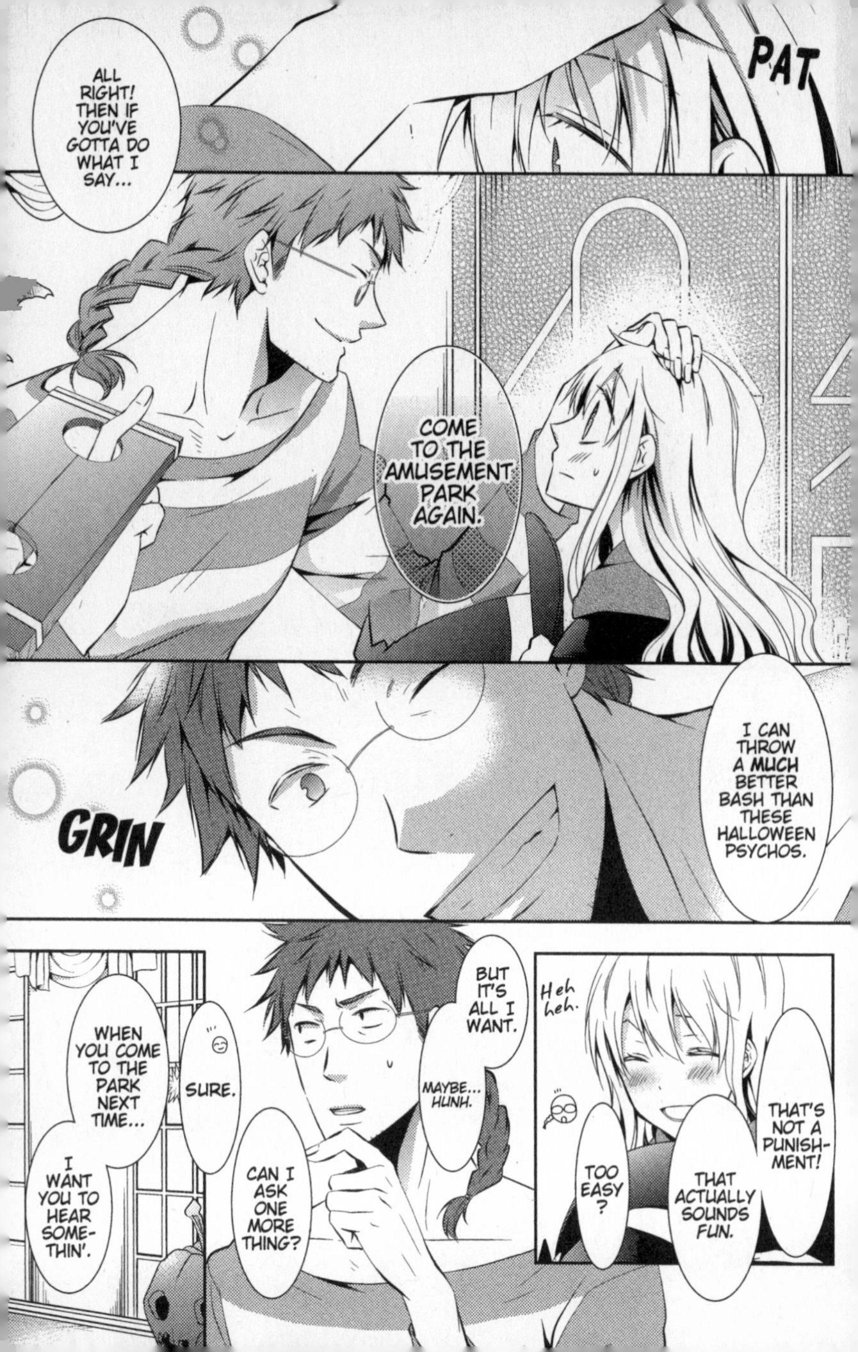
PAT
ALL RIGHT! THEN IF YOU'VE GOTTA DO WHAT I SAY...
COME TO THE AMUSEMENT PARK AGAIN.
I CAN THROW A MUCH BETTER BASH THAN THESE HALLOWEEN PSYCHOS.
GRIN
THAT'S NOT A PUNISHMENT!
Heh heh.
THAT ACTUALLY SOUNDS FUN.
TOO EASY?
BUT IT'S ALL I WANT.
MAYBE... HUNH.
CAN I ASK ONE MORE THING?
SURE.
WHEN YOU COME TO THE PARK NEXT TIME...
I WANT YOU TO HEAR SOMETHIN'.

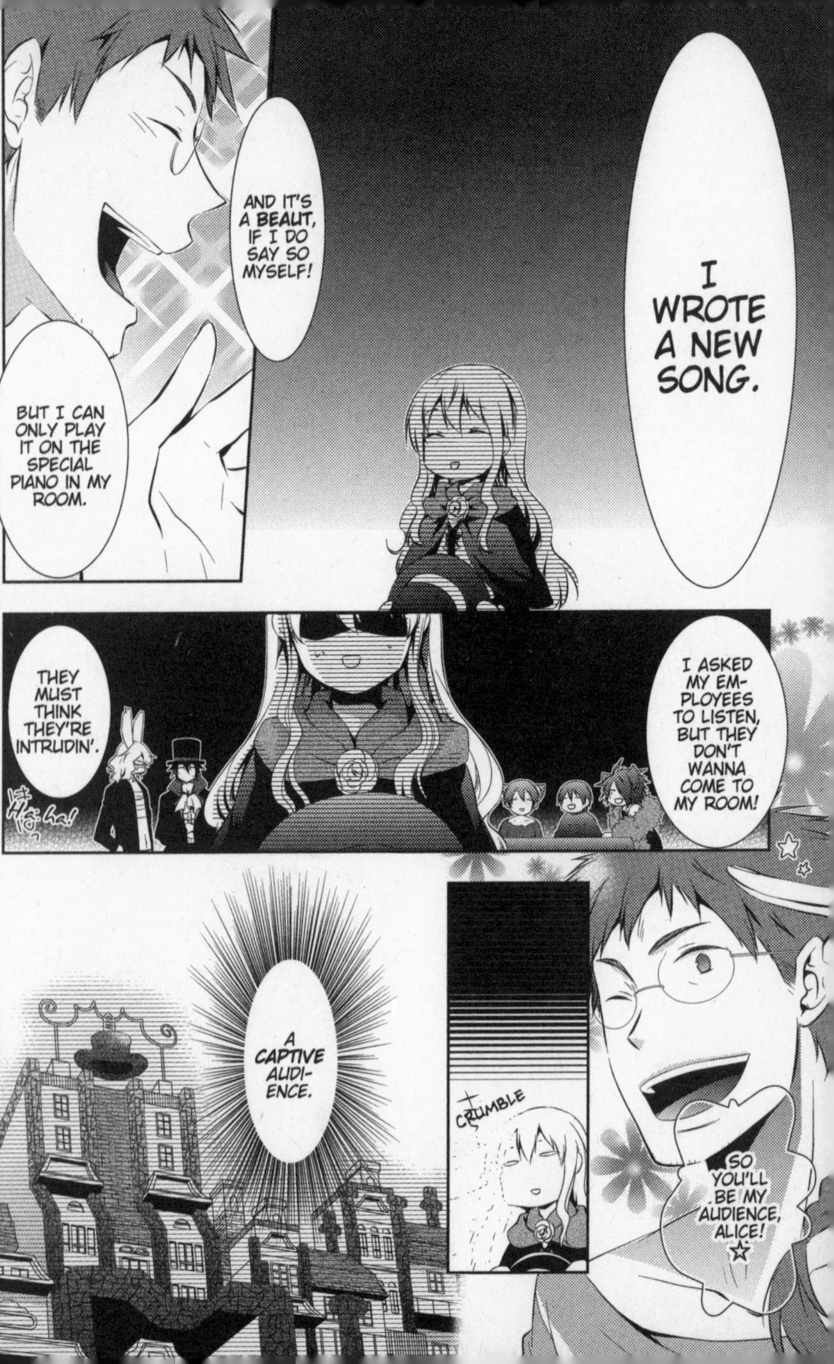
I WROTE A NEW SONG.
AND IT'S A BEAUT, IF I DO SAY SO MYSELF!
BUT I CAN ONLY PLAY IT ON THE SPECIAL PIANO IN MY ROOM.
I ASKED MY EM-PLOYEES TO LISTEN, BUT THEY DON'T WANNA COME TO MY ROOM!
THEY MUST THINK THEY'RE INTRUDIN'.
ha!
SO YOU'LL BE MY AUDIENCE, ALICE! ☆
CRUMBLE
A CAPTIVE AUDI-ENCE.

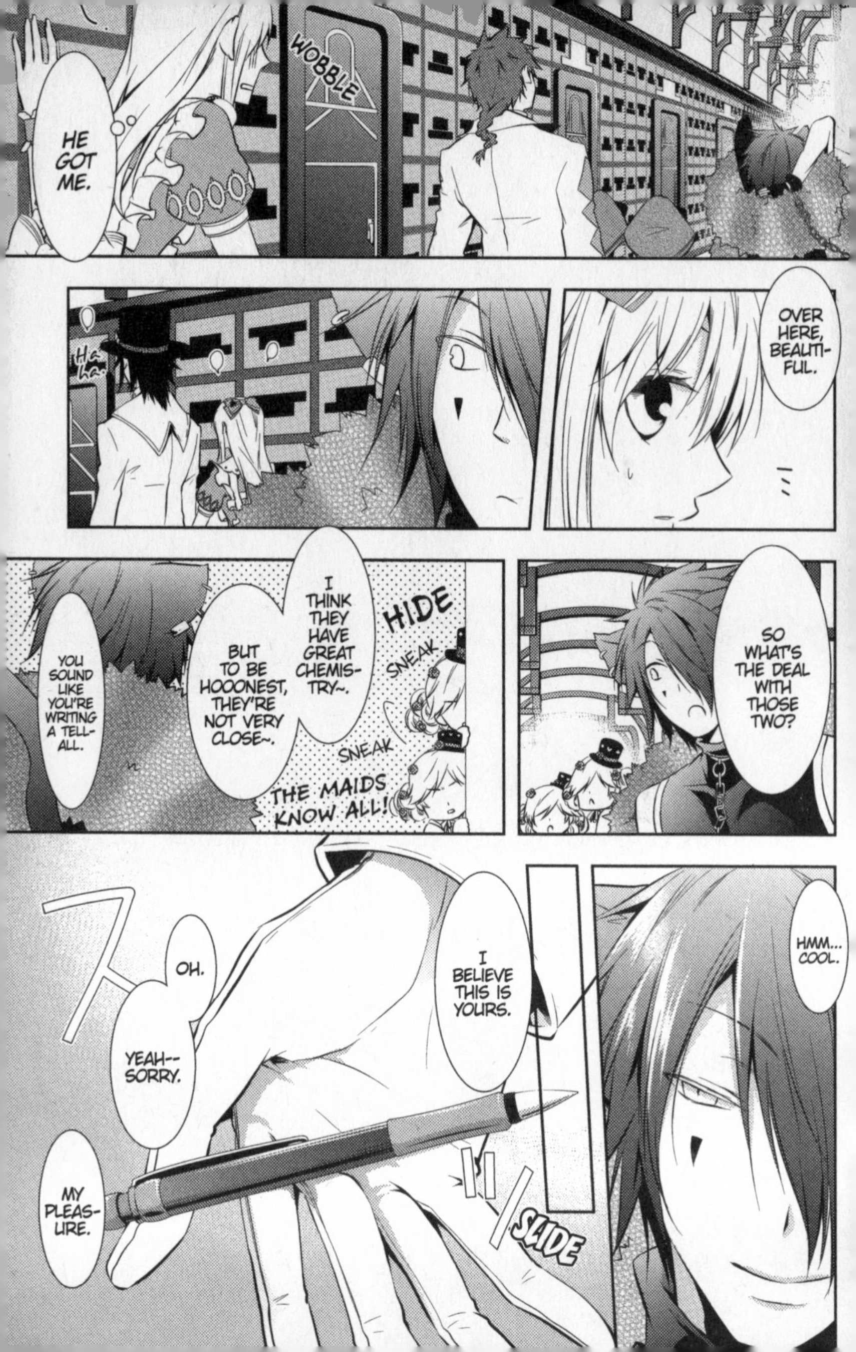
WOBBLE
HE GOT ME.
OVER HERE, BEAUTIFUL.
Ha ha.
SO WHAT'S THE DEAL WITH THOSE TWO?
I THINK THEY HAVE GREAT CHEMISTRY~.
HIDE
SNEAK
BUT TO BE HOOONEST, THEY'RE NOT VERY CLOSE~.
SNEAK
THE MAIDS KNOW ALL!
YOU SOUND LIKE YOU'RE WRITING A TELL-ALL.
HMM... COOL.
I BELIEVE THIS IS YOURS.
SLIDE
OH.
YEAH--SORRY.
MY PLEASURE.

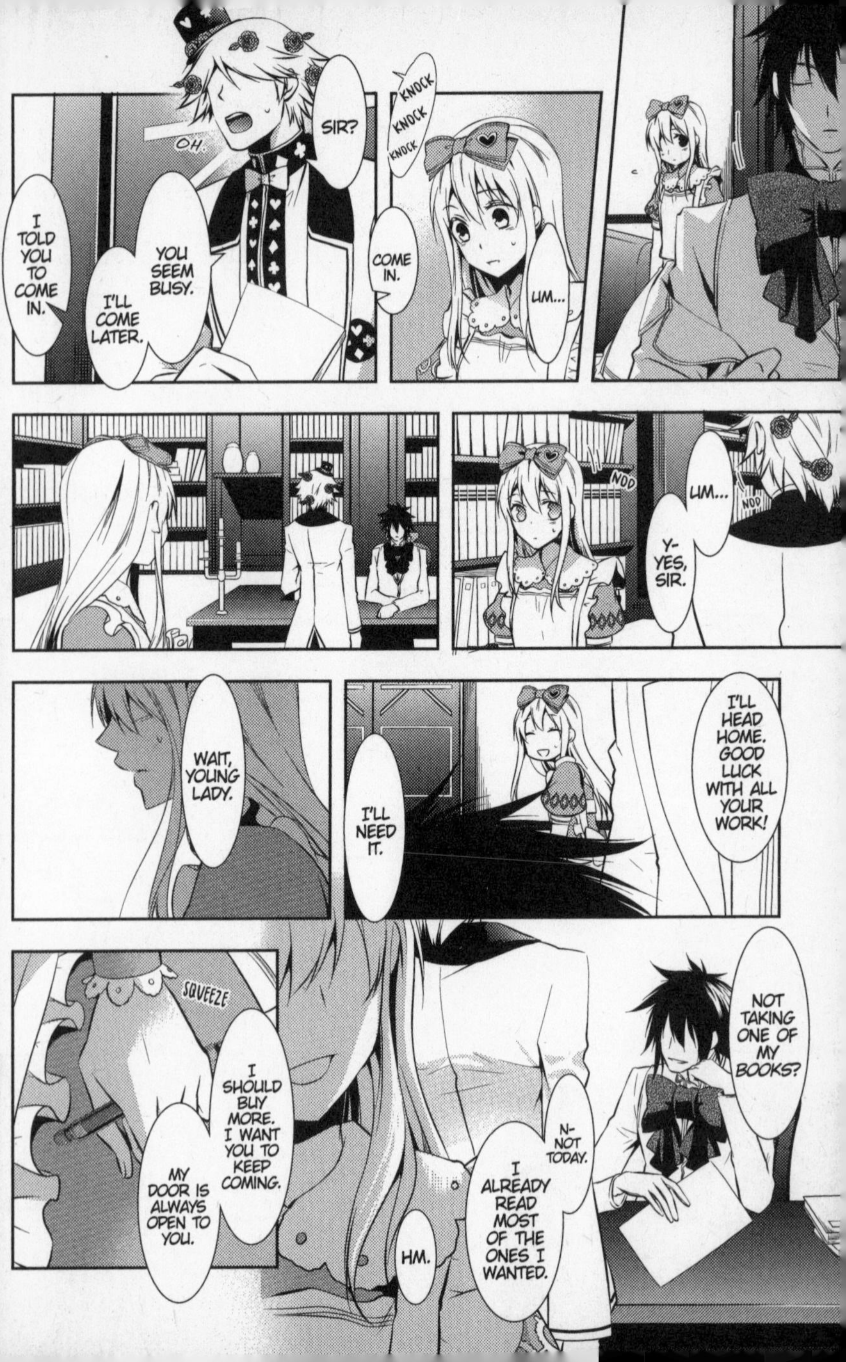
KNOCK KNOCK KNOCK
COME IN.
UM...
SIR?
OH.
YOU SEEM BUSY. I'LL COME LATER.
I TOLD YOU TO COME IN.
UM...
NOD NOD
Y-YES, SIR.
I'LL HEAD HOME. GOOD LUCK WITH ALL YOUR WORK!
I'LL NEED IT.
WAIT, YOUNG LADY.
NOT TAKING ONE OF MY BOOKS?
N-NOT TODAY.
I ALREADY READ MOST OF THE ONES I WANTED.
HM.
I SHOULD BUY MORE. I WANT YOU TO KEEP COMING.
MY DOOR IS ALWAYS OPEN TO YOU.
SQUEEZE

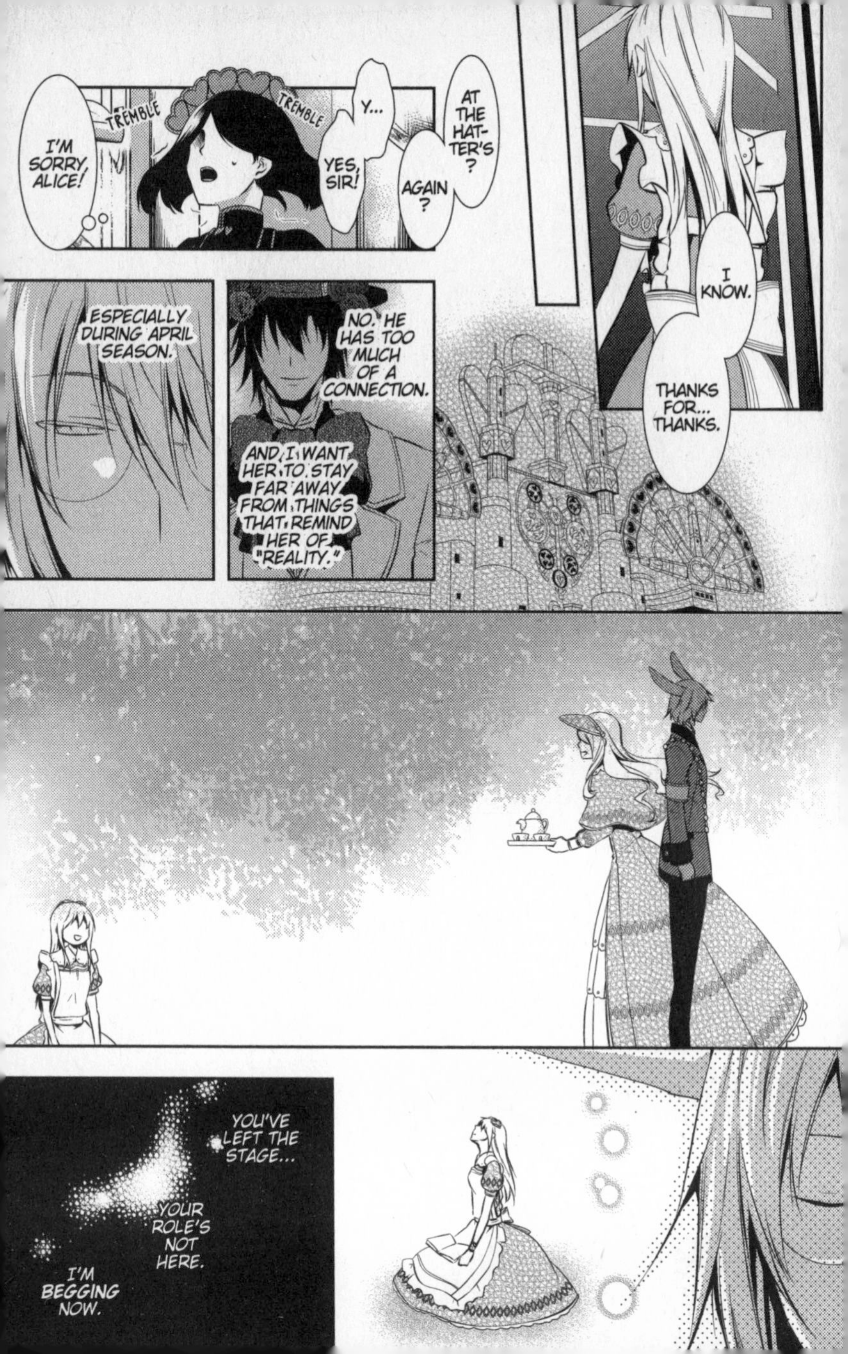
I KNOW.
THANKS FOR... THANKS.
AT THE HATTER'S?
AGAIN?
Y...
YES, SIR!
TREMBLE
TREMBLE
I'M SORRY, ALICE!
NO. HE HAS TOO MUCH OF A CONNECTION.
AND I WANT HER TO STAY FAR AWAY FROM THINGS THAT REMIND HER OF "REALITY."
ESPECIALLY DURING APRIL SEASON.
YOU'VE LEFT THE STAGE...
YOUR ROLE'S NOT HERE.
I'M BEGGING NOW.

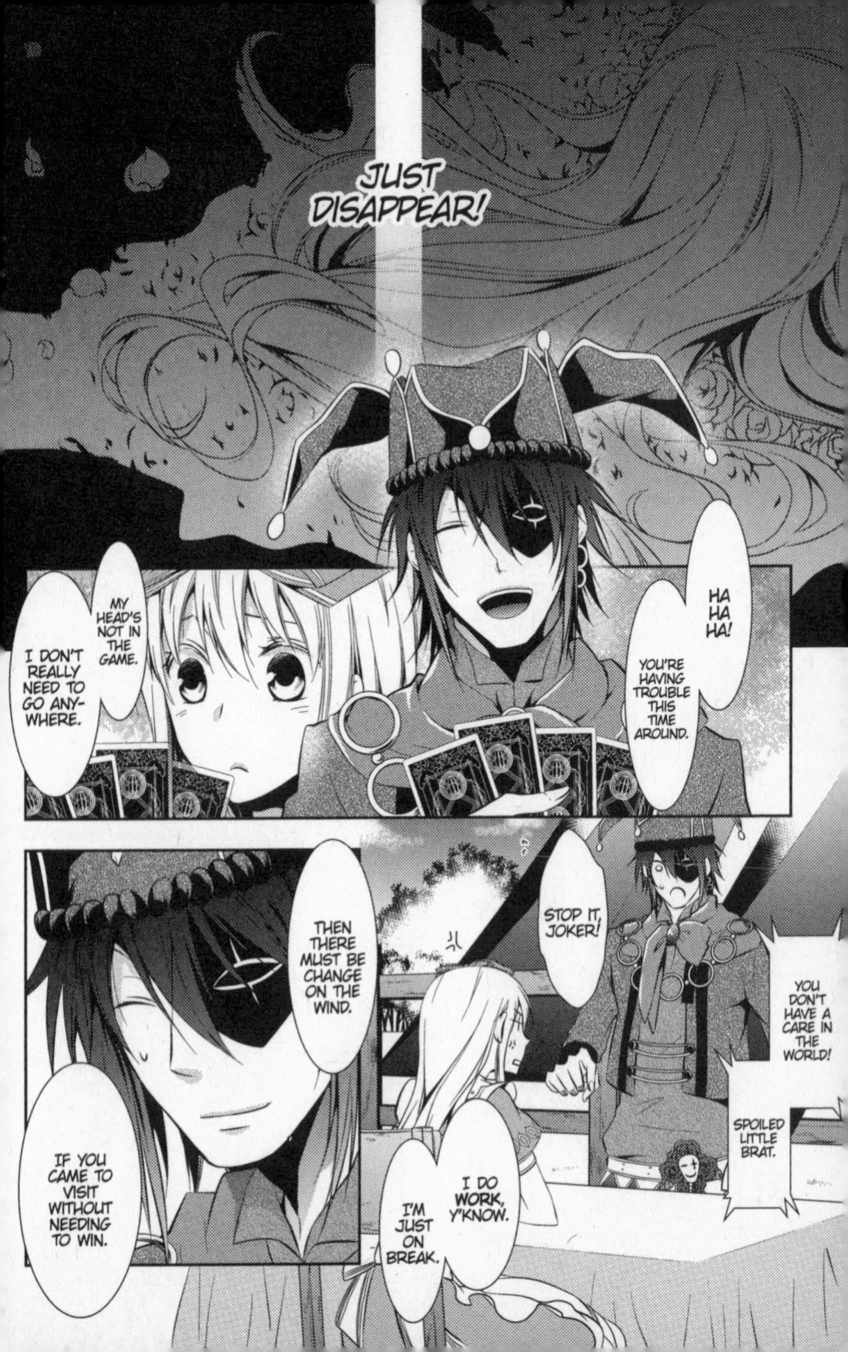
JUST DISAPPEAR!
HA HA HA!
YOU'RE HAVING TROUBLE THIS TIME AROUND.
MY HEAD'S NOT IN THE GAME.
I DON'T REALLY NEED TO GO ANY-WHERE.
YOU DON'T HAVE A CARE IN THE WORLD!
SPOILED LITTLE BRAT.
STOP IT, JOKER!
I DO WORK, Y'KNOW.
I'M JUST ON BREAK.
THEN THERE MUST BE CHANGE ON THE WIND.
IF YOU CAME TO VISIT WITHOUT NEEDING TO WIN.

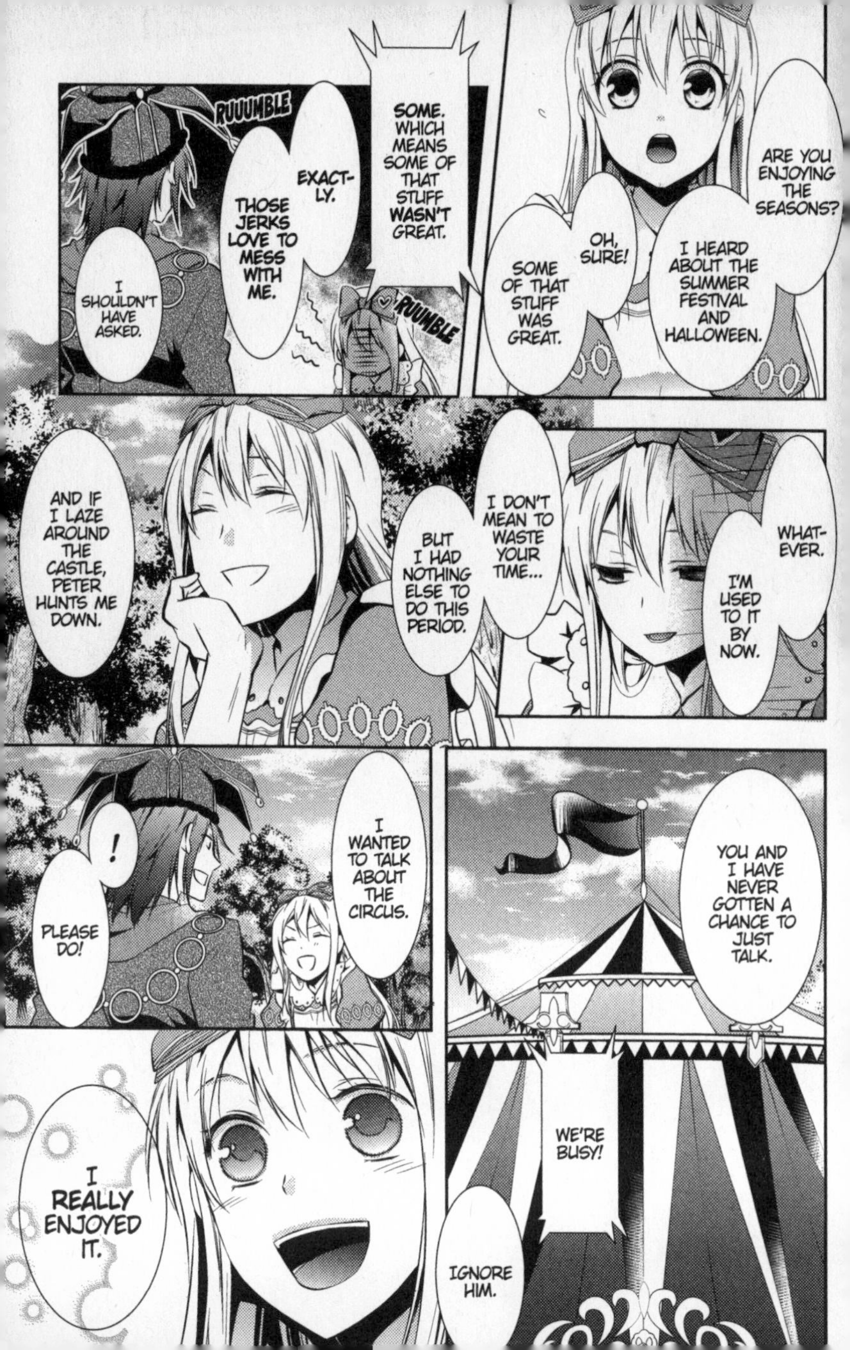
ARE YOU ENJOYING THE SEASONS?
I HEARD ABOUT THE SUMMER FESTIVAL AND HALLOWEEN.
OH, SURE!
SOME OF THAT STUFF WAS GREAT.
SOME. WHICH MEANS SOME OF THAT STUFF WASN'T GREAT.
RUUMBLE
EXACTLY.
THOSE JERKS LOVE TO MESS WITH ME.
RUUUMBLE
I SHOULDN'T HAVE ASKED.
WHAT-EVER.
I'M USED TO IT BY NOW.
I DON'T MEAN TO WASTE YOUR TIME...
BUT I HAD NOTHING ELSE TO DO THIS PERIOD.
AND IF I LAZE AROUND THE CASTLE, PETER HUNTS ME DOWN.
YOU AND I HAVE NEVER GOTTEN A CHANCE TO JUST TALK.
I WANTED TO TALK ABOUT THE CIRCUS.
!
PLEASE DO!
WE'RE BUSY!
IGNORE HIM.
I REALLY ENJOYED IT.

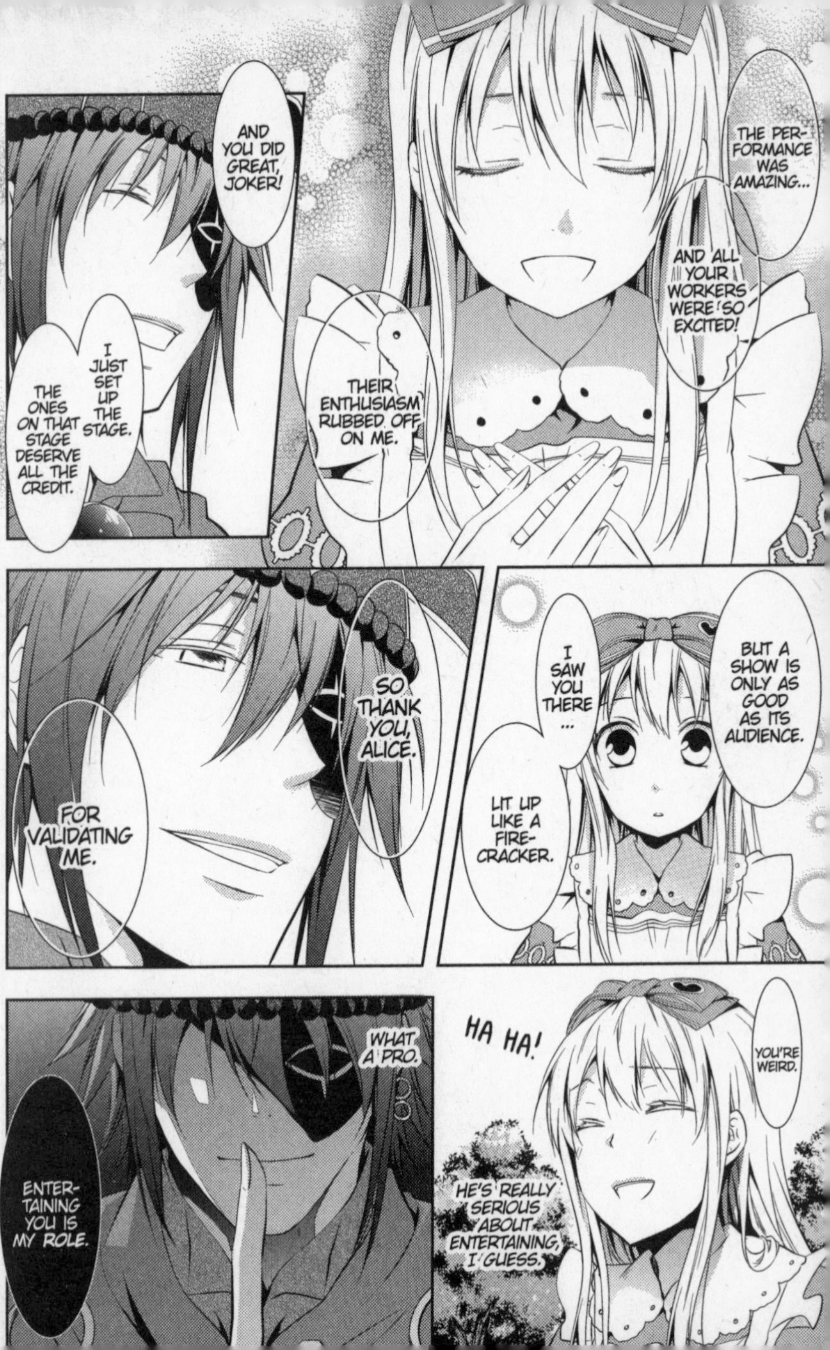
THE PERFORMANCE WAS AMAZING...
AND ALL YOUR WORKERS WERE SO EXCITED!
THEIR ENTHUSIASM RUBBED OFF ON ME.
AND YOU DID GREAT, JOKER!
I JUST SET UP THE STAGE.
THE ONES ON THAT STAGE DESERVE ALL THE CREDIT.
BUT A SHOW IS ONLY AS GOOD AS ITS AUDIENCE.
I SAW YOU THERE...
LIT UP LIKE A FIRECRACKER.
SO THANK YOU, ALICE.
FOR VALIDATING ME.
YOU'RE WEIRD.
HA HA!
HE'S REALLY SERIOUS ABOUT ENTERTAINING, I GUESS.
WHAT A PRO.
ENTERTAINING YOU IS MY ROLE.

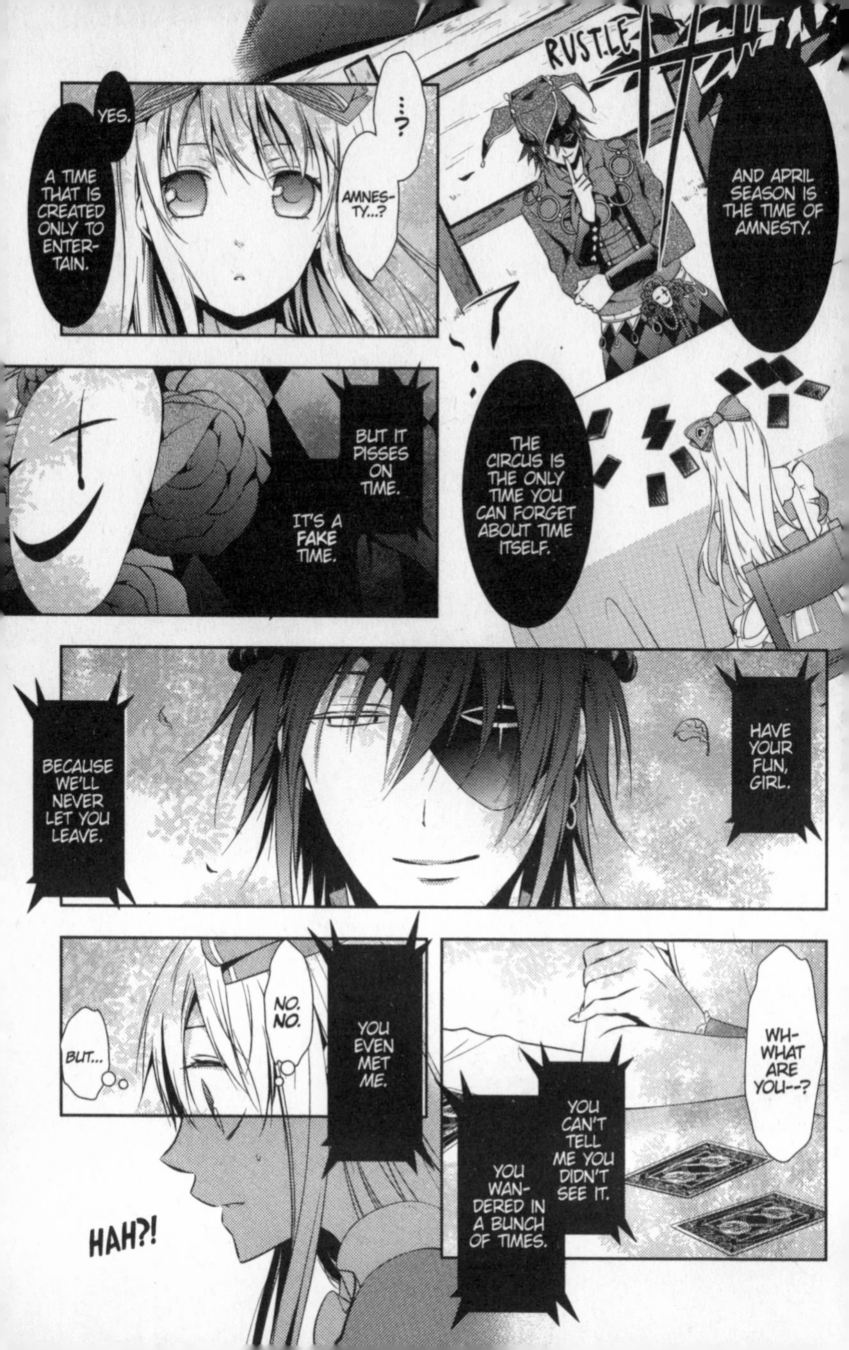
RUSTLE
AND APRIL SEASON IS THE TIME OF AMNESTY.
THE CIRCUS IS THE ONLY TIME YOU CAN FORGET ABOUT TIME ITSELF.
...?
AMNESTY...?
YES.
A TIME THAT IS CREATED ONLY TO ENTERTAIN.
BUT IT PISSES ON TIME.
IT'S A FAKE TIME.
HAVE YOUR FUN, GIRL.
BECAUSE WE'LL NEVER LET YOU LEAVE.
WH-WHAT ARE YOU--?
YOU CAN'T TELL ME YOU DIDN'T SEE IT.
YOU WANDERED IN A BUNCH OF TIMES.
YOU EVEN MET ME.
NO. NO.
BUT...
HAH?!

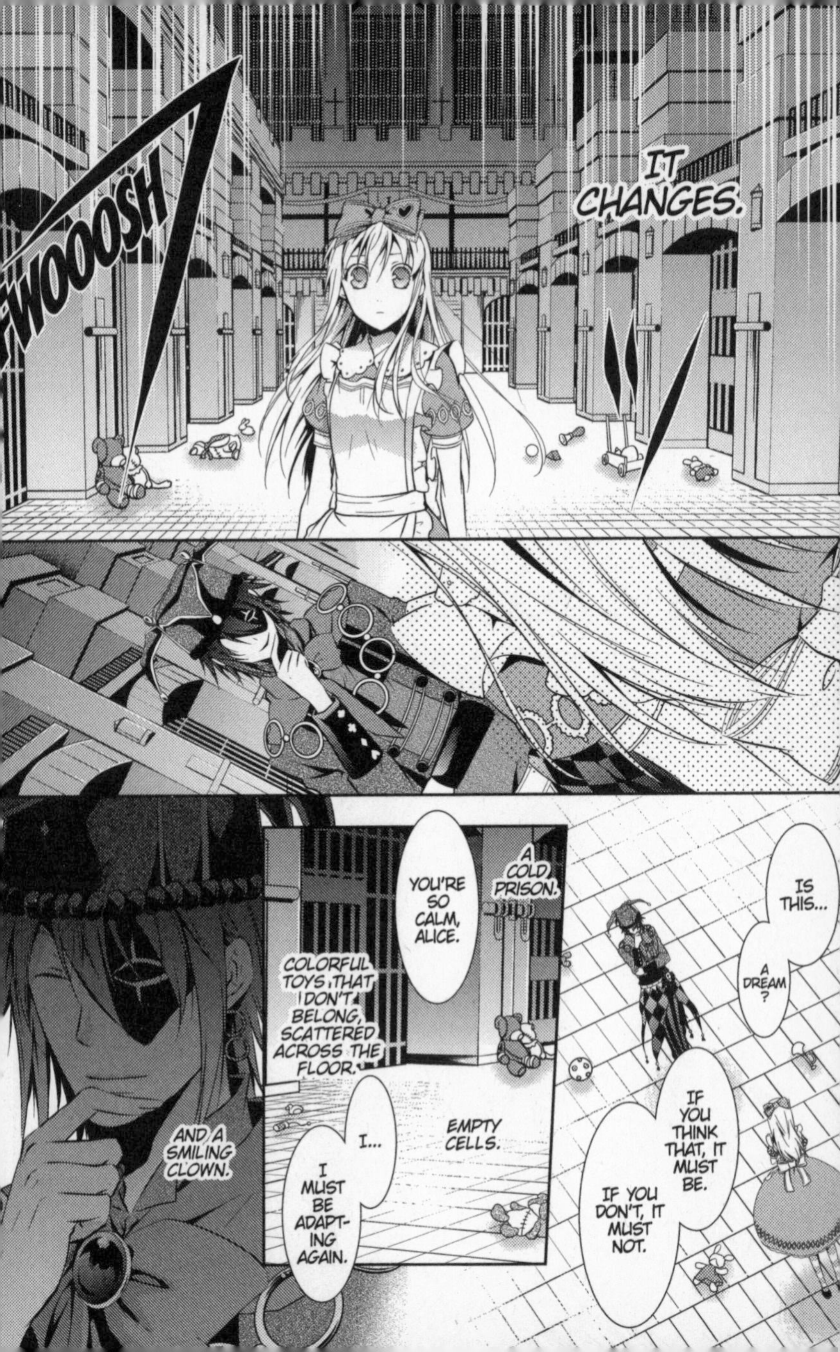
IT CHANGES.
WOOOSH
IS THIS...
A DREAM?
IF YOU THINK THAT, IT MUST BE.
IF YOU DON'T, IT MUST NOT.
A COLD PRISON.
YOU'RE SO CALM, ALICE.
COLORFUL TOYS THAT DON'T BELONG, SCATTERED ACROSS THE FLOOR.
EMPTY CELLS.
I...
I MUST BE ADAPTING AGAIN.
AND A SMILING CLOWN.

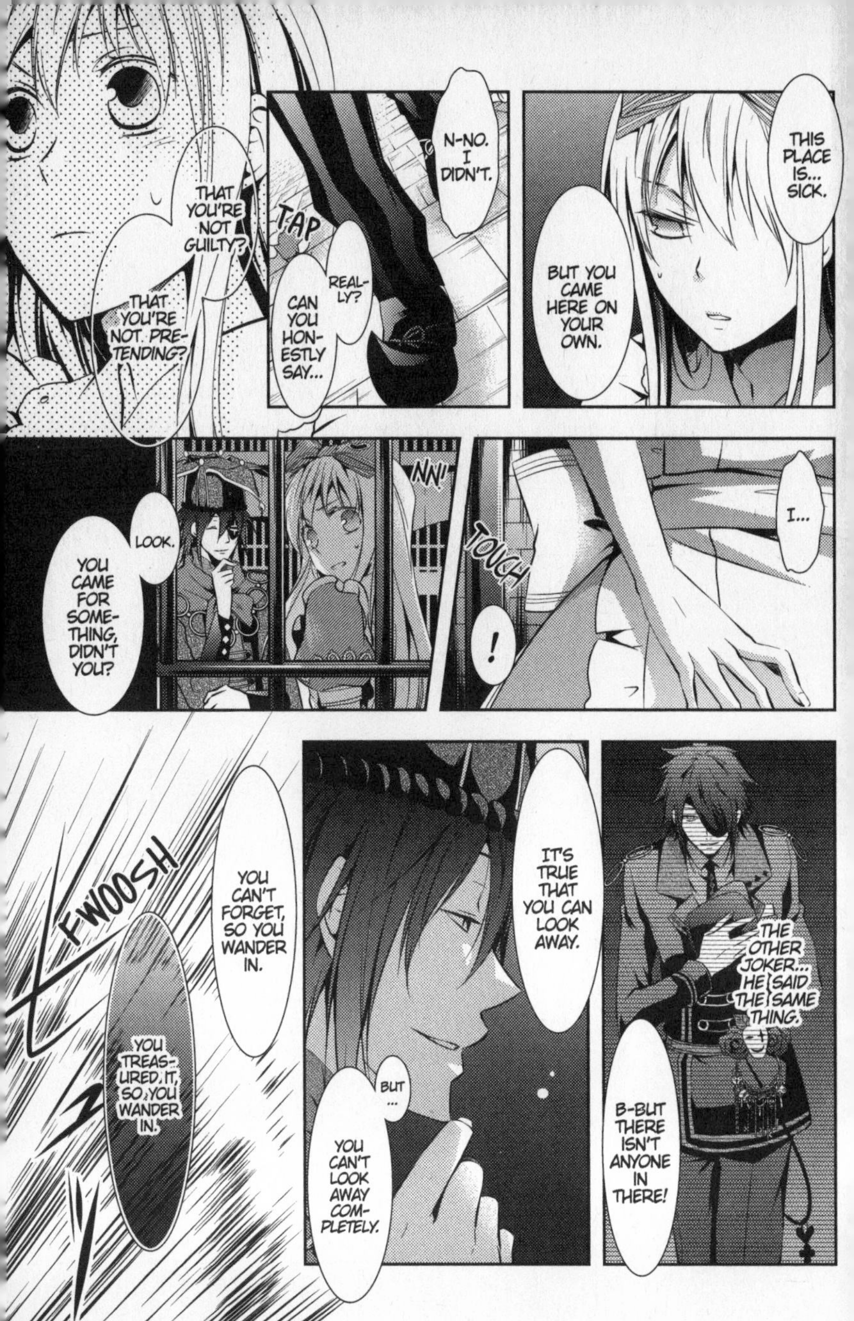
THIS PLACE IS... SICK.
BUT YOU CAME HERE ON YOUR OWN.
N-NO. I DIDN'T.
TAP
REALLY?
CAN YOU HONESTLY SAY...
THAT YOU'RE NOT GUILTY?
THAT YOU'RE NOT. PRETENDING?
I...
TOUCH
!
NN!
LOOK.
YOU CAME FOR SOMETHING, DIDN'T YOU?
THE OTHER JOKER... HE SAID THE SAME THING.
B-BUT THERE ISN'T ANYONE IN THERE!
IT'S TRUE THAT YOU CAN LOOK AWAY.
YOU CAN'T FORGET, SO YOU WANDER IN.
BUT...
YOU CAN'T LOOK AWAY COMPLETELY.
FWOOSH
YOU TREASURED IT, SO YOU WANDER IN.

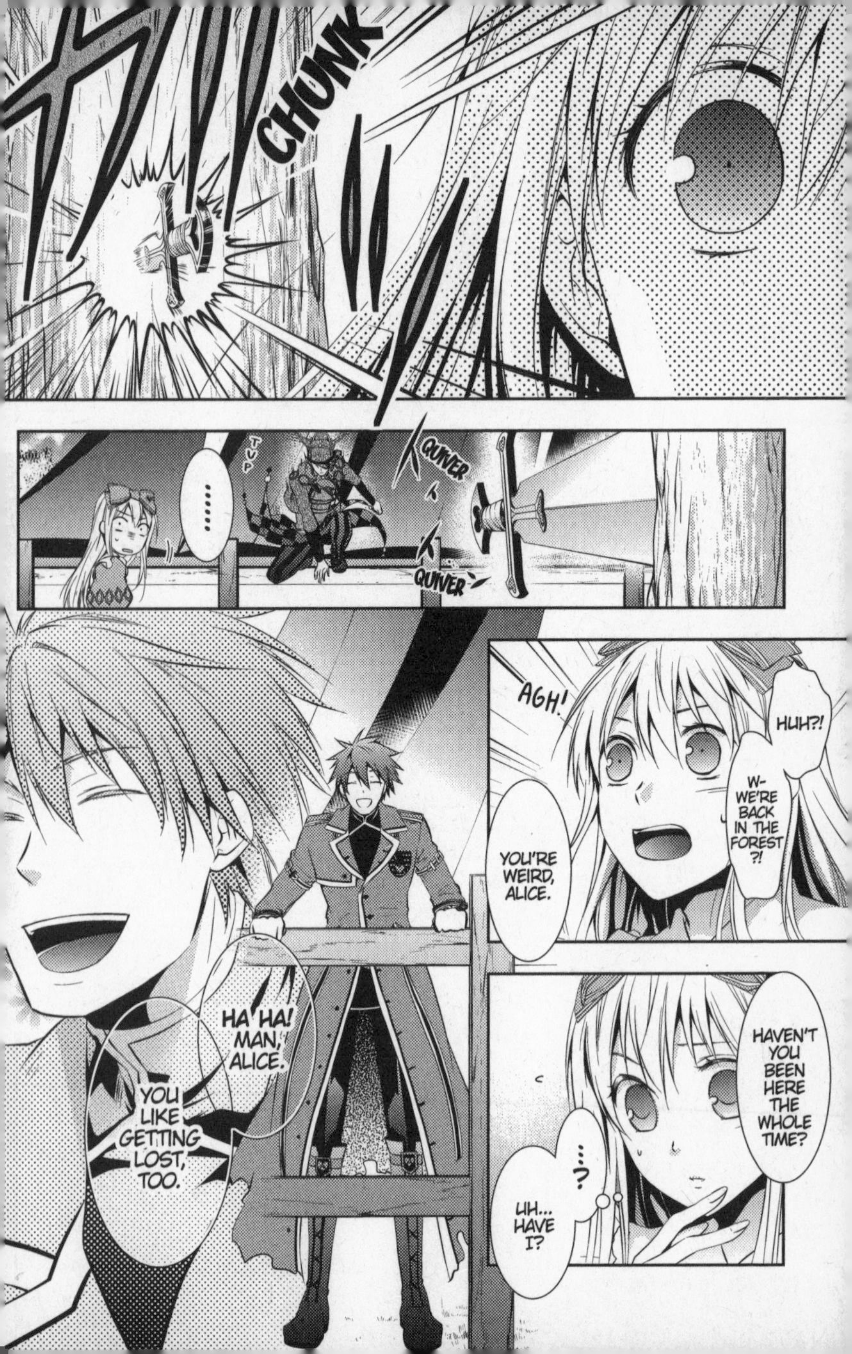
CHUNK
QUIVER
QUIVER
TUP
......
HUH?!
AGH!
W-WE'RE BACK IN THE FOREST?!
YOU'RE WEIRD, ALICE.
HAVEN'T YOU BEEN HERE THE WHOLE TIME?
...?
UH... HAVE I?
HA HA! MAN, ALICE.
YOU LIKE GETTING LOST, TOO.

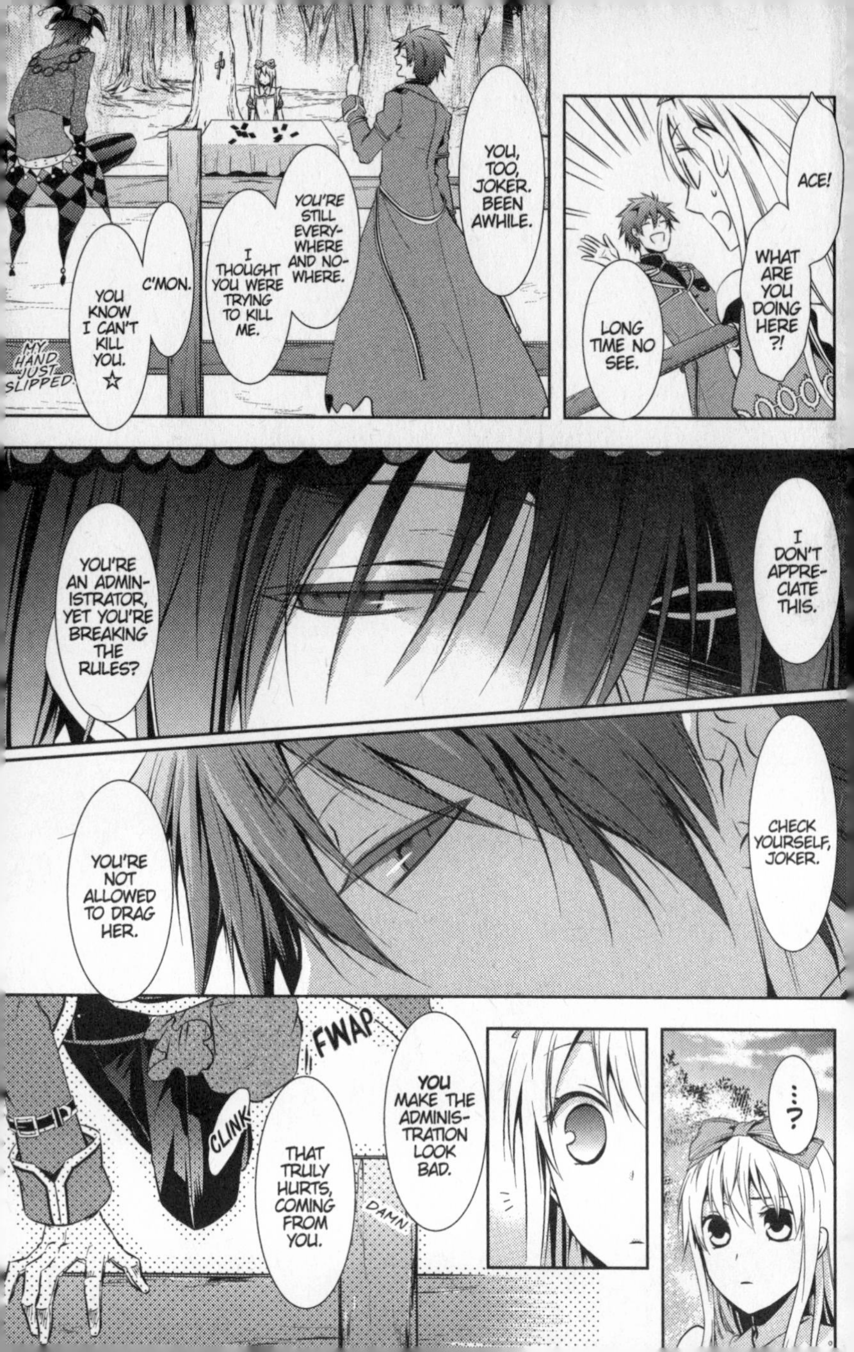
ACE!
WHAT ARE YOU DOING HERE?!
LONG TIME NO SEE.
YOU, TOO, JOKER. BEEN AWHILE.
YOU'RE STILL EVERYWHERE AND NOWHERE.
I THOUGHT YOU WERE TRYING TO KILL ME.
C'MON.
YOU KNOW I CAN'T KILL YOU. ☆
MY HAND JUST SLIPPED.
I DON'T APPRECIATE THIS.
YOU'RE AN ADMINISTRATOR, YET YOU'RE BREAKING THE RULES?
CHECK YOURSELF, JOKER.
YOU'RE NOT ALLOWED TO DRAG HER.
...?
FWAP
YOU MAKE THE ADMINISTRATION LOOK BAD.
THAT TRULY HURTS, COMING FROM YOU.
CLINK
DAMN

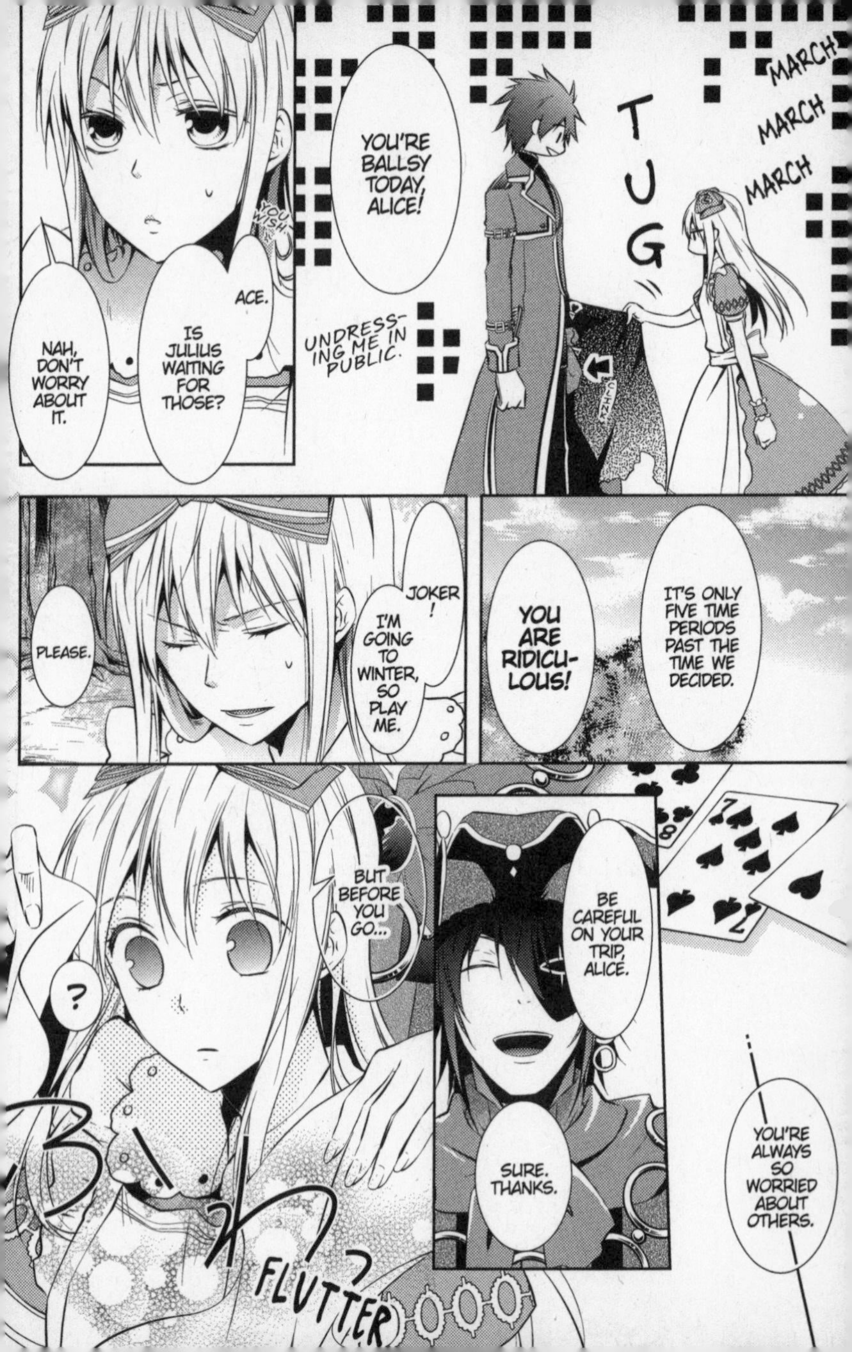
MARCH
MARCH
MARCH
YOU'RE BALLSY TODAY, ALICE!
TUG
CLINK
UNDRESSING ME IN PUBLIC.
ACE.
IS JULIUS WAITING FOR THOSE?
YOU WISH.
NAH, DON'T WORRY ABOUT IT.
IT'S ONLY FIVE TIME PERIODS PAST THE TIME WE DECIDED.
YOU ARE RIDICULOUS!
JOKER!
I'M GOING TO WINTER, SO PLAY ME.
PLEASE.
YOU'RE ALWAYS SO WORRIED ABOUT OTHERS.
BE CAREFUL ON YOUR TRIP, ALICE.
SURE. THANKS.
BUT BEFORE YOU GO...
?
FLUTTER

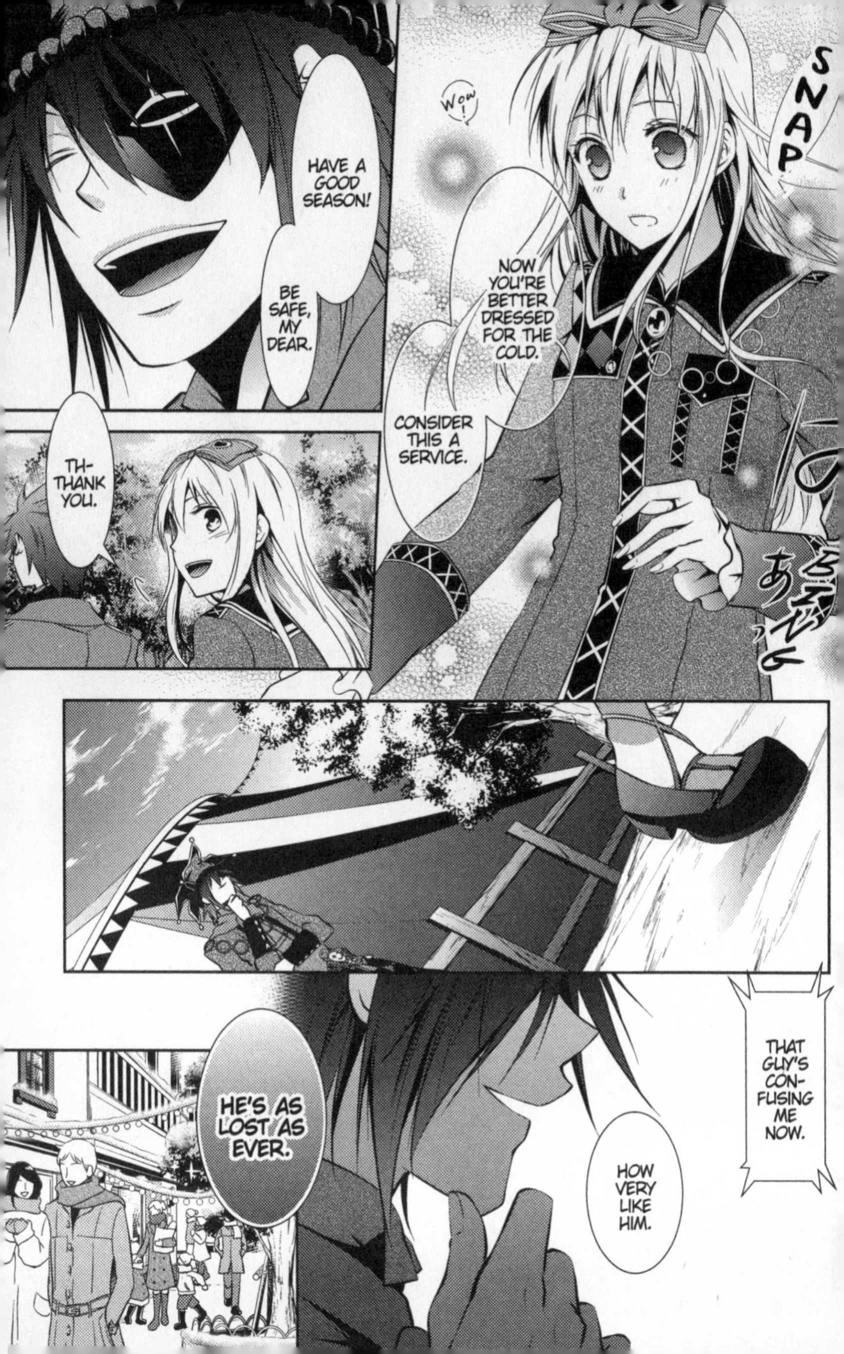
SNAP
WOW!
NOW YOU'RE BETTER DRESSED FOR THE COLD.
CONSIDER THIS A SERVICE.
HAVE A GOOD SEASON!
BE SAFE, MY DEAR.
TH-THANK YOU.
THAT GUY'S CONFUSING ME NOW.
HOW VERY LIKE HIM.
HE'S AS LOST AS EVER.

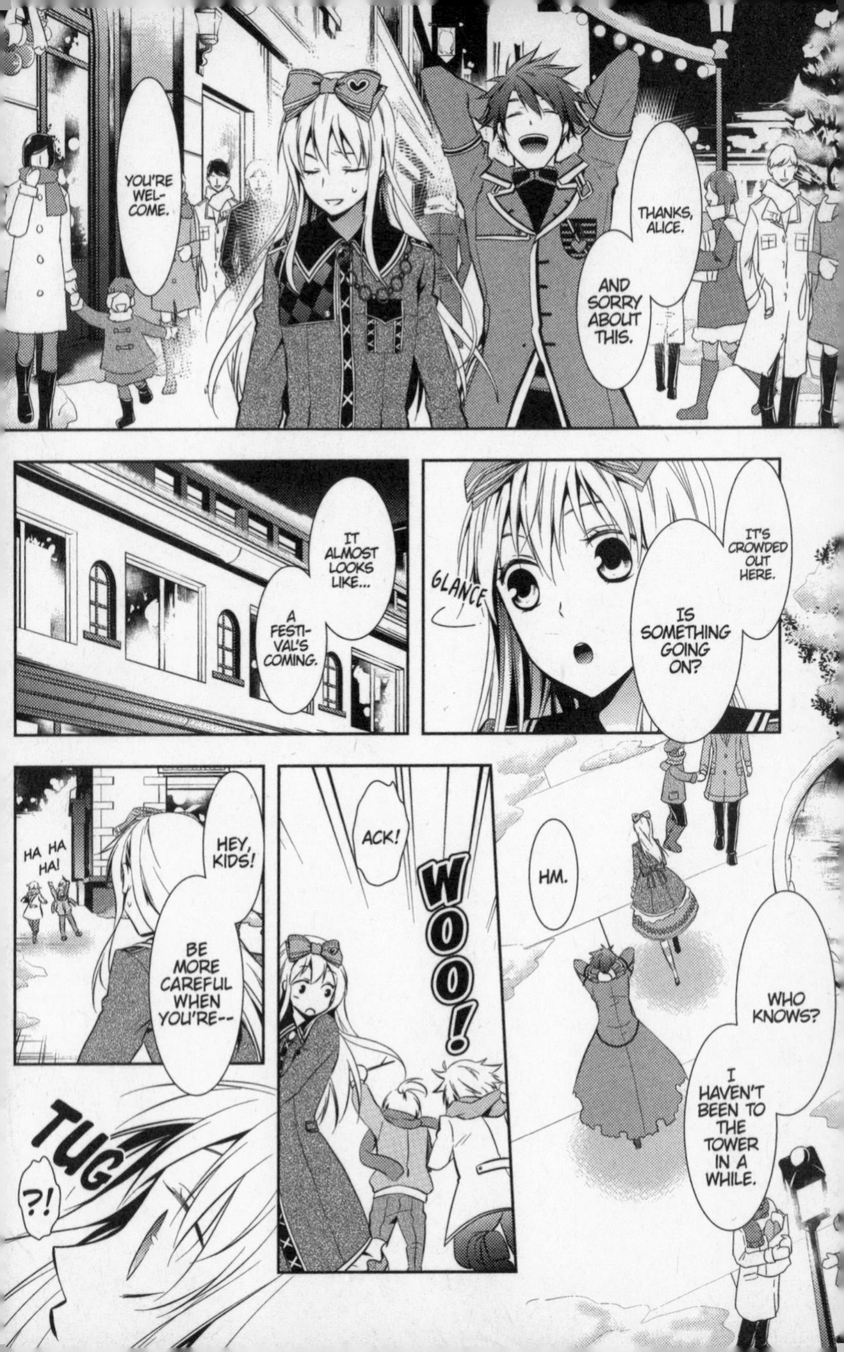
THANKS, ALICE.
AND SORRY ABOUT THIS.
YOU'RE WEL-COME.
IT'S CROWDED OUT HERE.
IS SOMETHING GOING ON?
GLANCE
IT ALMOST LOOKS LIKE...
A FESTI-VAL'S COMING.
HM.
WHO KNOWS?
I HAVEN'T BEEN TO THE TOWER IN A WHILE.
ACK!
WOOO!
HEY, KIDS!
BE MORE CAREFUL WHEN YOU'RE--
HA HA HA!
TUG
?!

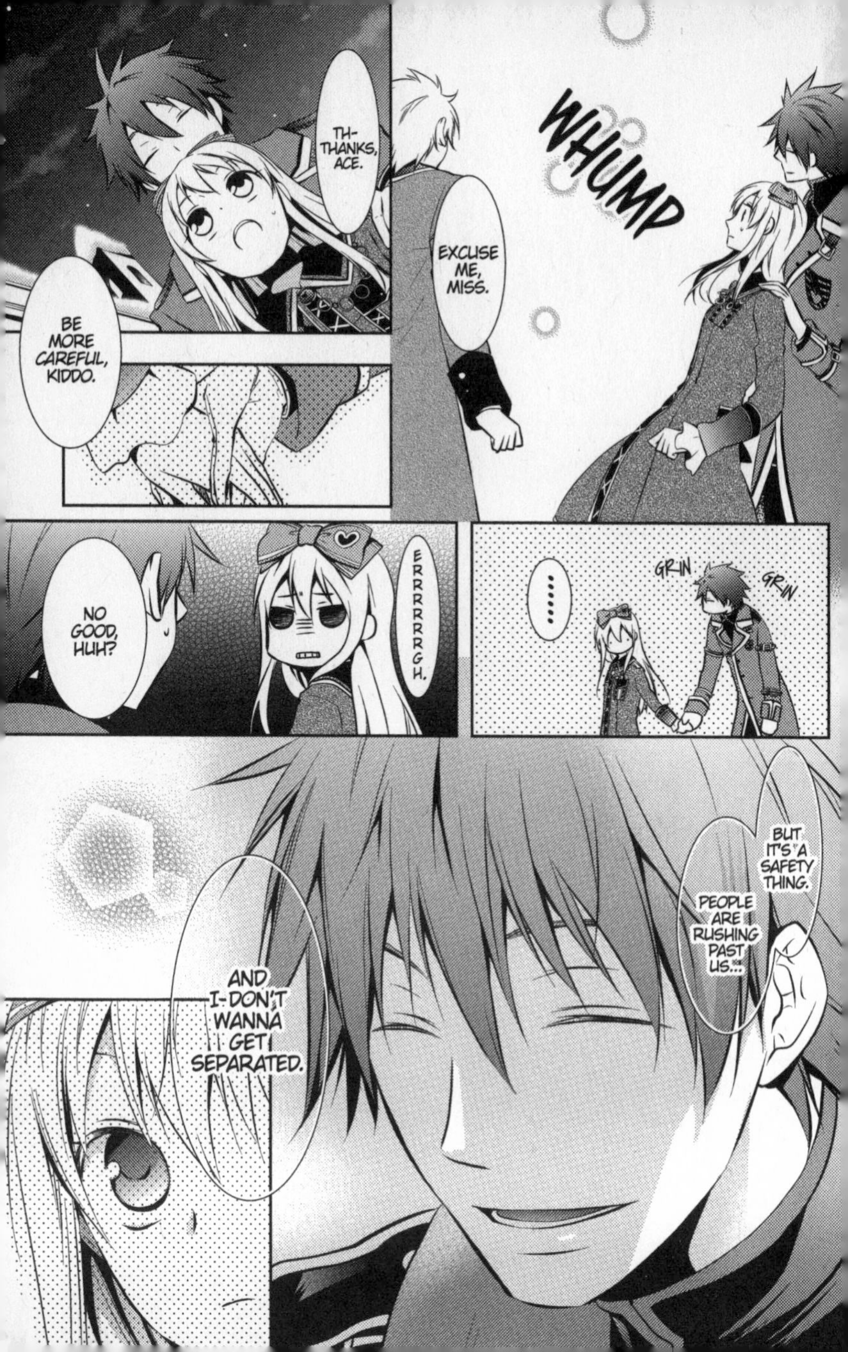
WHUMP
EXCUSE ME, MISS.
TH-THANKS, ACE.
BE MORE CAREFUL, KIDDO.
......
GRIN
GRIN
ERRRRRRGH.
NO GOOD, HUH?
BUT IT'S A SAFETY THING.
PEOPLE ARE RUSHING PAST US...
AND I-DON'T WANNA GET SEPARATED.

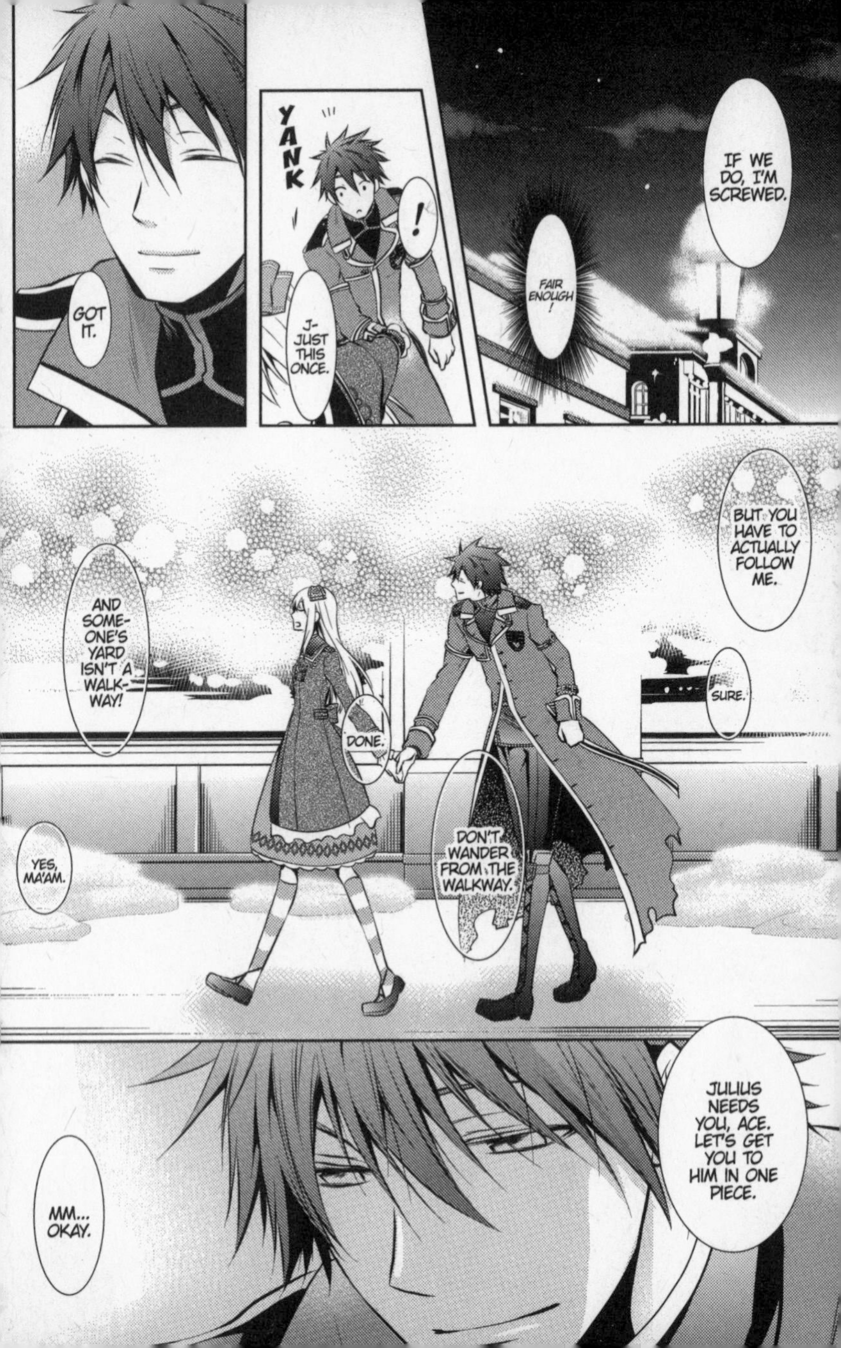
IF WE DO, I'M SCREWED.
FAIR ENOUGH!
YANK
!
J-JUST THIS ONCE.
GOT IT.
BUT YOU HAVE TO ACTUALLY FOLLOW ME.
SURE.
DON'T WANDER FROM THE WALKWAY.
DONE.
AND SOMEONE'S YARD ISN'T A WALK-WAY!
YES, MA'AM.
JULIUS NEEDS YOU, ACE. LET'S GET YOU TO HIM IN ONE PIECE.
MM... OKAY.

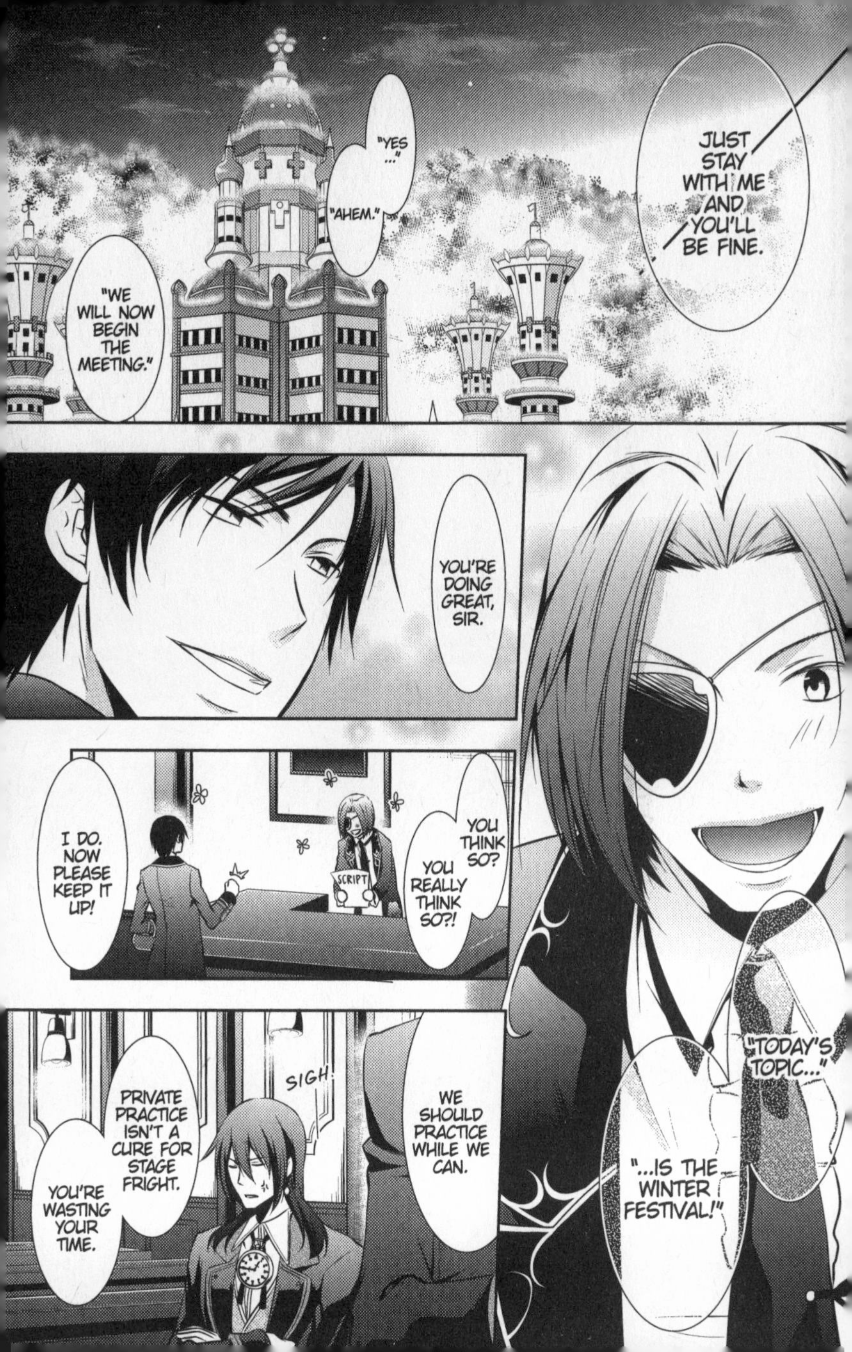
JUST STAY WITH ME AND YOU'LL BE FINE.
"YES..."
"AHEM."
"WE WILL NOW BEGIN THE MEETING."
"TODAY'S TOPIC..."
"...IS THE WINTER FESTIVAL!"
YOU'RE DOING GREAT, SIR.
YOU THINK SO?
YOU REALLY THINK SO?!
SCRIPT
I DO. NOW PLEASE KEEP IT UP!
WE SHOULD PRACTICE WHILE WE CAN.
SIGH!
PRIVATE PRACTICE ISN'T A CURE FOR STAGE FRIGHT.
YOU'RE WASTING YOUR TIME.

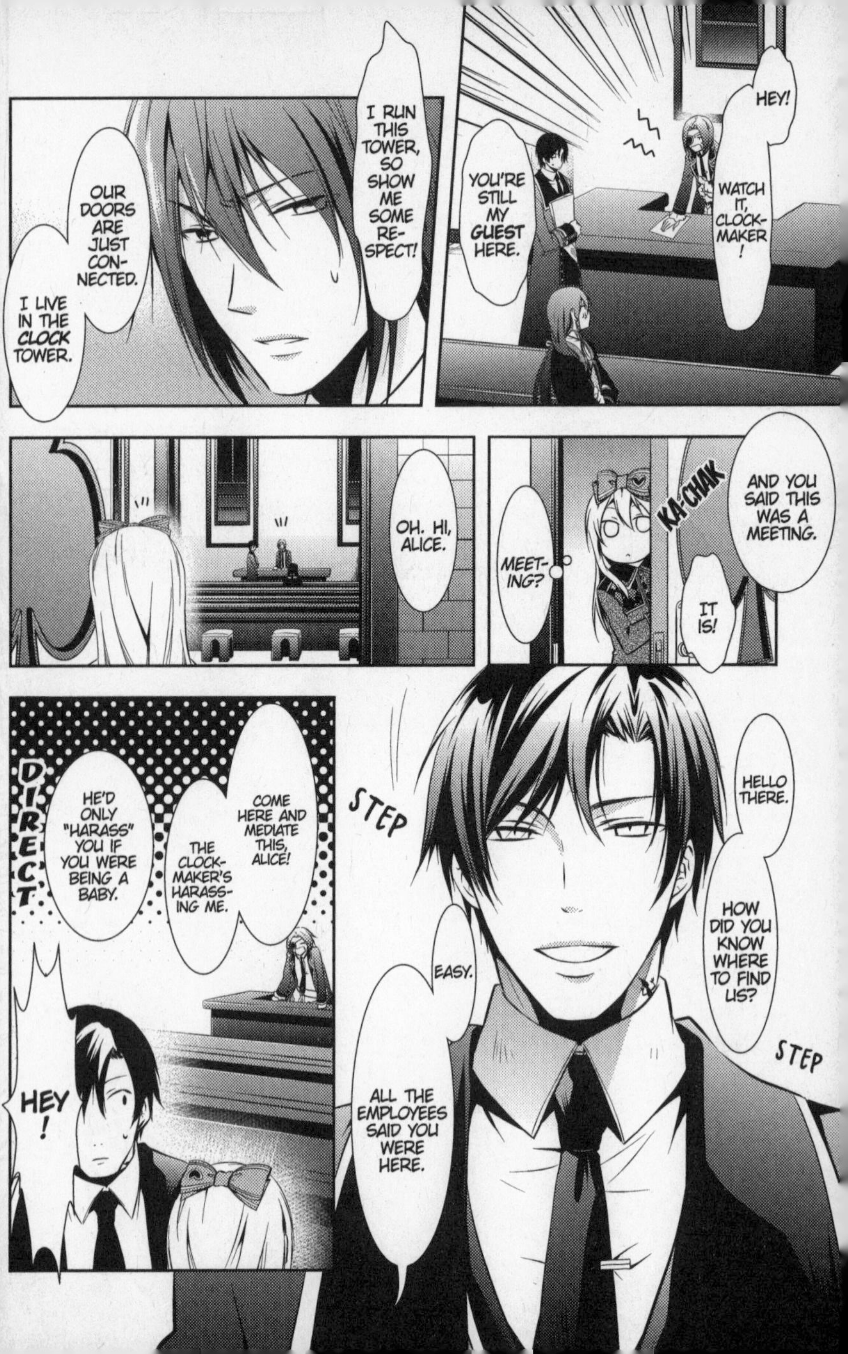
HEY!
WATCH IT, CLOCKMAKER!
YOU'RE STILL MY GUEST HERE.
I RUN THIS TOWER, SO SHOW ME SOME RESPECT!
OUR DOORS ARE JUST CONNECTED.
I LIVE IN THE CLOCK TOWER.
KA-CHAK
AND YOU SAID THIS WAS A MEETING.
IT IS!
MEETING?
OH. HI, ALICE.
HELLO THERE.
STEP
HOW DID YOU KNOW WHERE TO FIND US?
STEP
EASY.
ALL THE EMPLOYEES SAID YOU WERE HERE.
COME HERE AND MEDIATE THIS, ALICE!
THE CLOCKMAKER'S HARASSING ME.
HE'D ONLY "HARASS" YOU IF YOU WERE BEING A BABY.
DIRECT
HEY!

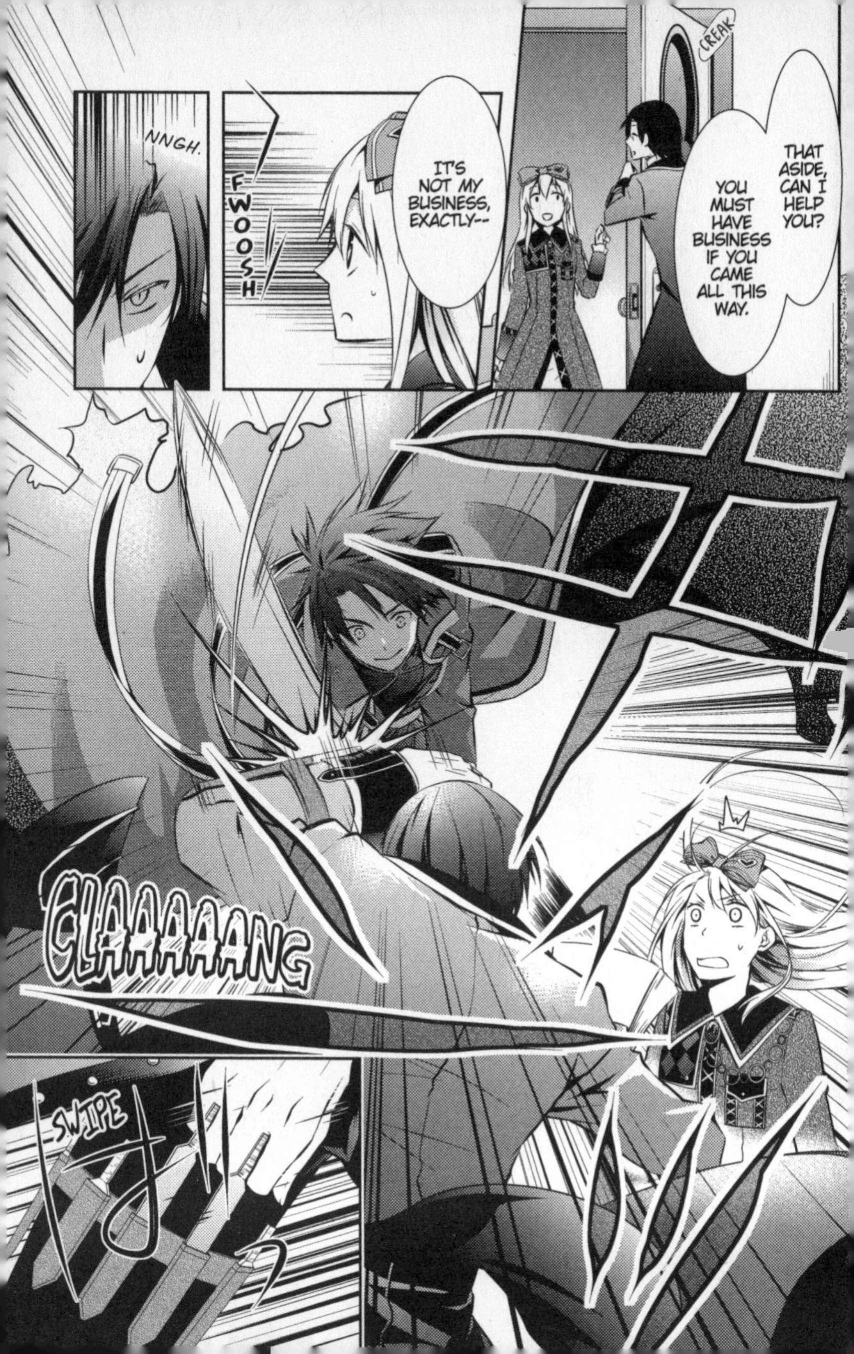
CREAK
THAT ASIDE, CAN I HELP YOU?
YOU MUST HAVE BUSINESS IF YOU CAME ALL THIS WAY.
FWOOSH
IT'S NOT MY BUSINESS, EXACTLY--
NNGH.
CLAAAAAANG
SWIPE

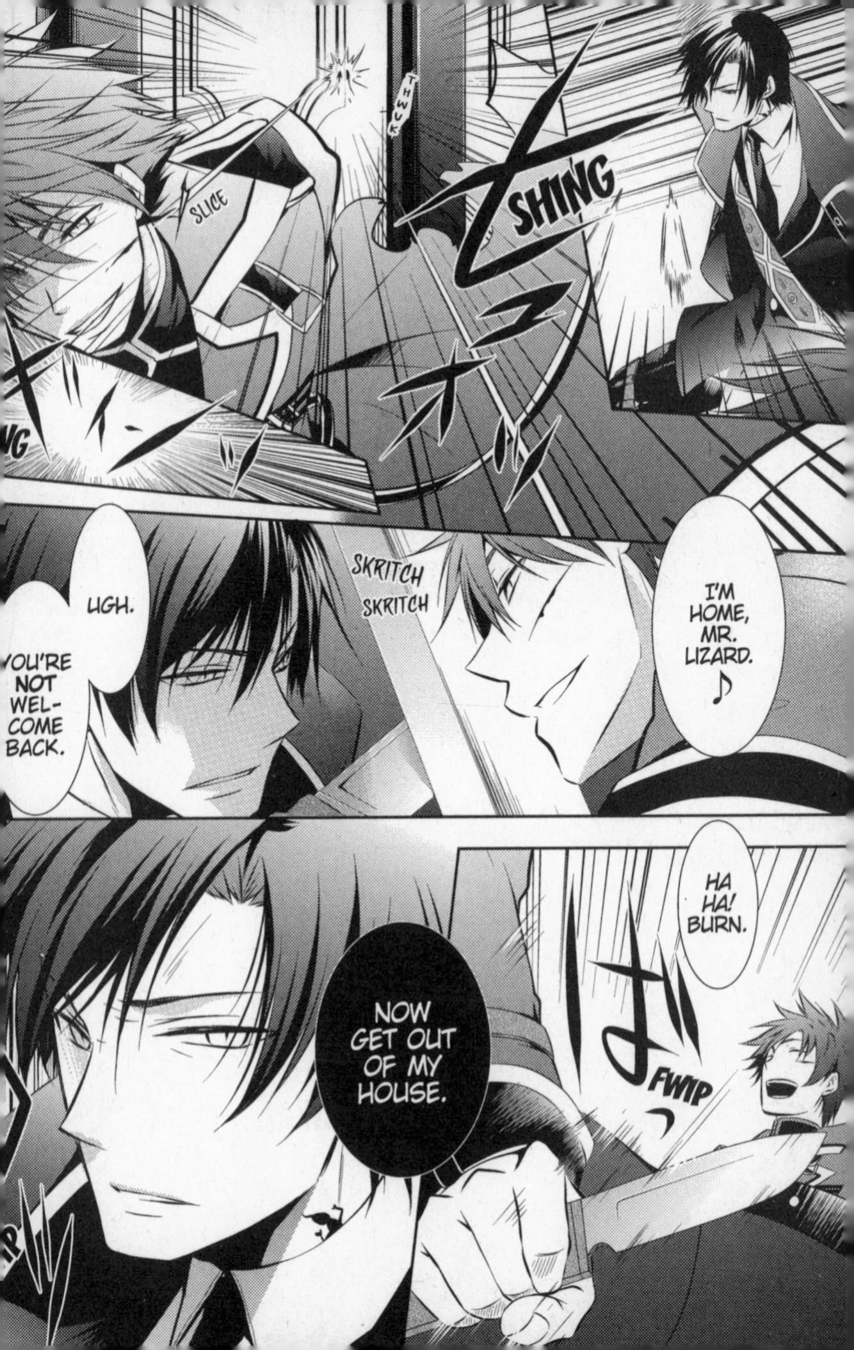
SHING
THWUK
SLICE
I'M HOME, MR. LIZARD. ♪
SKRITCH SKRITCH
UGH.
YOU'RE NOT WEL-COME BACK.
HA HA! BURN.
FWIP
NOW GET OUT OF MY HOUSE.

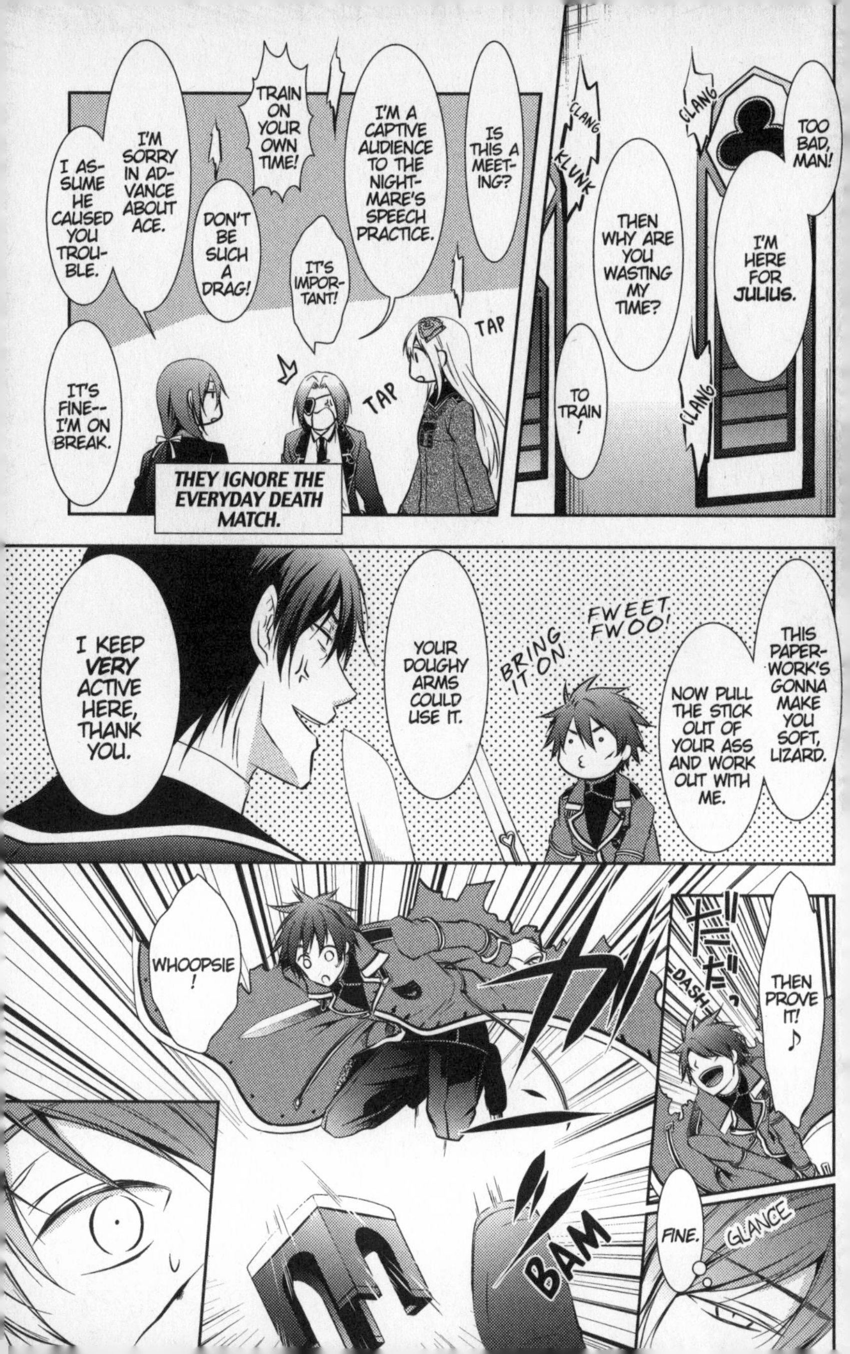
TOO BAD, MAN!
CLANG
I'M HERE FOR JULIUS.
CLANG
KLUNK
THEN WHY ARE YOU WASTING MY TIME?
TO TRAIN!
CLANG
IS THIS A MEETING?
I'M A CAPTIVE AUDIENCE TO THE NIGHTMARE'S SPEECH PRACTICE.
TRAIN ON YOUR OWN TIME!
IT'S IMPORTANT!
I'M SORRY IN ADVANCE ABOUT ACE.
DON'T BE SUCH A DRAG!
I ASSUME HE CAUSED YOU TROUBLE.
TAP
TAP
IT'S FINE--I'M ON BREAK.
THEY IGNORE THE EVERYDAY DEATH MATCH.
THIS PAPERWORK'S GONNA MAKE YOU SOFT, LIZARD.
NOW PULL THE STICK OUT OF YOUR ASS AND WORK OUT WITH ME.
FWEET FWOO!
BRING IT ON
YOUR DOUGHY ARMS COULD USE IT.
I KEEP VERY ACTIVE HERE, THANK YOU.
THEN PROVE IT! ♪
DASH
FINE.
GLANCE
WHOOPSIE!
BAM

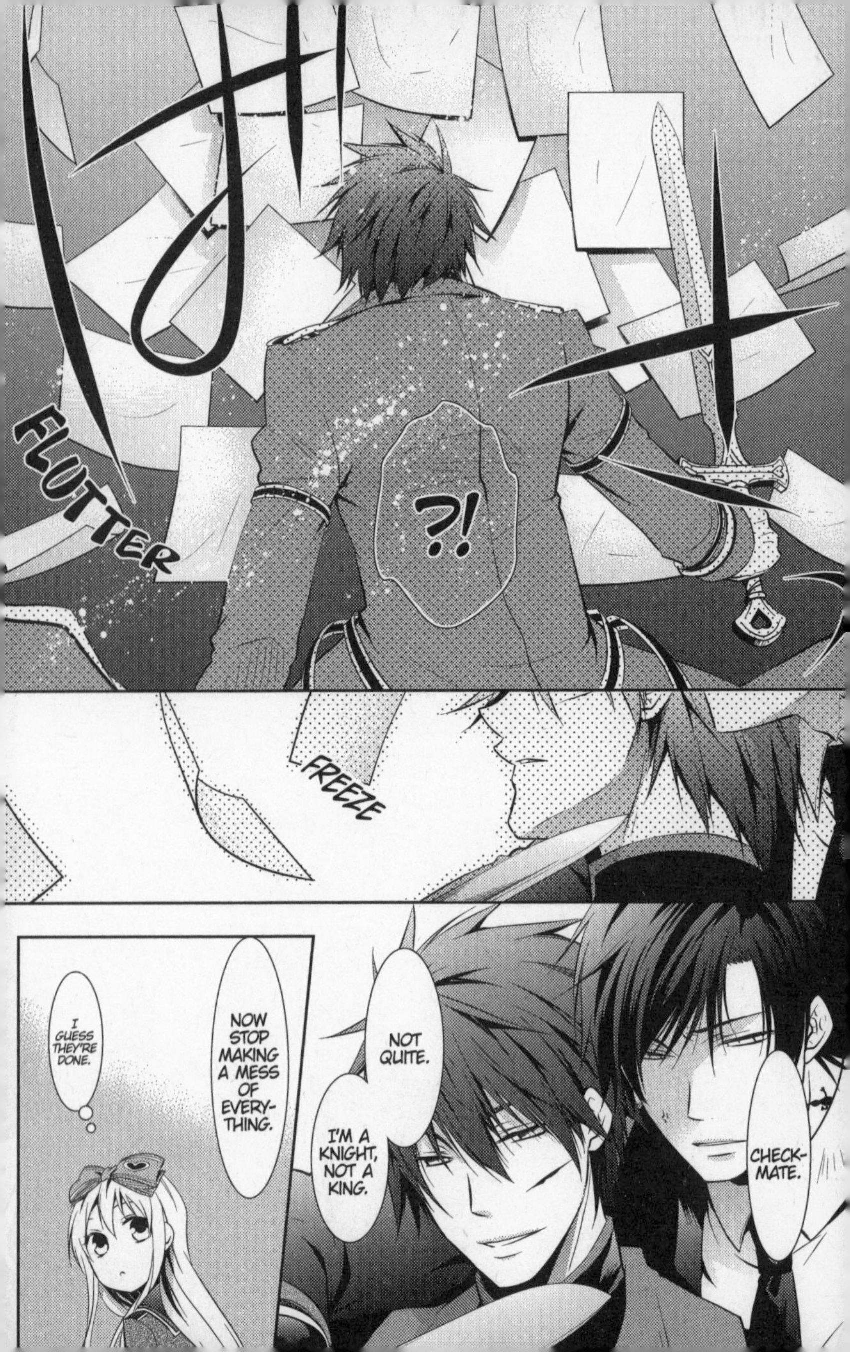
FLUTTER
?!
FREEZE
CHECK-MATE.
NOT QUITE.
I'M A KNIGHT, NOT A KING.
NOW STOP MAKING A MESS OF EVERY-THING.
I GUESS THEY'RE DONE.

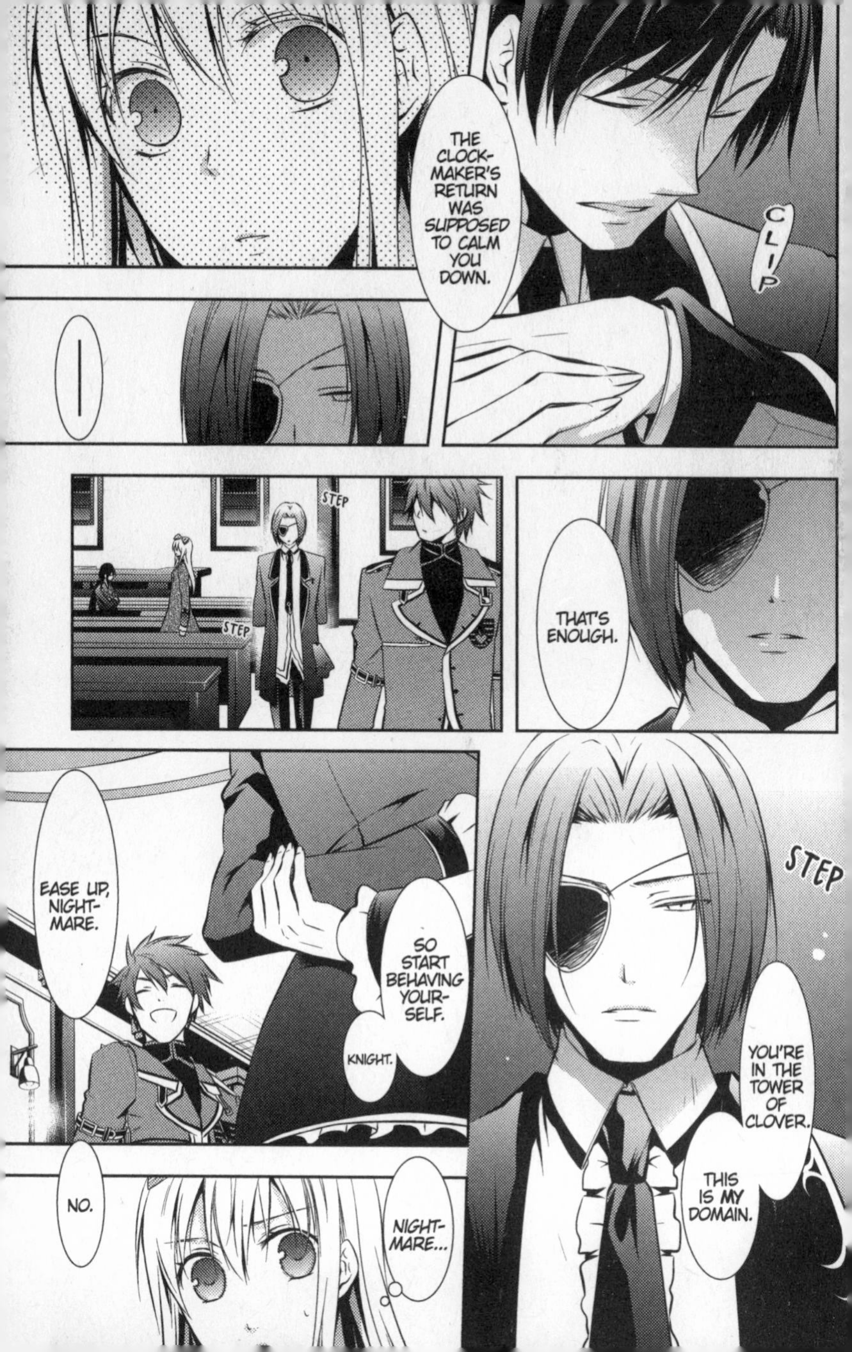

THE CLOCK-MAKER'S RETURN WAS SUPPOSED TO CALM YOU DOWN.
CLIP
—
THAT'S ENOUGH.
STEP
STEP
STEP
YOU'RE IN THE TOWER OF CLOVER.
THIS IS MY DOMAIN.
SO START BEHAVING YOURSELF.
KNIGHT.
EASE UP, NIGHT-MARE.
NIGHT-MARE...
NO.

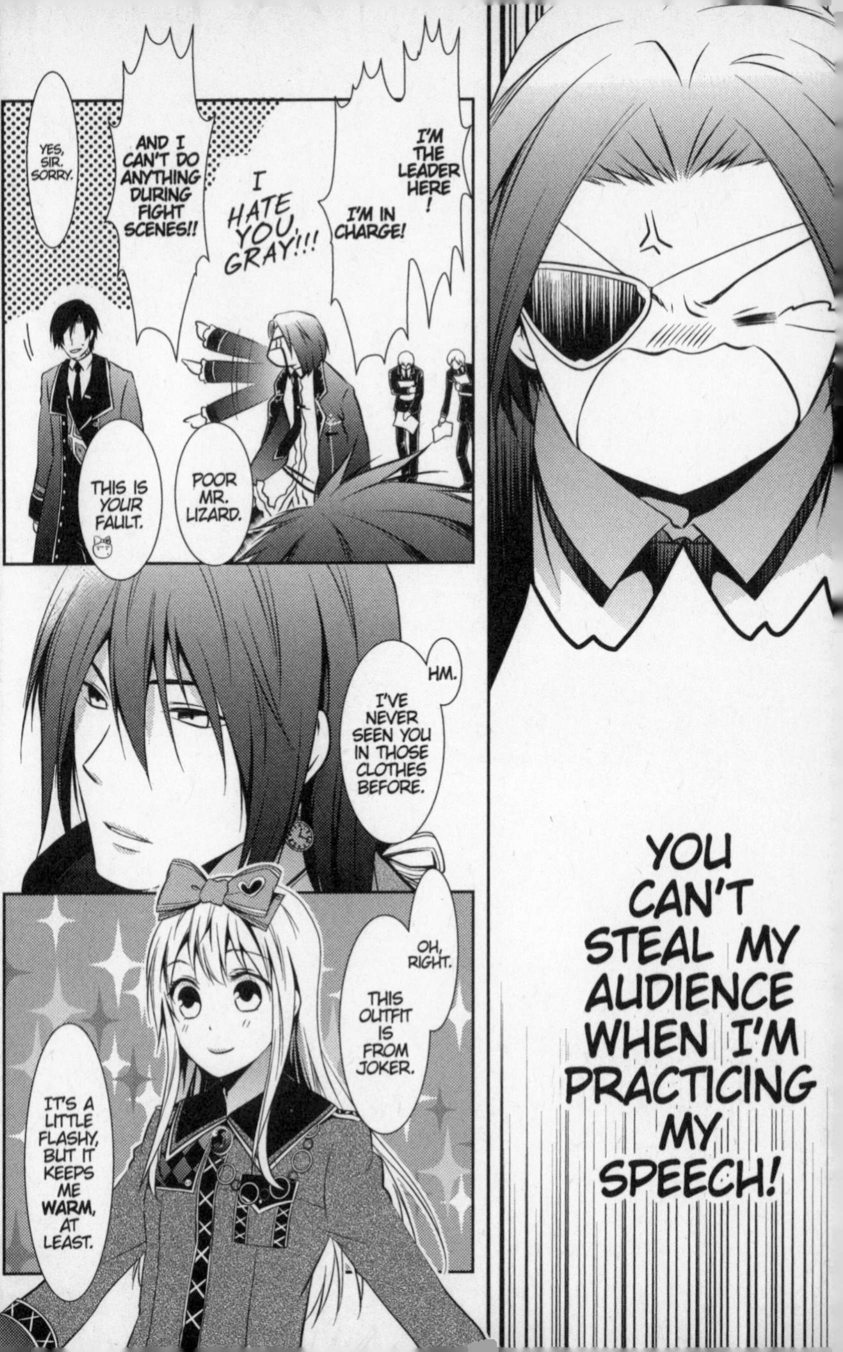
YOU CAN'T STEAL MY AUDIENCE WHEN I'M PRACTICING MY SPEECH!
I'M THE LEADER HERE!
I'M IN CHARGE!
I HATE YOU, GRAY!!!
AND I CAN'T DO ANYTHING DURING FIGHT SCENES!!
YES, SIR. SORRY.
POOR MR. LIZARD.
THIS IS YOUR FAULT.
HM.
I'VE NEVER SEEN YOU IN THOSE CLOTHES BEFORE.
OH, RIGHT.
THIS OUTFIT IS FROM JOKER.
IT'S A LITTLE FLASHY, BUT IT KEEPS ME WARM, AT LEAST.

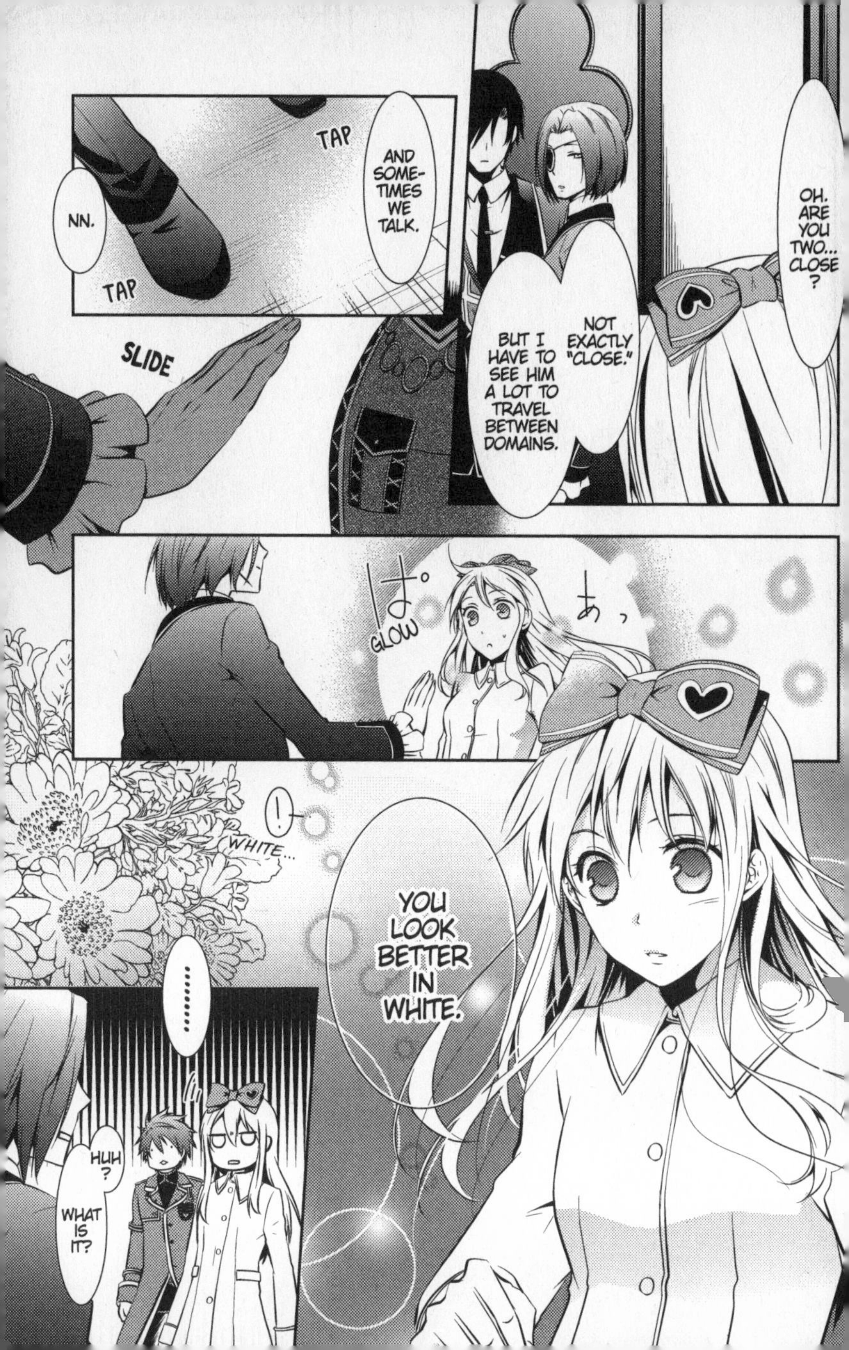
OH. ARE YOU TWO... CLOSE?
NOT EXACTLY "CLOSE."
BUT I HAVE TO SEE HIM A LOT TO TRAVEL BETWEEN DOMAINS.
AND SOME-TIMES WE TALK.
TAP
NN.
TAP
SLIDE
あっ
ぱ
GLOW
!
WHITE...
YOU LOOK BETTER IN WHITE.
......
HUH?
WHAT IS IT?

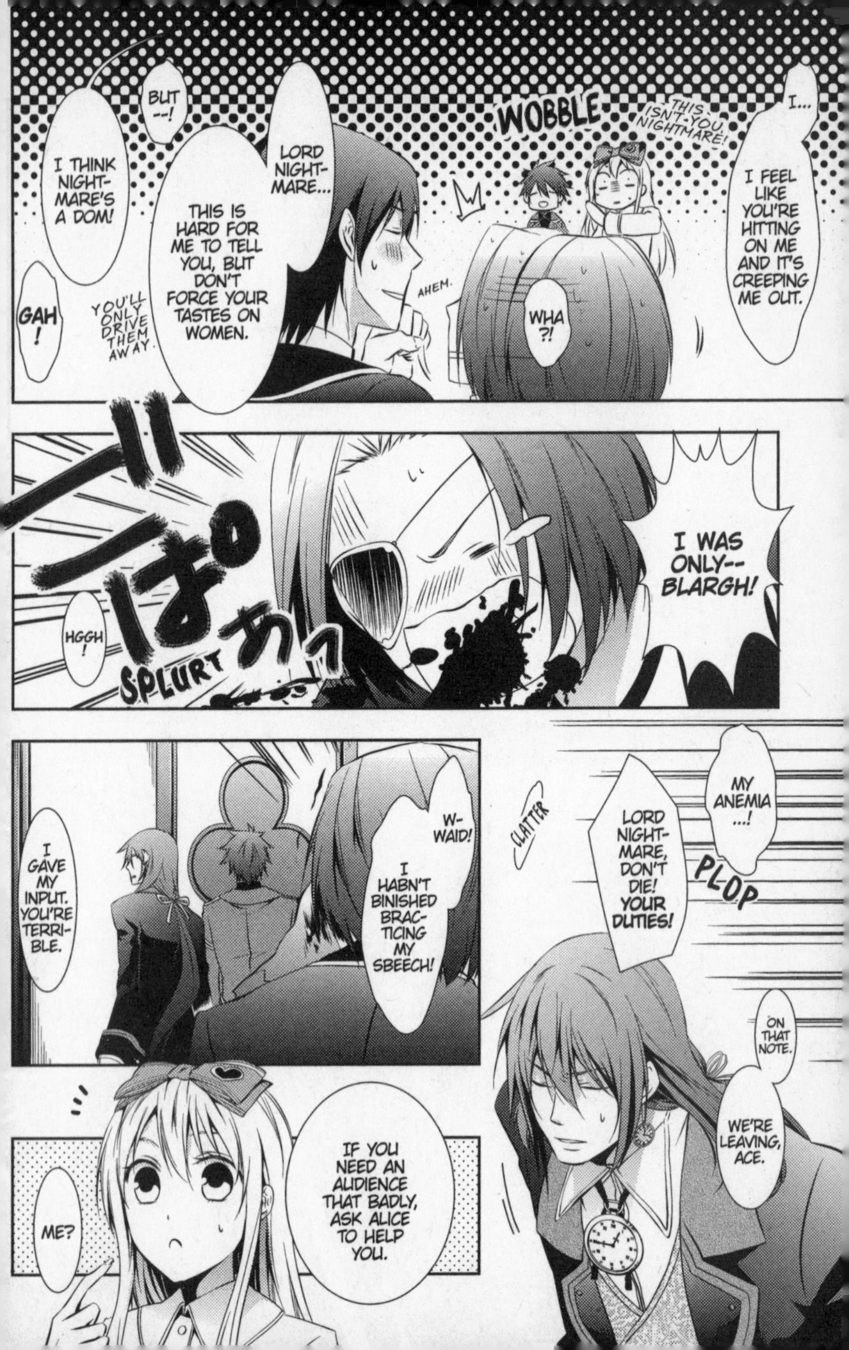

I...
I FEEL LIKE YOU'RE HITTING ON ME AND IT'S CREEPING ME OUT.
THIS ISN'T YOU, NIGHTMARE!
WOBBLE
WHA?!
AHEM.
LORD NIGHTMARE...
THIS IS HARD FOR ME TO TELL YOU, BUT DON'T FORCE YOUR TASTES ON WOMEN.
YOU'LL ONLY DRIVE THEM AWAY.
BUT--!
I THINK NIGHTMARE'S A DOM!
GAH!
I WAS ONLY--BLARGH!
SPLURT
HGGH!
MY ANEMIA...!
LORD NIGHTMARE, DON'T DIE! YOUR DUTIES!
PLOP
CLATTER
ON THAT NOTE.
WE'RE LEAVING, ACE.
W-WAID!
I HABN'T BINISHED BRACTICING MY SBEECH!
I GAVE MY INPUT. YOU'RE TERRIBLE.
IF YOU NEED AN AUDIENCE THAT BADLY, ASK ALICE TO HELP YOU.
ME?

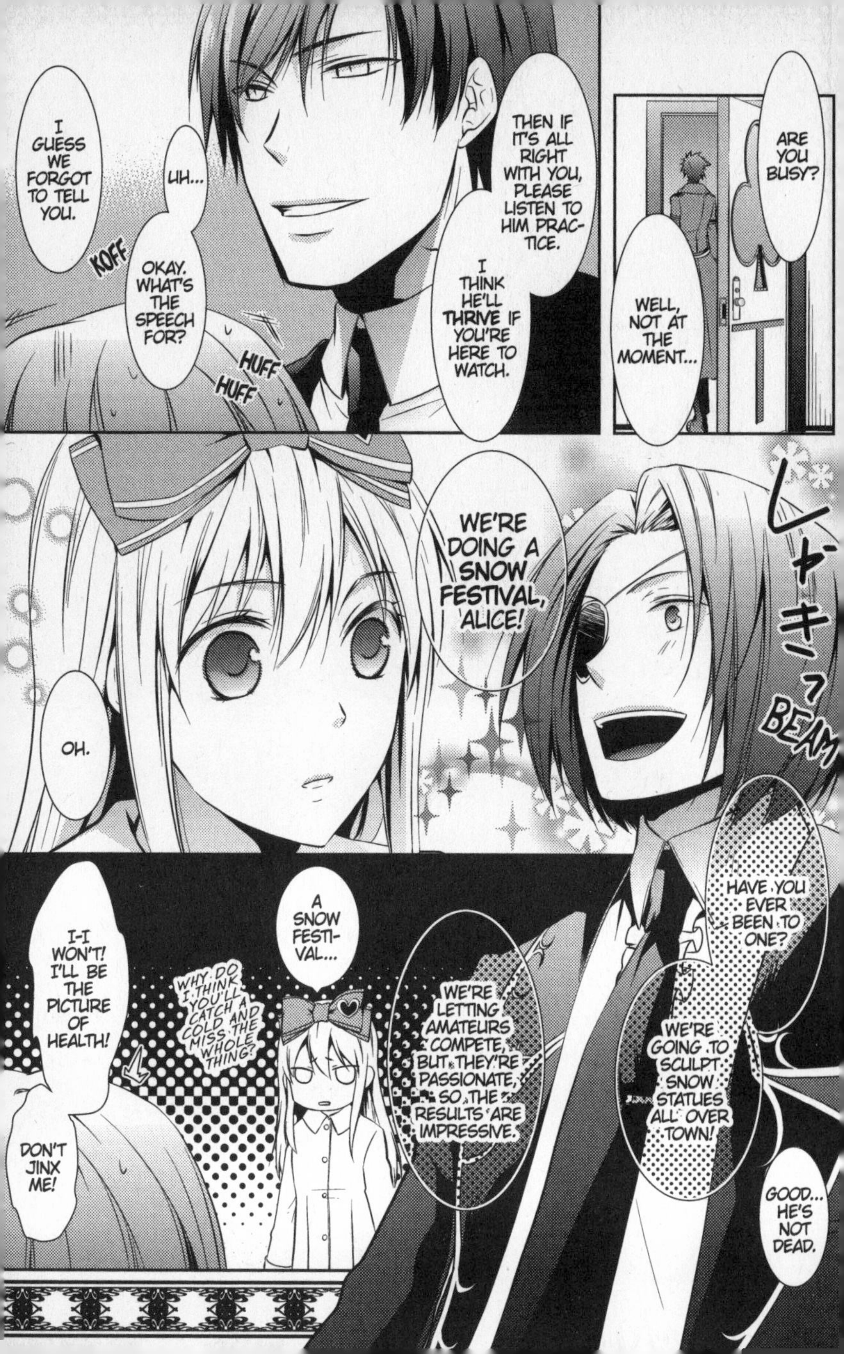
ARE YOU BUSY?
WELL, NOT AT THE MOMENT...
THEN IF IT'S ALL RIGHT WITH YOU, PLEASE LISTEN TO HIM PRACTICE.
I THINK HE'LL THRIVE IF YOU'RE HERE TO WATCH.
UH...
I GUESS WE FORGOT TO TELL YOU.
KOFF
OKAY. WHAT'S THE SPEECH FOR?
HUFF
HUFF
BEAM
WE'RE DOING A SNOW FESTIVAL, ALICE!
OH.
HAVE YOU EVER BEEN TO ONE?
WE'RE GOING TO SCULPT SNOW STATUES ALL OVER TOWN!
GOOD... HE'S NOT DEAD.
WE'RE LETTING AMATEURS COMPETE, BUT THEY'RE PASSIONATE, SO THE RESULTS ARE IMPRESSIVE.
A SNOW FESTIVAL...
WHY DO I THINK YOU'LL CATCH A COLD AND MISS THE WHOLE THING?
I-I WON'T! I'LL BE THE PICTURE OF HEALTH!
DON'T JINX ME!

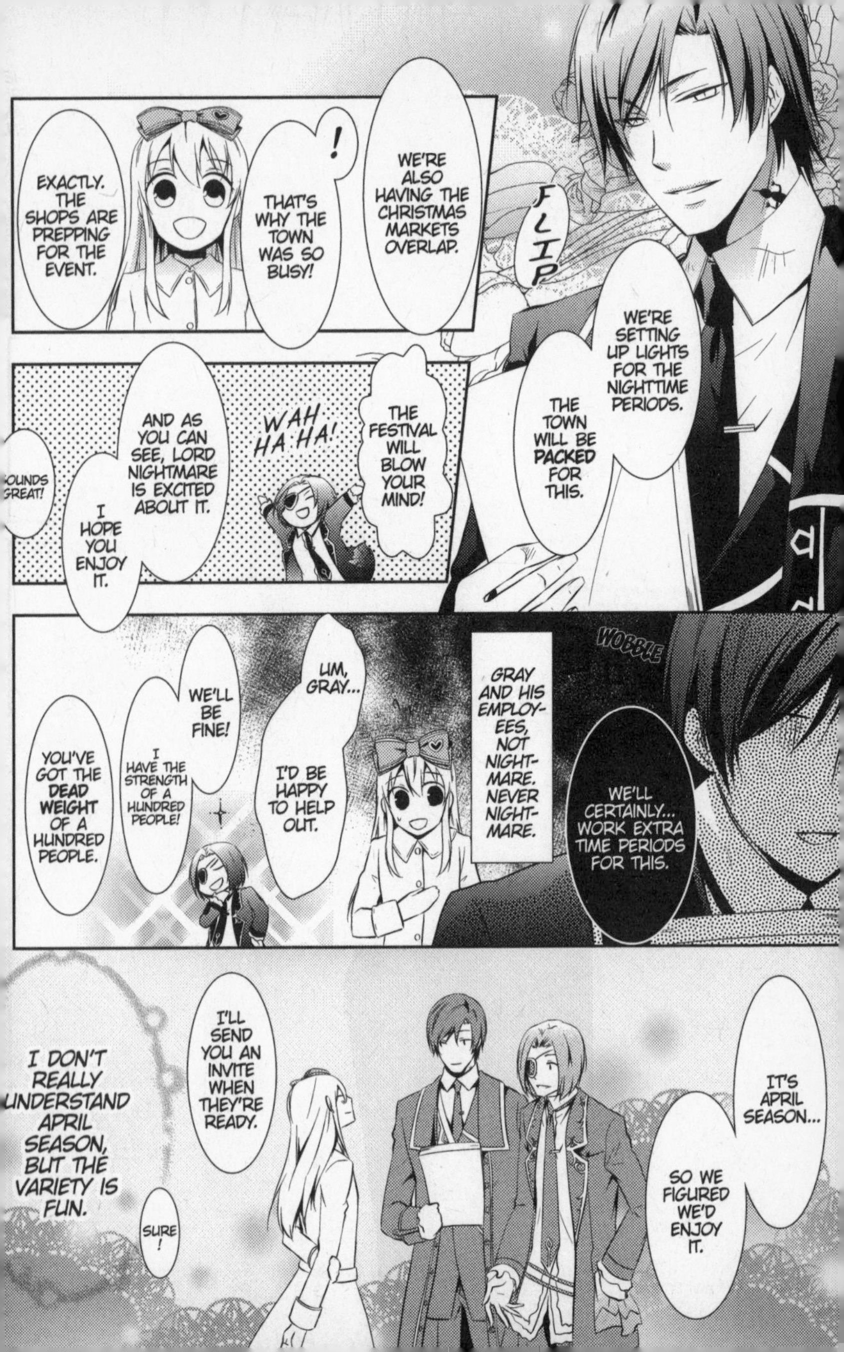

FLIP
WE'RE SETTING UP LIGHTS FOR THE NIGHTTIME PERIODS.
THE TOWN WILL BE **PACKED** FOR THIS.
WE'RE ALSO HAVING THE CHRISTMAS MARKETS OVERLAP.
!
THAT'S WHY THE TOWN WAS SO BUSY!
EXACTLY. THE SHOPS ARE PREPPING FOR THE EVENT.
THE FESTIVAL WILL BLOW YOUR MIND!
WAH HA HA!
AND AS YOU CAN SEE, LORD NIGHTMARE IS EXCITED ABOUT IT.
I HOPE YOU ENJOY IT.
OUNDS GREAT!
WOBBLE
WE'LL CERTAINLY... WORK EXTRA TIME PERIODS FOR THIS.
GRAY AND HIS EMPLOYEES, NOT NIGHTMARE. NEVER NIGHTMARE.
UM, GRAY...
I'D BE HAPPY TO HELP OUT.
WE'LL BE FINE!
I HAVE THE STRENGTH OF A HUNDRED PEOPLE!
YOU'VE GOT THE **DEAD WEIGHT** OF A HUNDRED PEOPLE.
IT'S APRIL SEASON...
SO WE FIGURED WE'D ENJOY IT.
I'LL SEND YOU AN INVITE WHEN THEY'RE READY.
SURE!
I DON'T REALLY UNDERSTAND APRIL SEASON, BUT THE VARIETY IS FUN.

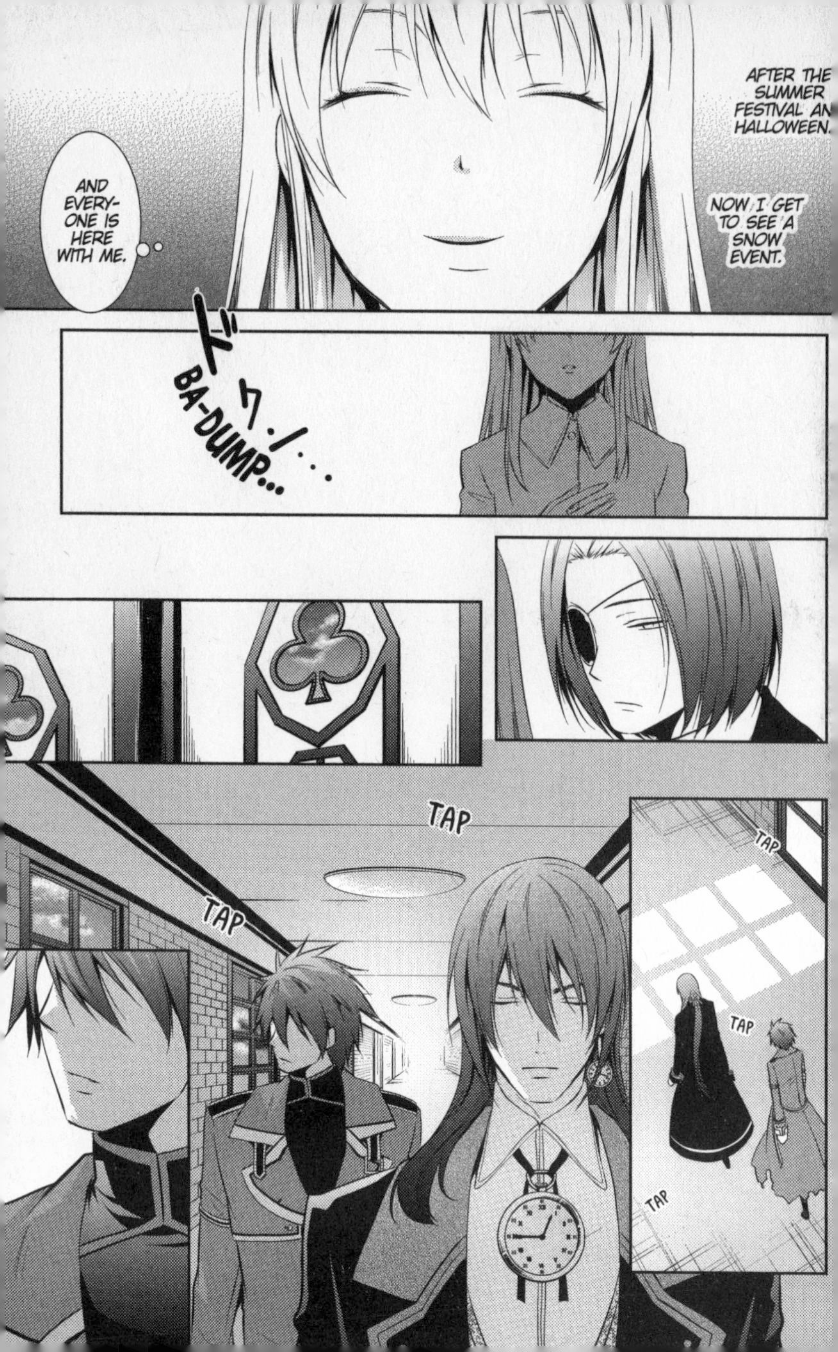
AFTER THE SUMMER FESTIVAL AN HALLOWEEN.
NOW I GET TO SEE A SNOW EVENT.
AND EVERY-ONE IS HERE WITH ME.
ドクン…
BA-DUMP...
TAP
TAP
TAP
TAP
TAP

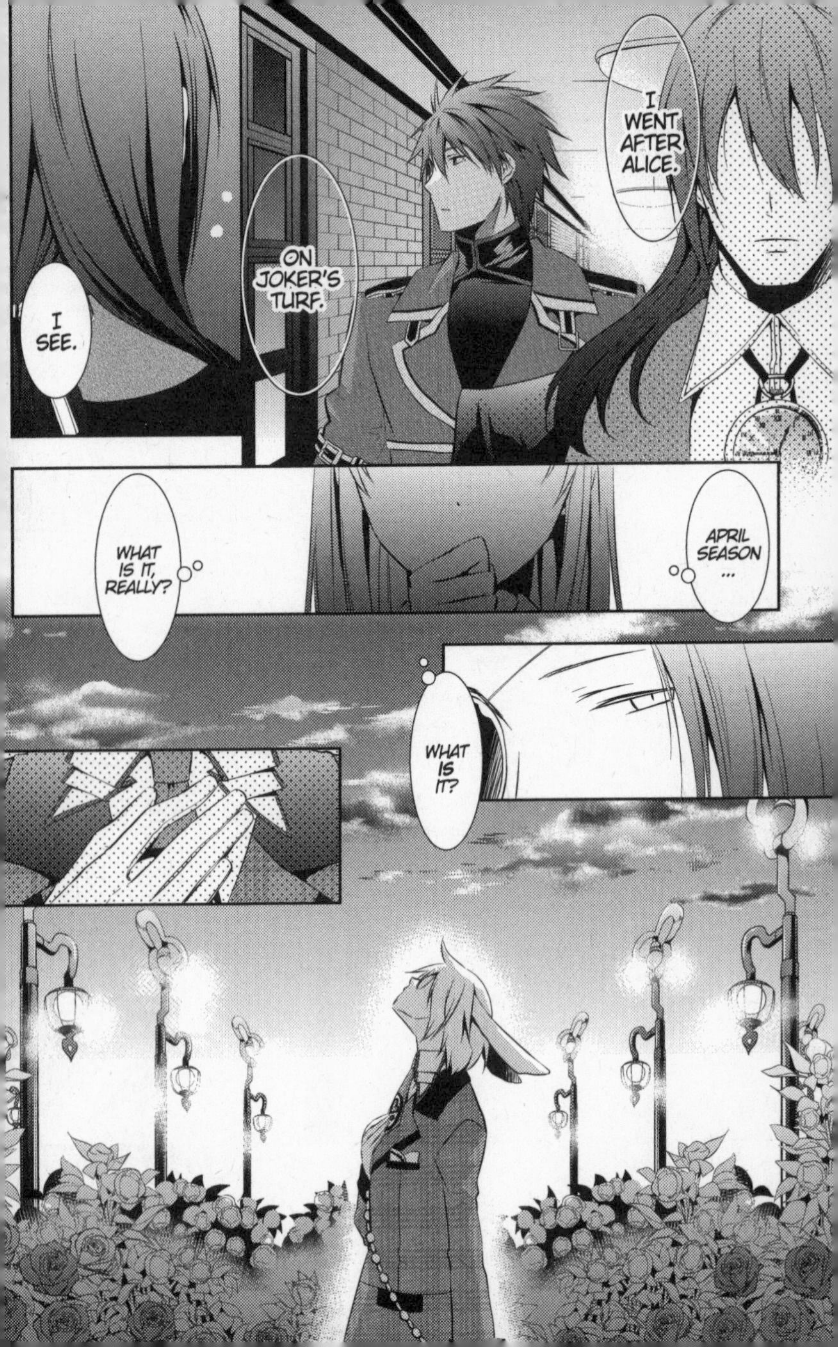
I WENT AFTER ALICE.
ON JOKER'S TURF.
I SEE.
APRIL SEASON ...
WHAT IS IT, REALLY?
WHAT IS IT?

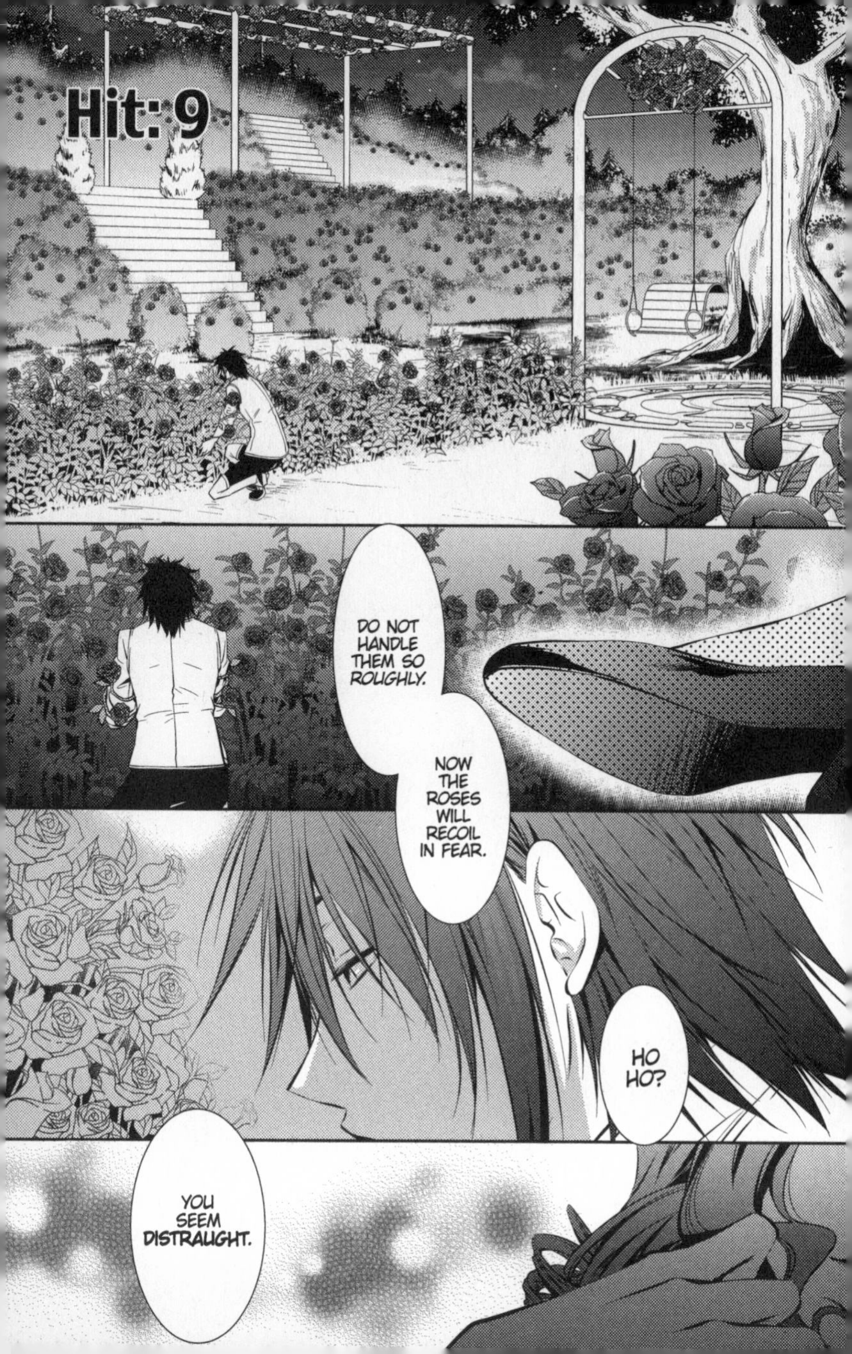
Hit: 9
DO NOT HANDLE THEM SO ROUGHLY.
NOW THE ROSES WILL RECOIL IN FEAR.
HO HO?
YOU SEEM DISTRAUGHT.

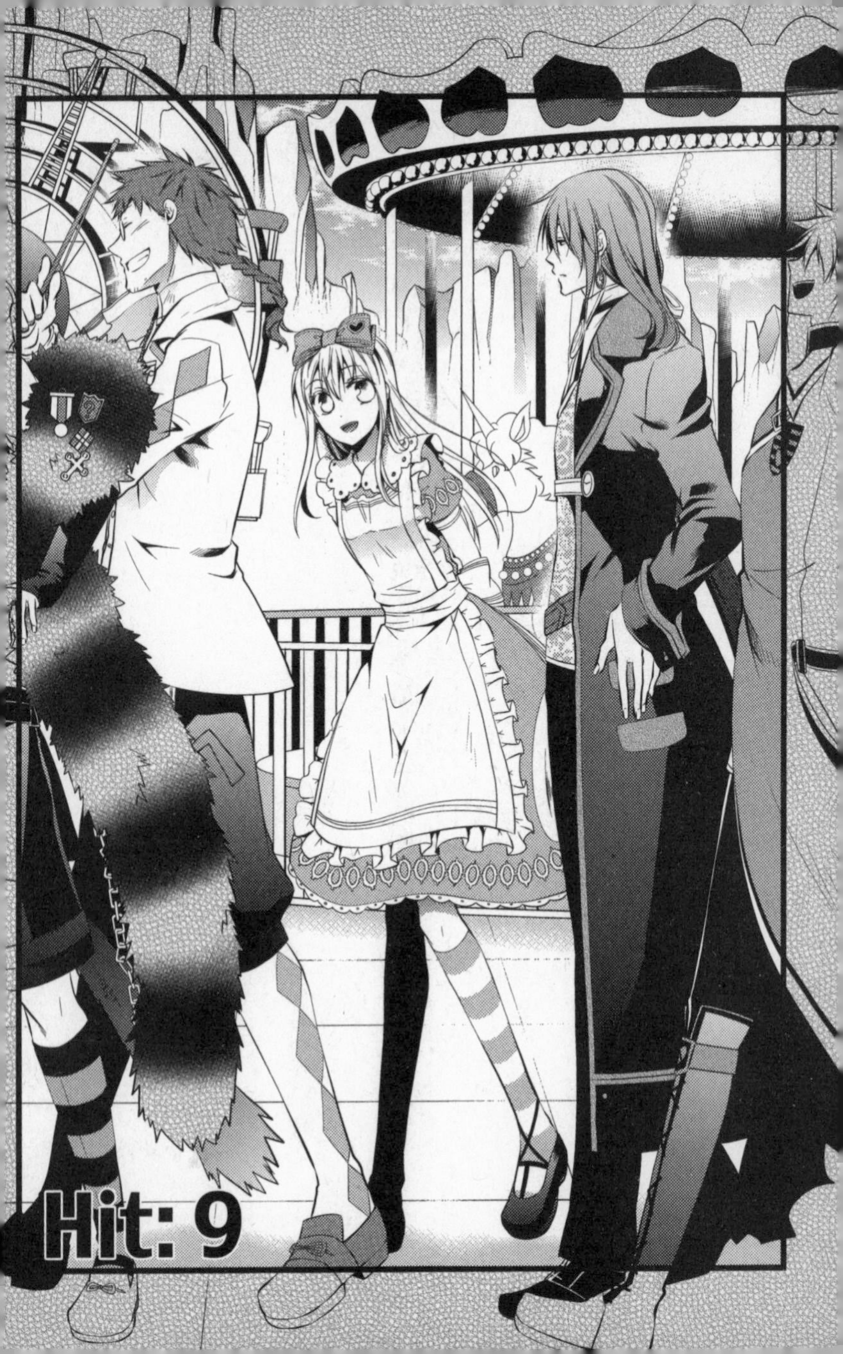
Hit: 9

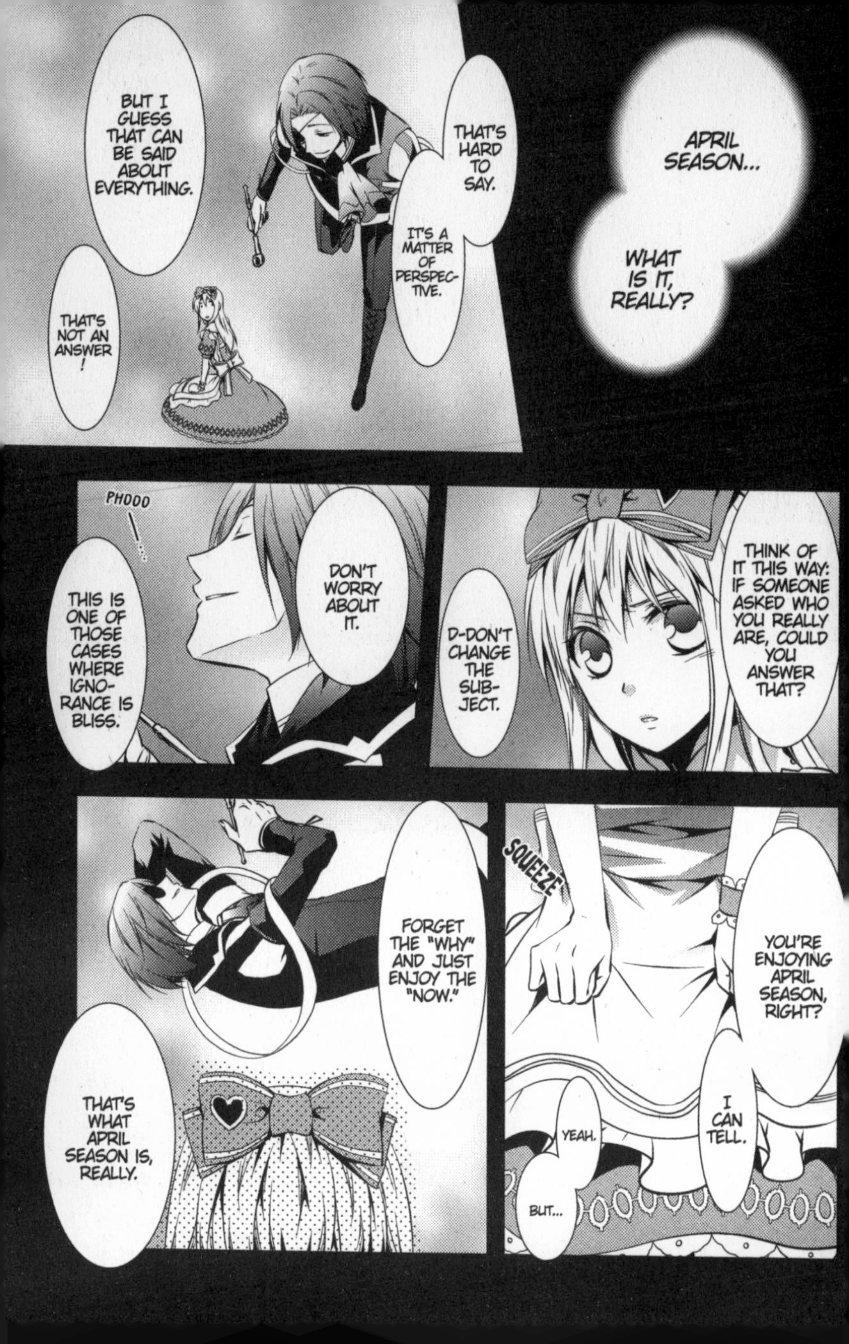
APRIL SEASON...
WHAT IS IT, REALLY?
THAT'S HARD TO SAY.
IT'S A MATTER OF PERSPECTIVE.
BUT I GUESS THAT CAN BE SAID ABOUT EVERYTHING.
THAT'S NOT AN ANSWER!
THINK OF IT THIS WAY: IF SOMEONE ASKED WHO YOU REALLY ARE, COULD YOU ANSWER THAT?
D-DON'T CHANGE THE SUBJECT.
PHOOO
DON'T WORRY ABOUT IT.
THIS IS ONE OF THOSE CASES WHERE IGNORANCE IS BLISS.
SQUEEZE
YOU'RE ENJOYING APRIL SEASON, RIGHT?
I CAN TELL.
YEAH.
BUT...
FORGET THE "WHY" AND JUST ENJOY THE "NOW."
THAT'S WHAT APRIL SEASON IS, REALLY.

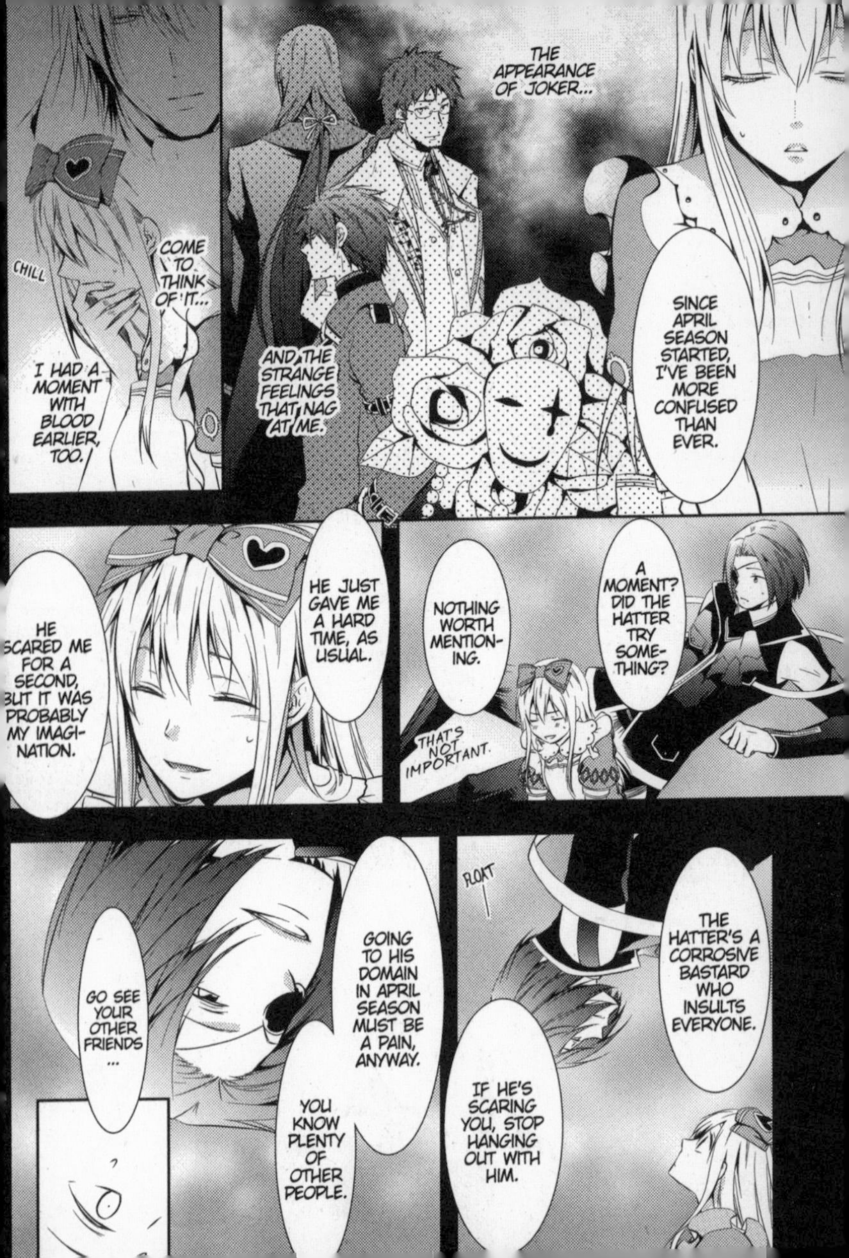
SINCE APRIL SEASON STARTED, I'VE BEEN MORE CONFUSED THAN EVER.
THE APPEARANCE OF JOKER...
AND THE STRANGE FEELINGS THAT NAG AT ME.
COME TO THINK OF IT...
I HAD A MOMENT WITH BLOOD EARLIER, TOO.
CHILL
A MOMENT? DID THE HATTER TRY SOMETHING?
NOTHING WORTH MENTIONING.
THAT'S NOT IMPORTANT.
HE JUST GAVE ME A HARD TIME, AS USUAL.
HE SCARED ME FOR A SECOND, BUT IT WAS PROBABLY MY IMAGINATION.
FLOAT
THE HATTER'S A CORROSIVE BASTARD WHO INSULTS EVERYONE.
IF HE'S SCARING YOU, STOP HANGING OUT WITH HIM.
GOING TO HIS DOMAIN IN APRIL SEASON MUST BE A PAIN, ANYWAY.
YOU KNOW PLENTY OF OTHER PEOPLE.
GO SEE YOUR OTHER FRIENDS...
?

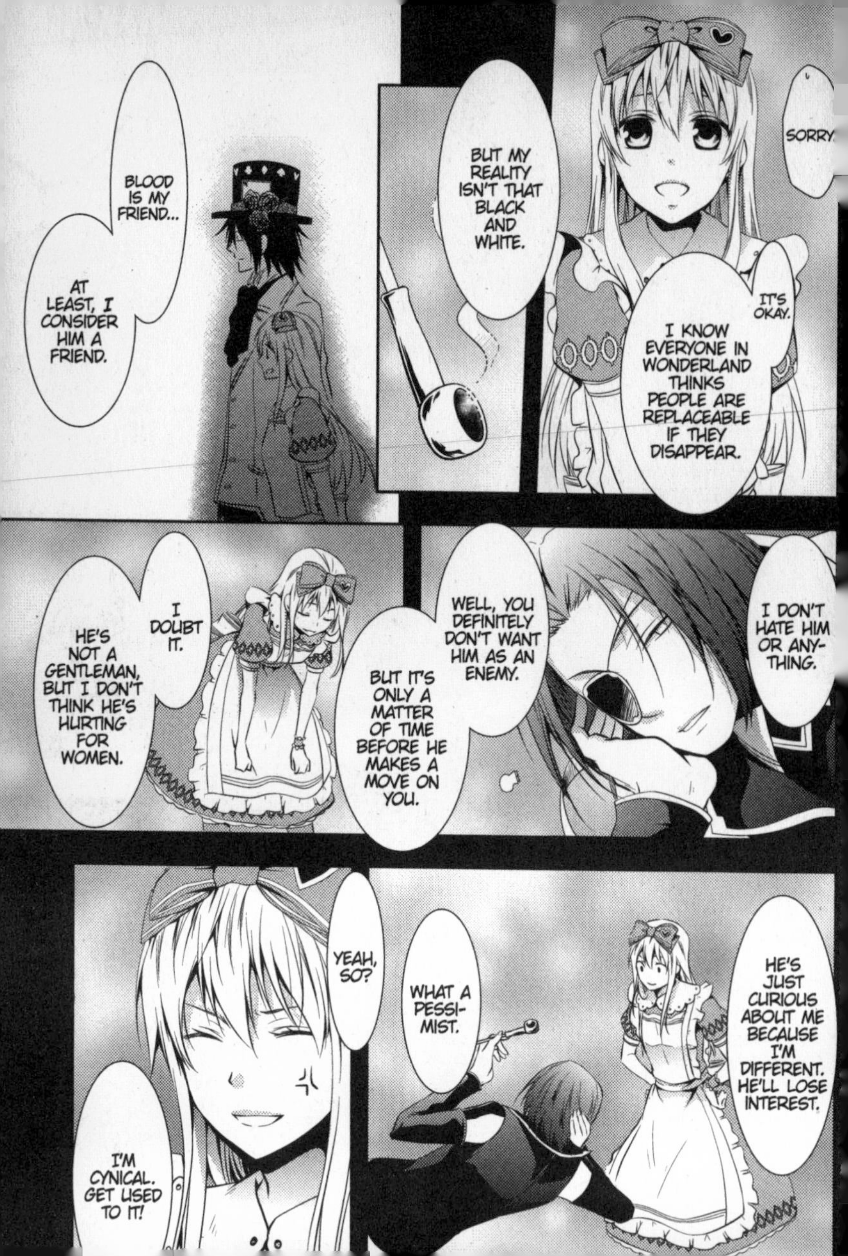
SORRY.
IT'S OKAY.
I KNOW EVERYONE IN WONDERLAND THINKS PEOPLE ARE REPLACEABLE IF THEY DISAPPEAR.
BUT MY REALITY ISN'T THAT BLACK AND WHITE.
BLOOD IS MY FRIEND...
AT LEAST, I CONSIDER HIM A FRIEND.
I DON'T HATE HIM OR ANY-THING.
WELL, YOU DEFINITELY DON'T WANT HIM AS AN ENEMY.
BUT IT'S ONLY A MATTER OF TIME BEFORE HE MAKES A MOVE ON YOU.
I DOUBT IT.
HE'S NOT A GENTLEMAN, BUT I DON'T THINK HE'S HURTING FOR WOMEN.
HE'S JUST CURIOUS ABOUT ME BECAUSE I'M DIFFERENT. HE'LL LOSE INTEREST.
WHAT A PESSI-MIST.
YEAH, SO?
I'M CYNICAL. GET USED TO IT!

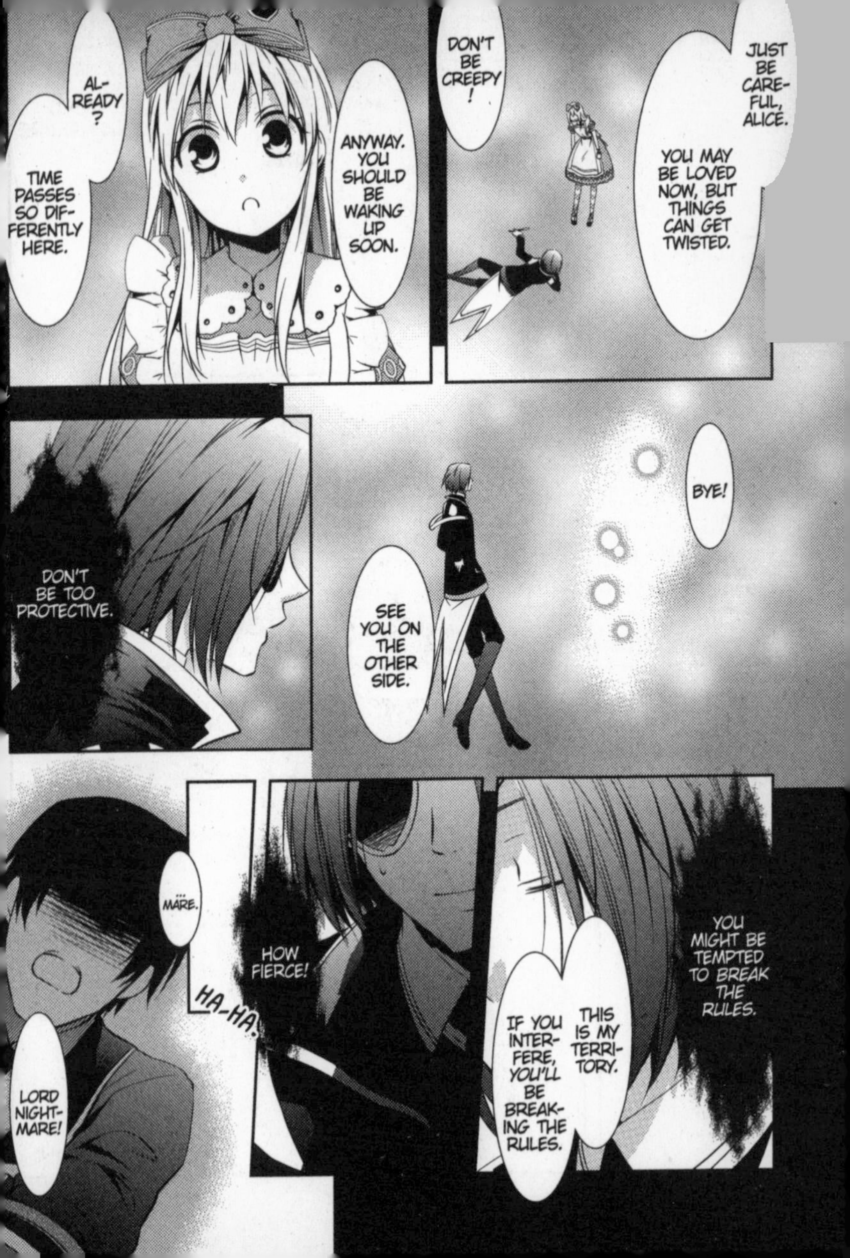
JUST BE CARE-FUL, ALICE.
YOU MAY BE LOVED NOW, BUT THINGS CAN GET TWISTED.
DON'T BE CREEPY!
ANYWAY. YOU SHOULD BE WAKING UP SOON.
AL-READY?
TIME PASSES SO DIF-FERENTLY HERE.
BYE!
SEE YOU ON THE OTHER SIDE.
DON'T BE TOO PROTECTIVE.
YOU MIGHT BE TEMPTED TO BREAK THE RULES.
THIS IS MY TERRI-TORY.
IF YOU INTER-FERE, YOU'LL BE BREAK-ING THE RULES.
HOW FIERCE!
HA-HA
MÄRE.
LORD NIGHT-MARE!

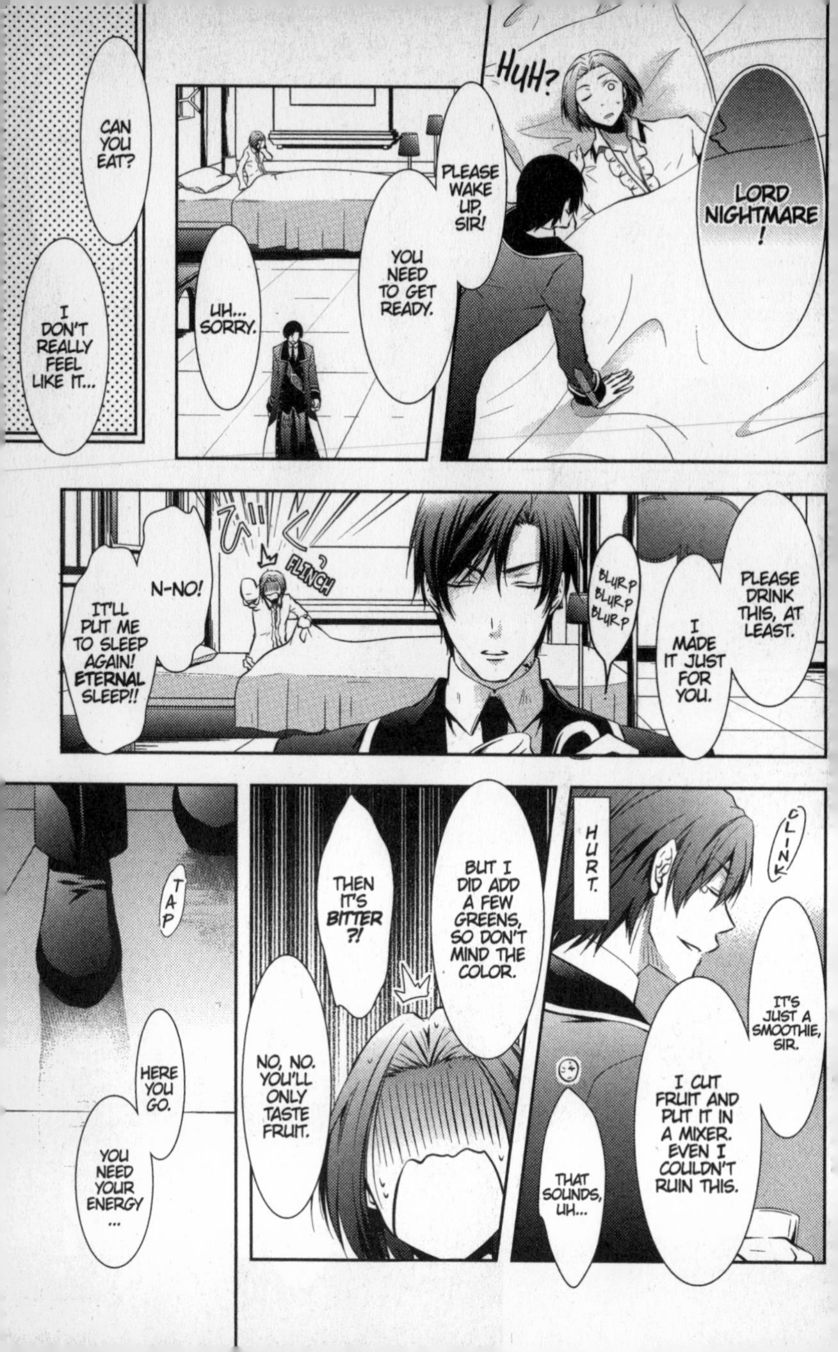
HUH?
LORD NIGHTMARE!
PLEASE WAKE UP, SIR!
YOU NEED TO GET READY.
UH... SORRY.
CAN YOU EAT?
I DON'T REALLY FEEL LIKE IT...
PLEASE DRINK THIS, AT LEAST.
I MADE IT JUST FOR YOU.
BLURP BLURP BLURP
FLINCH
N-NO!
IT'LL PUT ME TO SLEEP AGAIN! ETERNAL SLEEP!!
CLINK
HURT.
IT'S JUST A SMOOTHIE, SIR.
I CUT FRUIT AND PUT IT IN A MIXER. EVEN I COULDN'T RUIN THIS.
THAT SOUNDS, UH...
BUT I DID ADD A FEW GREENS, SO DON'T MIND THE COLOR.
THEN IT'S BITTER?!
NO, NO. YOU'LL ONLY TASTE FRUIT.
TAP
HERE YOU GO.
YOU NEED YOUR ENERGY...

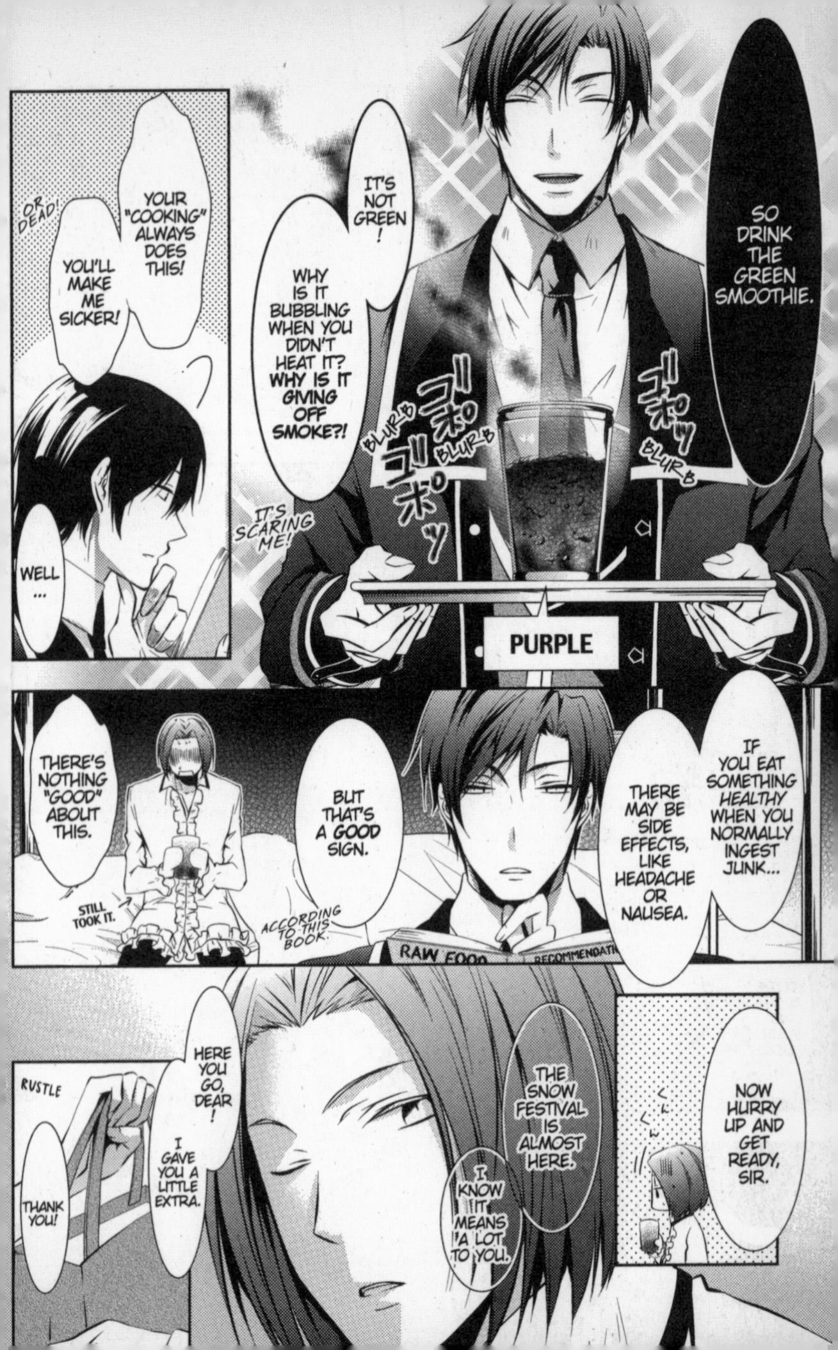
SO DRINK THE GREEN SMOOTHIE.
IT'S NOT GREEN!
WHY IS IT BUBBLING WHEN YOU DIDN'T HEAT IT? WHY IS IT GIVING OFF SMOKE?!
ゴポッ
BLURB
ゴポ
BLURB
ゴポッ
BLURB
PURPLE
IT'S SCARING ME!
YOUR "COOKING" ALWAYS DOES THIS!
OR DEAD!
YOU'LL MAKE ME SICKER!
WELL...
IF YOU EAT SOMETHING HEALTHY WHEN YOU NORMALLY INGEST JUNK...
THERE MAY BE SIDE EFFECTS, LIKE HEADACHE OR NAUSEA.
ACCORDING TO THIS BOOK.
RAW FOOD
BUT THAT'S A GOOD SIGN.
STILL TOOK IT.
THERE'S NOTHING "GOOD" ABOUT THIS.
NOW HURRY UP AND GET READY, SIR.
くん くん
THE SNOW FESTIVAL IS ALMOST HERE.
I KNOW IT MEANS A LOT TO YOU.
HERE YOU GO, DEAR!
I GAVE YOU A LITTLE EXTRA.
RUSTLE
THANK YOU!

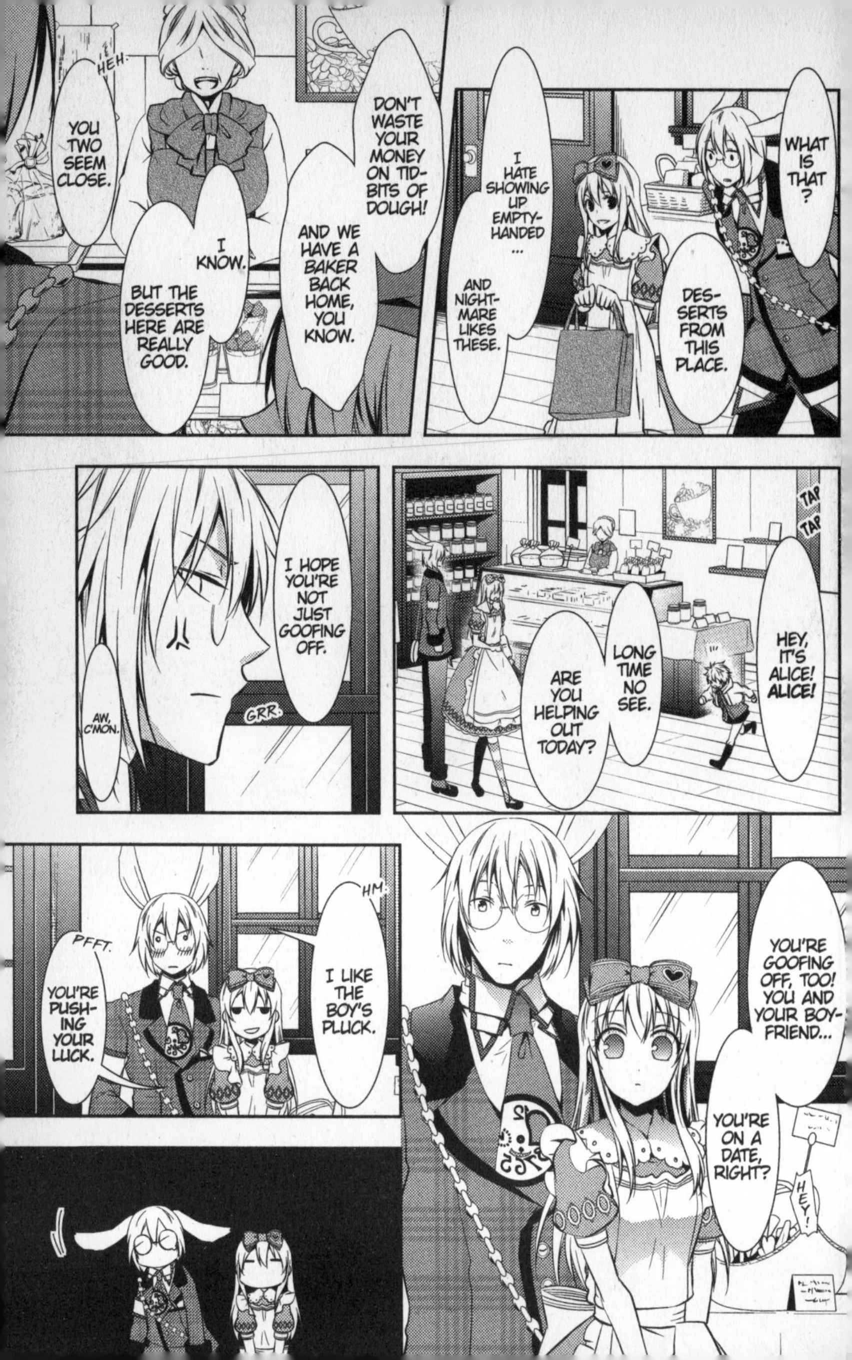
WHAT IS THAT?
DESSERTS FROM THIS PLACE.
I HATE SHOWING UP EMPTY-HANDED...
AND NIGHTMARE LIKES THESE.
DON'T WASTE YOUR MONEY ON TID-BITS OF DOUGH!
AND WE HAVE A BAKER BACK HOME, YOU KNOW.
HEH.
YOU TWO SEEM CLOSE.
I KNOW.
BUT THE DESSERTS HERE ARE REALLY GOOD.
TAP TAP
HEY, IT'S ALICE! ALICE!
LONG TIME NO SEE.
ARE YOU HELPING OUT TODAY?
I HOPE YOU'RE NOT JUST GOOFING OFF.
GRR.
AW, C'MON.
YOU'RE GOOFING OFF, TOO! YOU AND YOUR BOY-FRIEND...
YOU'RE ON A DATE, RIGHT?
HEY!
HM.
I LIKE THE BOY'S PLUCK.
PFFT.
YOU'RE PUSHING YOUR LUCK.

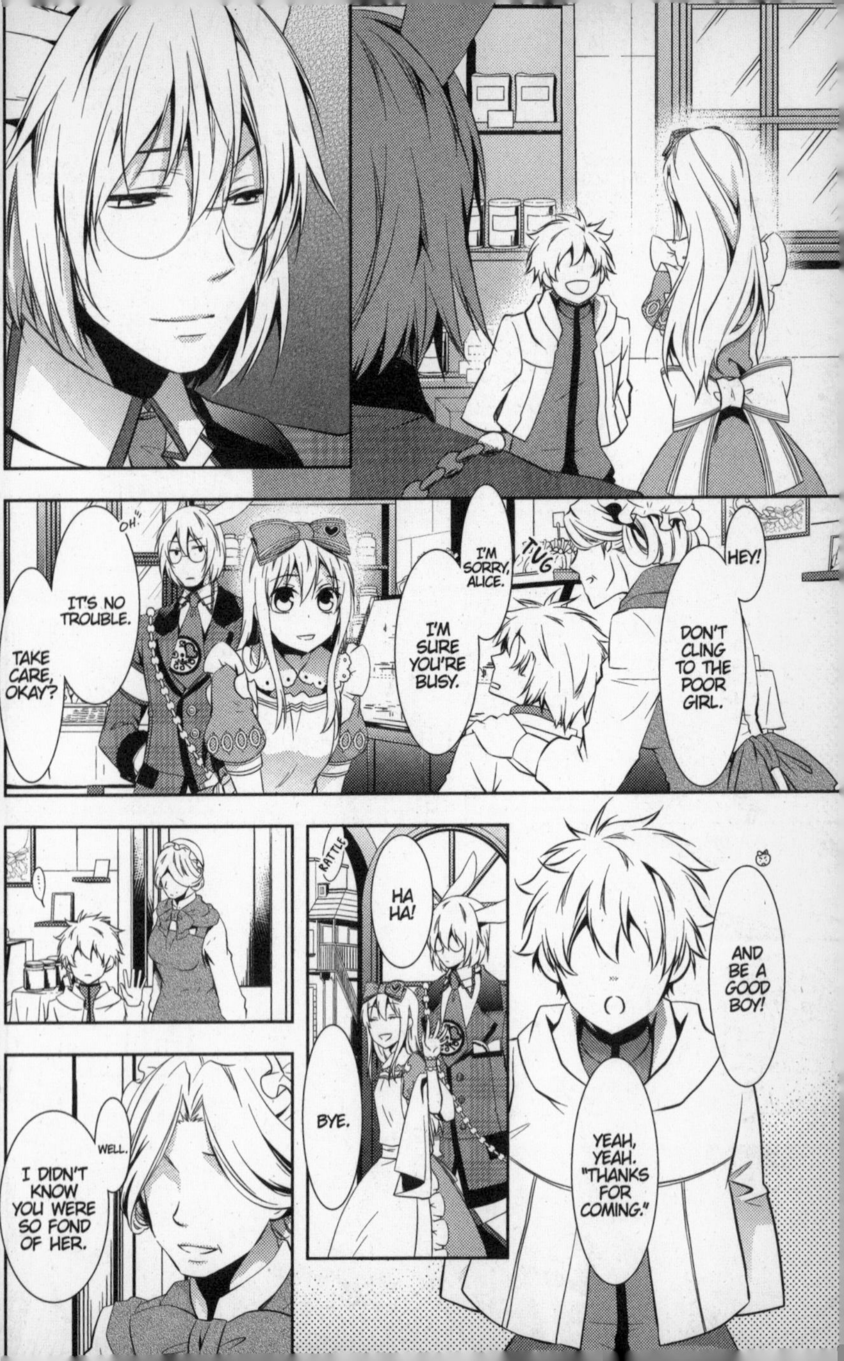
HEY!
TUG
DON'T CLING TO THE POOR GIRL.
I'M SORRY, ALICE.
I'M SURE YOU'RE BUSY.
OH...
IT'S NO TROUBLE.
TAKE CARE, OKAY?
AND BE A GOOD BOY!
YEAH, YEAH. "THANKS FOR COMING."
RATTLE
HA HA!
BYE.
...
WELL.
I DIDN'T KNOW YOU WERE SO FOND OF HER.

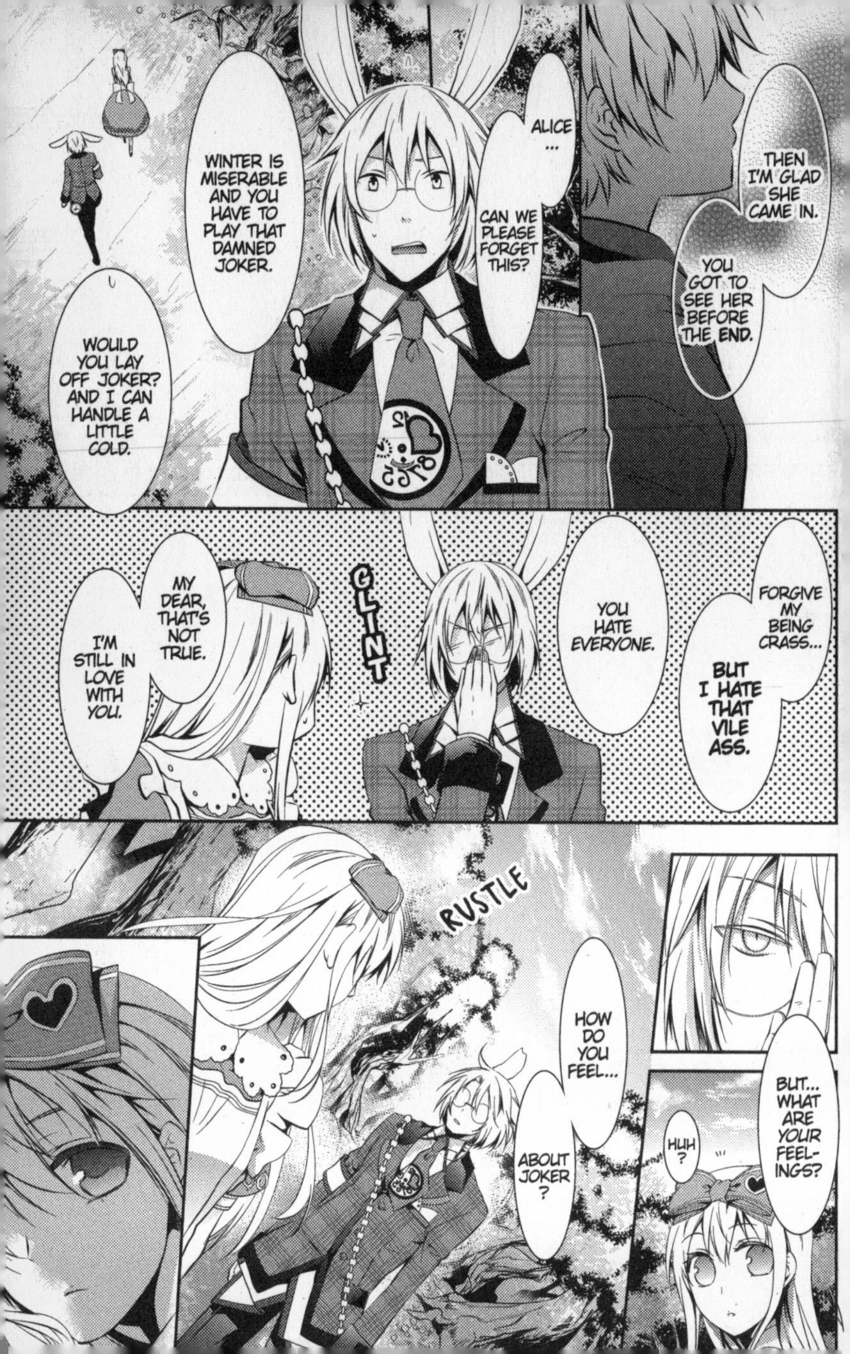

THEN I'M GLAD SHE CAME IN.
YOU GOT TO SEE HER BEFORE THE END.
ALICE ...
CAN WE PLEASE FORGET THIS?
WINTER IS MISERABLE AND YOU HAVE TO PLAY THAT DAMNED JOKER.
WOULD YOU LAY OFF JOKER? AND I CAN HANDLE A LITTLE COLD.
FORGIVE MY BEING CRASS...
BUT I HATE THAT VILE ASS.
YOU HATE EVERYONE.
GLINT
MY DEAR, THAT'S NOT TRUE.
I'M STILL IN LOVE WITH YOU.
BUT... WHAT ARE YOUR FEEL-INGS?
HUH?
RUSTLE
HOW DO YOU FEEL...
ABOUT JOKER?

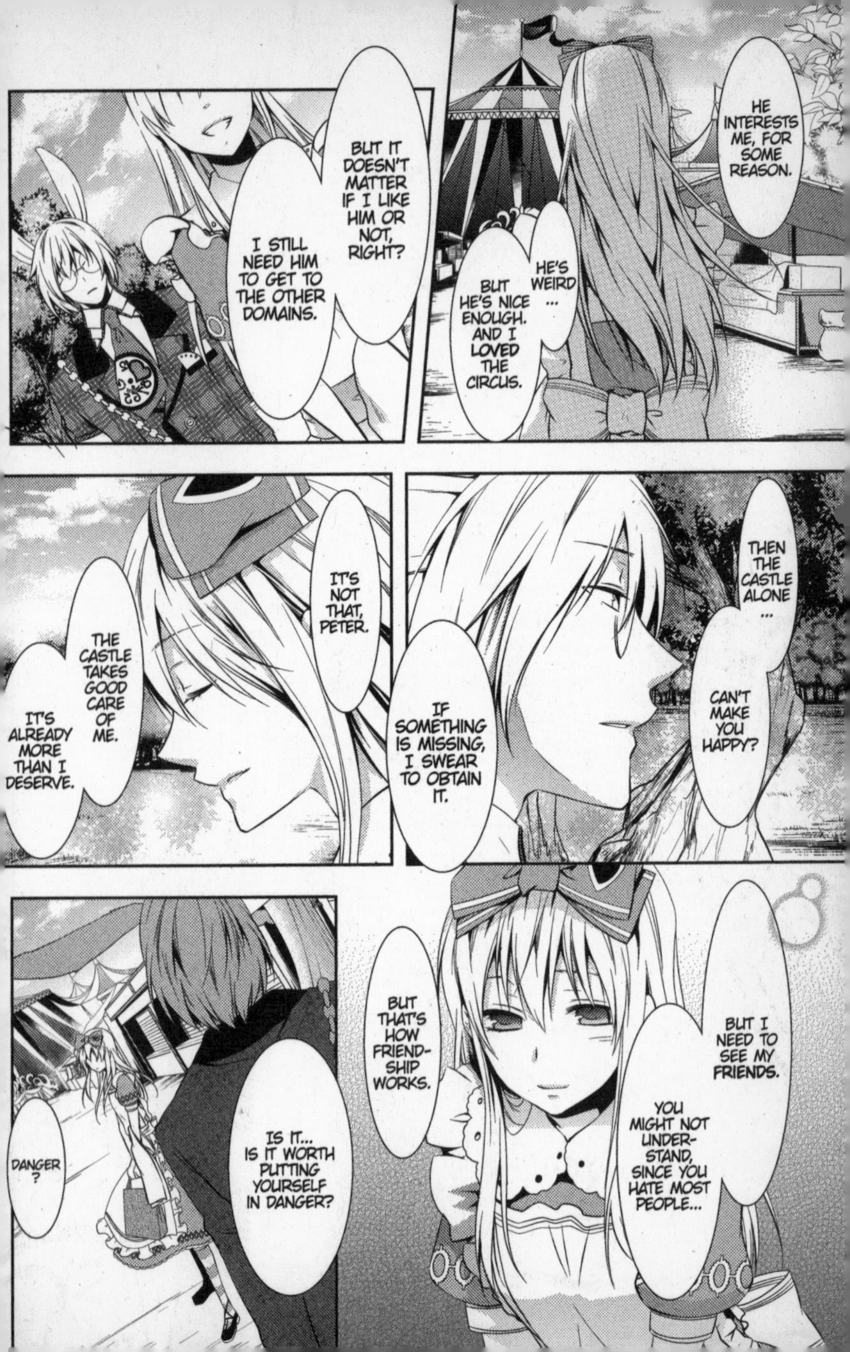
HE INTERESTS ME, FOR SOME REASON.
HE'S WEIRD...
BUT HE'S NICE ENOUGH. AND I LOVED THE CIRCUS.
BUT IT DOESN'T MATTER IF I LIKE HIM OR NOT, RIGHT?
I STILL NEED HIM TO GET TO THE OTHER DOMAINS.
THEN THE CASTLE ALONE...
CAN'T MAKE YOU HAPPY?
IF SOMETHING IS MISSING, I SWEAR TO OBTAIN IT.
IT'S NOT THAT, PETER.
THE CASTLE TAKES GOOD CARE OF ME.
IT'S ALREADY MORE THAN I DESERVE.
BUT I NEED TO SEE MY FRIENDS.
YOU MIGHT NOT UNDER-STAND, SINCE YOU HATE MOST PEOPLE...
BUT THAT'S HOW FRIEND-SHIP WORKS.
IS IT... IS IT WORTH PUTTING YOURSELF IN DANGER?
DANGER?

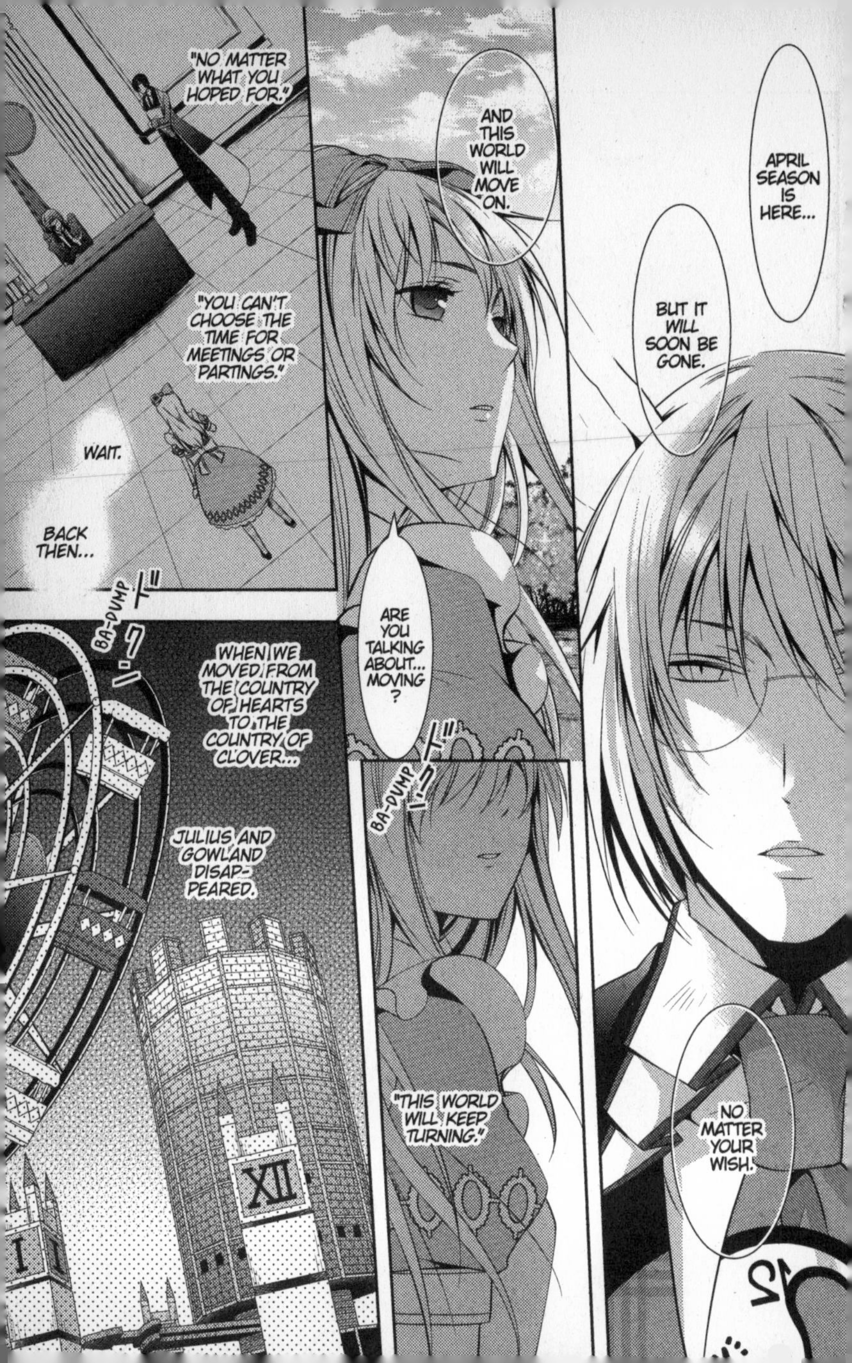
APRIL SEASON IS HERE...
BUT IT WILL SOON BE GONE.
NO MATTER YOUR WISH.
AND THIS WORLD WILL MOVE ON.
ARE YOU TALKING ABOUT... MOVING?
BA-DUMP
"THIS WORLD WILL KEEP TURNING."
"NO MATTER WHAT YOU HOPED FOR."
"YOU CAN'T CHOOSE THE TIME FOR MEETINGS OR PARTINGS."
WAIT.
BACK THEN...
BA-DUMP
WHEN WE MOVED FROM THE COUNTRY OF HEARTS TO THE COUNTRY OF CLOVER...
JULIUS AND GOWLAND DISAP-PEARED.

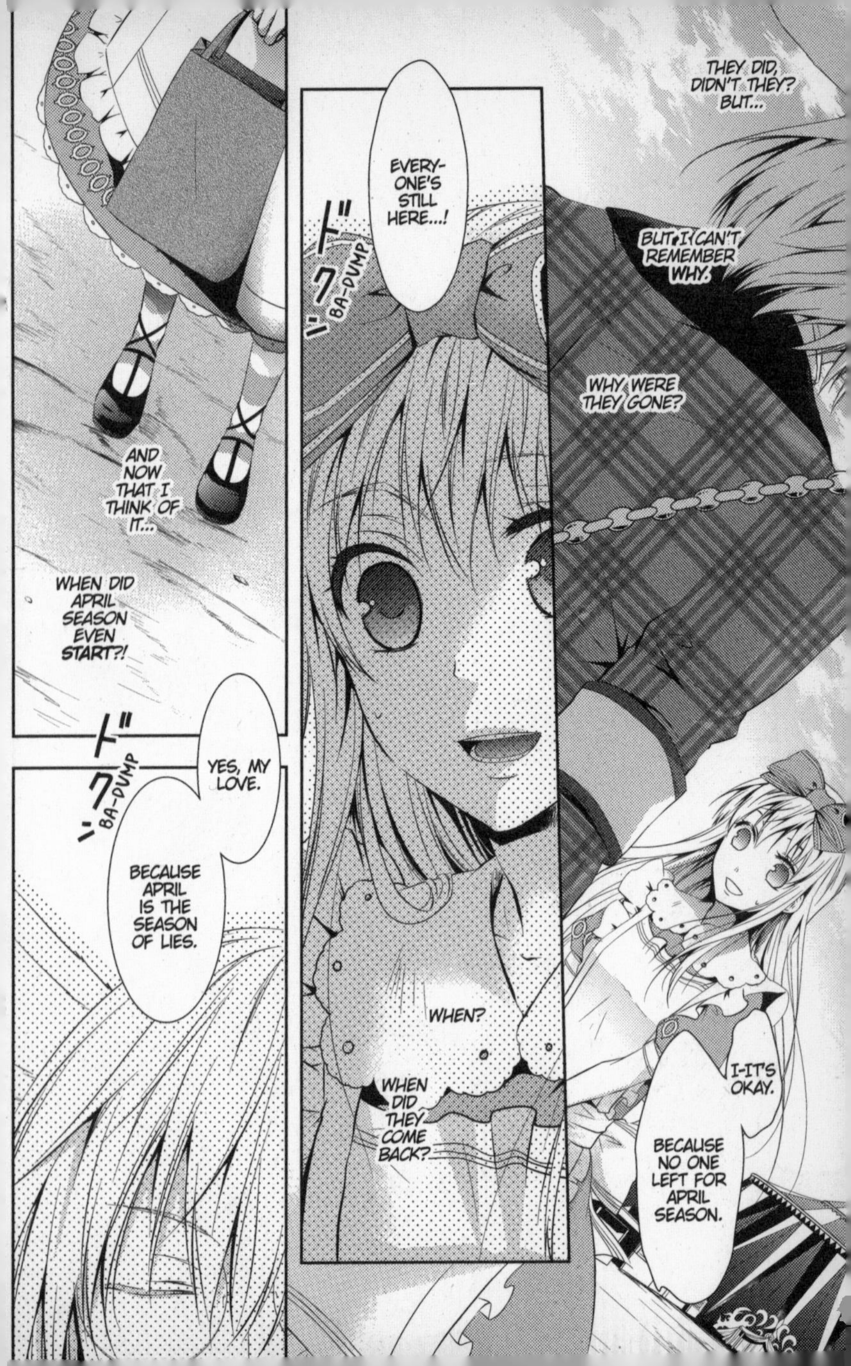
THEY DID, DIDN'T THEY? BUT...
BUT I CAN'T REMEMBER WHY.
WHY WERE THEY GONE?
I-IT'S OKAY.
BECAUSE NO ONE LEFT FOR APRIL SEASON.
BA-DUMP
EVERY-ONE'S STILL HERE...!
WHEN?
WHEN DID THEY COME BACK?
AND NOW THAT I THINK OF IT...
WHEN DID APRIL SEASON EVEN START?!
BA-DUMP
YES, MY LOVE.
BECAUSE APRIL IS THE SEASON OF LIES.

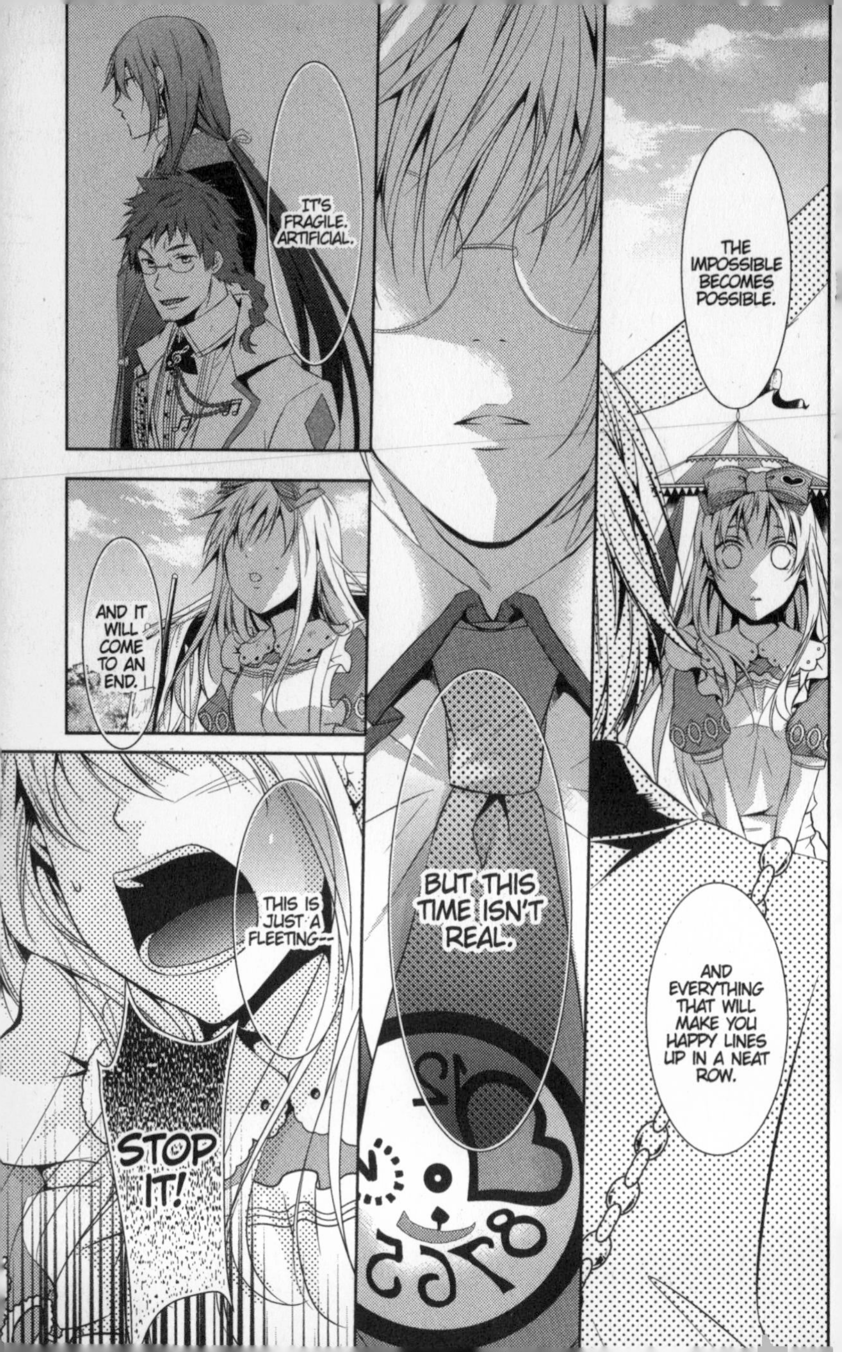
THE IMPOSSIBLE BECOMES POSSIBLE.
AND EVERYTHING THAT WILL MAKE YOU HAPPY LINES UP IN A NEAT ROW.
BUT THIS TIME ISN'T REAL.
IT'S FRAGILE. ARTIFICIAL.
AND IT WILL COME TO AN END.
THIS IS JUST A FLEETING--
STOP IT!

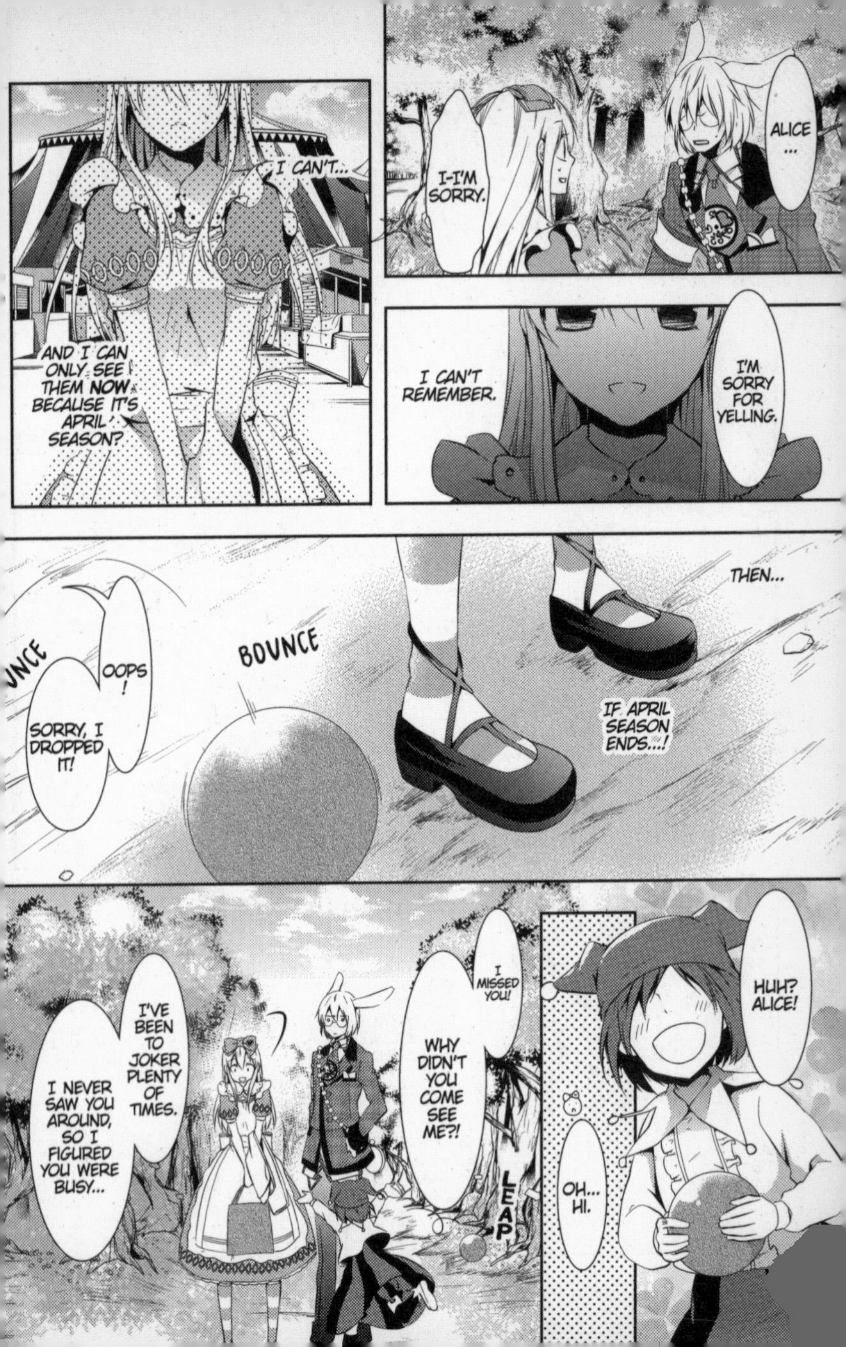
ALICE ...
I-I'M SORRY.
I'M SORRY FOR YELLING.
I CAN'T REMEMBER.
I CAN'T...
AND I CAN ONLY SEE THEM NOW BECAUSE IT'S APRIL SEASON?
THEN...
IF APRIL SEASON ENDS...!
BOUNCE
OOPS!
SORRY, I DROPPED IT!
UNCE
HUH? ALICE!
OH... HI.
I MISSED YOU!
WHY DIDN'T YOU COME SEE ME?!
LEAP
I'VE BEEN TO JOKER PLENTY OF TIMES.
I NEVER SAW YOU AROUND, SO I FIGURED YOU WERE BUSY...

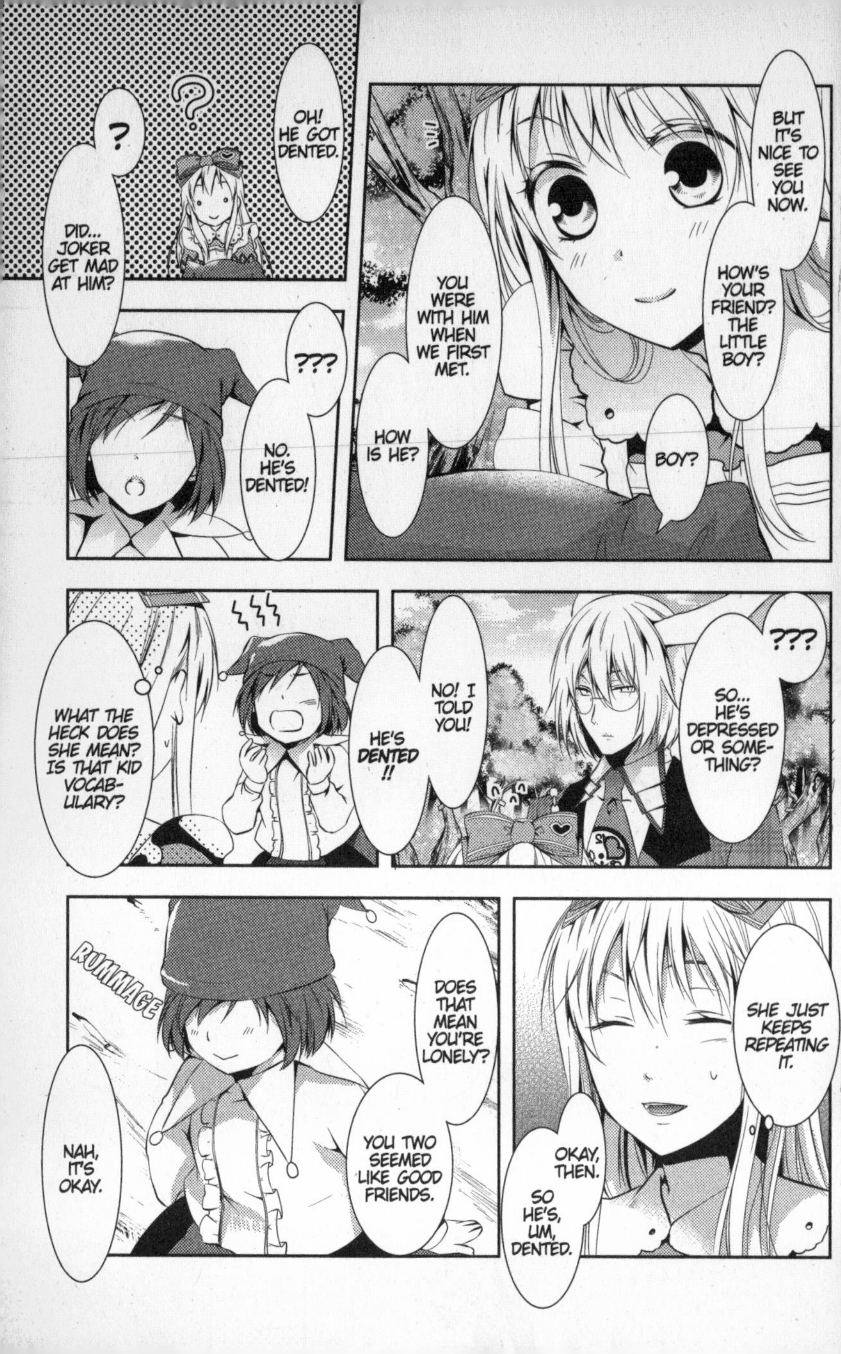
BUT IT'S NICE TO SEE YOU NOW.
HOW'S YOUR FRIEND? THE LITTLE BOY?
BOY?
YOU WERE WITH HIM WHEN WE FIRST MET.
HOW IS HE?
OH! HE GOT DENTED.
?
DID... JOKER GET MAD AT HIM?
???
NO. HE'S DENTED!
???
SO... HE'S DEPRESSED OR SOME-THING?
NO! I TOLD YOU!
HE'S DENTED!!
WHAT THE HECK DOES SHE MEAN? IS THAT KID VOCAB-ULARY?
SHE JUST KEEPS REPEATING IT.
OKAY, THEN.
SO HE'S, UM, DENTED.
RUMMAGE
DOES THAT MEAN YOU'RE LONELY?
YOU TWO SEEMED LIKE GOOD FRIENDS.
NAH, IT'S OKAY.

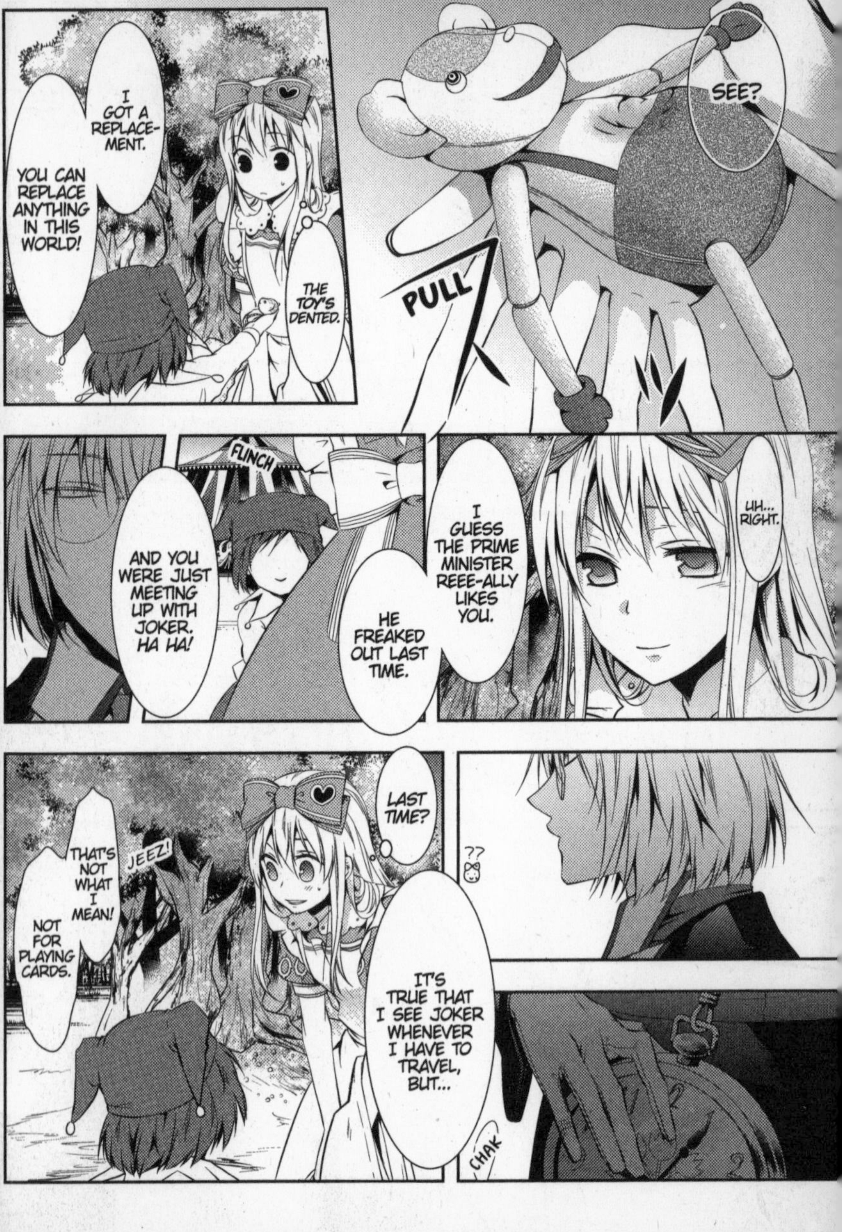
SEE?
PULL
THE TOY'S DENTED.
I GOT A REPLACE-MENT.
YOU CAN REPLACE ANYTHING IN THIS WORLD!
UH... RIGHT.
I GUESS THE PRIME MINISTER REEE-ALLY LIKES YOU.
HE FREAKED OUT LAST TIME.
FLINCH
AND YOU WERE JUST MEETING UP WITH JOKER. HA HA!
??
CHAK
LAST TIME?
IT'S TRUE THAT I SEE JOKER WHENEVER I HAVE TO TRAVEL, BUT...
JEEZ!
THAT'S NOT WHAT I MEAN!
NOT FOR PLAYING CARDS.

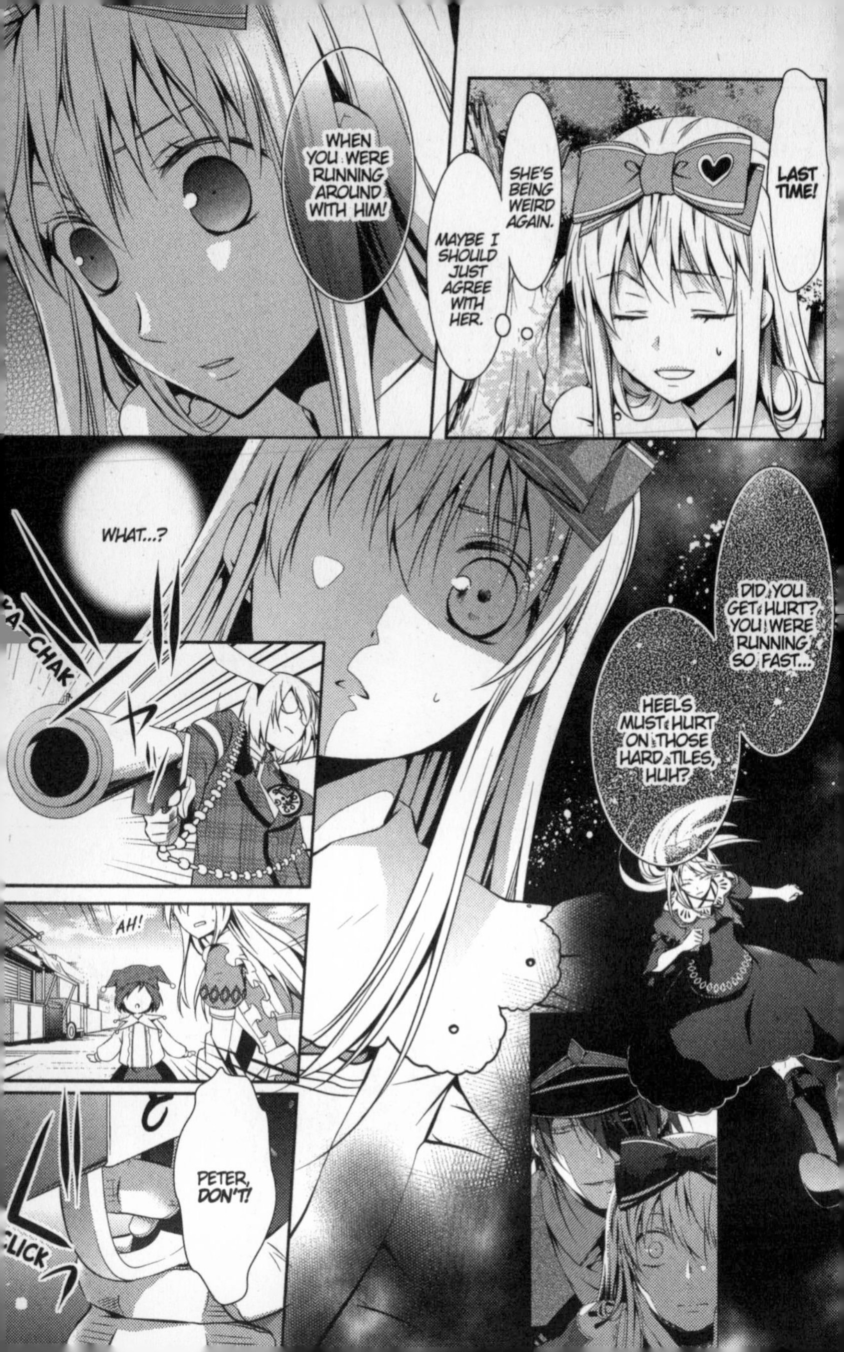
LAST TIME!
SHE'S BEING WEIRD AGAIN.
MAYBE I SHOULD JUST AGREE WITH HER.
WHEN YOU WERE RUNNING AROUND WITH HIM!
DID YOU GET HURT? YOU WERE RUNNING SO FAST...
HEELS MUST HURT ON THOSE HARD TILES, HUH?
WHAT...?
A-CHAK
AH!
PETER, DON'T!
CLICK

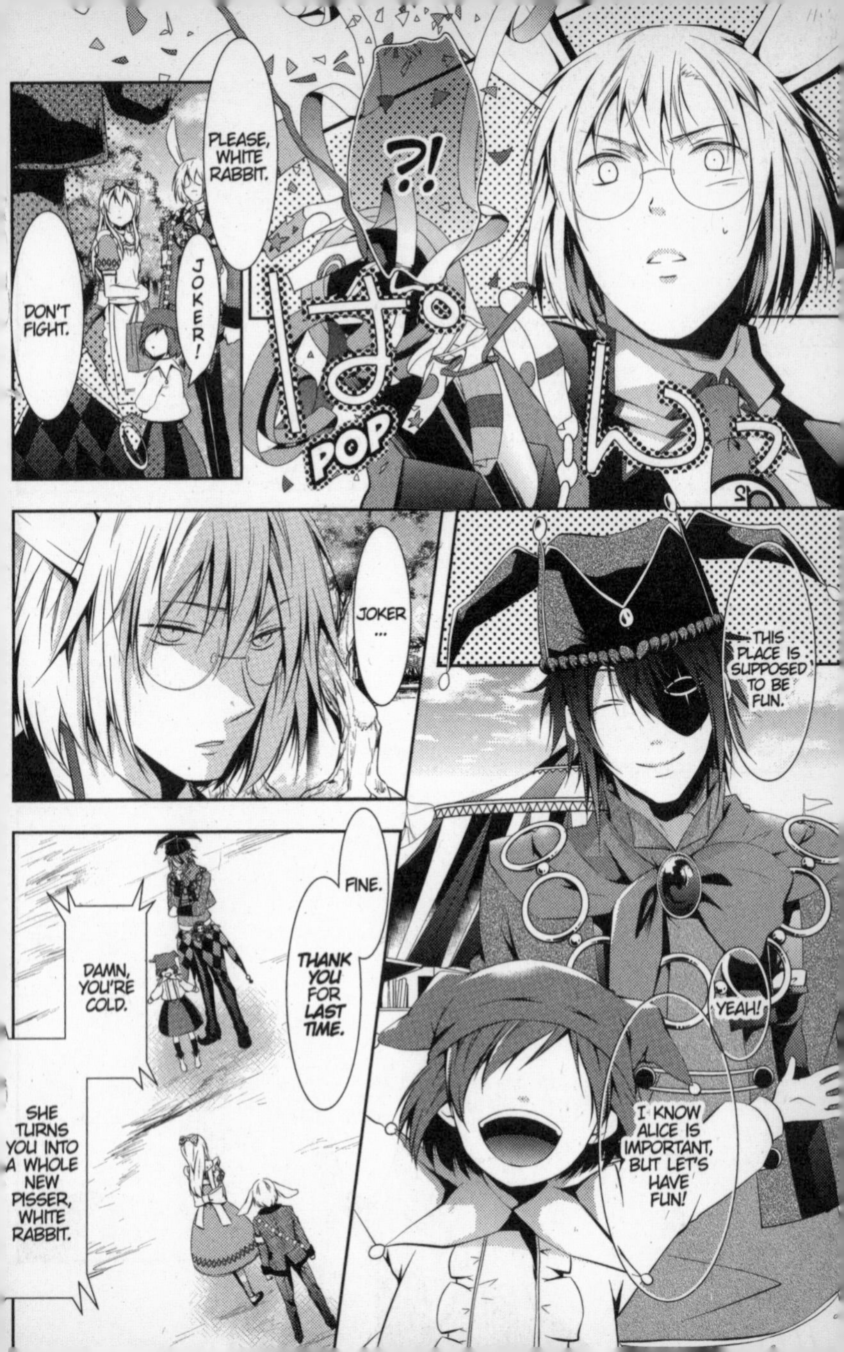
?!
POP
PLEASE, WHITE RABBIT.
JOKER!
DON'T FIGHT.
THIS PLACE IS SUPPOSED TO BE FUN.
JOKER ...
YEAH!
I KNOW ALICE IS IMPORTANT, BUT LET'S HAVE FUN!
FINE.
THANK YOU FOR LAST TIME.
DAMN, YOU'RE COLD.
SHE TURNS YOU INTO A WHOLE NEW PISSER, WHITE RABBIT.

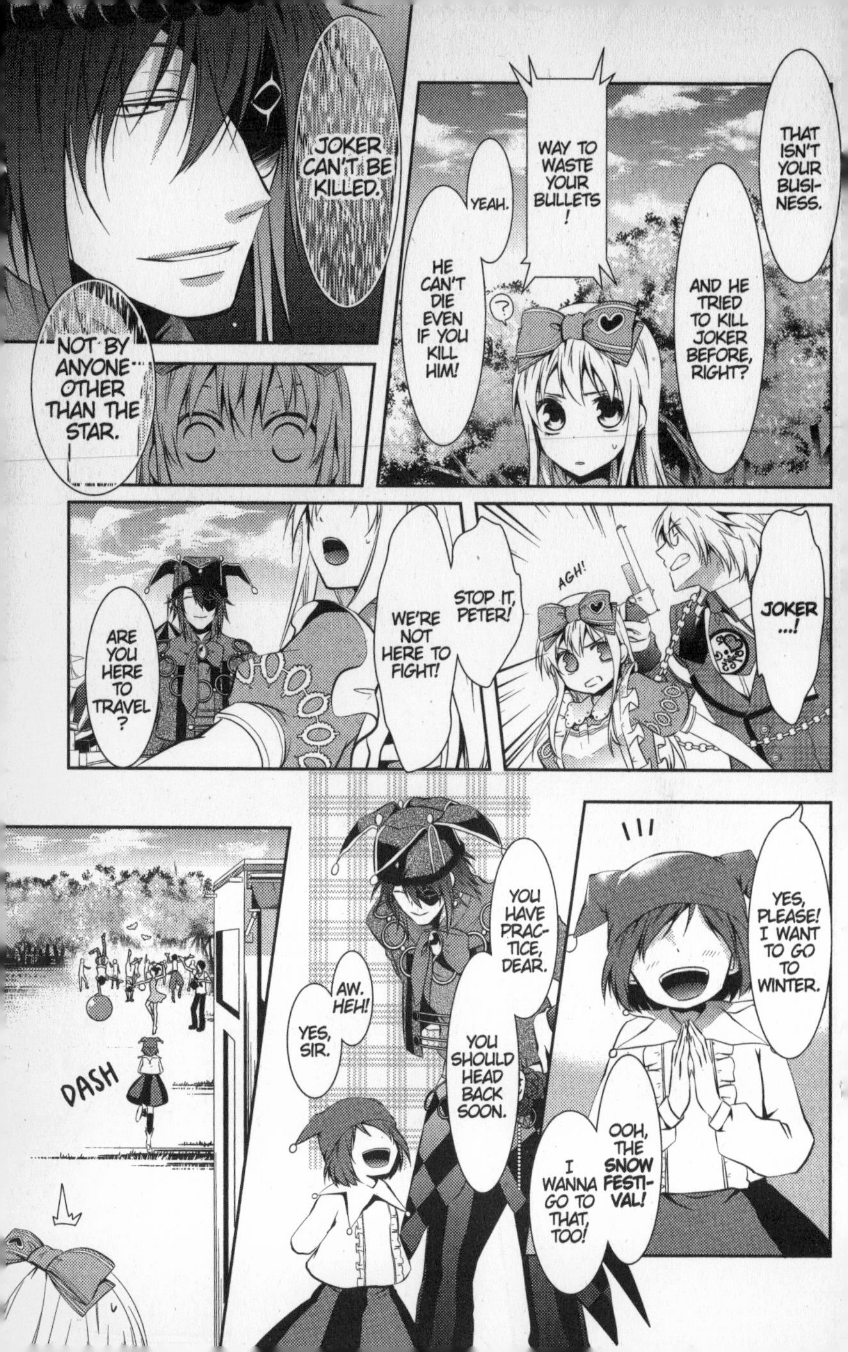
THAT ISN'T YOUR BUSINESS.
WAY TO WASTE YOUR BULLETS!
AND HE TRIED TO KILL JOKER BEFORE, RIGHT?
YEAH.
HE CAN'T DIE EVEN IF YOU KILL HIM!
?
JOKER CAN'T BE KILLED.
NOT BY ANYONE... OTHER THAN THE STAR.
JOKER...!
AGH!
STOP IT, PETER!
WE'RE NOT HERE TO FIGHT!
ARE YOU HERE TO TRAVEL?
YES, PLEASE! I WANT TO GO TO WINTER.
OOH, THE SNOW FESTIVAL!
I WANNA GO TO THAT, TOO!
YOU HAVE PRACTICE, DEAR.
YOU SHOULD HEAD BACK SOON.
AW. HEH!
YES, SIR.
DASH

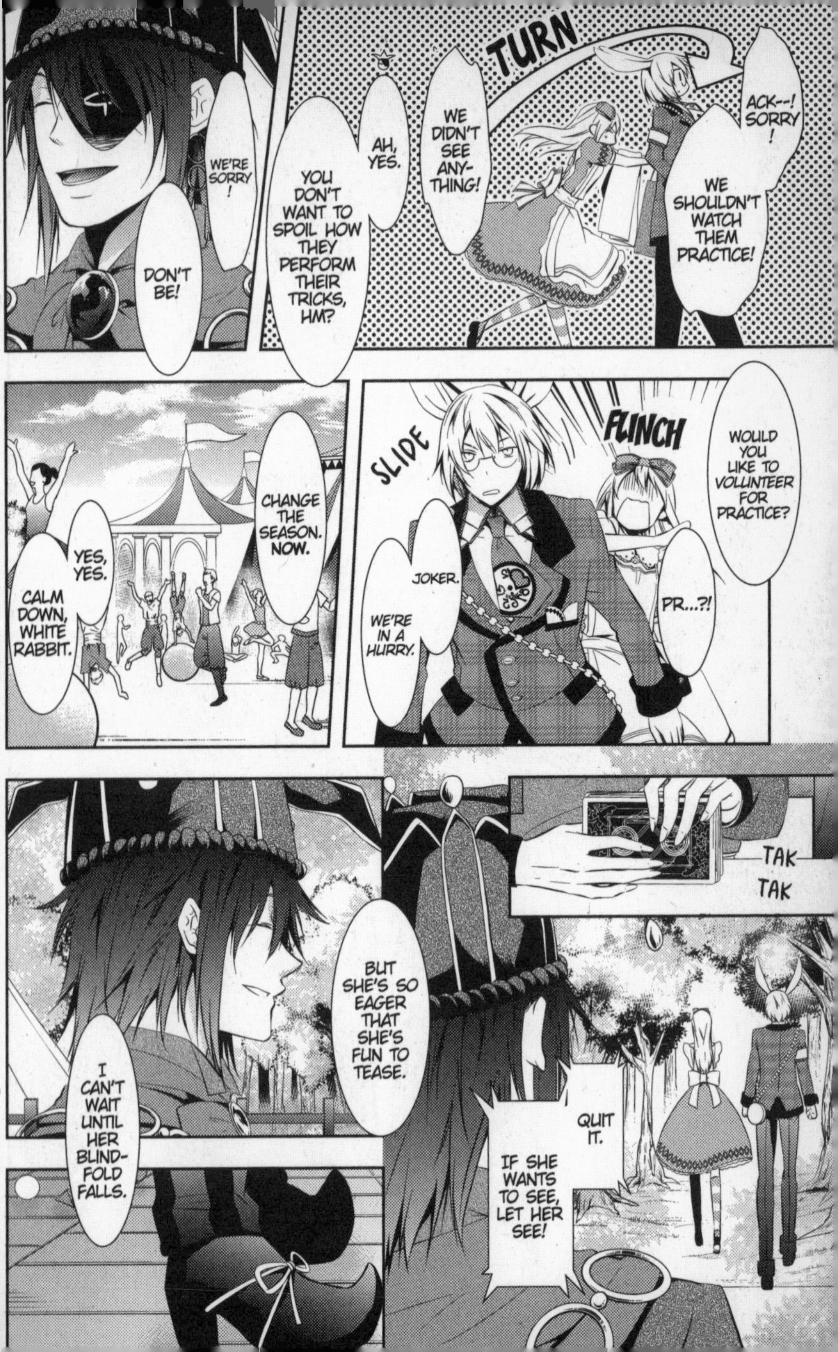
ACK--! SORRY!
WE SHOULDN'T WATCH THEM PRACTICE!
TURN
WE DIDN'T SEE ANY-THING!
AH, YES.
YOU DON'T WANT TO SPOIL HOW THEY PERFORM THEIR TRICKS, HM?
WE'RE SORRY!
DON'T BE!
WOULD YOU LIKE TO VOLUNTEER FOR PRACTICE?
FLINCH
PR...?!
SLIDE
JOKER.
WE'RE IN A HURRY.
CHANGE THE SEASON. NOW.
YES, YES.
CALM DOWN, WHITE RABBIT.
TAK TAK
QUIT IT.
IF SHE WANTS TO SEE, LET HER SEE!
BUT SHE'S SO EAGER THAT SHE'S FUN TO TEASE.
I CAN'T WAIT UNTIL HER BLIND-FOLD FALLS.

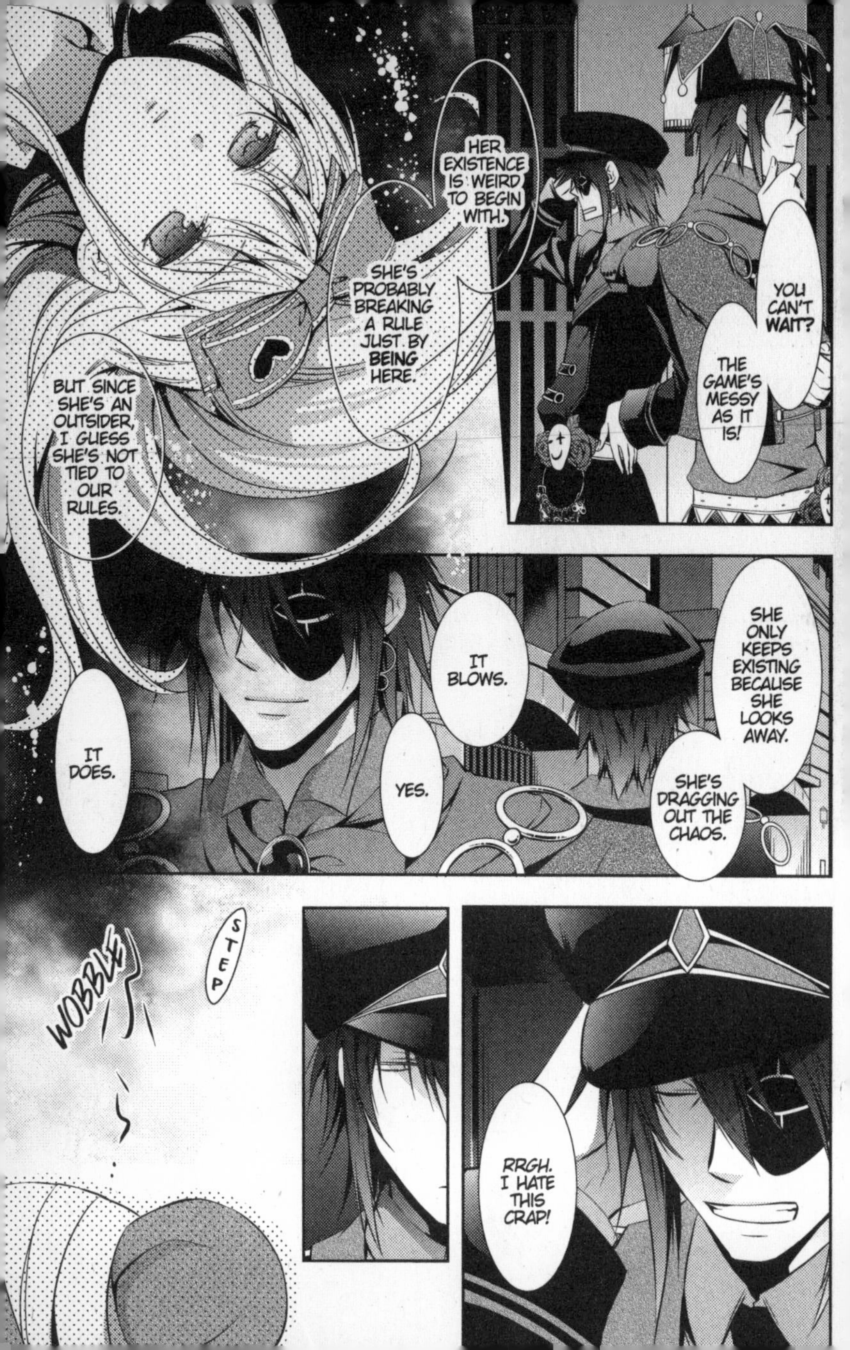
YOU CAN'T WAIT?
THE GAME'S MESSY AS IT IS!
HER EXISTENCE IS WEIRD TO BEGIN WITH.
SHE'S PROBABLY BREAKING A RULE JUST BY BEING HERE.
BUT SINCE SHE'S AN OUTSIDER, I GUESS SHE'S NOT TIED TO OUR RULES.
SHE ONLY KEEPS EXISTING BECAUSE SHE LOOKS AWAY.
SHE'S DRAGGING OUT THE CHAOS.
IT BLOWS.
YES.
IT DOES.
RRGH. I HATE THIS CRAP!
STEP
WOBBLE

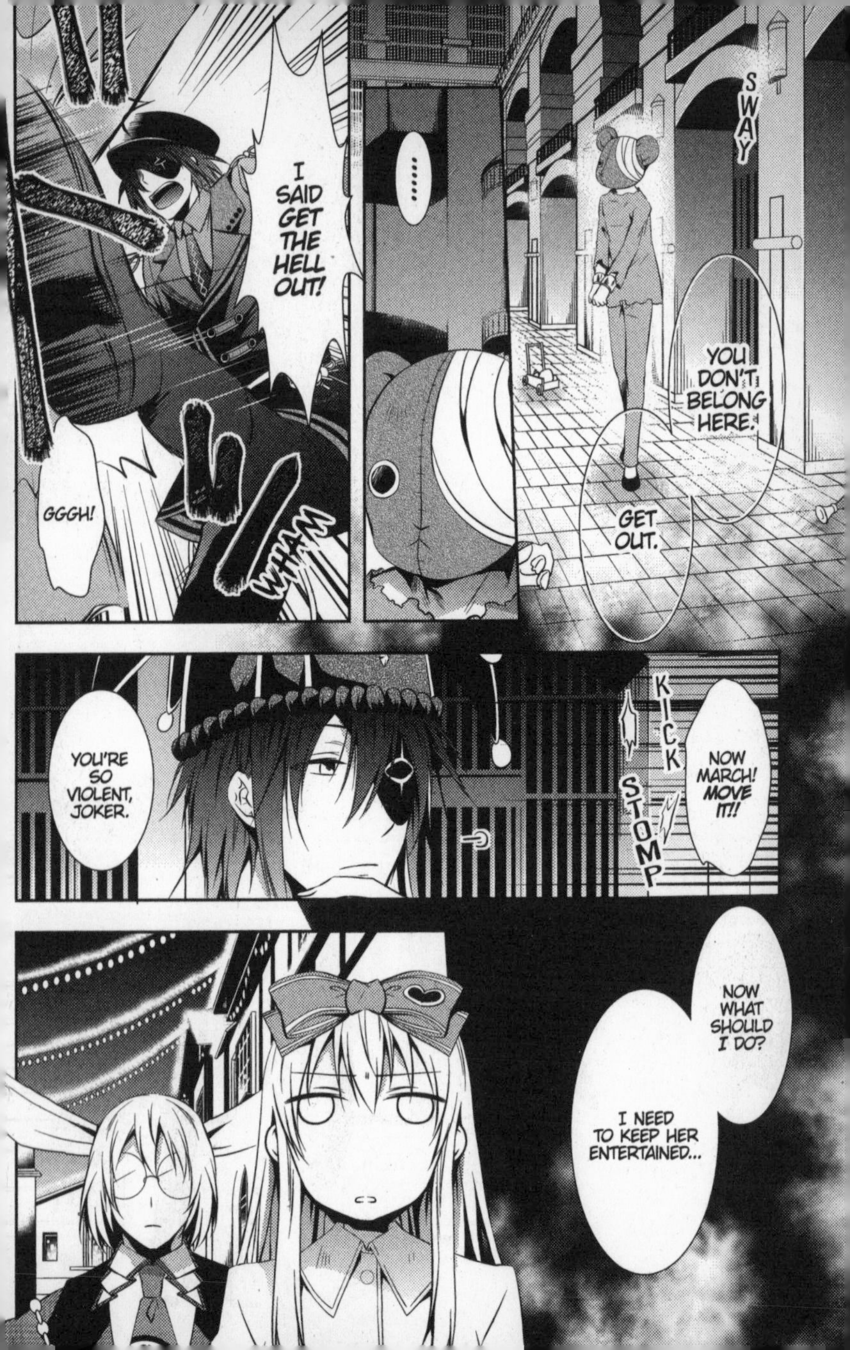
SWAY
YOU DON'T BELONG HERE.
GET OUT.
......
I SAID GET THE HELL OUT!
GGGH!
WHAM
NOW MARCH! MOVE IT!!
KICK
STOMP
YOU'RE SO VIOLENT, JOKER.
NOW WHAT SHOULD I DO?
I NEED TO KEEP HER ENTERTAINED...

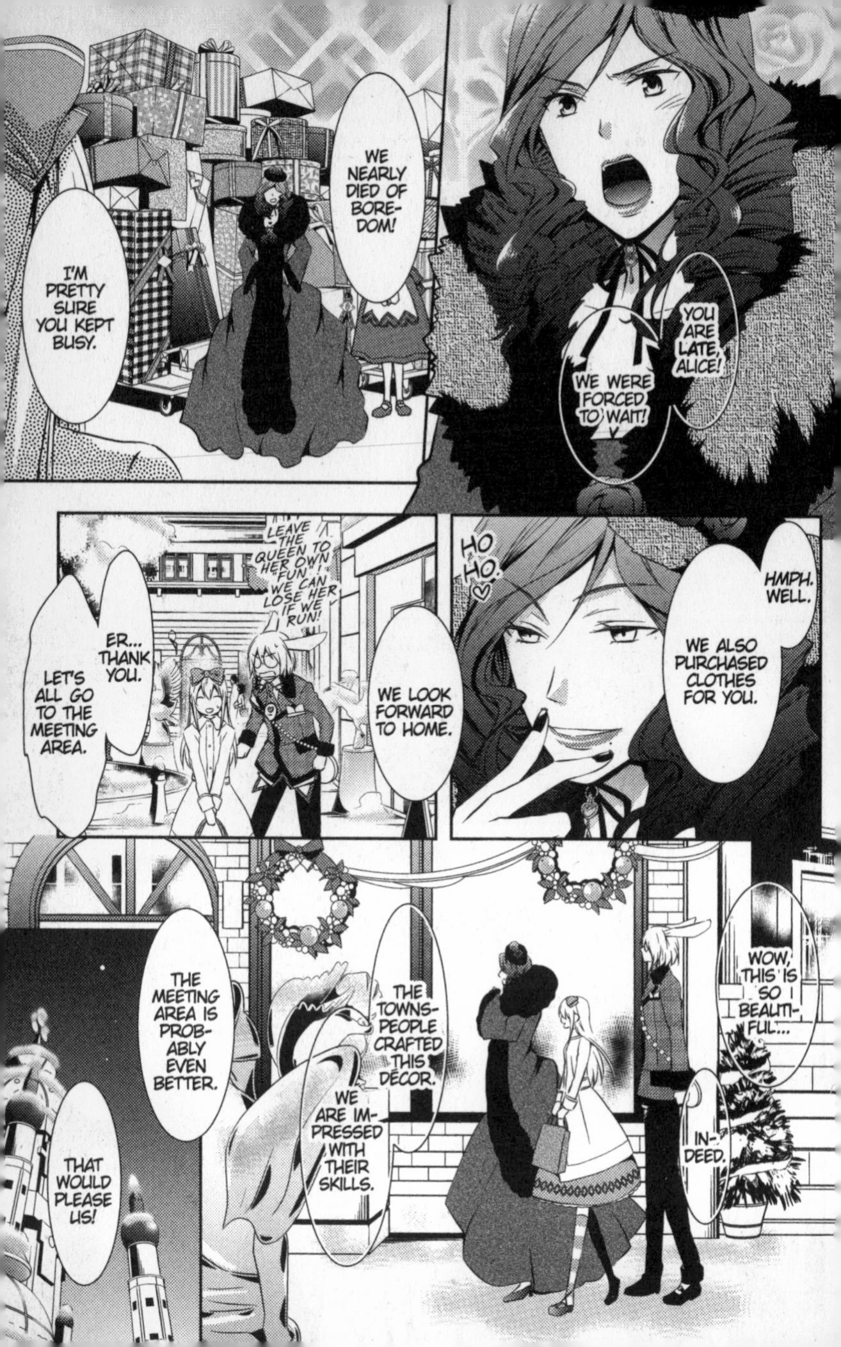
YOU ARE LATE, ALICE!
WE WERE FORCED TO WAIT!
WE NEARLY DIED OF BORE-DOM!
I'M PRETTY SURE YOU KEPT BUSY.
HO HO.
HMPH. WELL.
WE ALSO PURCHASED CLOTHES FOR YOU.
WE LOOK FORWARD TO HOME.
LEAVE THE QUEEN TO HER OWN "FUN"! WE CAN LOSE HER IF WE RUN!
ER... THANK YOU.
LET'S ALL GO TO THE MEETING AREA.
WOW, THIS IS SO BEAUTI-FUL...
IN-DEED.
THE TOWNS-PEOPLE CRAFTED THIS DÉCOR.
WE ARE IM-PRESSED WITH THEIR SKILLS.
THE MEETING AREA IS PROB-ABLY EVEN BETTER.
THAT WOULD PLEASE US!

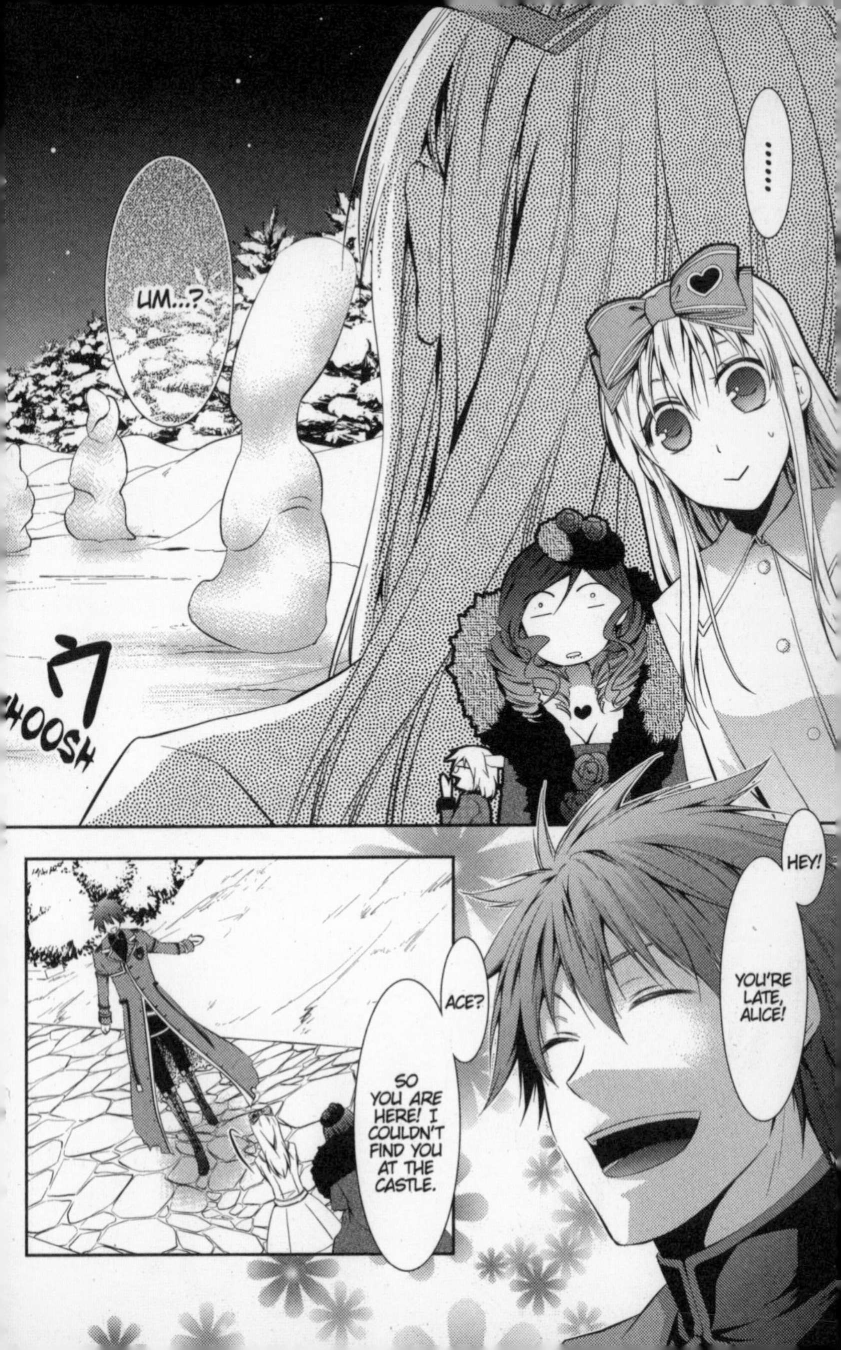
......
UM...?
HOOSH
HEY!
YOU'RE LATE, ALICE!
ACE?
SO YOU ARE HERE! I COULDN'T FIND YOU AT THE CASTLE.

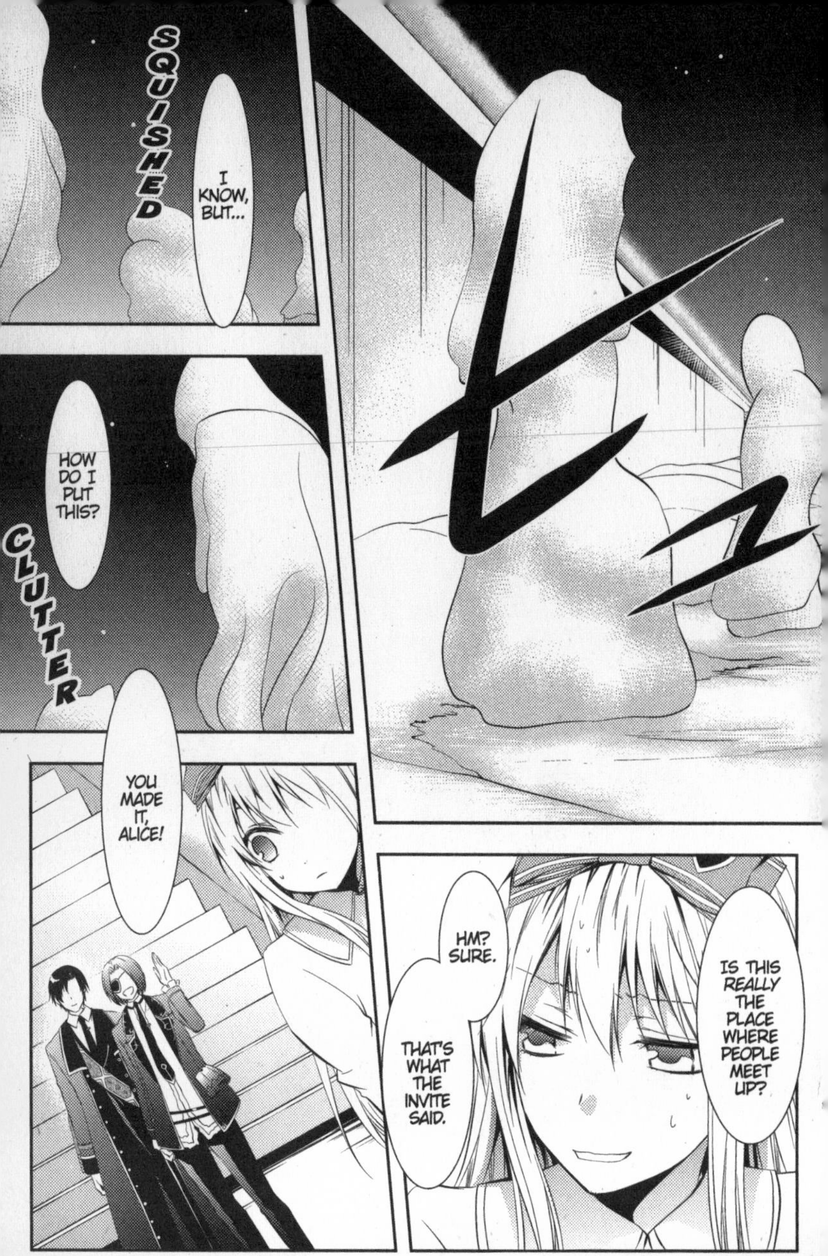
I KNOW, BUT...
SQUISHED
HOW DO I PUT THIS?
CLUTTER
IS THIS REALLY THE PLACE WHERE PEOPLE MEET UP?
HM? SURE.
THAT'S WHAT THE INVITE SAID.
YOU MADE IT, ALICE!

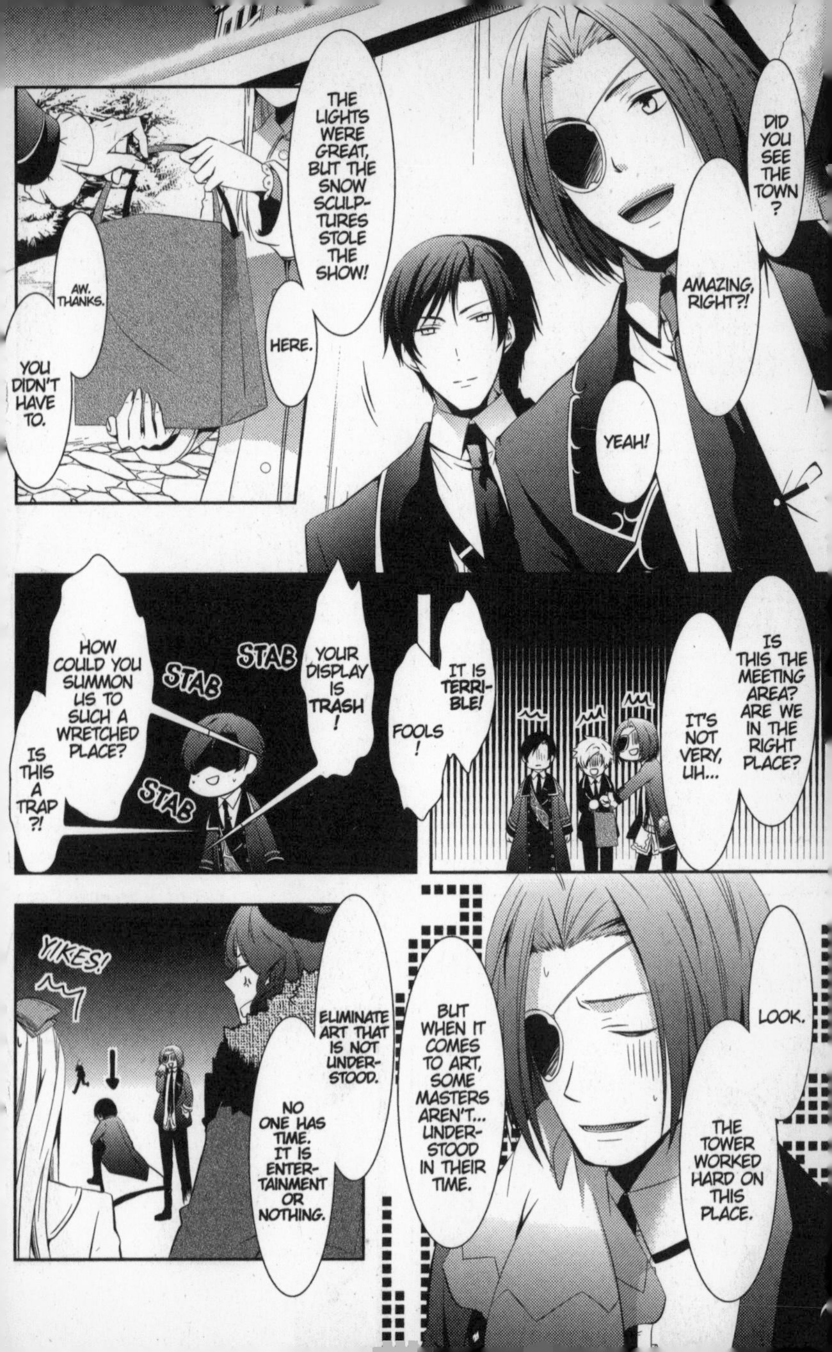
DID YOU SEE THE TOWN?
AMAZING, RIGHT?!
YEAH!
THE LIGHTS WERE GREAT, BUT THE SNOW SCULPTURES STOLE THE SHOW!
HERE.
AW. THANKS.
YOU DIDN'T HAVE TO.
IS THIS THE MEETING AREA? ARE WE IN THE RIGHT PLACE?
IT'S NOT VERY, UH...
IT IS TERRIBLE!
FOOLS!
YOUR DISPLAY IS TRASH!
STAB
STAB
HOW COULD YOU SUMMON US TO SUCH A WRETCHED PLACE?
STAB
IS THIS A TRAP?!
LOOK.
THE TOWER WORKED HARD ON THIS PLACE.
BUT WHEN IT COMES TO ART, SOME MASTERS AREN'T... UNDERSTOOD IN THEIR TIME.
ELIMINATE ART THAT IS NOT UNDERSTOOD.
NO ONE HAS TIME. IT IS ENTERTAINMENT OR NOTHING.
YIKES!

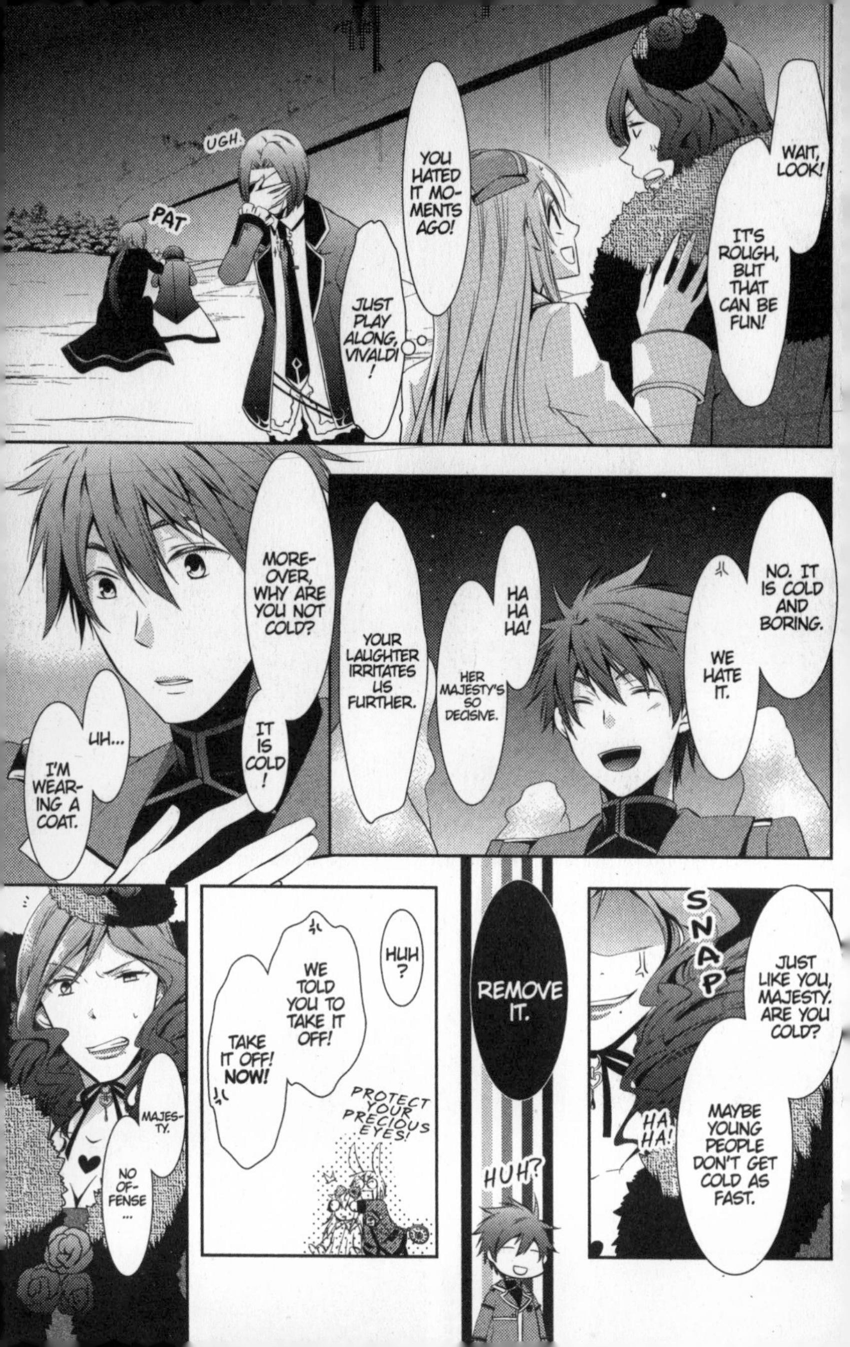

WAIT, LOOK!
IT'S ROUGH, BUT THAT CAN BE FUN!
YOU HATED IT MOMENTS AGO!
JUST PLAY ALONG, VIVALDI!
UGH.
PAT
NO. IT IS COLD AND BORING.
WE HATE IT.
HA HA HA!
HER MAJESTY'S SO DECISIVE.
YOUR LAUGHTER IRRITATES US FURTHER.
MOREOVER, WHY ARE YOU NOT COLD?
IT IS COLD!
UH...
I'M WEARING A COAT.
SNAP
JUST LIKE YOU, MAJESTY. ARE YOU COLD?
MAYBE YOUNG PEOPLE DON'T GET COLD AS FAST.
HA HA!
REMOVE IT.
HUH?
HUH?
WE TOLD YOU TO TAKE IT OFF!
TAKE IT OFF! NOW!
PROTECT YOUR PRECIOUS EYES!
MAJESTY.
NO OFFENSE...

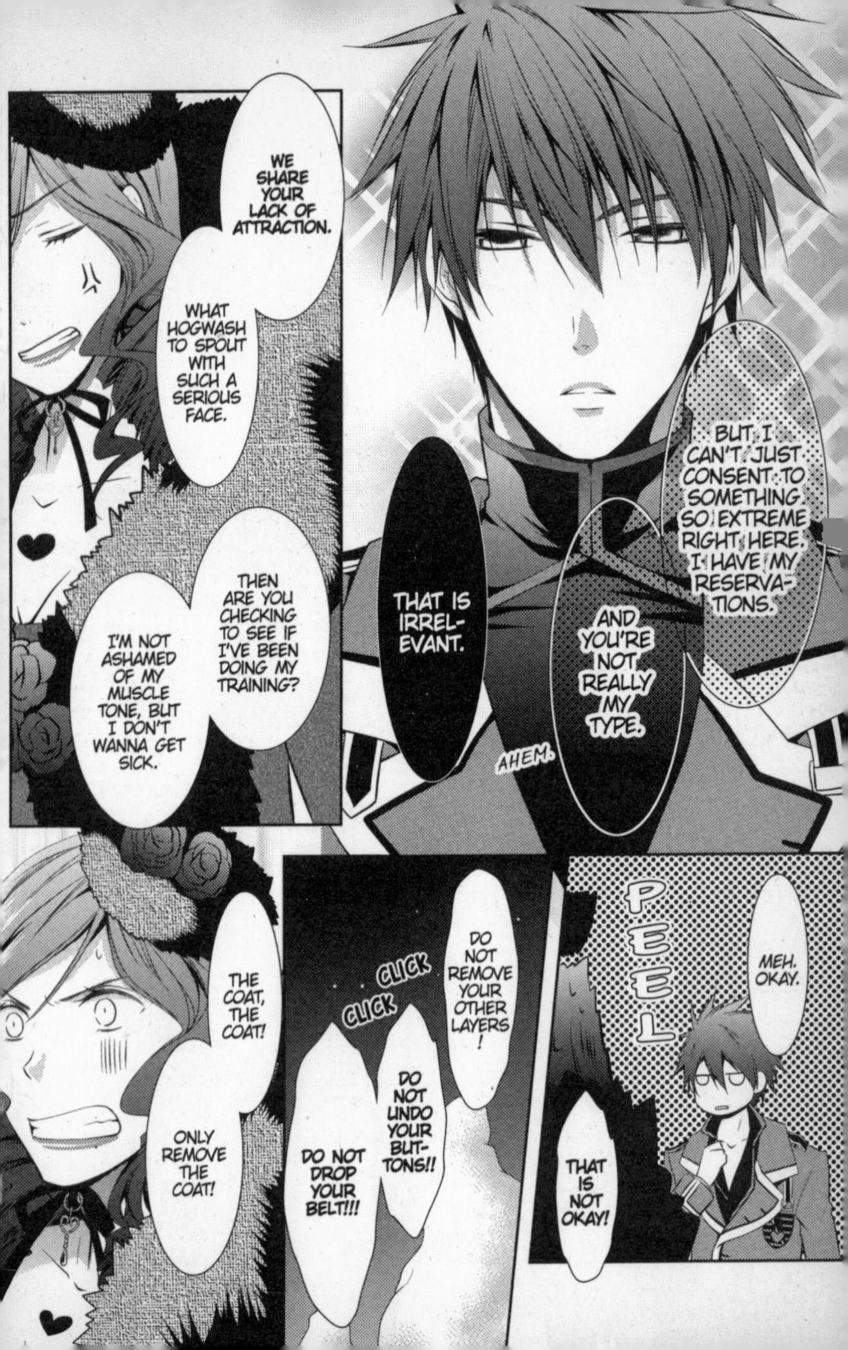
BUT I CAN'T JUST CONSENT TO SOMETHING SO EXTREME RIGHT HERE. I HAVE MY RESERVATIONS.
AND YOU'RE NOT REALLY MY TYPE.
AHEM.
THAT IS IRRELEVANT.
WE SHARE YOUR LACK OF ATTRACTION.
WHAT HOGWASH TO SPOUT WITH SUCH A SERIOUS FACE.
THEN ARE YOU CHECKING TO SEE IF I'VE BEEN DOING MY TRAINING?
I'M NOT ASHAMED OF MY MUSCLE TONE, BUT I DON'T WANNA GET SICK.
PEEL
MEH. OKAY.
THAT IS NOT OKAY!
DO NOT REMOVE YOUR OTHER LAYERS!
CLICK
CLICK
DO NOT UNDO YOUR BUTTONS!!
DO NOT DROP YOUR BELT!!!
THE COAT, THE COAT!
ONLY REMOVE THE COAT!

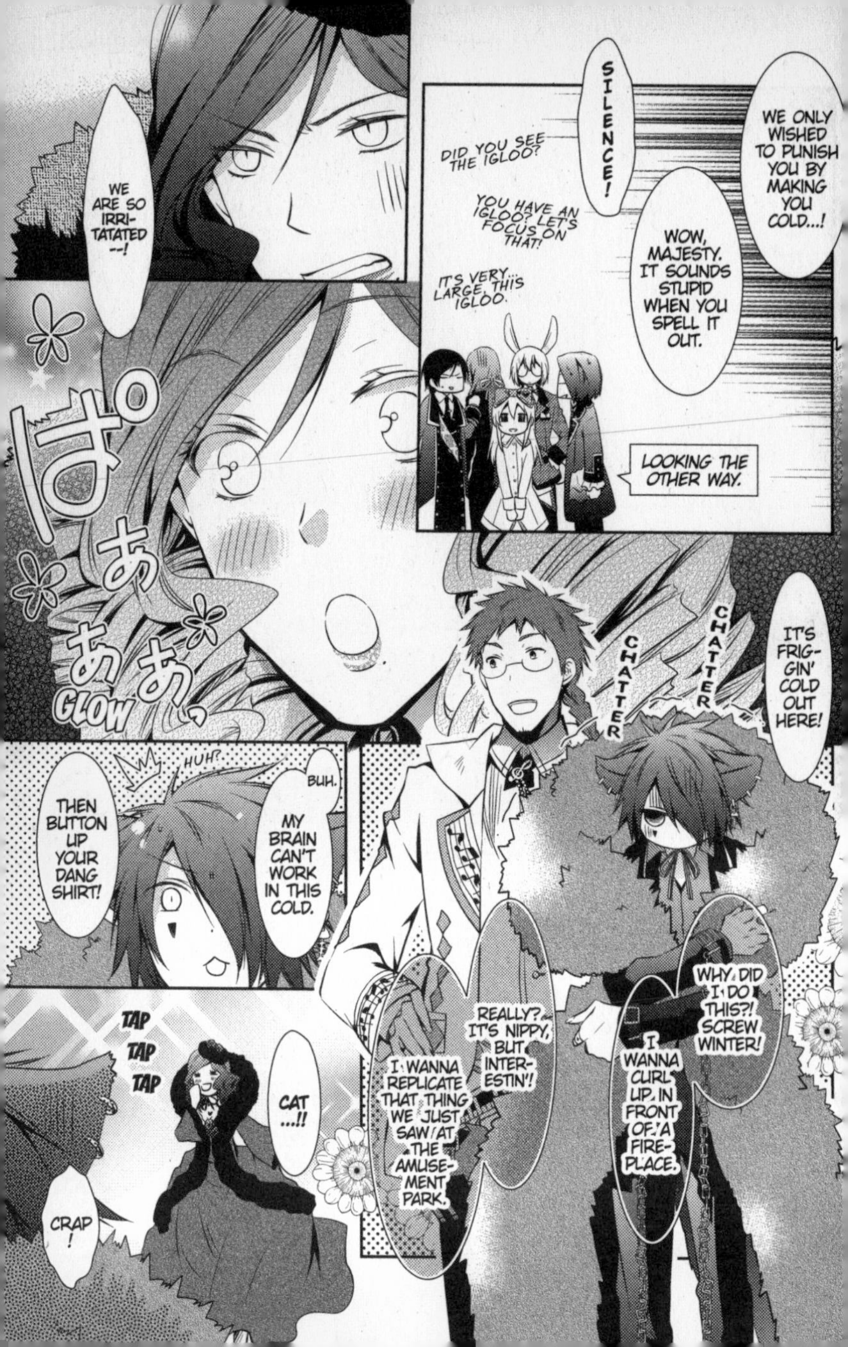

WE ONLY WISHED TO PUNISH YOU BY MAKING YOU COLD...!
SILENCE!
WOW, MAJESTY. IT SOUNDS STUPID WHEN YOU SPELL IT OUT.
DID YOU SEE THE IGLOO?
YOU HAVE AN IGLOO? LET'S FOCUS ON THAT!
IT'S VERY... LARGE, THIS IGLOO.
LOOKING THE OTHER WAY.
WE ARE SO IRRI-TATATED --!
ぱぁあ、
GLOW
IT'S FRIG-GIN' COLD OUT HERE!
CHATTER CHATTER
WHY DID I DO THIS?! SCREW WINTER!
I WANNA CURL UP IN FRONT OF A FIRE-PLACE.
REALLY? IT'S NIPPY, BUT INTER-ESTIN'!
I WANNA REPLICATE THAT THING WE JUST SAW AT THE AMUSEMENT PARK.
BUH.
MY BRAIN CAN'T WORK IN THIS COLD.
HUH?
THEN BUTTON UP YOUR DANG SHIRT!
CAT ...!!
TAP TAP TAP
CRAP!

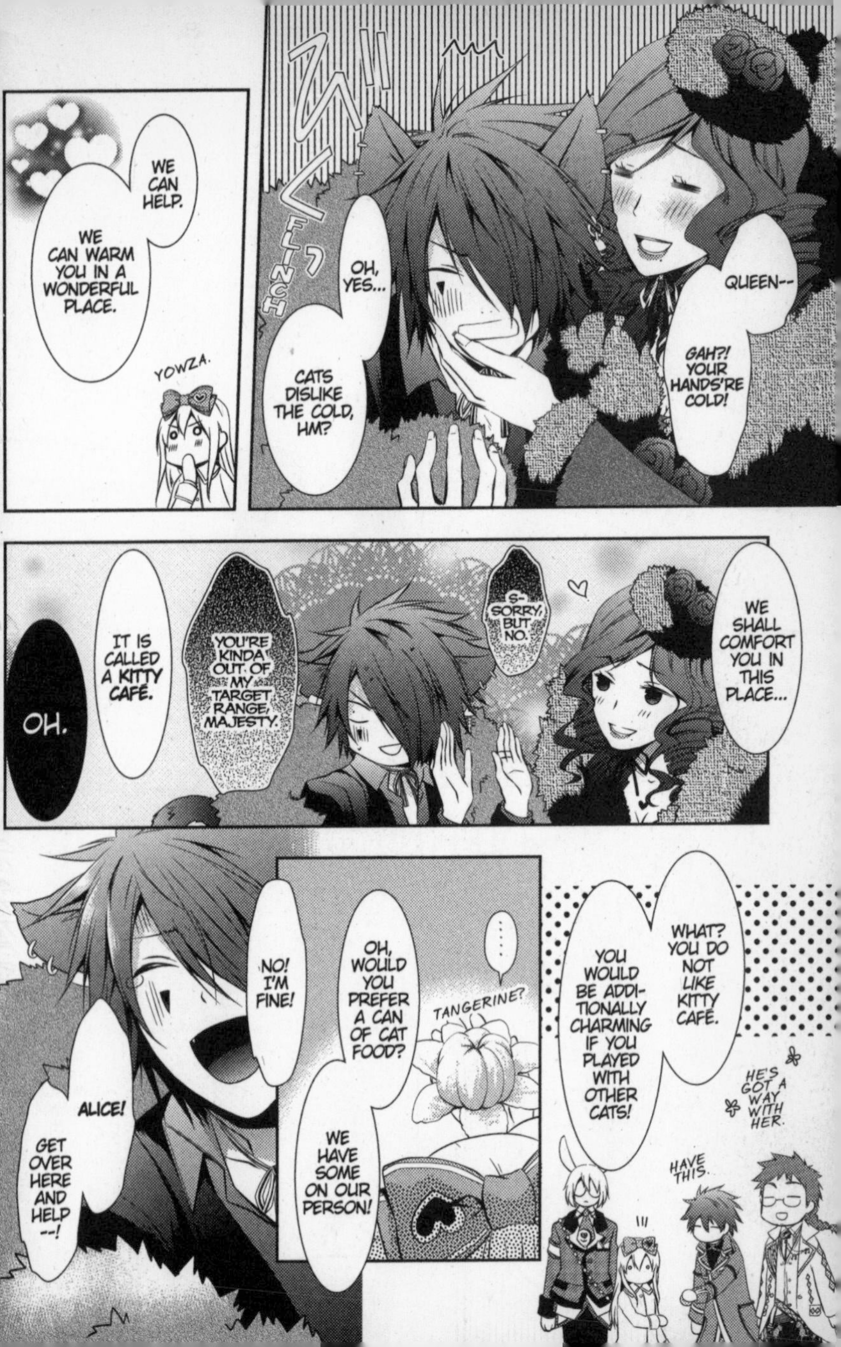
QUEEN--
GAH?! YOUR HANDS'RE COLD!
FLINCH
OH, YES...
CATS DISLIKE THE COLD, HM?
WE CAN HELP.
WE CAN WARM YOU IN A WONDERFUL PLACE.
YOWZA.
WE SHALL COMFORT YOU IN THIS PLACE...
S-SORRY, BUT NO.
YOU'RE KINDA OUT OF MY TARGET RANGE, MAJESTY.
IT IS CALLED A KITTY CAFÉ.
OH.
WHAT? YOU DO NOT LIKE KITTY CAFÉ.
YOU WOULD BE ADDITIONALLY CHARMING IF YOU PLAYED WITH OTHER CATS!
HE'S GOT A WAY WITH HER.
HAVE THIS.
!!!
.....
TANGERINE?
OH, WOULD YOU PREFER A CAN OF CAT FOOD?
WE HAVE SOME ON OUR PERSON!
NO! I'M FINE!
ALICE!
GET OVER HERE AND HELP--!

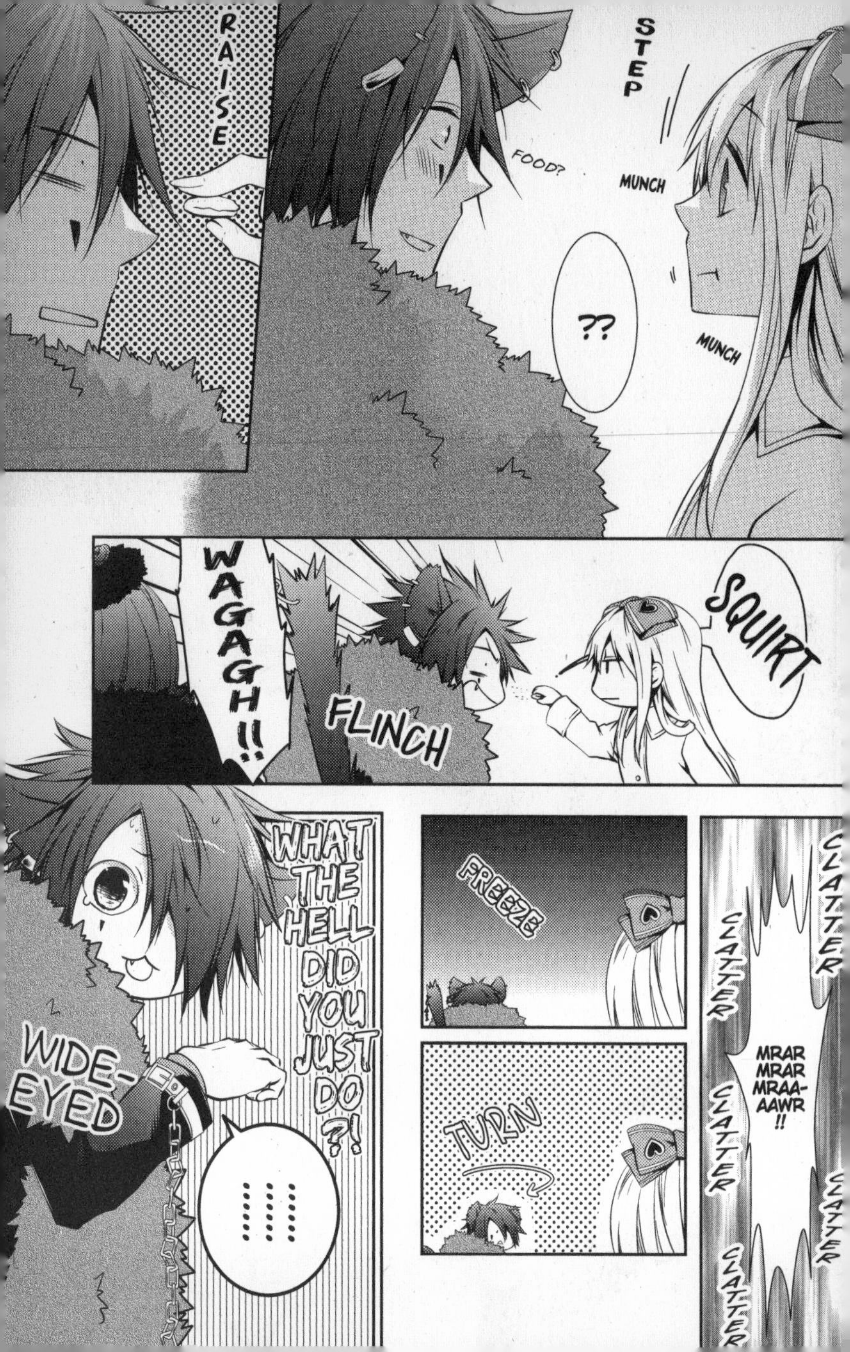
STEP
MUNCH
FOOD?
??
MUNCH
RAISE
SQUIRT
FLINCH
WAGAGH!!
CLATTER
CLATTER
MRAR MRAR MRAA-AAWR!!
CLATTER
CLATTER
CLATTER
FREEZE
TURN
WHAT THE HELL DID YOU JUST DO?!
WIDE-EYED
!!!!

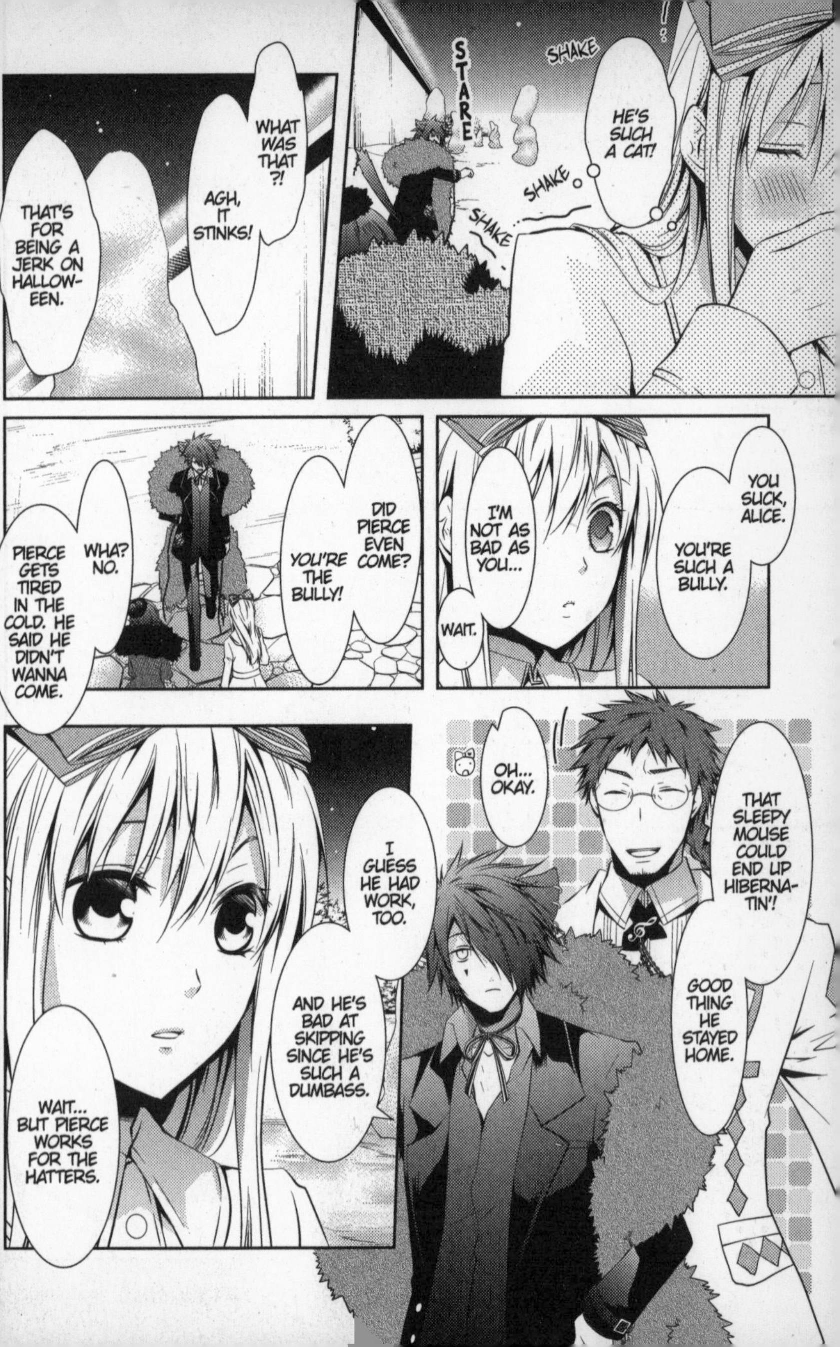
!?
SHAKE
HE'S SUCH A CAT!
STARE
SHAKE
SHAKE
SHAKE
WHAT WAS THAT ?!
AGH, IT STINKS!
THAT'S FOR BEING A JERK ON HALLOW-EEN.
YOU SUCK, ALICE.
YOU'RE SUCH A BULLY.
I'M NOT AS BAD AS YOU...
WAIT.
DID PIERCE EVEN COME?
YOU'RE THE BULLY!
WHA? NO.
PIERCE GETS TIRED IN THE COLD. HE SAID HE DIDN'T WANNA COME.
THAT SLEEPY MOUSE COULD END UP HIBERNA-TIN'!
OH... OKAY.
GOOD THING HE STAYED HOME.
AND HE'S BAD AT SKIPPING SINCE HE'S SUCH A DUMBASS.
I GUESS HE HAD WORK, TOO.
WAIT... BUT PIERCE WORKS FOR THE HATTERS.

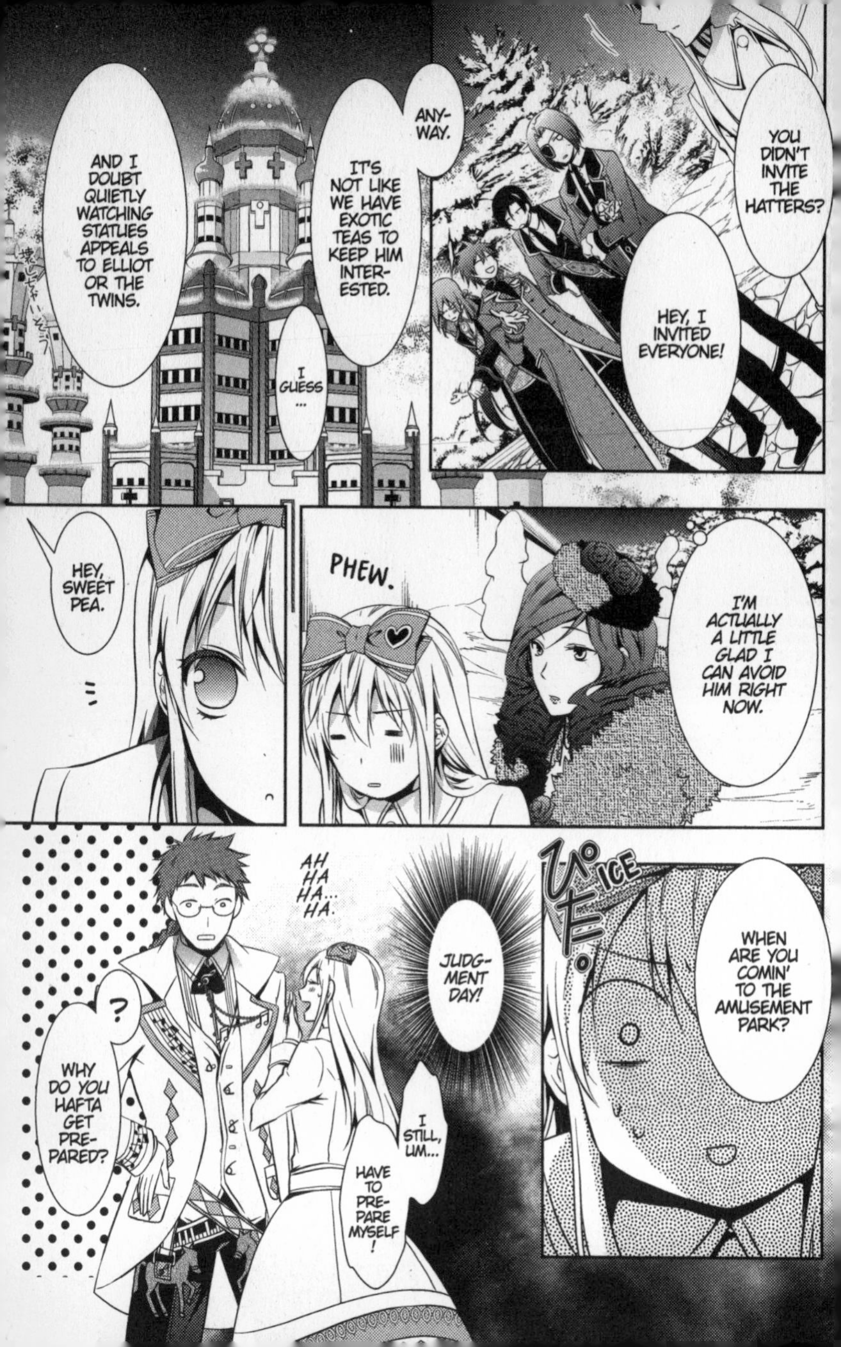

YOU DIDN'T INVITE THE HATTERS?
HEY, I INVITED EVERYONE!
ANY-WAY.
IT'S NOT LIKE WE HAVE EXOTIC TEAS TO KEEP HIM INTER-ESTED.
I GUESS...
AND I DOUBT QUIETLY WATCHING STATUES APPEALS TO ELLIOT OR THE TWINS.
I'M ACTUALLY A LITTLE GLAD I CAN AVOID HIM RIGHT NOW.
PHEW.
HEY, SWEET PEA.
ICE
WHEN ARE YOU COMIN' TO THE AMUSEMENT PARK?
JUDG-MENT DAY!
AH HA HA... HA.
I STILL, UM...
HAVE TO PRE-PARE MYSELF!
?
WHY DO YOU HAFTA GET PRE-PARED?

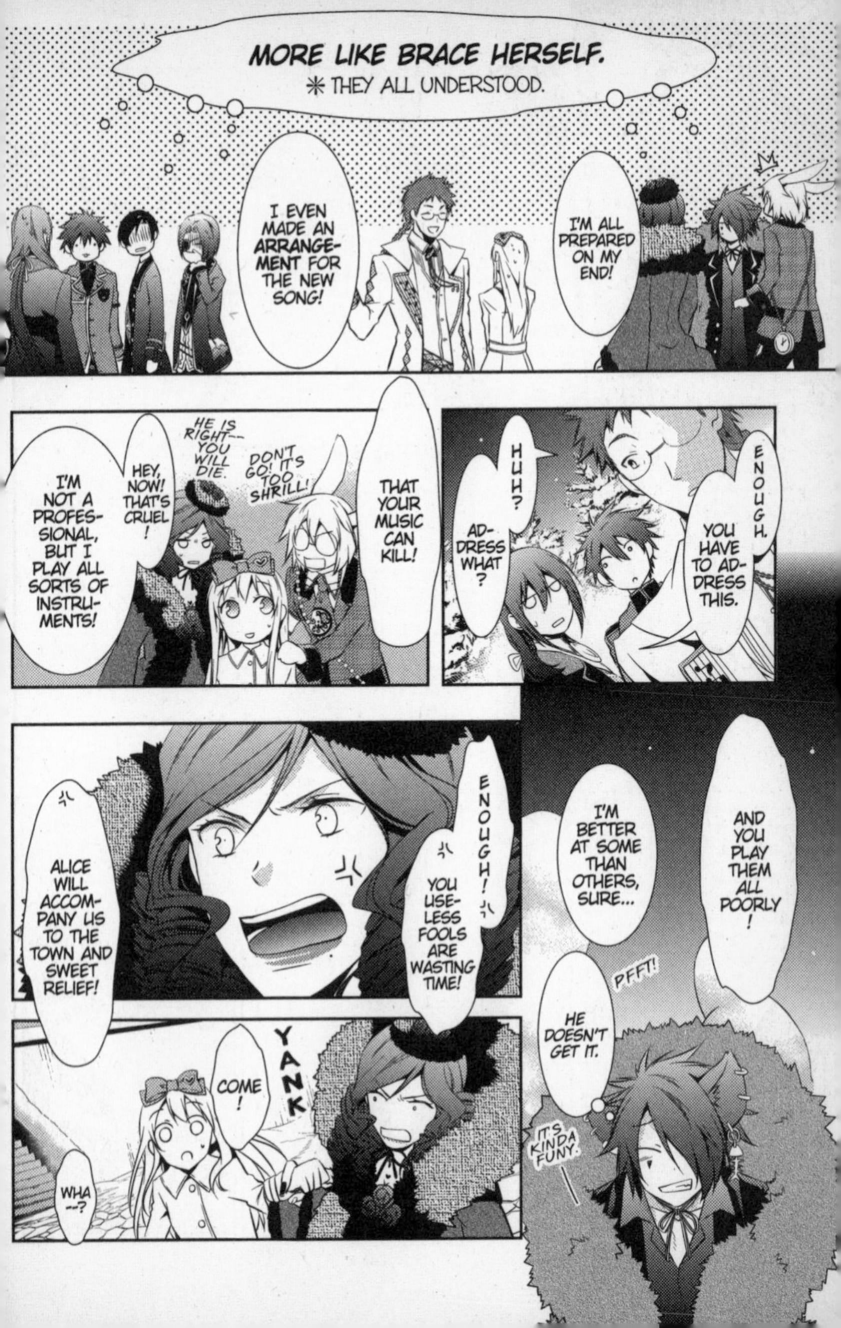

MORE LIKE BRACE HERSELF.
✻ THEY ALL UNDERSTOOD.
I'M ALL PREPARED ON MY END!
I EVEN MADE AN ARRANGEMENT FOR THE NEW SONG!
ENOUGH.
YOU HAVE TO ADDRESS THIS.
HUH?
ADDRESS WHAT?
THAT YOUR MUSIC CAN KILL!
DON'T GO! IT'S TOO SHRILL!
HE IS RIGHT-- YOU WILL DIE.
HEY, NOW! THAT'S CRUEL!
I'M NOT A PROFESSIONAL, BUT I PLAY ALL SORTS OF INSTRUMENTS!
AND YOU PLAY THEM ALL POORLY!
I'M BETTER AT SOME THAN OTHERS, SURE...
PFFT!
HE DOESN'T GET IT.
IT'S KINDA FUNY.
ENOUGH!
YOU USELESS FOOLS ARE WASTING TIME!
ALICE WILL ACCOMPANY US TO THE TOWN AND SWEET RELIEF!
YANK
COME!
WHA--?

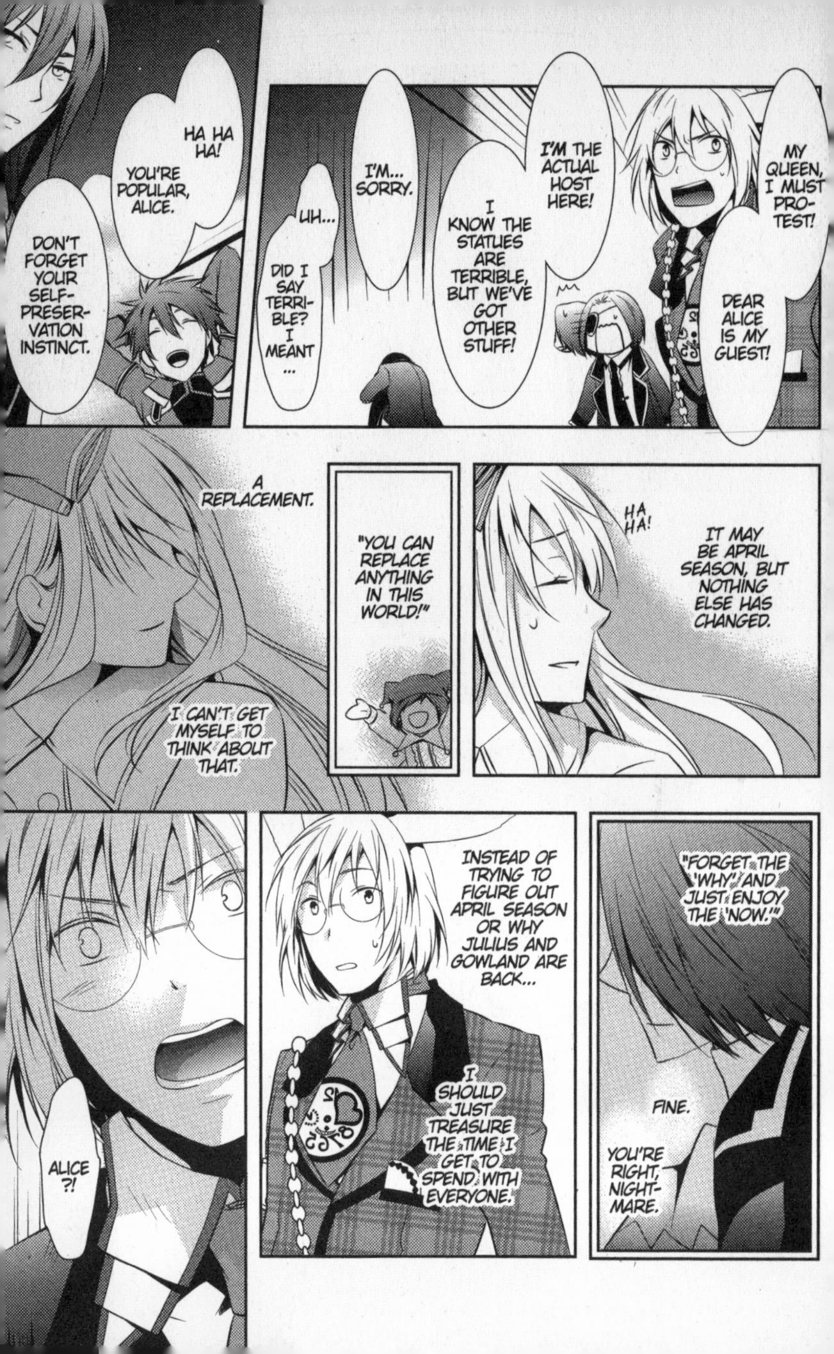
MY QUEEN, I MUST PRO-TEST!
DEAR ALICE IS MY GUEST!
I'M THE ACTUAL HOST HERE!
I KNOW THE STATUES ARE TERRIBLE, BUT WE'VE GOT OTHER STUFF!
I'M... SORRY.
UH...
DID I SAY TERRI-BLE? I MEANT ...
HA HA HA!
YOU'RE POPULAR, ALICE.
DON'T FORGET YOUR SELF-PRESER-VATION INSTINCT.
HA HA!
IT MAY BE APRIL SEASON, BUT NOTHING ELSE HAS CHANGED.
"YOU CAN REPLACE ANYTHING IN THIS WORLD!"
A REPLACEMENT.
I CAN'T GET MYSELF TO THINK ABOUT THAT.
"FORGET THE 'WHY' AND JUST ENJOY THE 'NOW.'"
FINE.
YOU'RE RIGHT, NIGHT-MARE.
INSTEAD OF TRYING TO FIGURE OUT APRIL SEASON OR WHY JULIUS AND GOWLAND ARE BACK...
I SHOULD JUST TREASURE THE TIME I GET TO SPEND WITH EVERYONE.
ALICE ?!

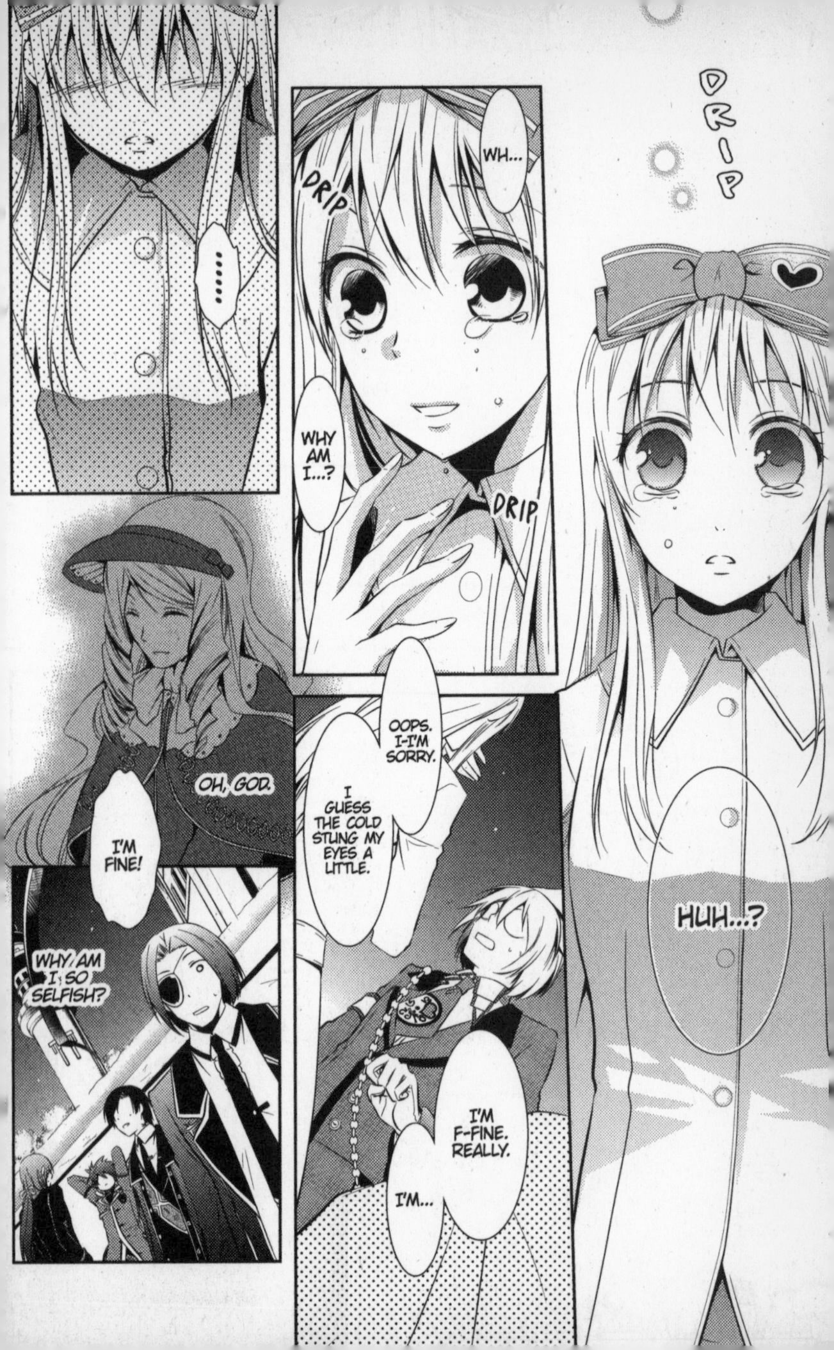
DRIP
DRIP
HUH...?
WH...
DRIP
WHY AM I...?
DRIP
......
OOPS. I-I'M SORRY.
I GUESS THE COLD STUNG MY EYES A LITTLE.
I'M F-FINE. REALLY.
I'M...
OH, GOD.
I'M FINE!
WHY AM I SO SELFISH?

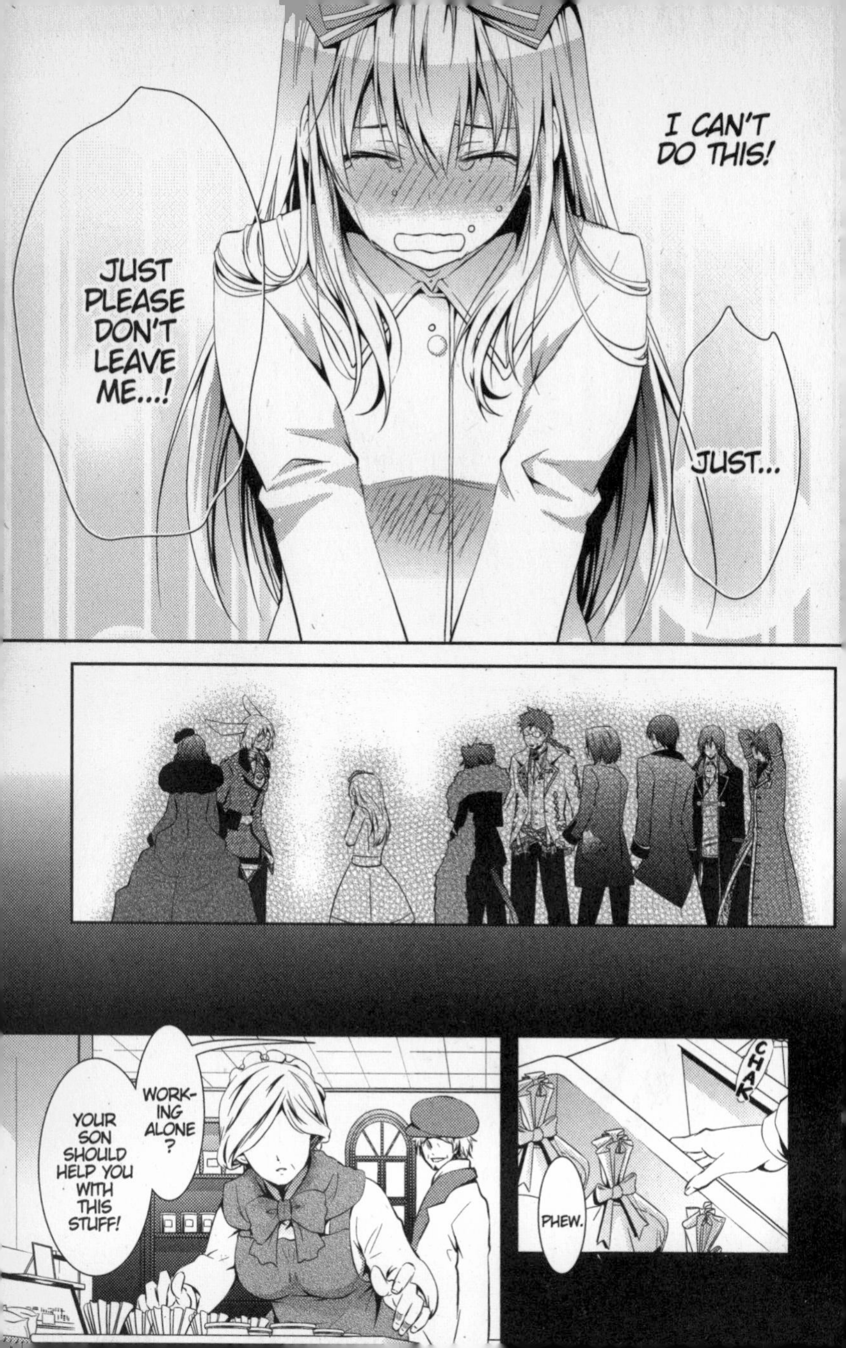
I CAN'T DO THIS!
JUST...
JUST PLEASE DON'T LEAVE ME...!
CHAK
PHEW.
WORKING ALONE?
YOUR SON SHOULD HELP YOU WITH THIS STUFF!

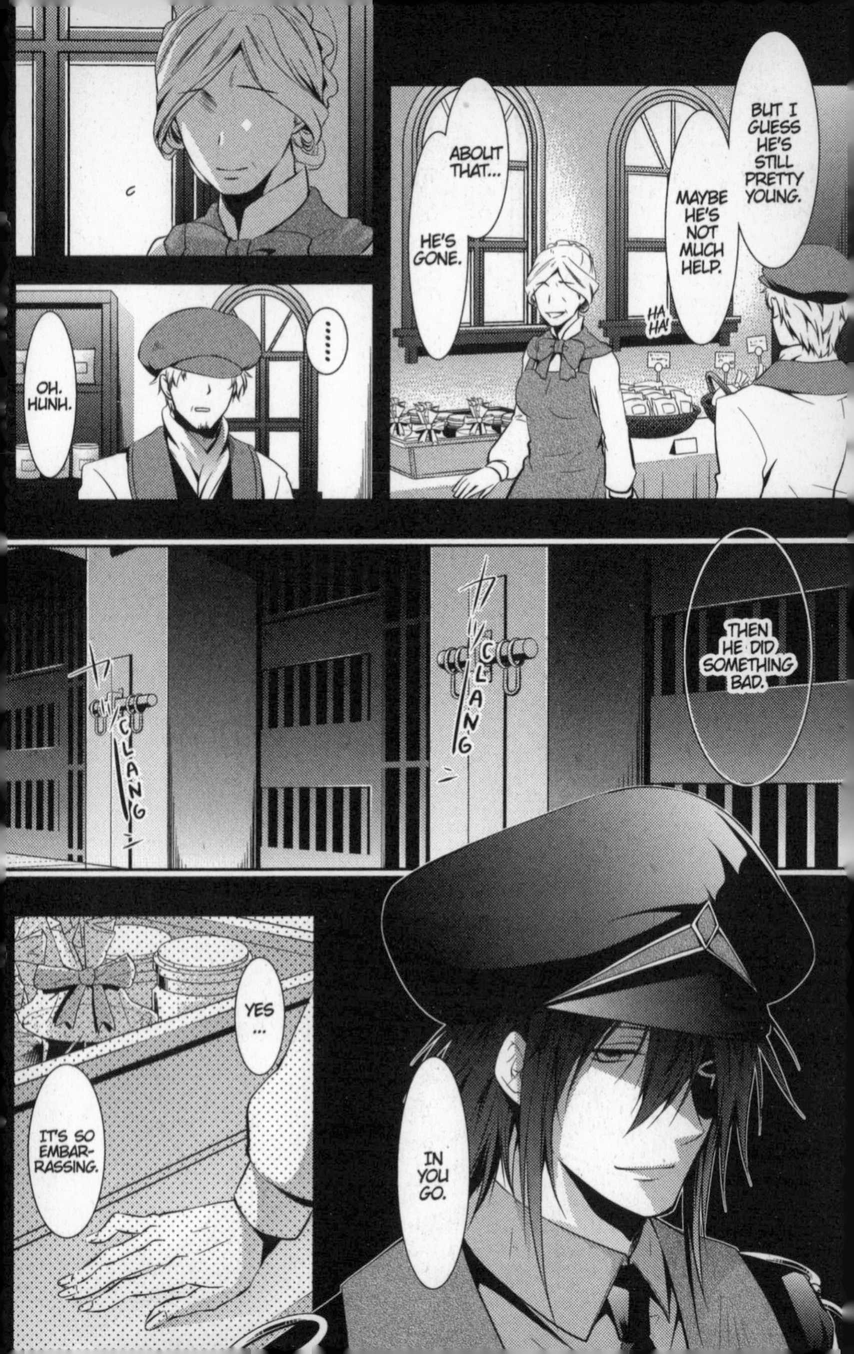
BUT I GUESS HE'S STILL PRETTY YOUNG.
MAYBE HE'S NOT MUCH HELP.
HA HA!
ABOUT THAT...
HE'S GONE.
......
OH. HUNH.
THEN HE DID SOMETHING BAD.
CLANG
CLANG
IN YOU GO.
YES...
IT'S SO EMBARRASSING.

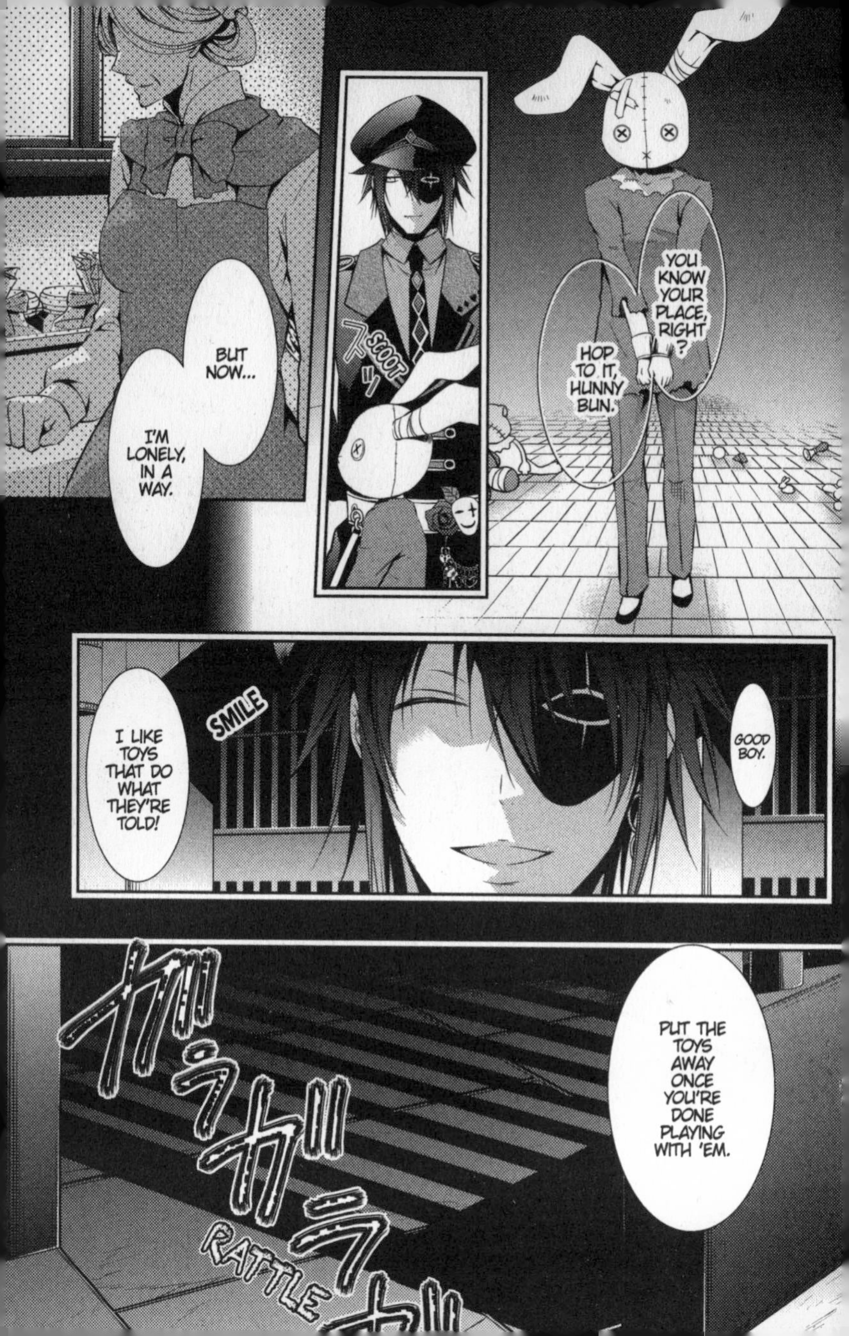
YOU KNOW YOUR PLACE, RIGHT?
HOP TO IT, HUNNY BUN.
SCOOT
BUT NOW...
I'M LONELY, IN A WAY.
GOOD BOY.
SMILE
I LIKE TOYS THAT DO WHAT THEY'RE TOLD!
PUT THE TOYS AWAY ONCE YOU'RE DONE PLAYING WITH 'EM.
RATTLE

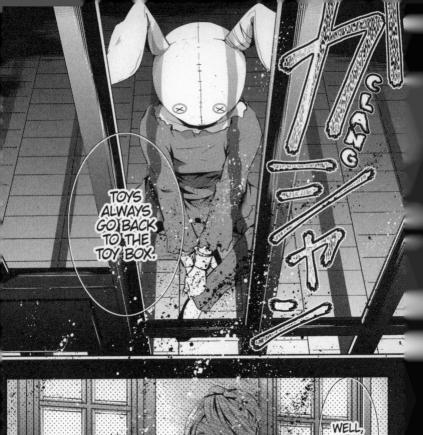

TOYS ALWAYS GO BACK TO THE TOY BOX.

CLANG

WELL, IT'S OKAY.

I'LL GET A REPLACEMENT SOON.

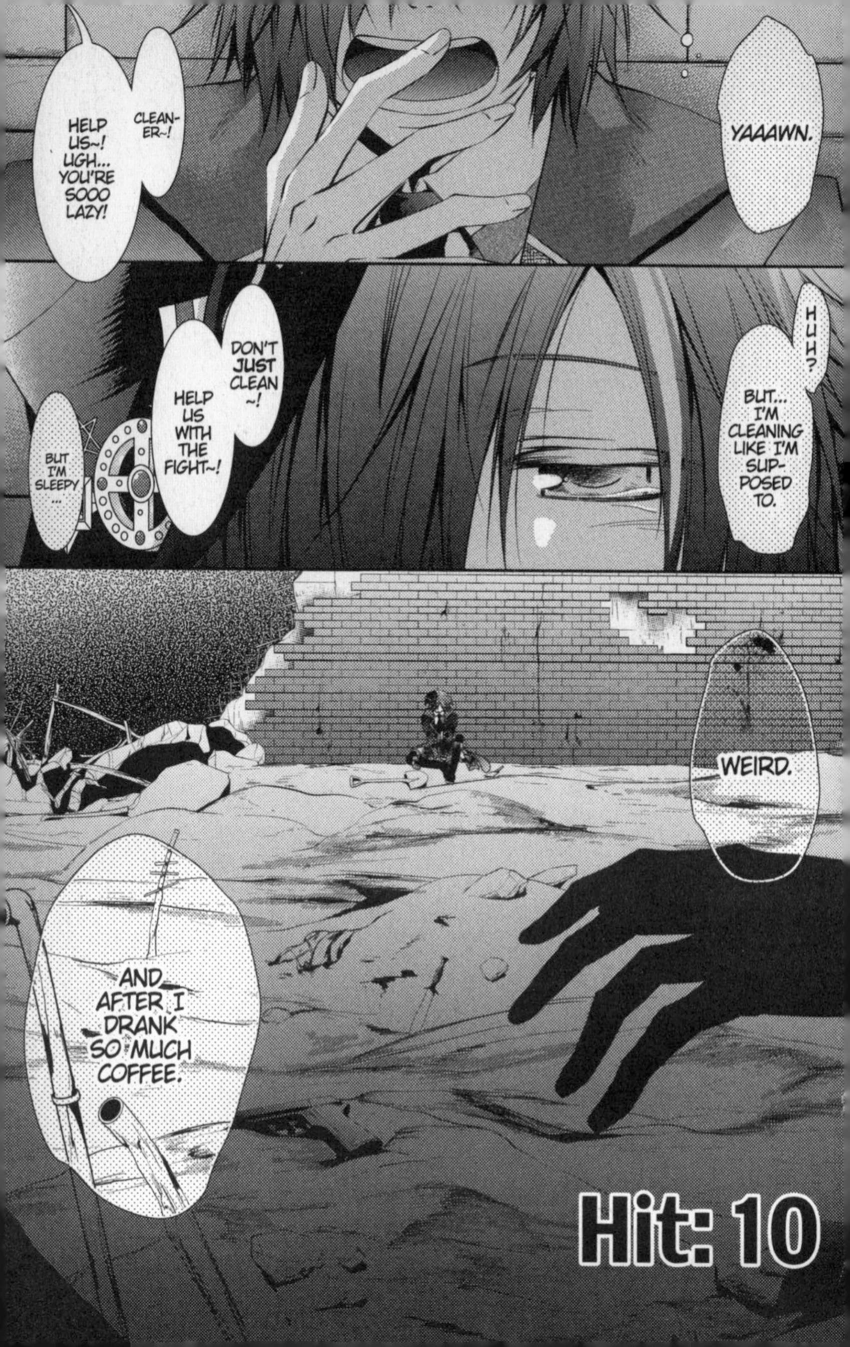
YAAAWN.
CLEAN-ER~!
HELP US~! UGH... YOU'RE SOOO LAZY!
HUH? BUT... I'M CLEANING LIKE I'M SUP-POSED TO.
DON'T JUST CLEAN ~!
HELP US WITH THE FIGHT~!
BUT I'M SLEEPY ...
WEIRD.
AND AFTER I DRANK SO MUCH COFFEE.
Hit: 10

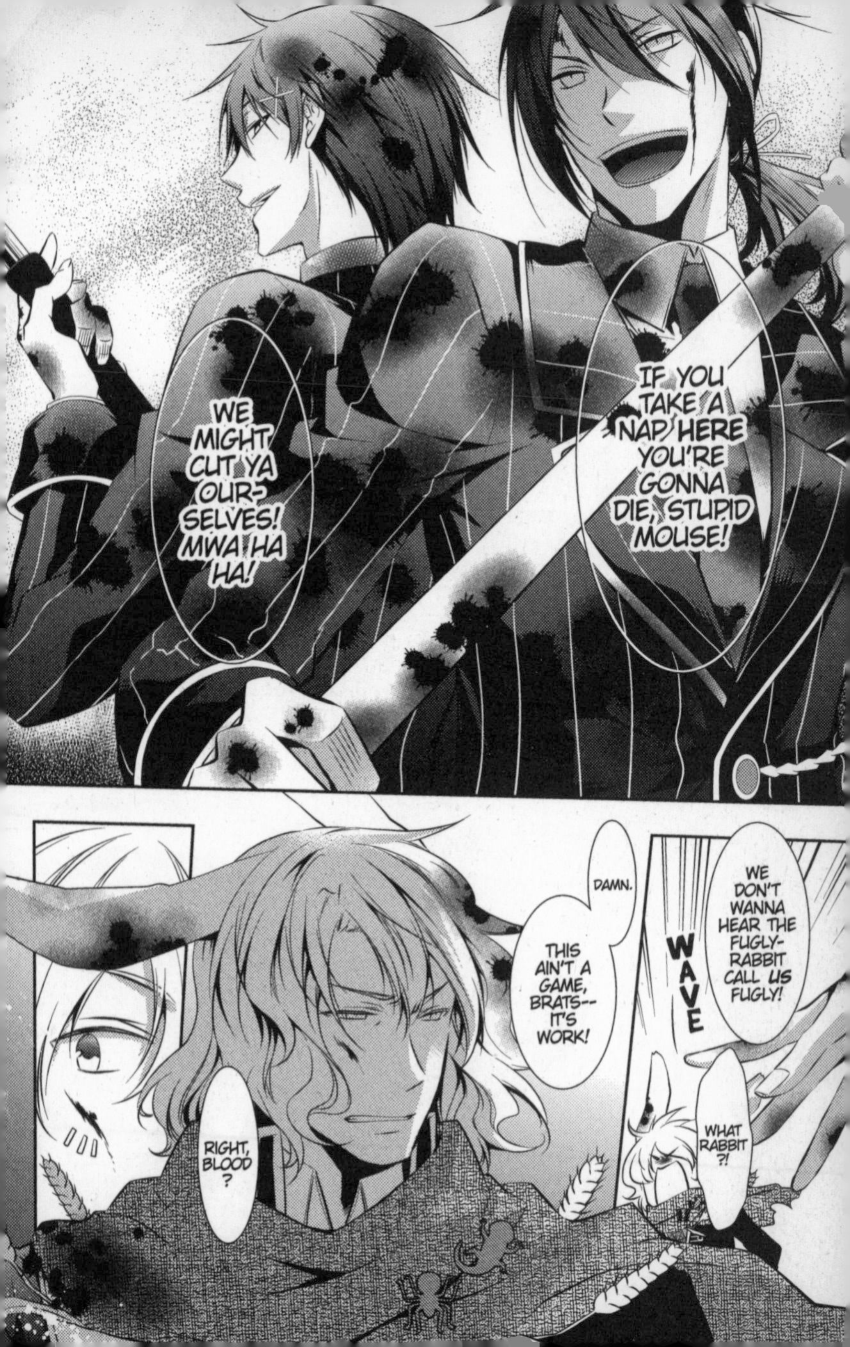
IF YOU TAKE A NAP HERE YOU'RE GONNA DIE, STUPID MOUSE!
WE MIGHT CUT YA OUR-SELVES! MWA HA HA!
WE DON'T WANNA HEAR THE FUGLY-RABBIT CALL US FUGLY!
WAVE
WHAT RABBIT?!
DAMN.
THIS AIN'T A GAME, BRATS-- IT'S WORK!
RIGHT, BLOOD?

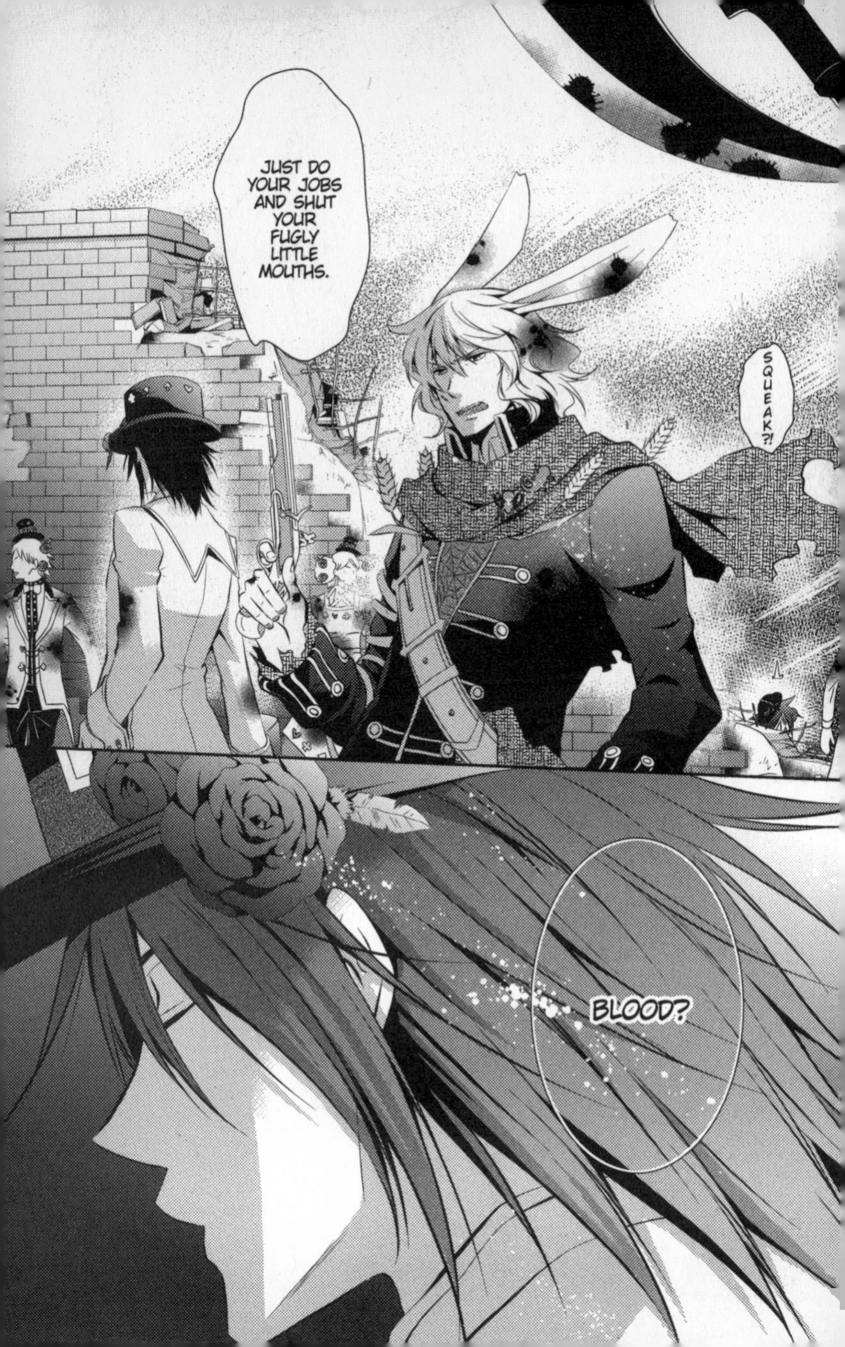
SQUEAK?!
JUST DO YOUR JOBS AND SHUT YOUR FUGLY LITTLE MOUTHS.
BLOOD?

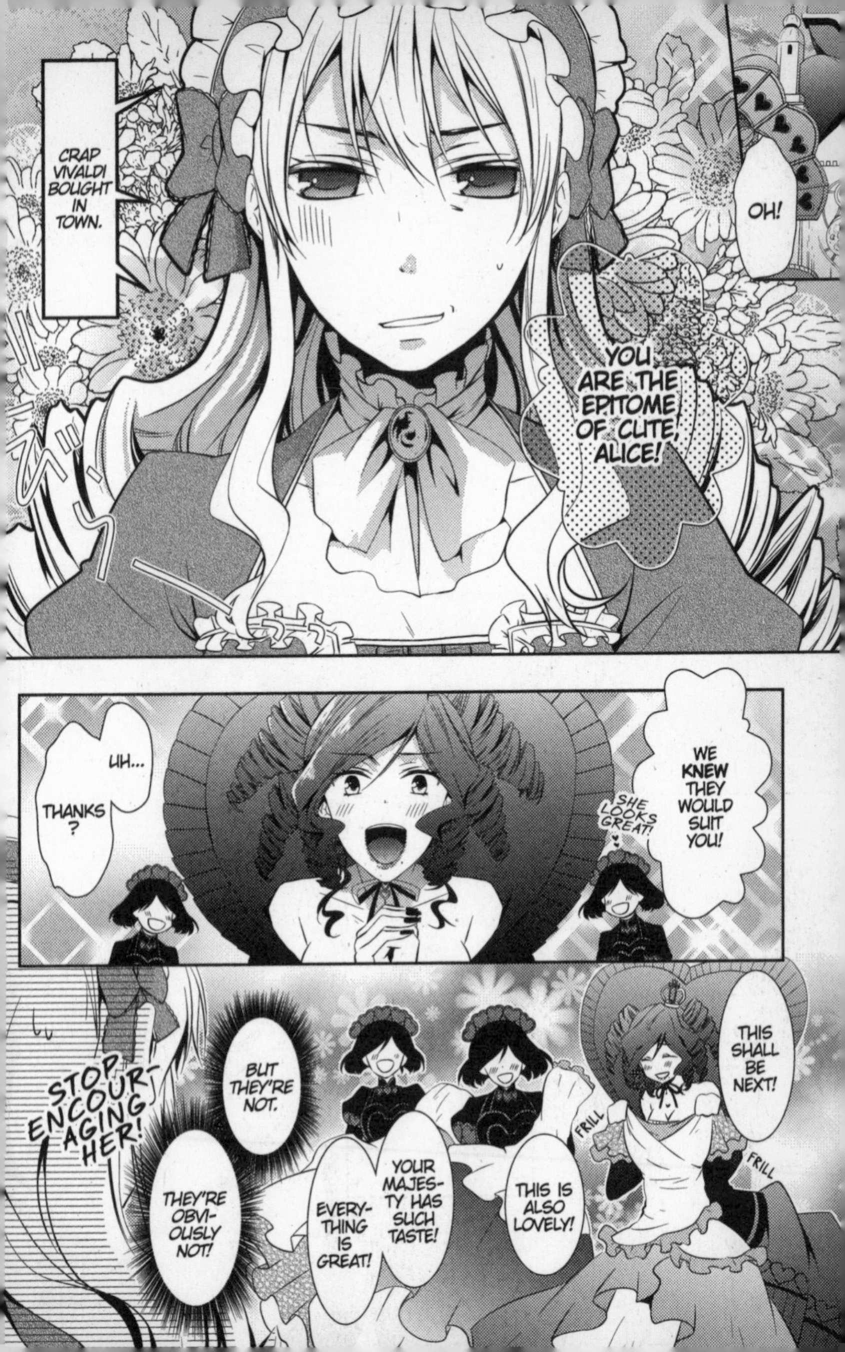
OH!
YOU ARE THE EPITOME OF CUTE, ALICE!
CRAP VIVALDI BOUGHT IN TOWN.
WE KNEW THEY WOULD SUIT YOU!
SHE LOOKS GREAT!
UH... THANKS?
THIS SHALL BE NEXT!
FRILL
FRILL
THIS IS ALSO LOVELY!
YOUR MAJESTY HAS SUCH TASTE!
EVERYTHING IS GREAT!
BUT THEY'RE NOT.
THEY'RE OBVIOUSLY NOT!
STOP ENCOURAGING HER!

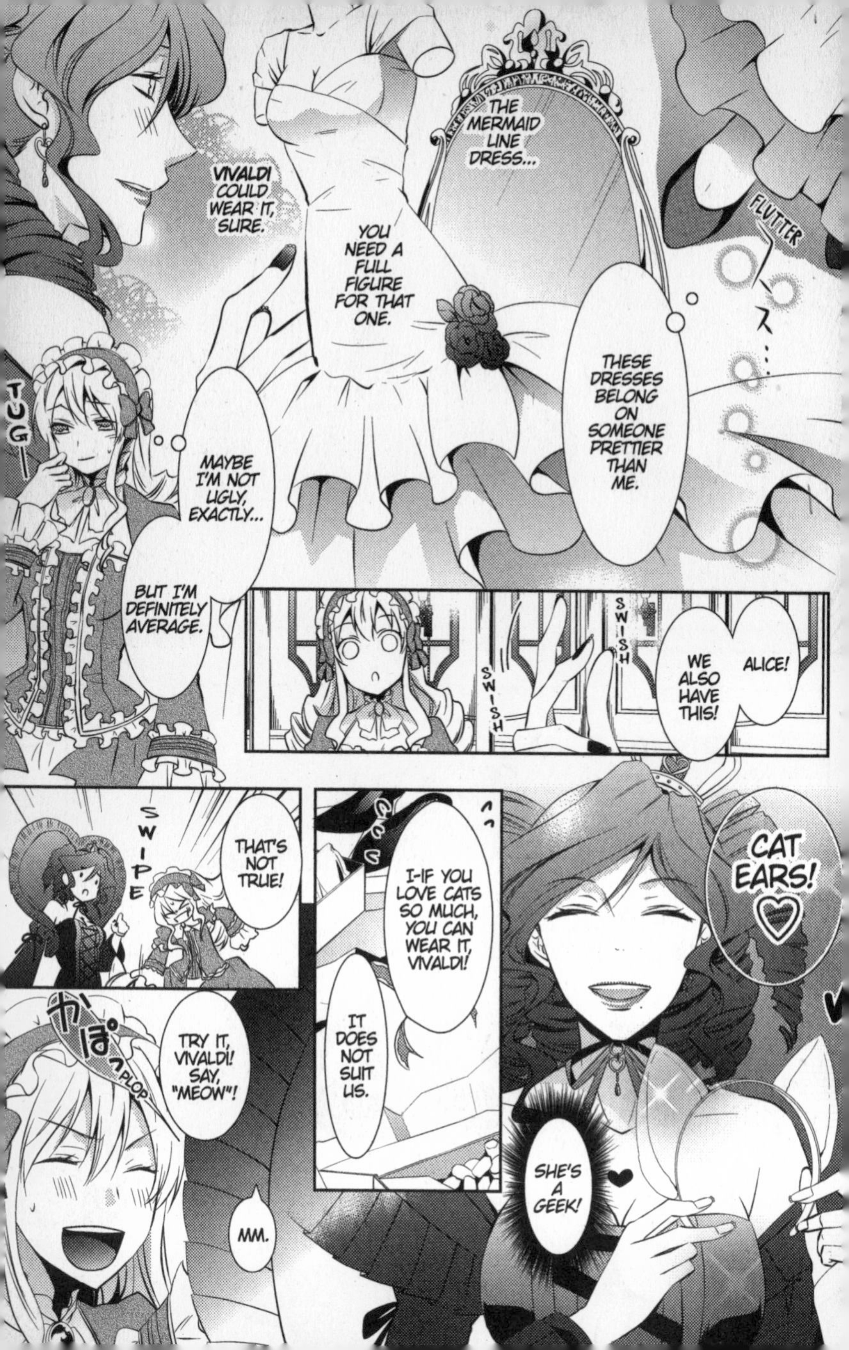
FLUTTER
THESE DRESSES BELONG ON SOMEONE PRETTIER THAN ME.
THE MERMAID LINE DRESS...
YOU NEED A FULL FIGURE FOR THAT ONE.
VIVALDI COULD WEAR IT, SURE.
TUG
MAYBE I'M NOT UGLY, EXACTLY...
BUT I'M DEFINITELY AVERAGE.
ALICE!
WE ALSO HAVE THIS!
SWISH
SWISH
CAT EARS! ♥
SHE'S A GEEK!
I-IF YOU LOVE CATS SO MUCH, YOU CAN WEAR IT, VIVALDI!
IT DOES NOT SUIT US.
THAT'S NOT TRUE!
SWIPE
PLOP
TRY IT, VIVALDI! SAY, "MEOW"!
MM.

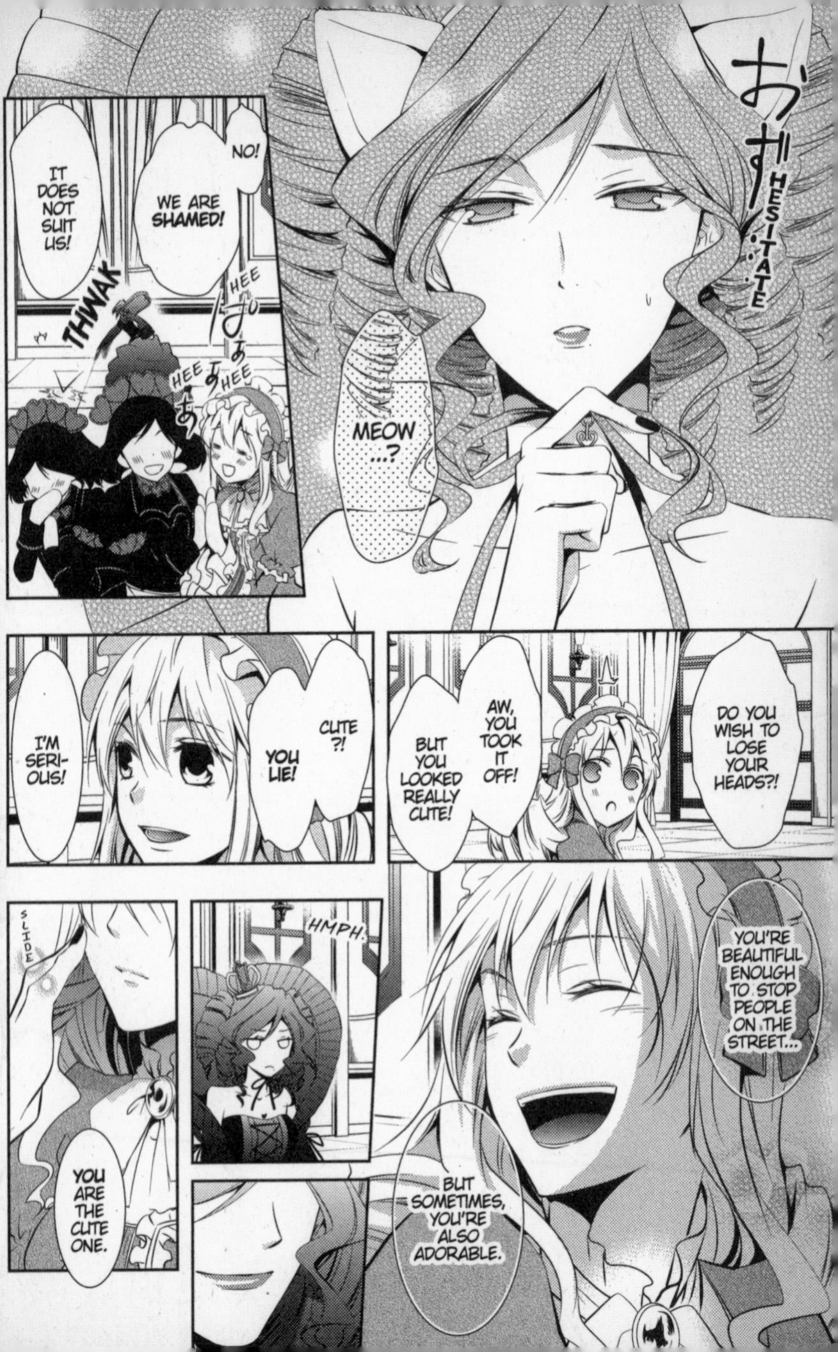
おず
HESITATE
MEOW...?
NO!
WE ARE SHAMED!
IT DOES NOT SUIT US!
THWAK
HEE HEE HEE
DO YOU WISH TO LOSE YOUR HEADS?!
AW, YOU TOOK IT OFF!
BUT YOU LOOKED REALLY CUTE!
CUTE?!
YOU LIE!
I'M SERI-OUS!
YOU'RE BEAUTIFUL ENOUGH TO STOP PEOPLE ON THE STREET...
BUT SOMETIMES, YOU'RE ALSO ADORABLE.
HMPH.
SLIDE
YOU ARE THE CUTE ONE.

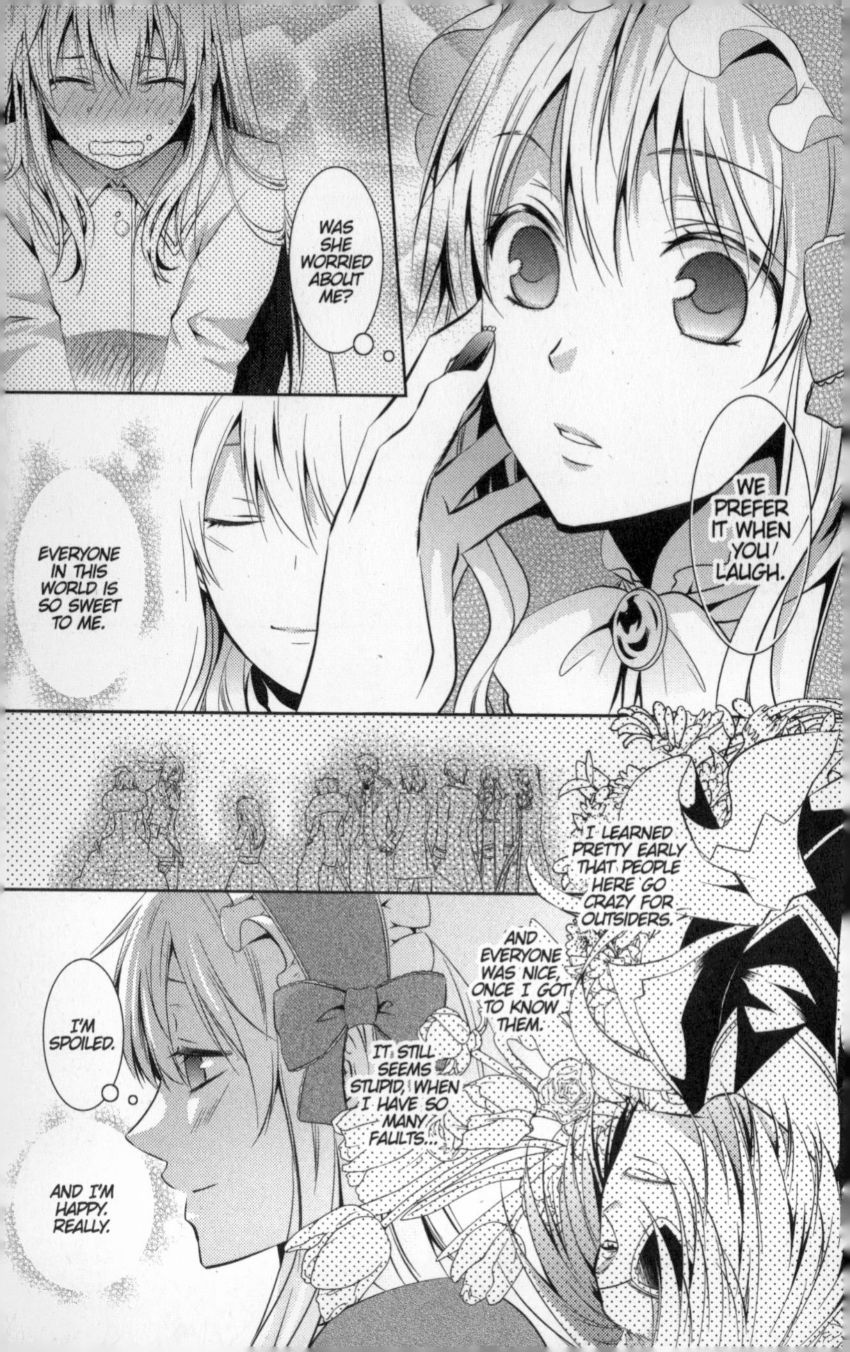
WE PREFER IT WHEN YOU LAUGH.
WAS SHE WORRIED ABOUT ME?
EVERYONE IN THIS WORLD IS SO SWEET TO ME.
I LEARNED PRETTY EARLY THAT PEOPLE HERE GO CRAZY FOR OUTSIDERS.
AND EVERYONE WAS NICE, ONCE I GOT TO KNOW THEM.
IT STILL SEEMS STUPID, WHEN I HAVE SO MANY FAULTS...
I'M SPOILED.
AND I'M HAPPY. REALLY.

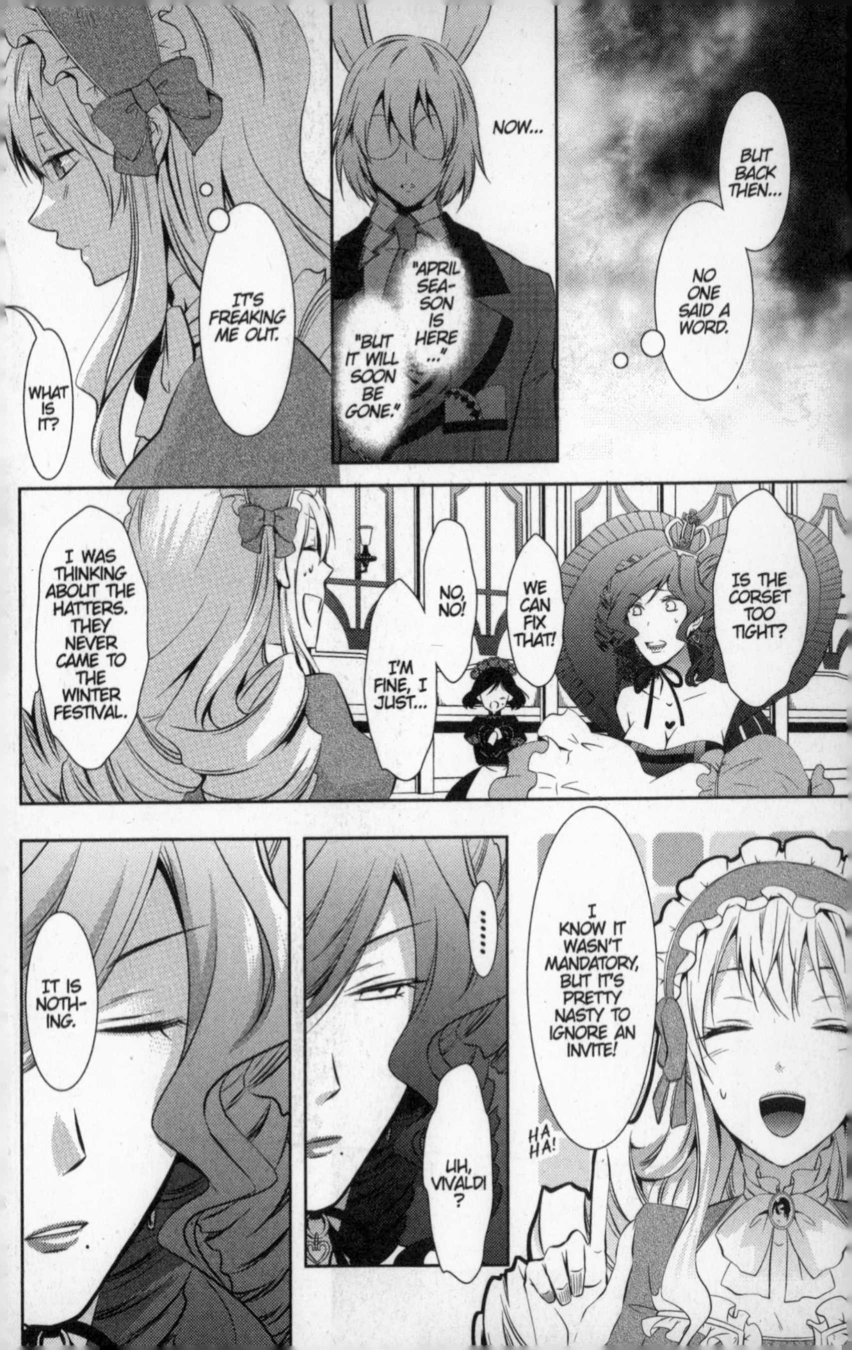
BUT BACK THEN...
NO ONE SAID A WORD.
NOW...
"APRIL SEASON IS HERE..."
"BUT IT WILL SOON BE GONE."
IT'S FREAKING ME OUT.
WHAT IS IT?
IS THE CORSET TOO TIGHT?
WE CAN FIX THAT!
NO, NO!
I'M FINE, I JUST...
I WAS THINKING ABOUT THE HATTERS. THEY NEVER CAME TO THE WINTER FESTIVAL.
I KNOW IT WASN'T MANDATORY, BUT IT'S PRETTY NASTY TO IGNORE AN INVITE!
HA HA!
......
UH, VIVALDI?
IT IS NOTHING.

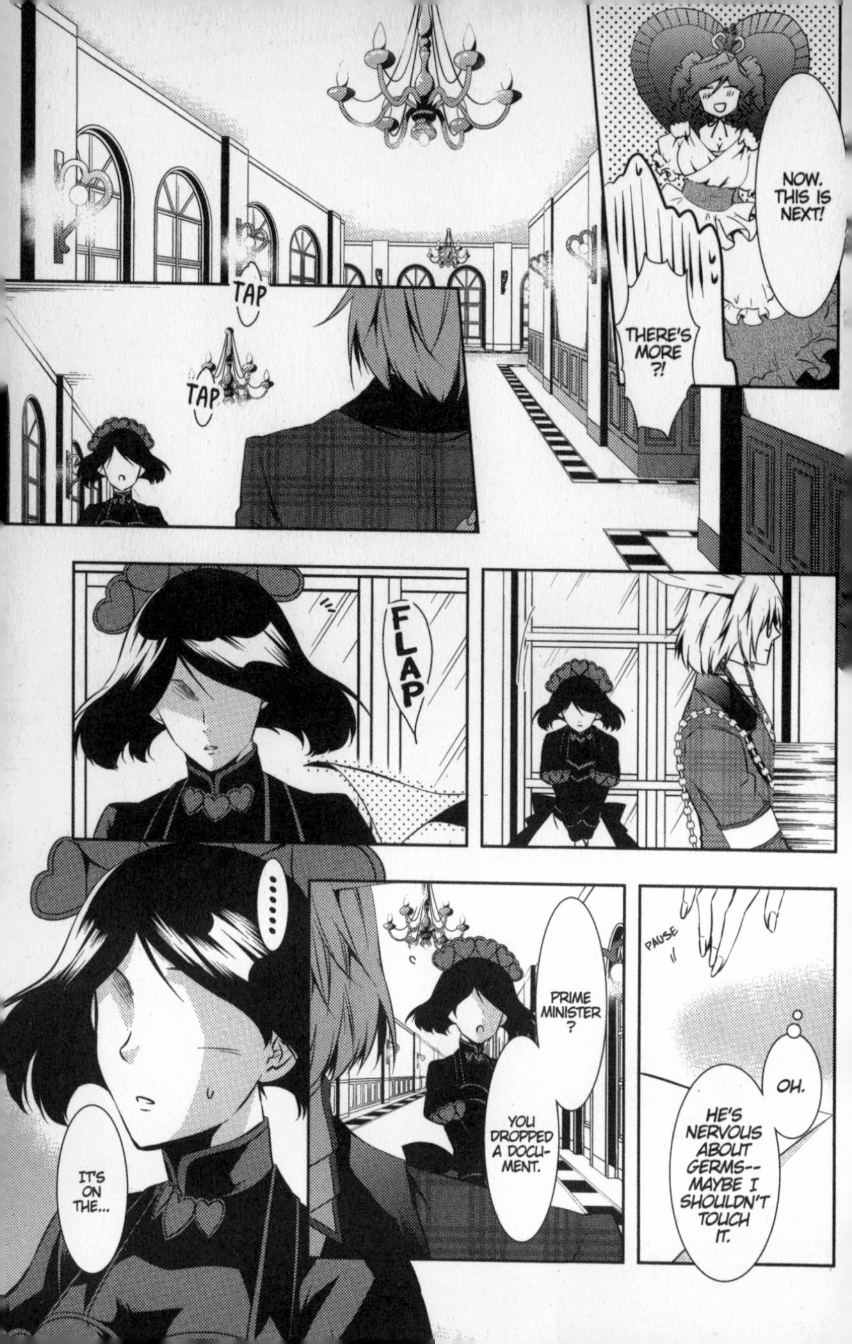
NOW. THIS IS NEXT!
THERE'S MORE ?!
TAP
TAP
FLAP
PAUSE
OH.
HE'S NERVOUS ABOUT GERMS-- MAYBE I SHOULDN'T TOUCH IT.
PRIME MINISTER ?
YOU DROPPED A DOCU- MENT.
......
IT'S ON THE...

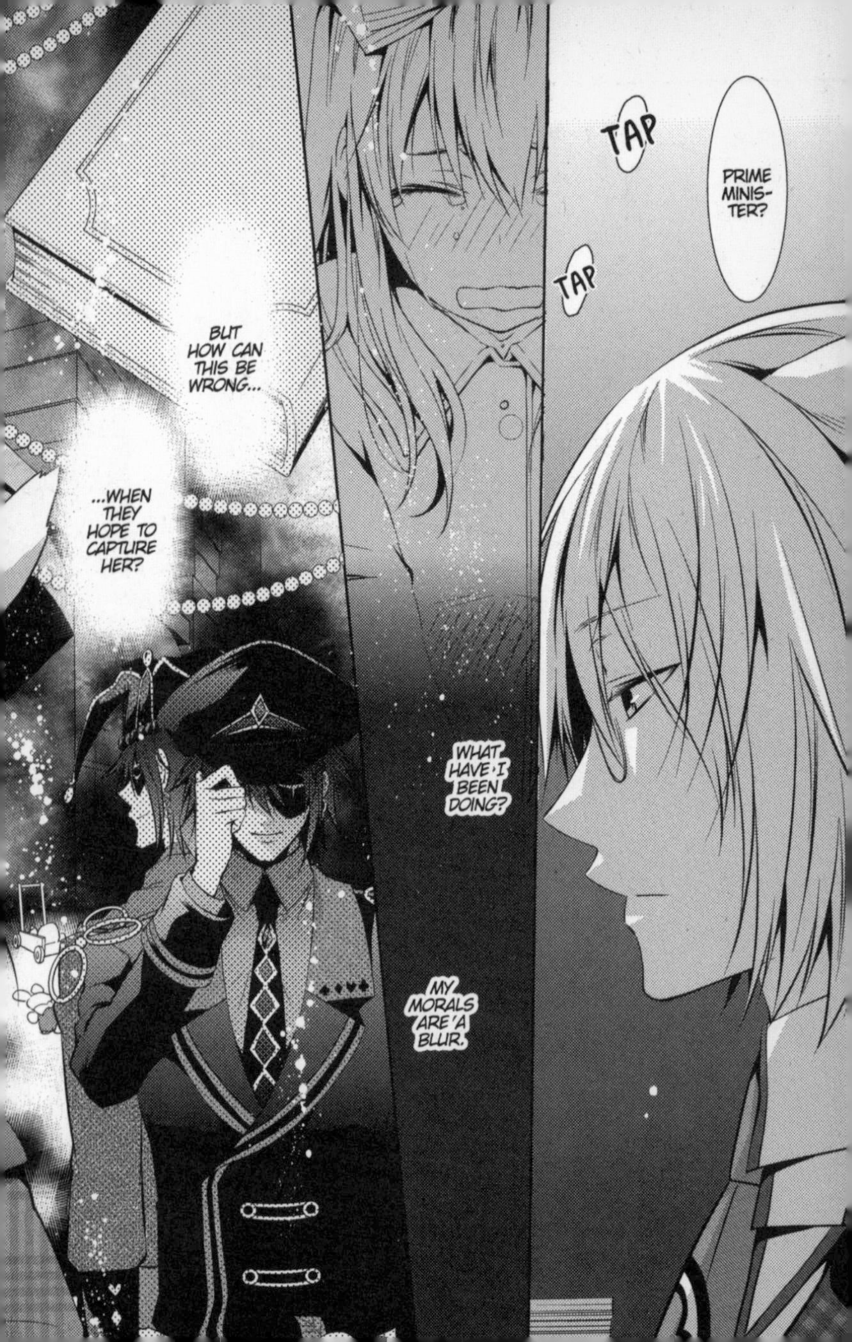
PRIME MINI-STER?
TAP
TAP
WHAT HAVE I BEEN DOING?
MY MORALS ARE A BLUR.
BUT HOW CAN THIS BE WRONG...
...WHEN THEY HOPE TO CAPTURE HER?

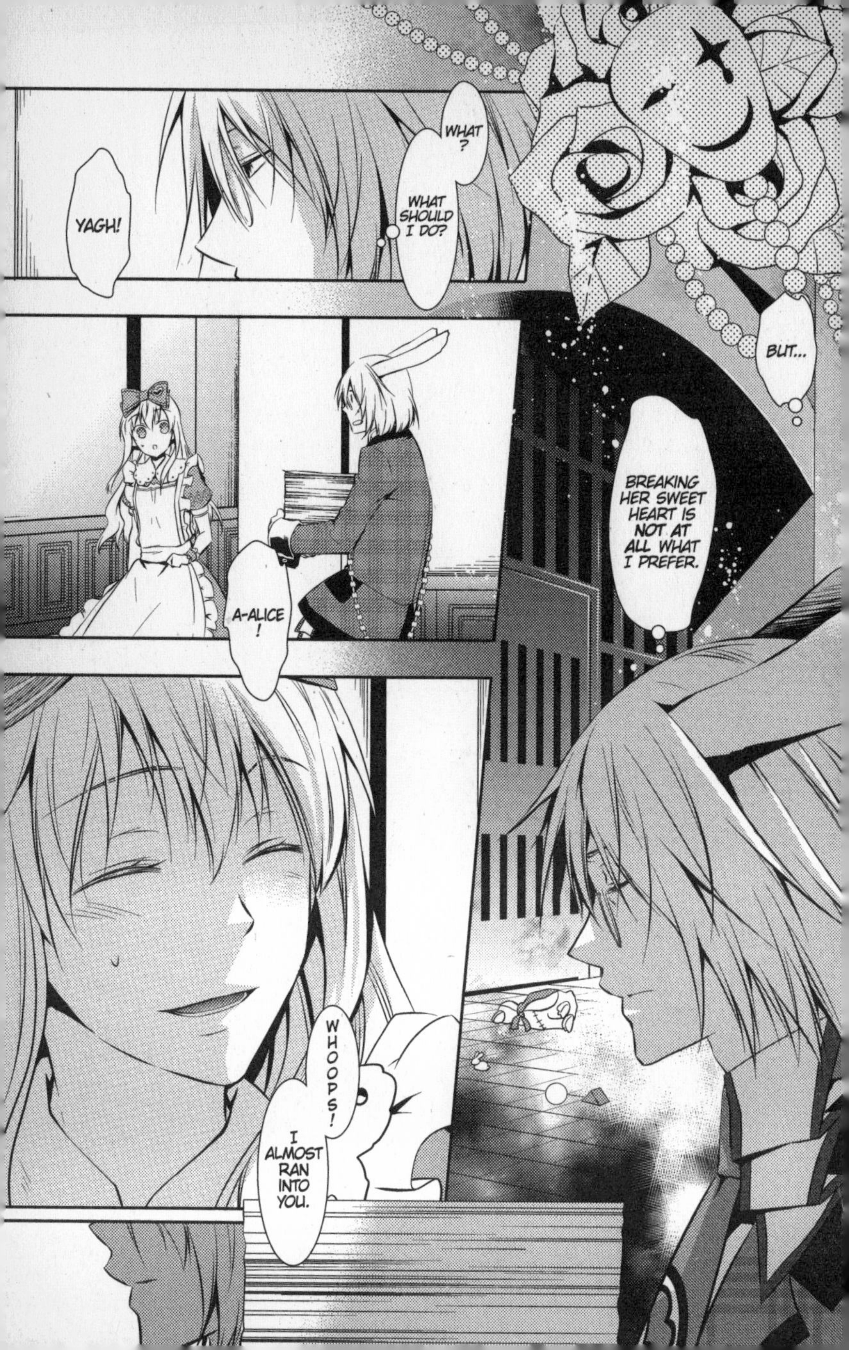
BUT...
BREAKING HER SWEET HEART IS NOT AT ALL WHAT I PREFER.
WHAT?
WHAT SHOULD I DO?
YAGH!
A-ALICE!
WHOOPS!
I ALMOST RAN INTO YOU.

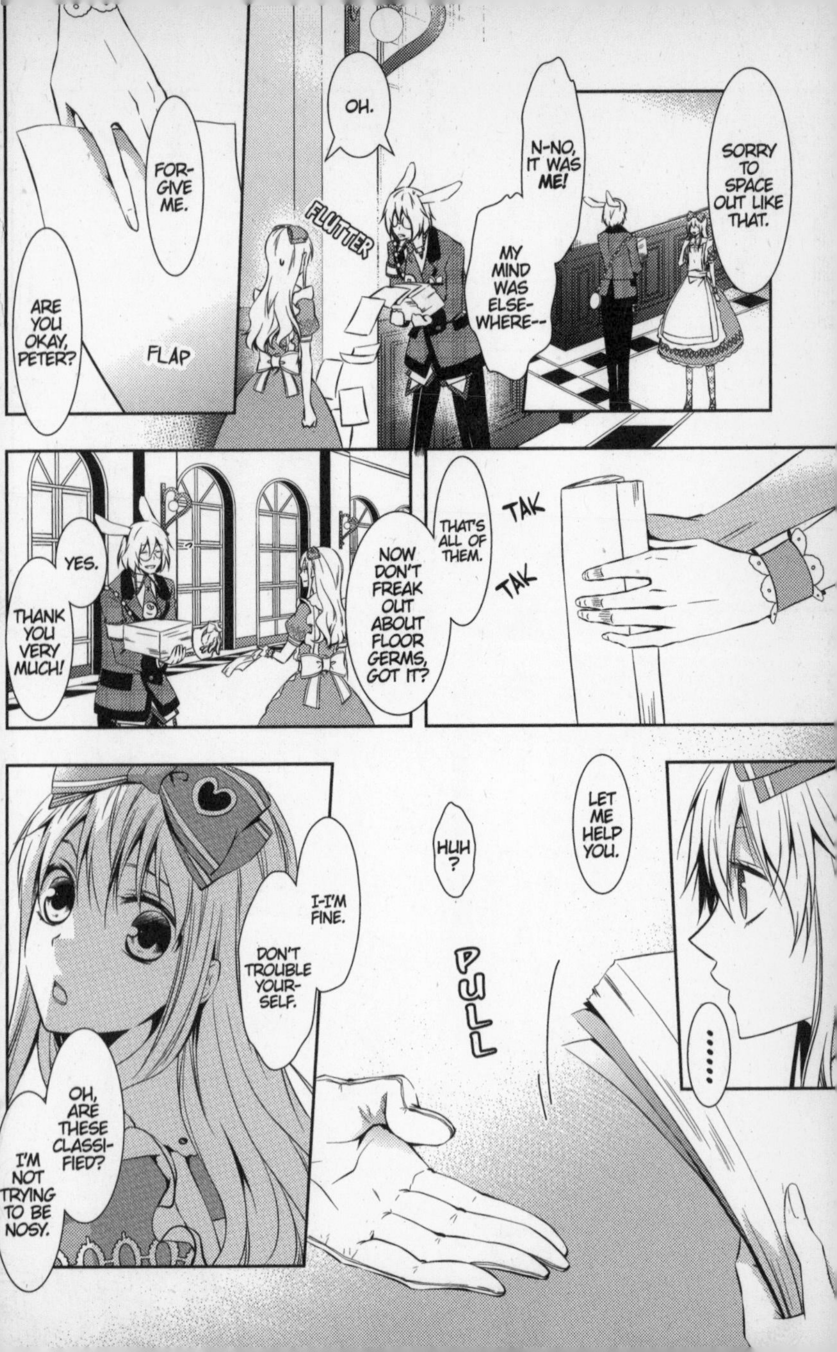
SORRY TO SPACE OUT LIKE THAT.
N-NO, IT WAS ME!
MY MIND WAS ELSE-WHERE--
OH.
FLUTTER
FOR-GIVE ME.
FLAP
ARE YOU OKAY, PETER?
TAK
TAK
THAT'S ALL OF THEM.
NOW DON'T FREAK OUT ABOUT FLOOR GERMS, GOT IT?
YES.
THANK YOU VERY MUCH!
......
LET ME HELP YOU.
HUH?
PULL
I-I'M FINE.
DON'T TROUBLE YOUR-SELF.
OH, ARE THESE CLASSI-FIED?
I'M NOT TRYING TO BE NOSY.

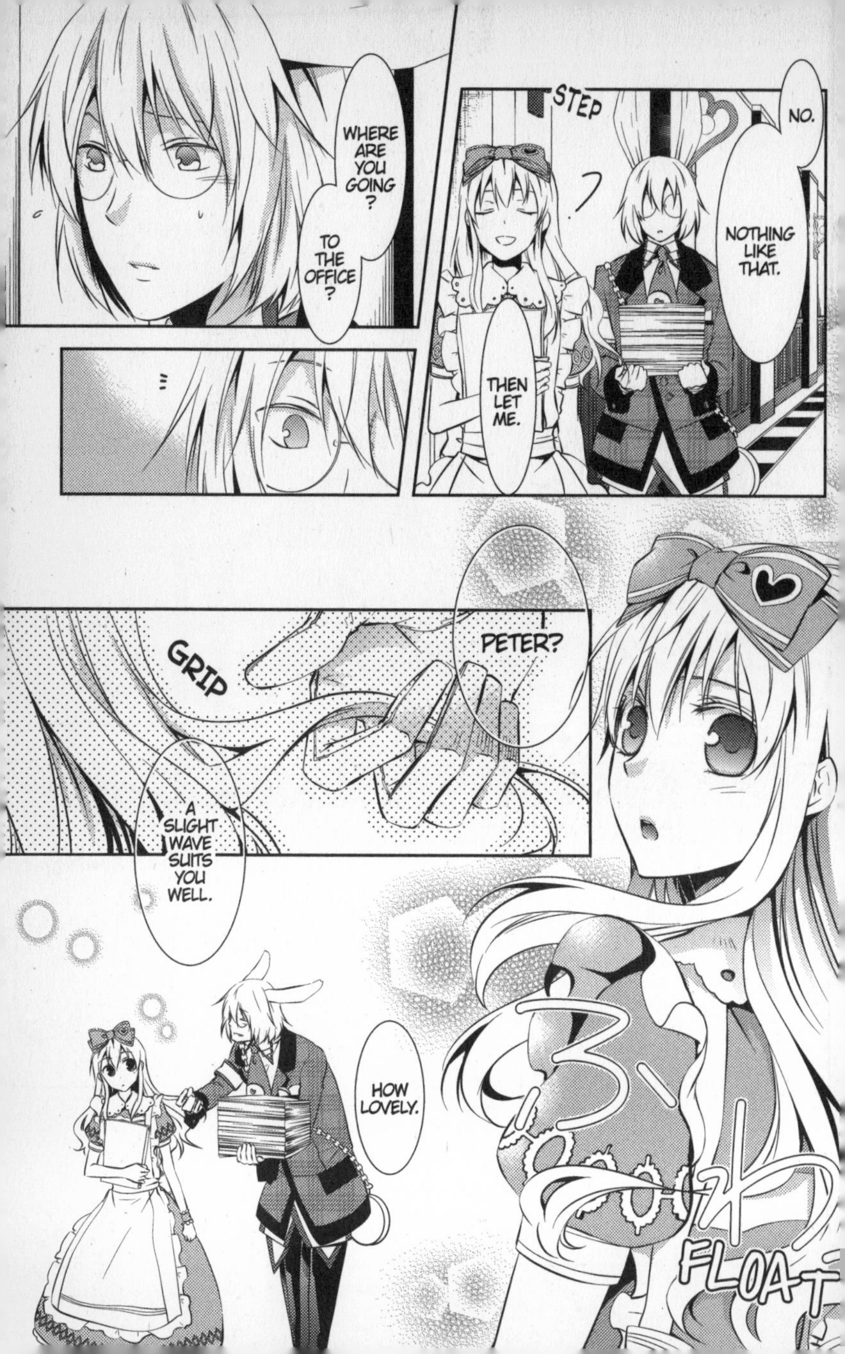
NO.
STEP
NOTHING LIKE THAT.
THEN LET ME.
WHERE ARE YOU GOING?
TO THE OFFICE?
...
PETER?
GRIP
A SLIGHT WAVE SUITS YOU WELL.
HOW LOVELY.
FLOAT

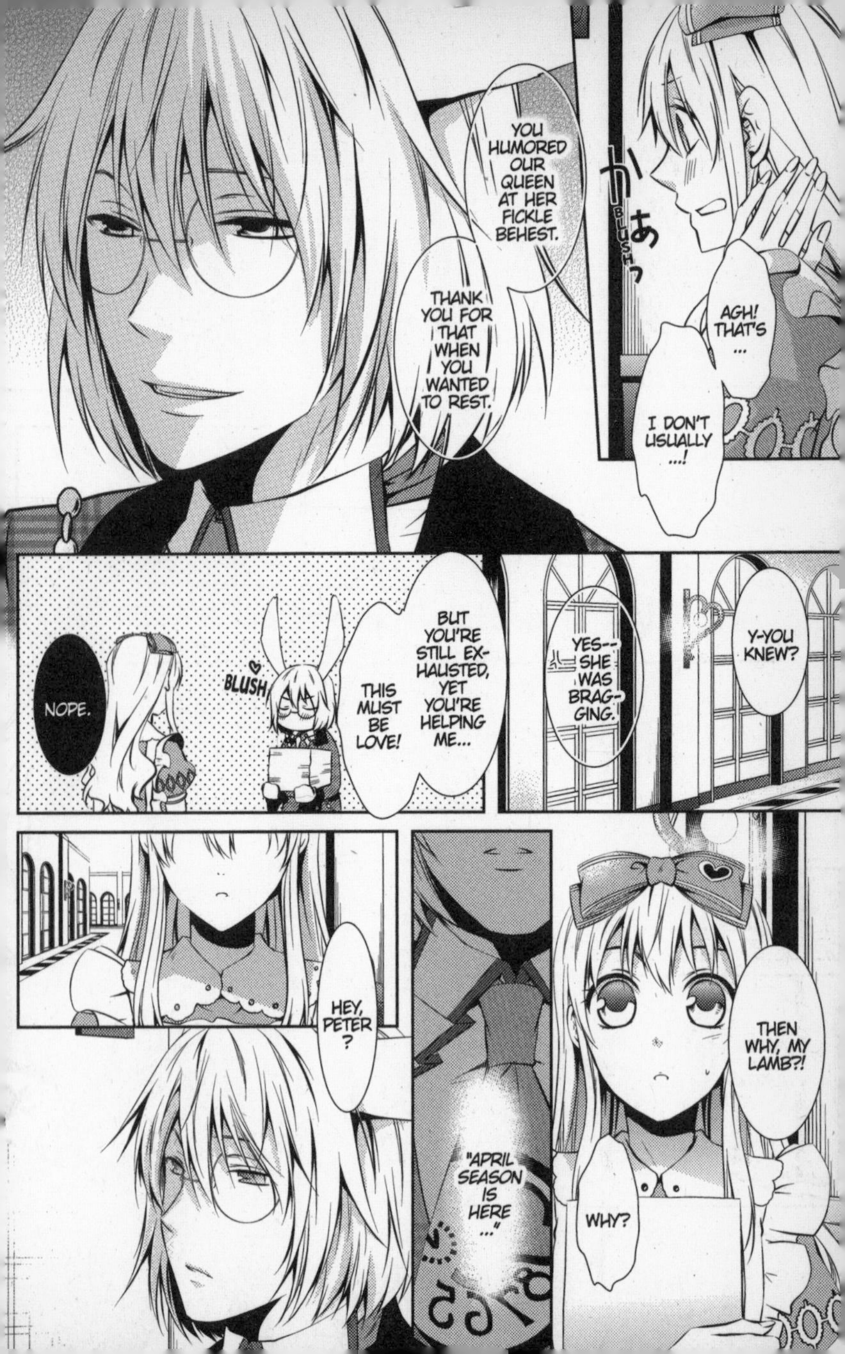
かあ
BLUSH
AGH! THAT'S ...
I DON'T USUALLY ...!
YOU HUMORED OUR QUEEN AT HER FICKLE BEHEST.
THANK YOU FOR THAT WHEN YOU WANTED TO REST.
Y-YOU KNEW?
YES-- SHE WAS BRAG-GING.
BUT YOU'RE STILL EX-HAUSTED, YET YOU'RE HELPING ME...
THIS MUST BE LOVE!
BLUSH
NOPE.
THEN WHY, MY LAMB?!
WHY?
"APRIL SEASON IS HERE ..."
HEY, PETER?

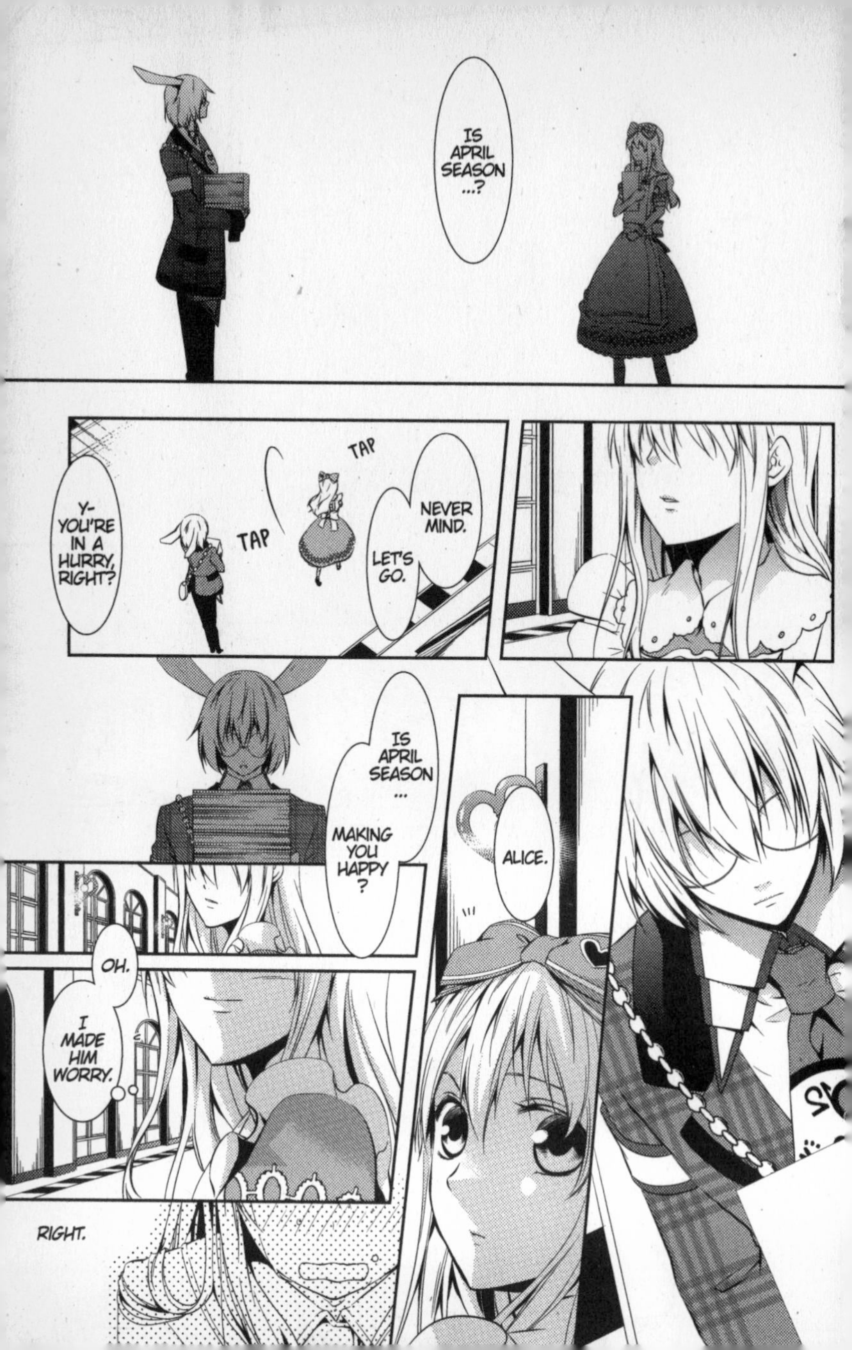
IS APRIL SEASON ...?
TAP
NEVER MIND.
LET'S GO.
TAP
Y-YOU'RE IN A HURRY, RIGHT?
ALICE.
IS APRIL SEASON ...
MAKING YOU HAPPY?
OH.
I MADE HIM WORRY.
RIGHT.

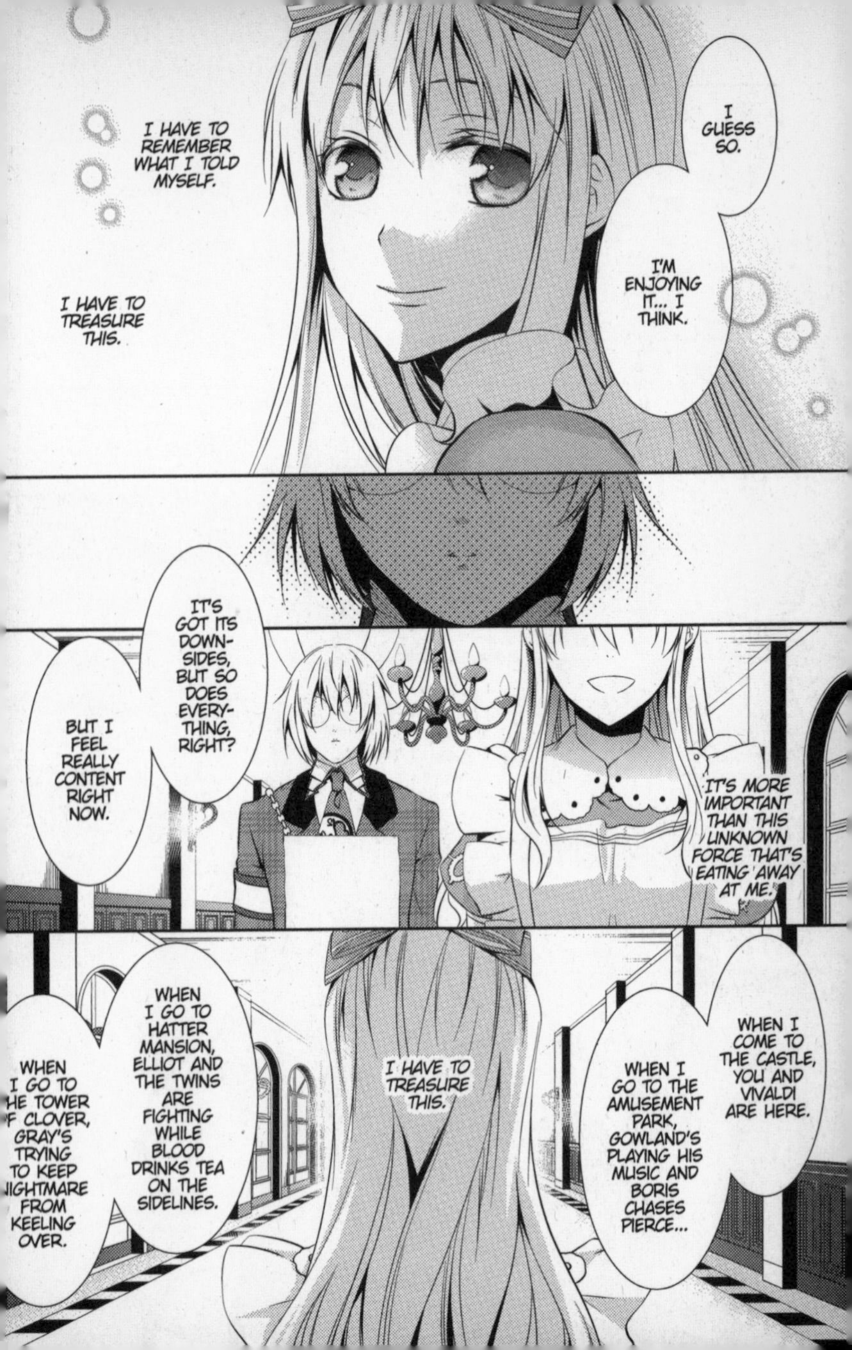
I GUESS SO.
I'M ENJOYING IT... I THINK.
I HAVE TO REMEMBER WHAT I TOLD MYSELF.
I HAVE TO TREASURE THIS.
IT'S MORE IMPORTANT THAN THIS UNKNOWN FORCE THAT'S EATING AWAY AT ME.
IT'S GOT ITS DOWN-SIDES, BUT SO DOES EVERY-THING, RIGHT?
BUT I FEEL REALLY CONTENT RIGHT NOW.
WHEN I COME TO THE CASTLE, YOU AND VIVALDI ARE HERE.
WHEN I GO TO THE AMUSEMENT PARK, GOWLAND'S PLAYING HIS MUSIC AND BORIS CHASES PIERCE...
I HAVE TO TREASURE THIS.
WHEN I GO TO HATTER MANSION, ELLIOT AND THE TWINS ARE FIGHTING WHILE BLOOD DRINKS TEA ON THE SIDELINES.
WHEN I GO TO HE TOWER F CLOVER, GRAY'S TRYING TO KEEP IGHTMARE FROM KEELING OVER.

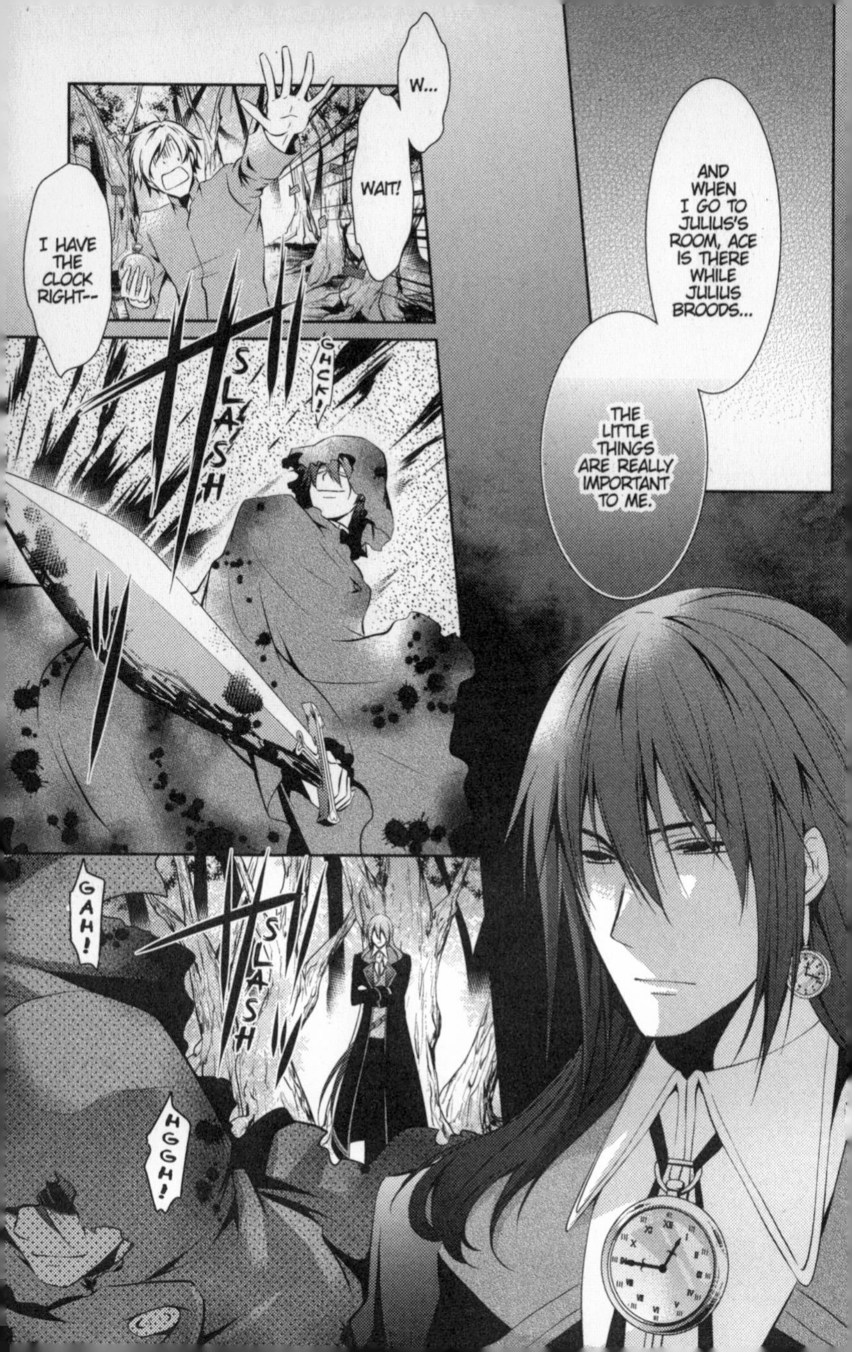
AND WHEN I GO TO JULIUS'S ROOM, ACE IS THERE WHILE JULIUS BROODS...
THE LITTLE THINGS ARE REALLY IMPORTANT TO ME.
W...
WAIT!
I HAVE THE CLOCK RIGHT--
GHCK!
SLASH
SLASH
GAH!
HGGH!

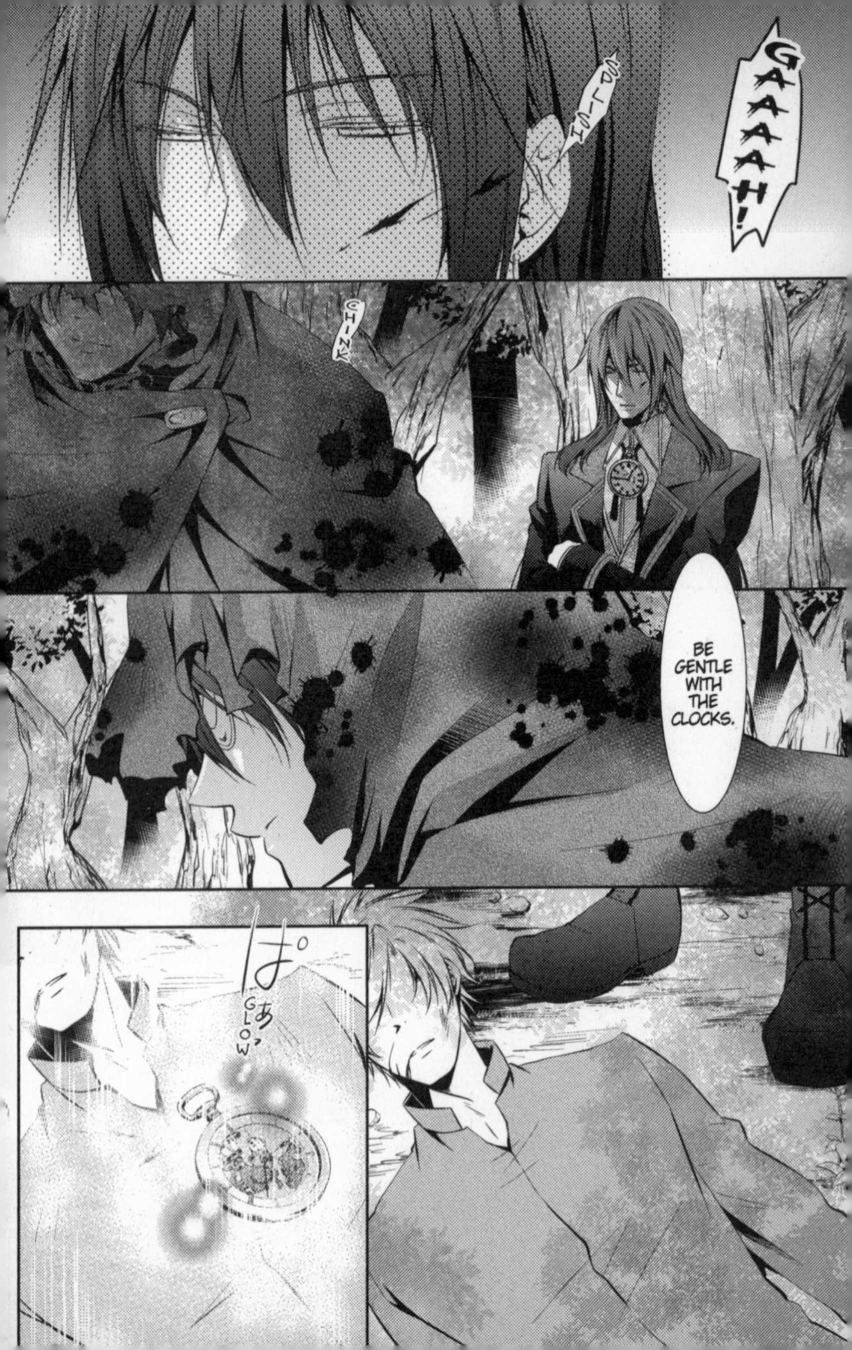
GAAAAH!
SPLISH
CHINK
BE GENTLE WITH THE CLOCKS.
ぽ
あ
GLOW

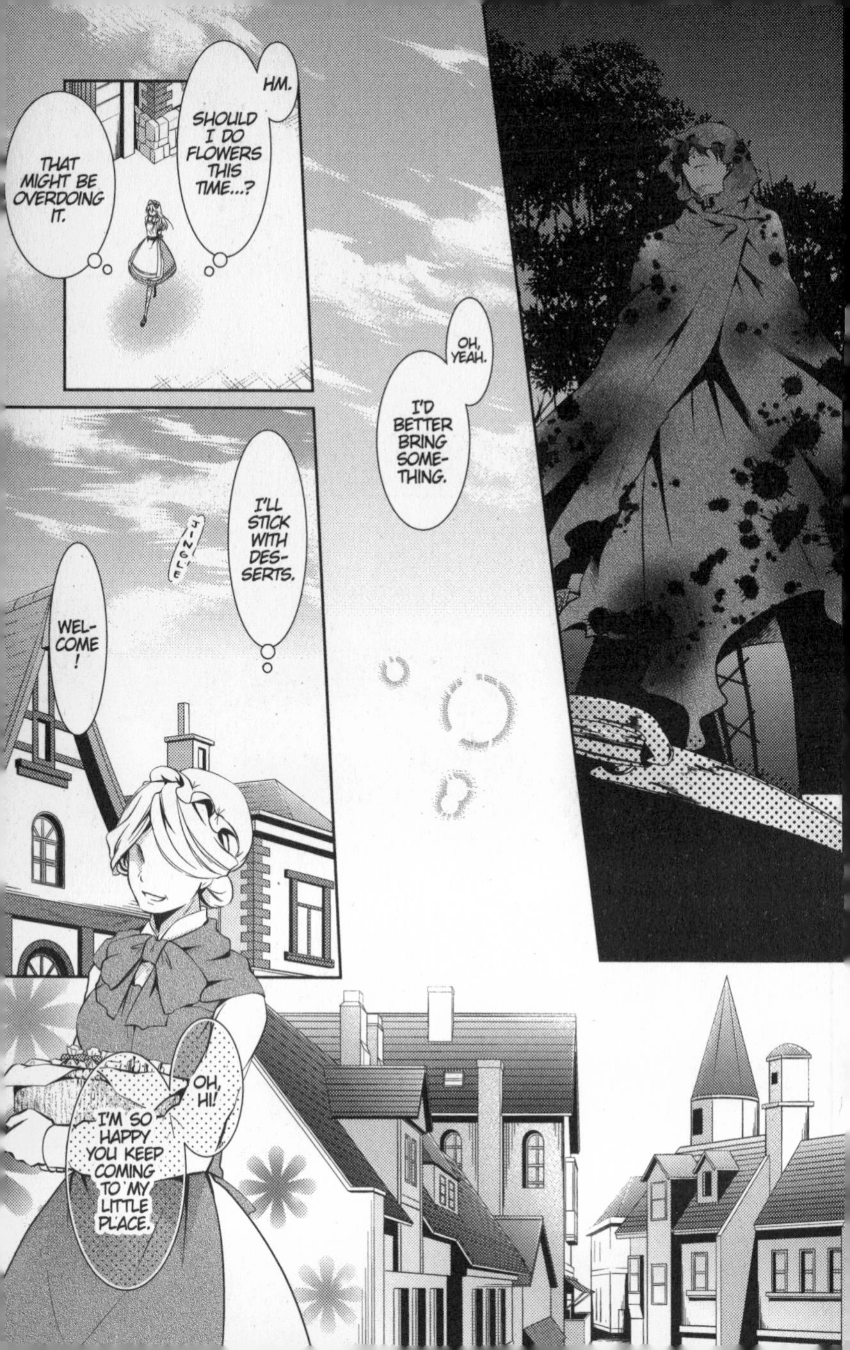
OH, YEAH.
I'D BETTER BRING SOME-THING.
HM.
SHOULD I DO FLOWERS THIS TIME...?
THAT MIGHT BE OVERDOING IT.
I'LL STICK WITH DES-SERTS.
JINGLE
WEL-COME!
OH, HI!
I'M SO HAPPY YOU KEEP COMING TO MY LITTLE PLACE.

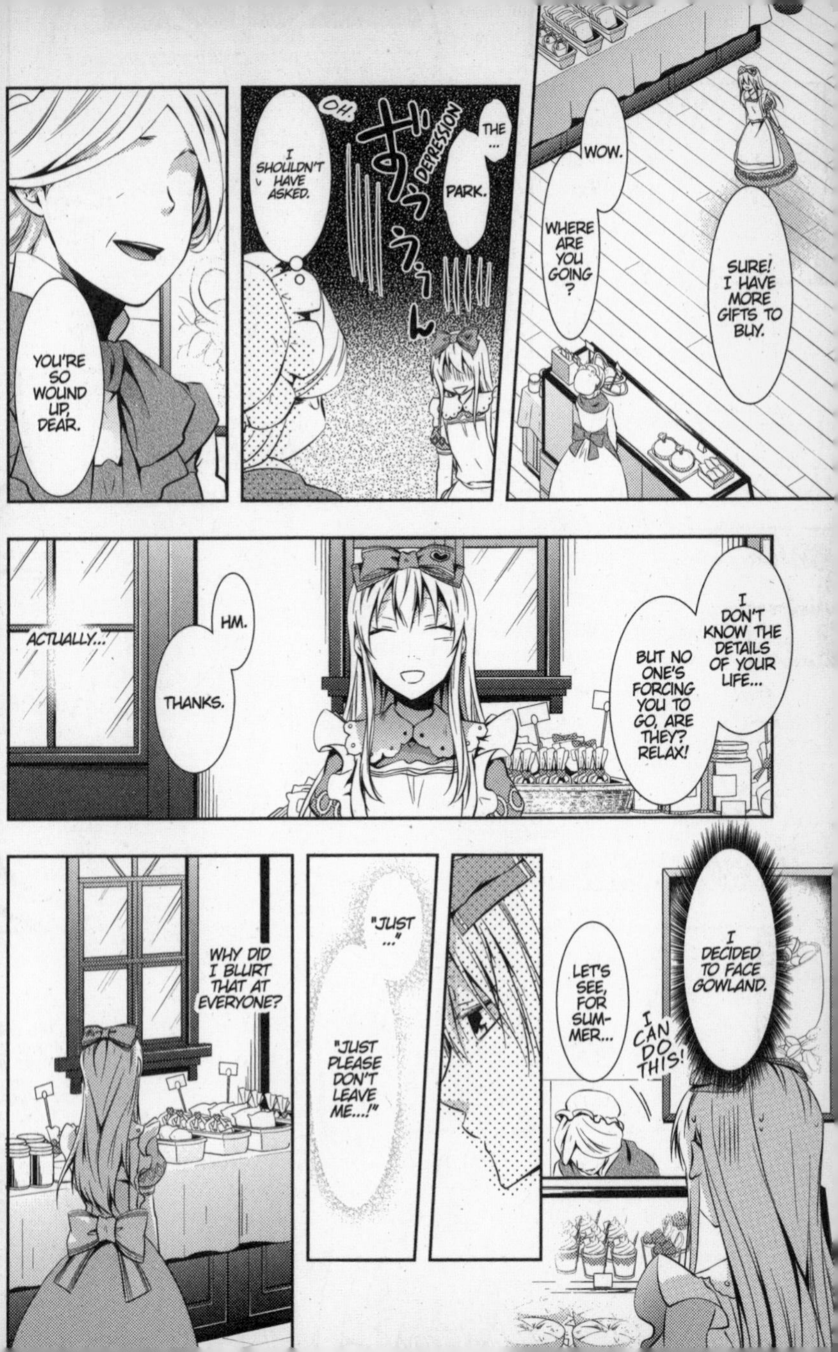
SURE! I HAVE MORE GIFTS TO BUY.
WOW.
WHERE ARE YOU GOING?
THE...
PARK.
DEPRESSION
OH.
I SHOULDN'T HAVE ASKED.
YOU'RE SO WOUND UP, DEAR.
I DON'T KNOW THE DETAILS OF YOUR LIFE...
BUT NO ONE'S FORCING YOU TO GO, ARE THEY? RELAX!
HM.
THANKS.
ACTUALLY...
I DECIDED TO FACE GOWLAND.
I CAN DO THIS!
LET'S SEE, FOR SUMMER...
"JUST..."
"JUST PLEASE DON'T LEAVE ME...!"
WHY DID I BLURT THAT AT EVERYONE?

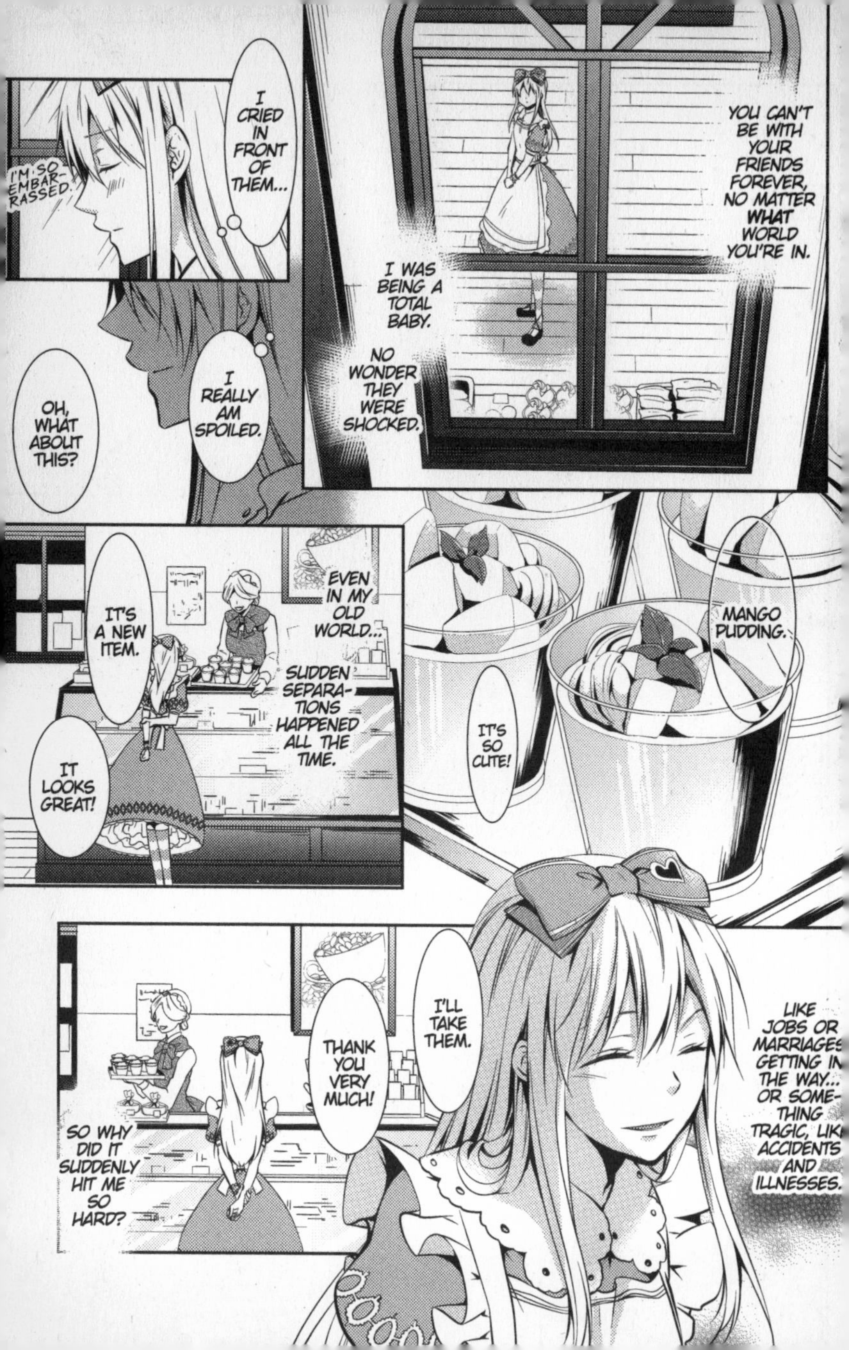
YOU CAN'T BE WITH YOUR FRIENDS FOREVER, NO MATTER WHAT WORLD YOU'RE IN.
I WAS BEING A TOTAL BABY.
NO WONDER THEY WERE SHOCKED.
I CRIED IN FRONT OF THEM...
I'M SO EMBAR-RASSED.
I REALLY AM SPOILED.
OH, WHAT ABOUT THIS?
MANGO PUDDING.
IT'S SO CUTE!
EVEN IN MY OLD WORLD...
SUDDEN SEPARA-TIONS HAPPENED ALL THE TIME.
IT'S A NEW ITEM.
IT LOOKS GREAT!
LIKE JOBS OR MARRIAGES GETTING IN THE WAY... OR SOME-THING TRAGIC, LIKE ACCIDENTS AND ILLNESSES.
I'LL TAKE THEM.
THANK YOU VERY MUCH!
SO WHY DID IT SUDDENLY HIT ME SO HARD?

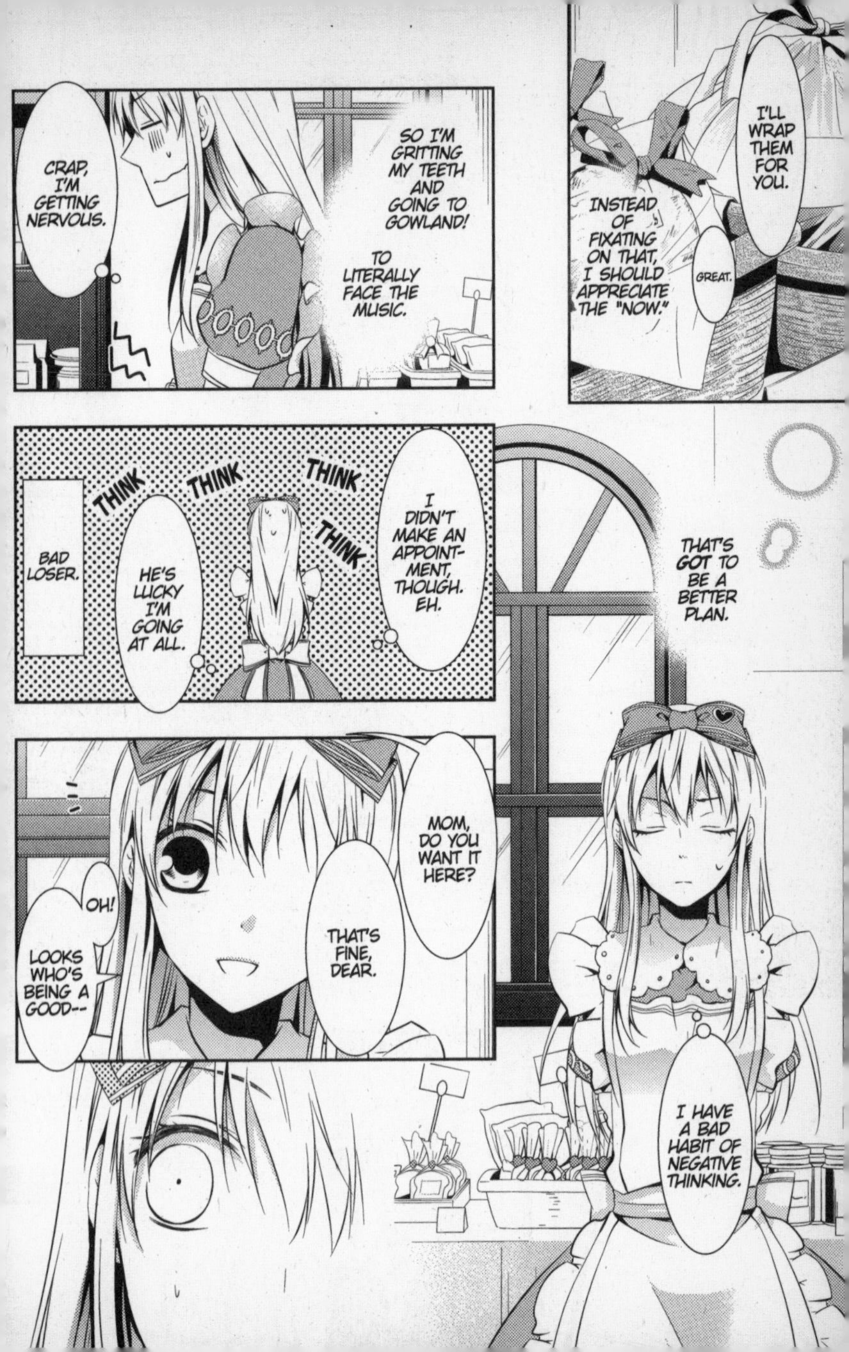
I'LL WRAP THEM FOR YOU.
GREAT.
INSTEAD OF FIXATING ON THAT, I SHOULD APPRECIATE THE "NOW."
SO I'M GRITTING MY TEETH AND GOING TO GOWLAND!
TO LITERALLY FACE THE MUSIC.
CRAP, I'M GETTING NERVOUS.
THAT'S GOT TO BE A BETTER PLAN.
I HAVE A BAD HABIT OF NEGATIVE THINKING.
I DIDN'T MAKE AN APPOINTMENT, THOUGH. EH.
THINK
THINK
THINK
THINK
HE'S LUCKY I'M GOING AT ALL.
BAD LOSER.
MOM, DO YOU WANT IT HERE?
THAT'S FINE, DEAR.
OH!
LOOKS WHO'S BEING A GOOD--

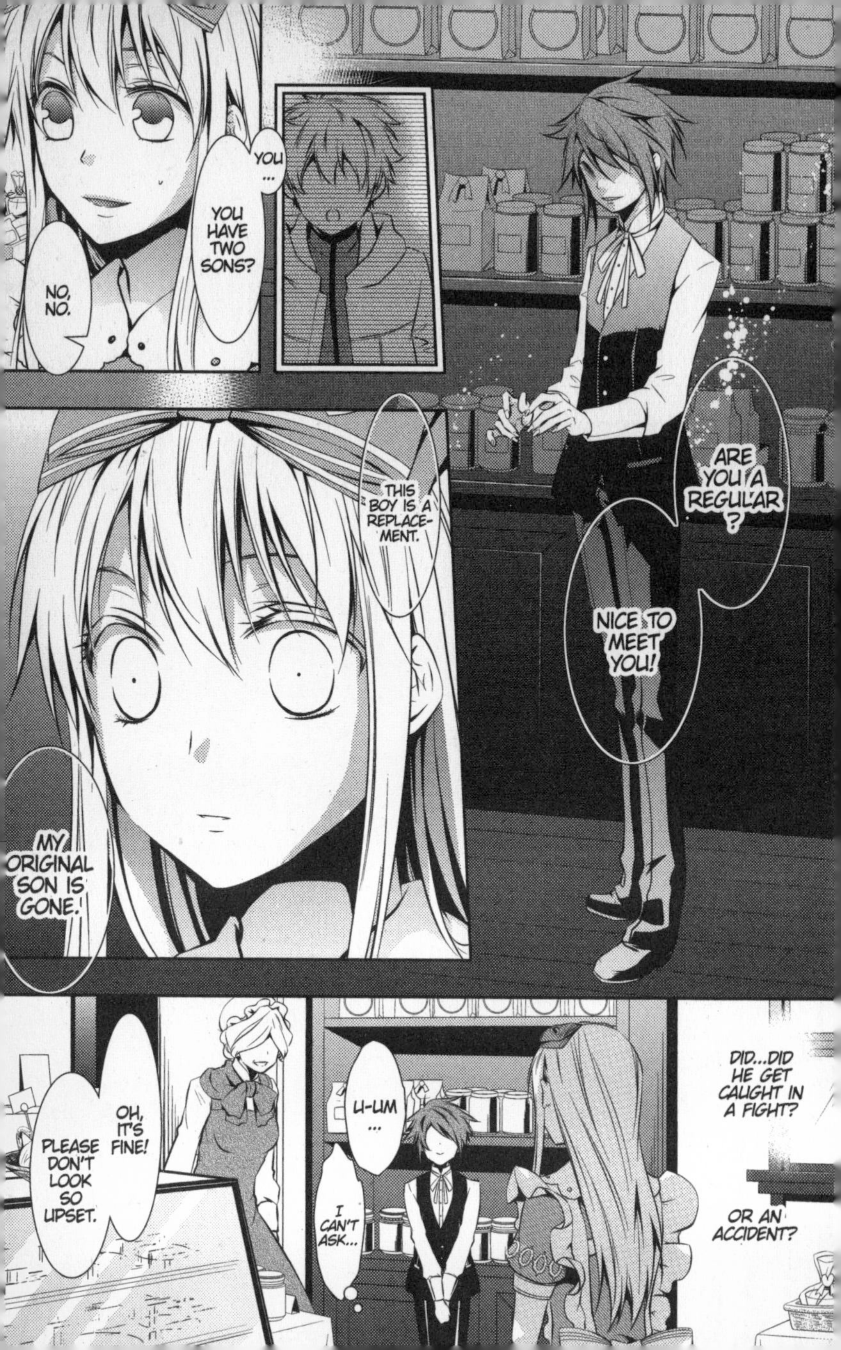
ARE YOU A REGULAR?
NICE TO MEET YOU!
YOU ...
YOU HAVE TWO SONS?
NO, NO.
THIS BOY IS A REPLACEMENT.
MY ORIGINAL SON IS GONE.
DID...DID HE GET CAUGHT IN A FIGHT?
OR AN ACCIDENT?
U-UM ...
I CAN'T ASK...
OH, IT'S FINE!
PLEASE DON'T LOOK SO UPSET.

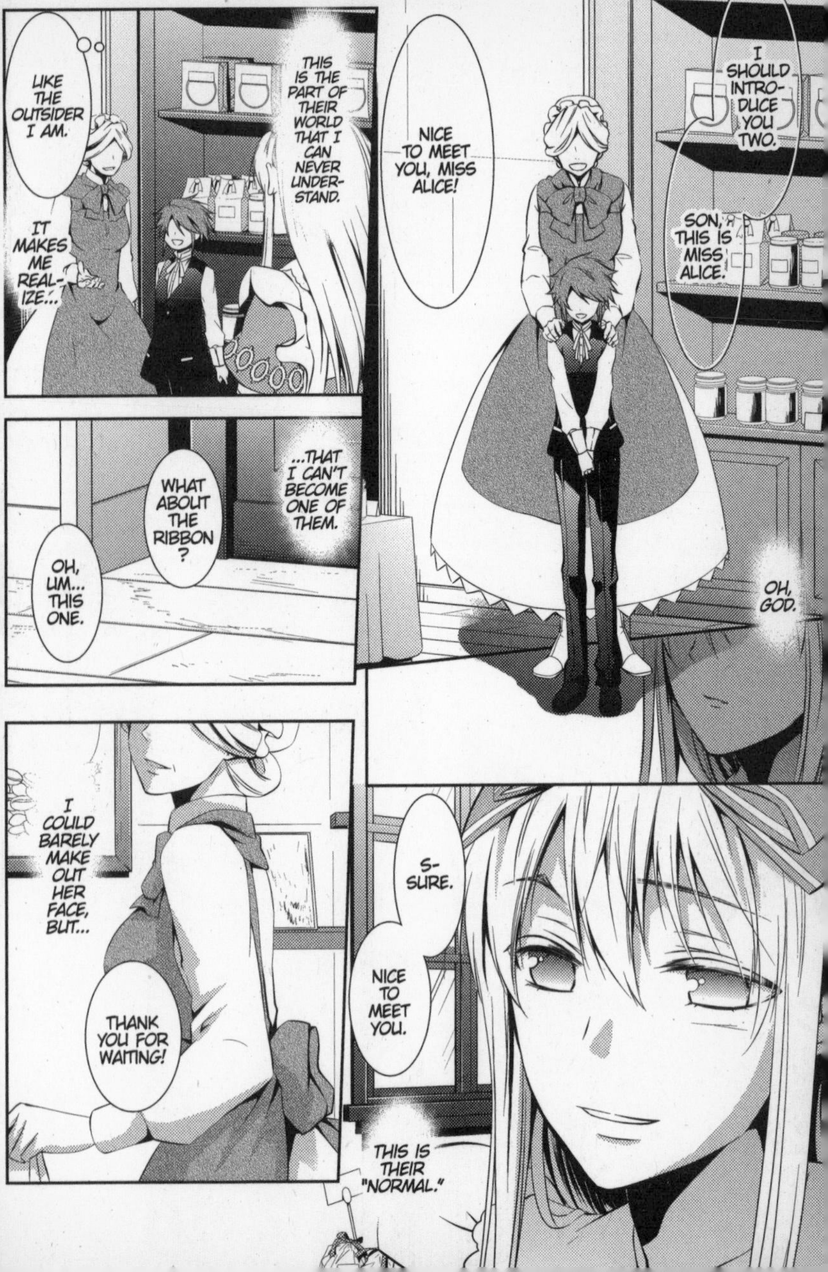
I SHOULD INTRODUCE YOU TWO.
SON, THIS IS MISS ALICE.
NICE TO MEET YOU, MISS ALICE!
OH, GOD.
THIS IS THE PART OF THEIR WORLD THAT I CAN NEVER UNDERSTAND.
LIKE THE OUTSIDER I AM.
IT MAKES ME REALIZE...
...THAT I CAN'T BECOME ONE OF THEM.
WHAT ABOUT THE RIBBON?
OH, UM... THIS ONE.
S-SURE.
NICE TO MEET YOU.
THIS IS THEIR "NORMAL."
I COULD BARELY MAKE OUT HER FACE, BUT...
THANK YOU FOR WAITING!

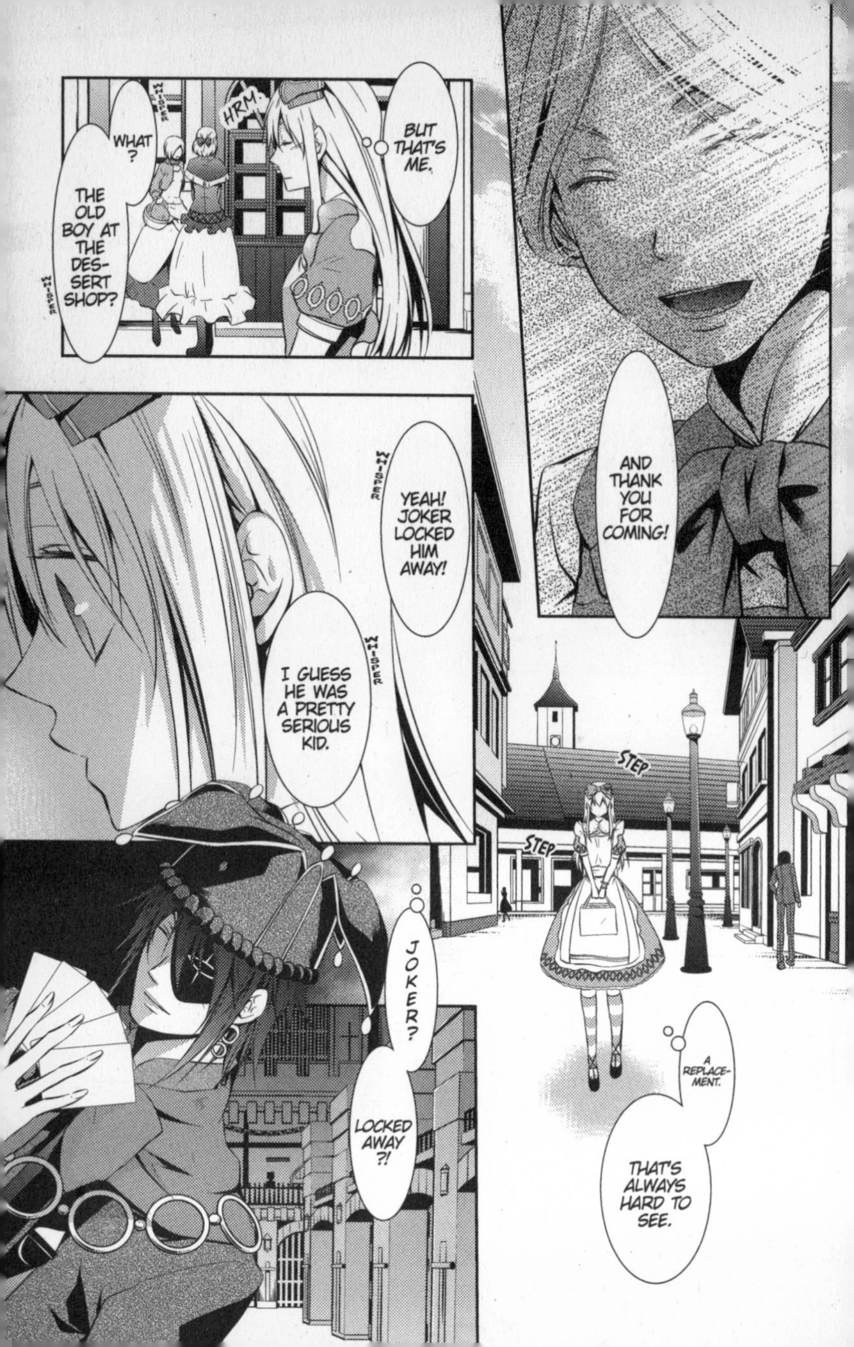
AND THANK YOU FOR COMING!
BUT THAT'S ME.
HRM.
WHISPER
WHAT?
THE OLD BOY AT THE DES-SERT SHOP?
WHISPER
WHISPER
YEAH! JOKER LOCKED HIM AWAY!
WHISPER
I GUESS HE WAS A PRETTY SERIOUS KID.
STEP
STEP
A REPLACE-MENT.
THAT'S ALWAYS HARD TO SEE.
JOKER?
LOCKED AWAY?!

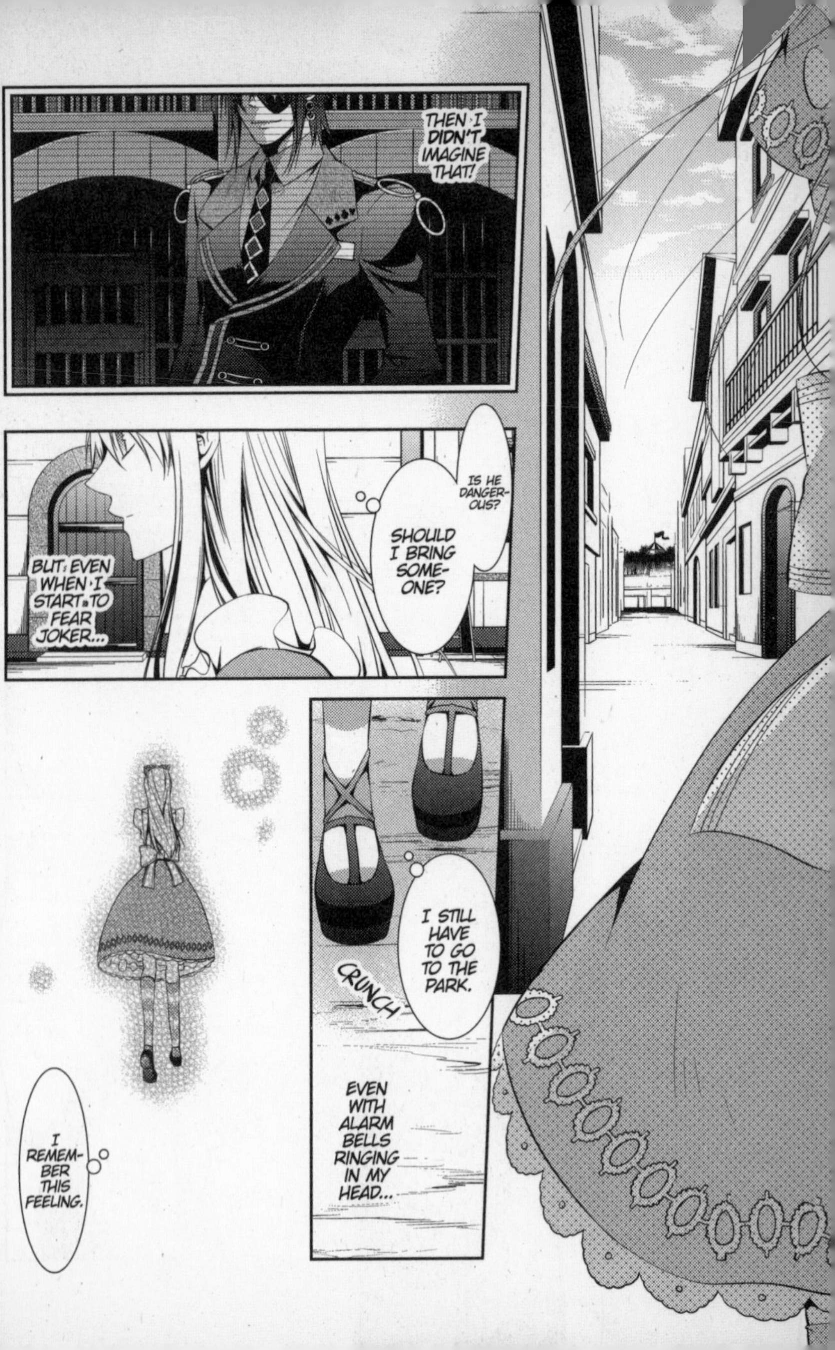
THEN I DIDN'T IMAGINE THAT!
IS HE DANGEROUS?
SHOULD I BRING SOMEONE?
BUT EVEN WHEN I START TO FEAR JOKER...
I STILL HAVE TO GO TO THE PARK.
CRUNCH
EVEN WITH ALARM BELLS RINGING IN MY HEAD...
I REMEMBER THIS FEELING.

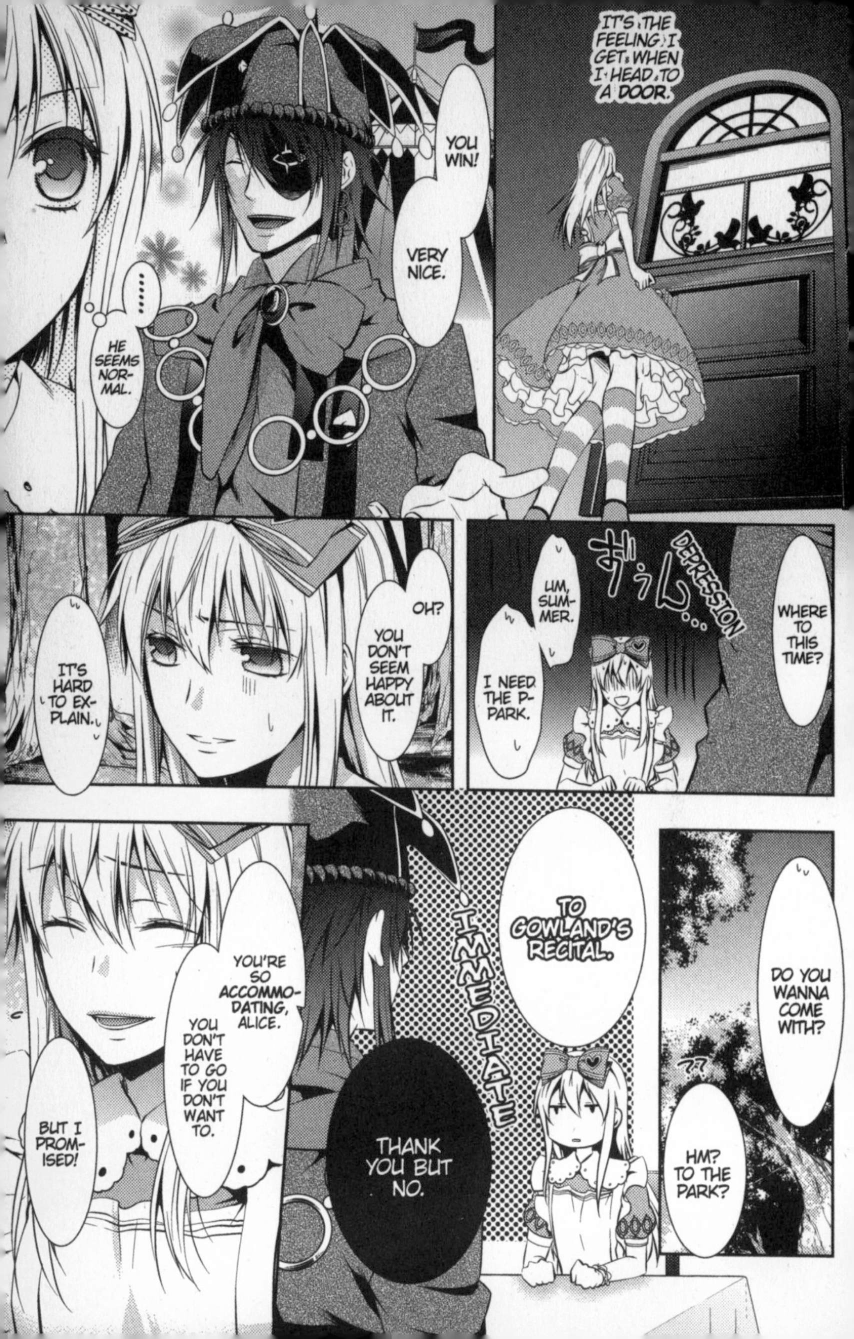
IT'S THE FEELING I GET WHEN I HEAD TO A DOOR.
YOU WIN!
VERY NICE.
......
HE SEEMS NOR-MAL.
WHERE TO THIS TIME?
DEPRESSION
ずぅん...
UM, SUM-MER.
I NEED THE P-PARK.
OH?
YOU DON'T SEEM HAPPY ABOUT IT.
IT'S HARD TO EX-PLAIN.
DO YOU WANNA COME WITH?
HM? TO THE PARK?
TO GOWLAND'S RECITAL.
IMMEDIATE
THANK YOU BUT NO.
YOU'RE SO ACCOMMO-DATING, ALICE.
YOU DON'T HAVE TO GO IF YOU DON'T WANT TO.
BUT I PROM-ISED!

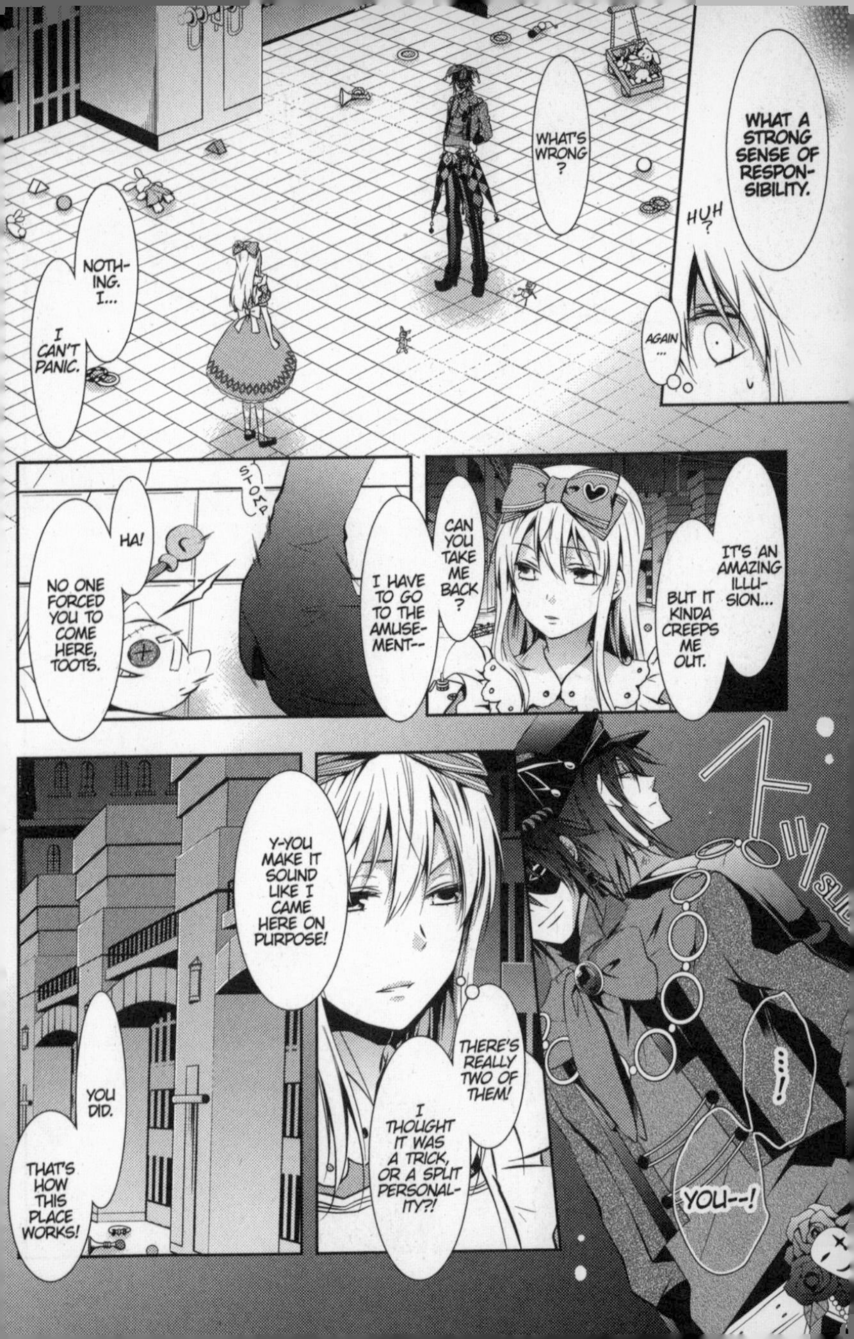
WHAT A STRONG SENSE OF RESPON-SIBILITY.
HUH?
AGAIN...
WHAT'S WRONG?
NOTH-ING. I...
I CAN'T PANIC.
IT'S AN AMAZING ILLU-SION...
BUT IT KINDA CREEPS ME OUT.
CAN YOU TAKE ME BACK?
I HAVE TO GO TO THE AMUSE-MENT--
STOMP
HA!
NO ONE FORCED YOU TO COME HERE, TOOTS.
SLID
...!
YOU--!
Y-YOU MAKE IT SOUND LIKE I CAME HERE ON PURPOSE!
THERE'S REALLY TWO OF THEM!
I THOUGHT IT WAS A TRICK, OR A SPLIT PERSONAL-ITY?!
YOU DID.
THAT'S HOW THIS PLACE WORKS!

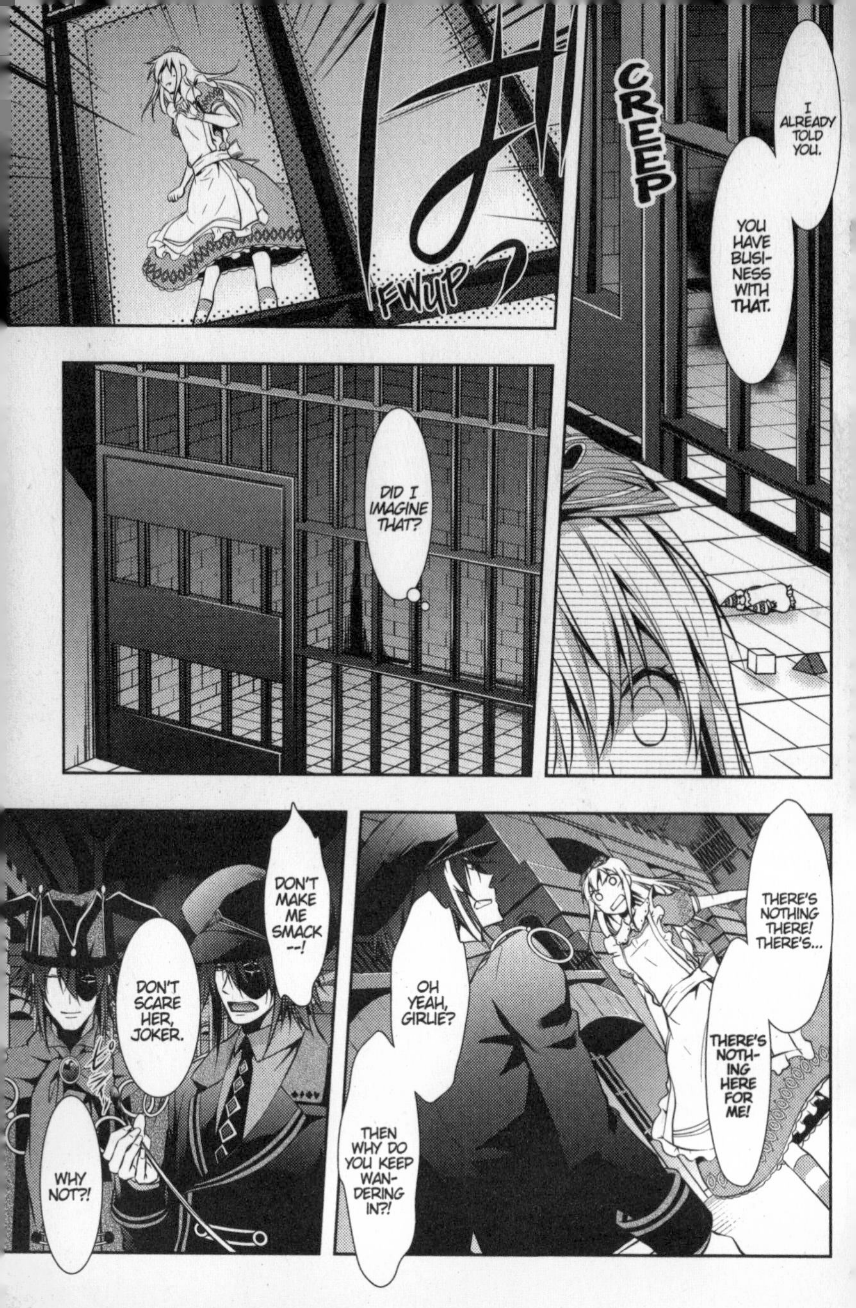
CREEP
I ALREADY TOLD YOU.
YOU HAVE BUSINESS WITH THAT.
FWUP
DID I IMAGINE THAT?
THERE'S NOTHING THERE! THERE'S...
THERE'S NOTHING HERE FOR ME!
OH YEAH, GIRLIE?
THEN WHY DO YOU KEEP WANDERING IN?!
DON'T MAKE ME SMACK--!
DON'T SCARE HER, JOKER.
WHY NOT?!

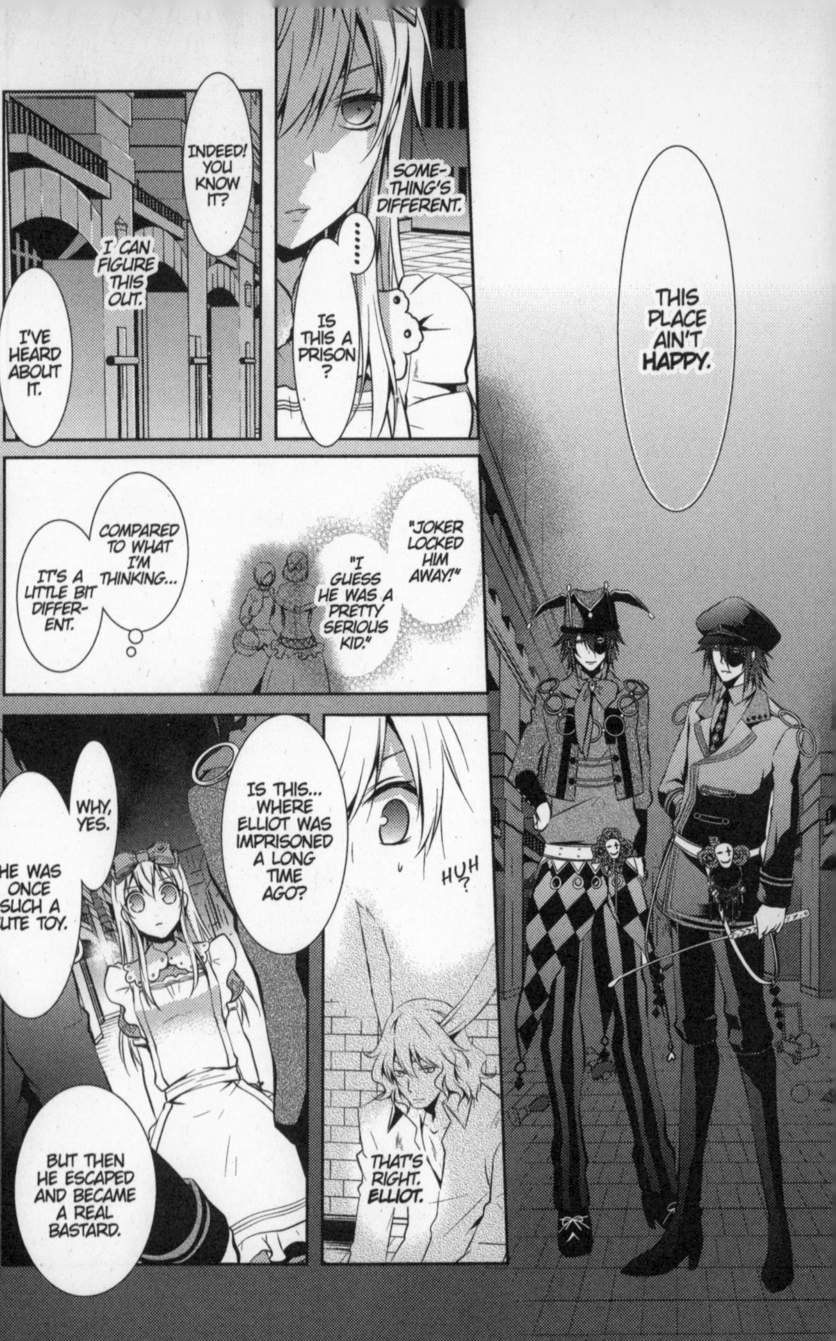
THIS PLACE AIN'T **HAPPY.**
SOME-THING'S DIFFERENT.
......
IS THIS A PRISON?
INDEED! YOU KNOW IT?
I CAN FIGURE THIS OUT.
I'VE HEARD ABOUT IT.
"JOKER LOCKED HIM AWAY!"
"I GUESS HE WAS A PRETTY SERIOUS KID."
COMPARED TO WHAT I'M THINKING...
IT'S A LITTLE BIT DIFFER-ENT.
IS THIS... WHERE ELLIOT WAS IMPRISONED A LONG TIME AGO?
HUH?
THAT'S RIGHT. **ELLIOT.**
WHY, YES.
HE WAS ONCE SUCH A CUTE TOY.
BUT THEN HE ESCAPED AND BECAME A REAL BASTARD.

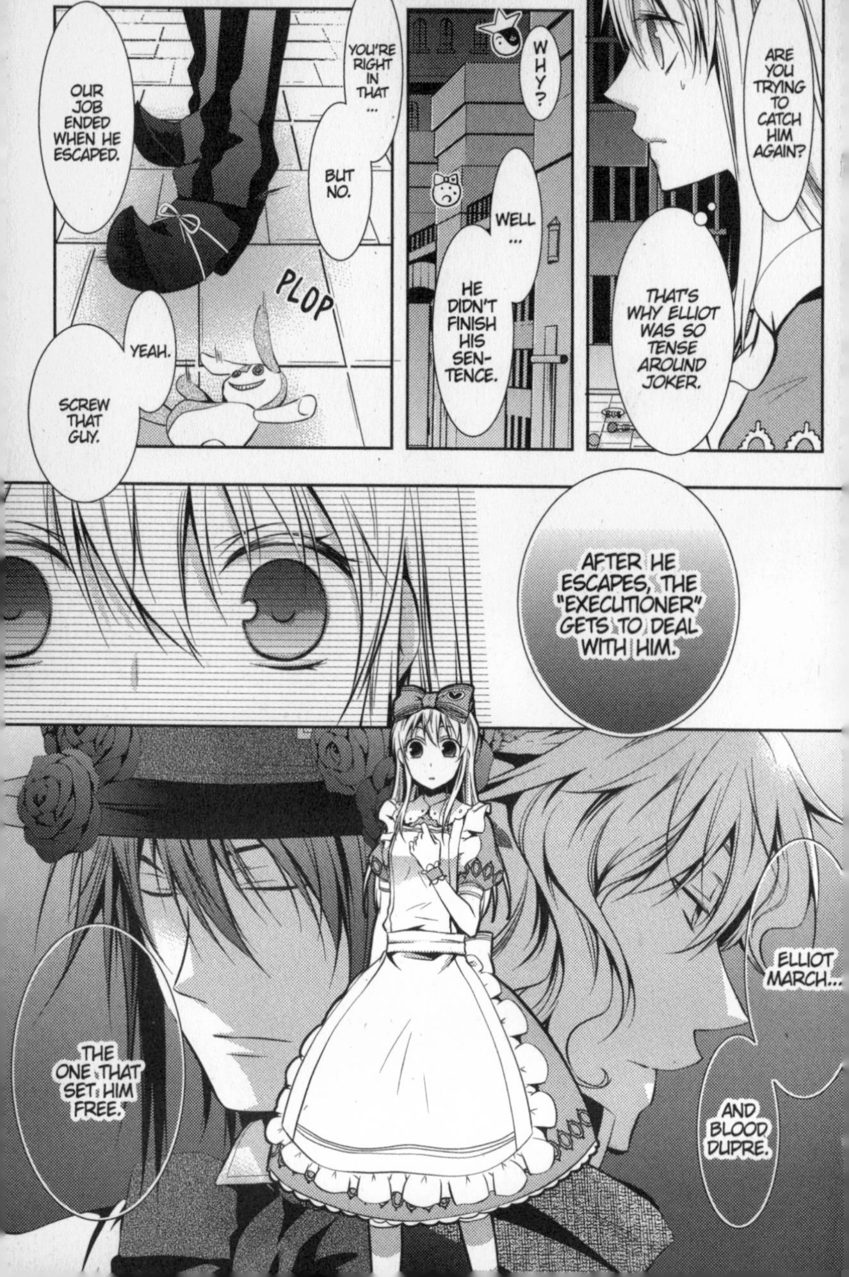
ARE YOU TRYING TO CATCH HIM AGAIN?
THAT'S WHY ELLIOT WAS SO TENSE AROUND JOKER.
WHY?
WELL...
HE DIDN'T FINISH HIS SEN-TENCE.
YOU'RE RIGHT IN THAT...
BUT NO.
OUR JOB ENDED WHEN HE ESCAPED.
PLOP
YEAH.
SCREW THAT GUY.
AFTER HE ESCAPES, THE "EXECUTIONER" GETS TO DEAL WITH HIM.
ELLIOT MARCH...
AND BLOOD DUPRE.
THE ONE THAT SET HIM FREE.

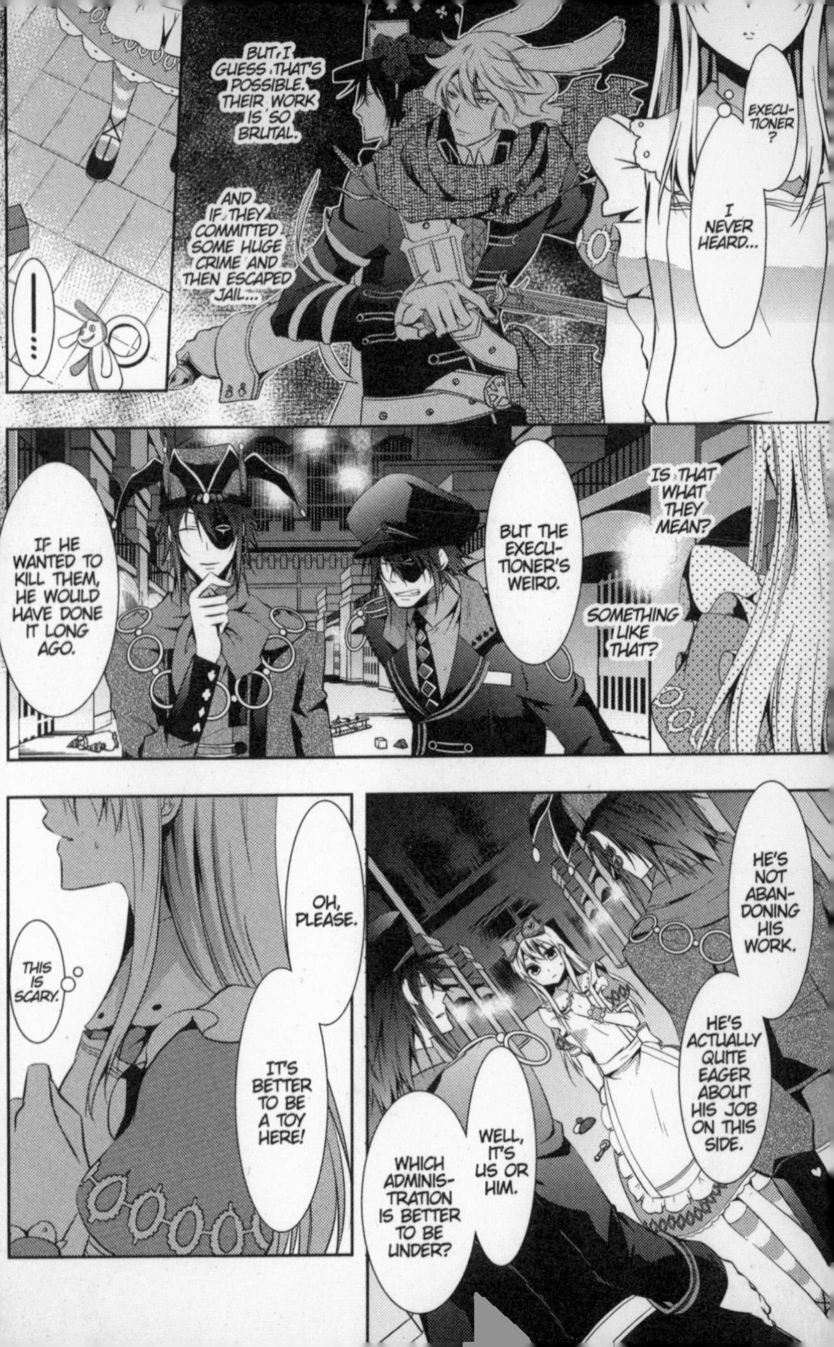
EXECUTIONER?
I NEVER HEARD...
BUT, I GUESS THAT'S POSSIBLE. THEIR WORK IS SO BRUTAL.
AND IF THEY COMMITTED SOME HUGE CRIME AND THEN ESCAPED JAIL...
!...
IS THAT WHAT THEY MEAN?
SOMETHING LIKE THAT?
BUT THE EXECUTIONER'S WEIRD.
IF HE WANTED TO KILL THEM, HE WOULD HAVE DONE IT LONG AGO.
HE'S NOT ABANDONING HIS WORK.
HE'S ACTUALLY QUITE EAGER ABOUT HIS JOB ON THIS SIDE.
WELL, IT'S US OR HIM.
WHICH ADMINISTRATION IS BETTER TO BE UNDER?
OH, PLEASE.
IT'S BETTER TO BE A TOY HERE!
THIS IS SCARY.

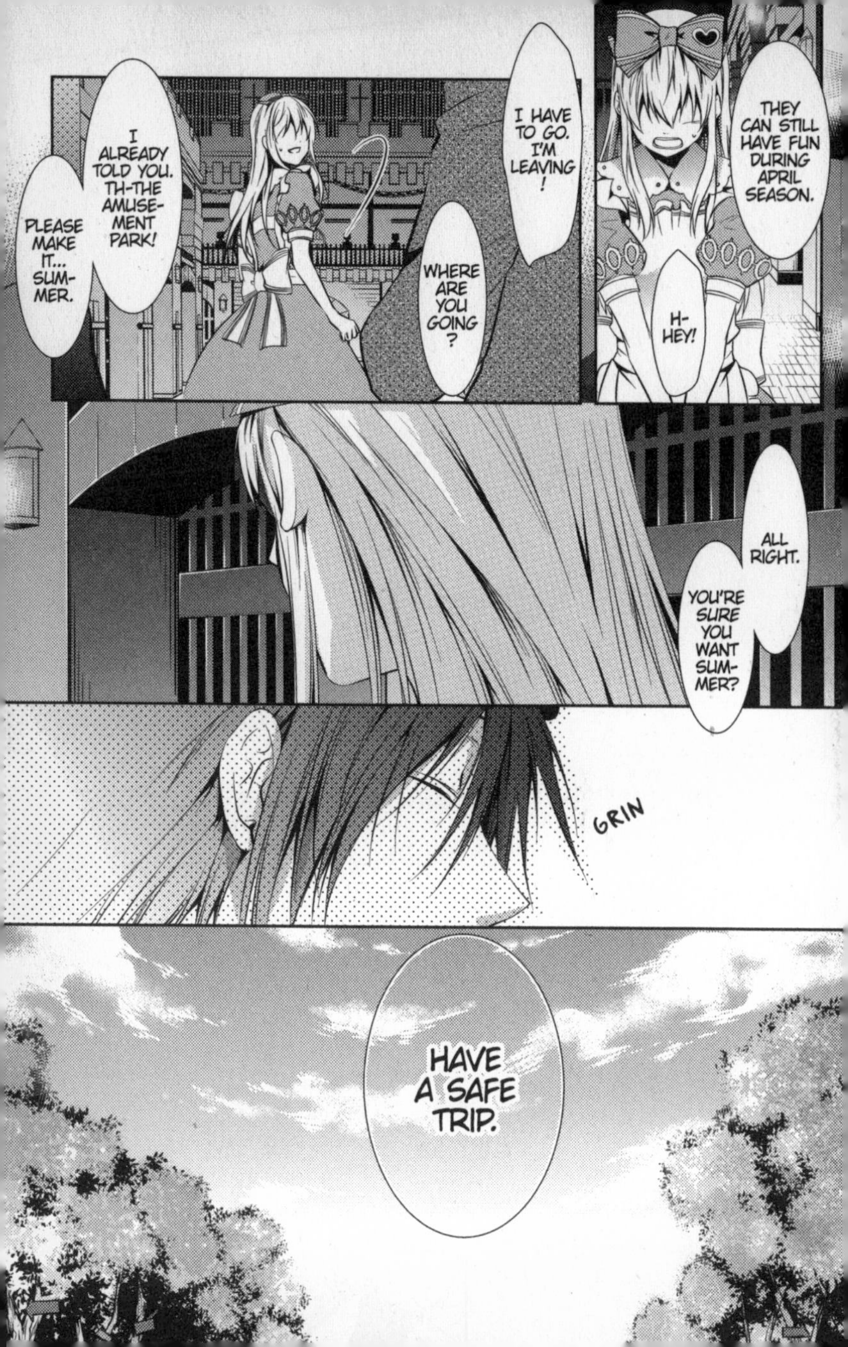
THEY CAN STILL HAVE FUN DURING APRIL SEASON.
H-HEY!
I HAVE TO GO. I'M LEAVING!
WHERE ARE YOU GOING?
I ALREADY TOLD YOU. TH-THE AMUSEMENT PARK!
PLEASE MAKE IT... SUMMER.
ALL RIGHT.
YOU'RE SURE YOU WANT SUMMER?
GRIN
HAVE A SAFE TRIP.

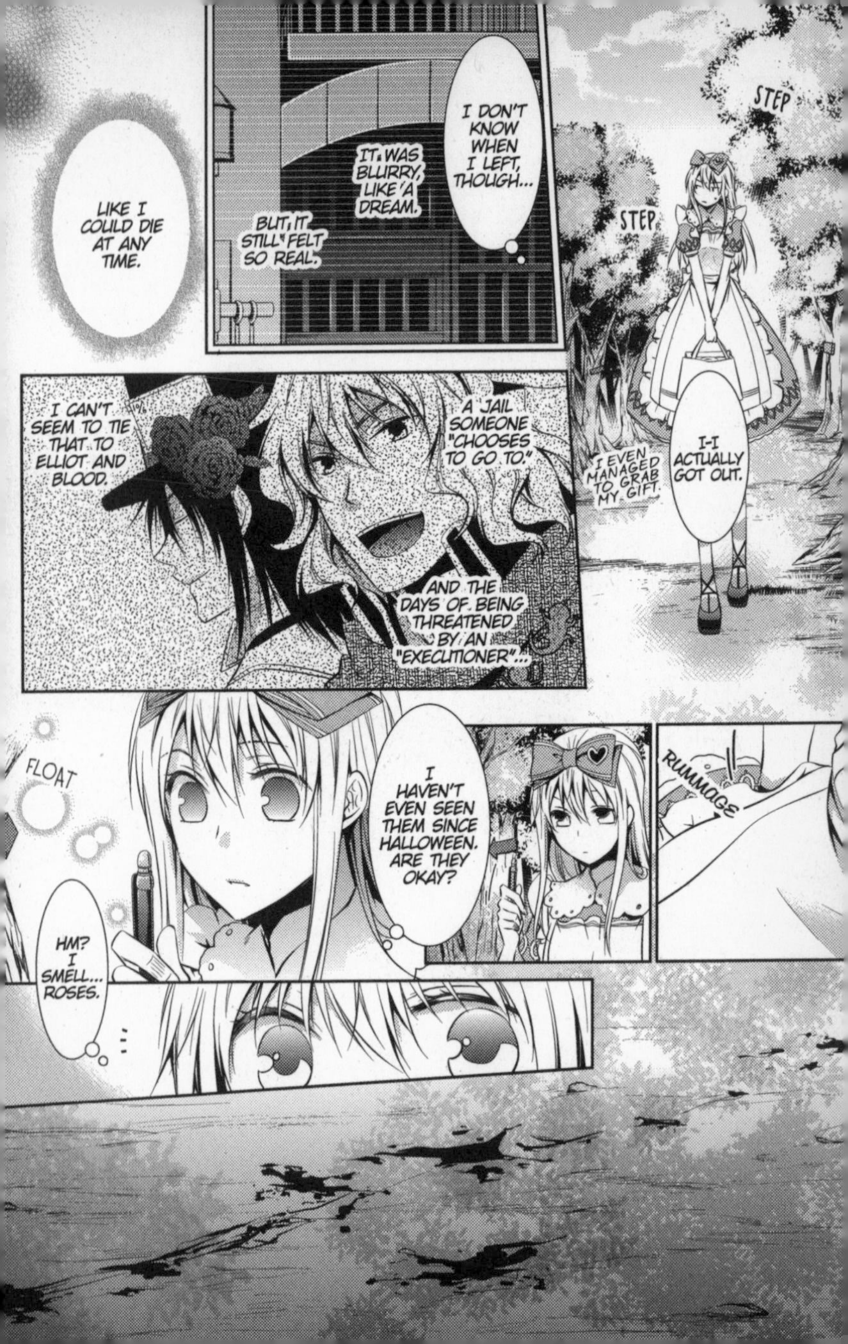
STEP
STEP
I-I ACTUALLY GOT OUT.
I EVEN MANAGED TO GRAB MY GIFT.
I DON'T KNOW WHEN I LEFT, THOUGH...
IT WAS BLURRY, LIKE A DREAM.
BUT, IT STILL FELT SO REAL.
LIKE I COULD DIE AT ANY TIME.
A JAIL SOMEONE "CHOOSES TO GO TO."
AND THE DAYS OF BEING THREATENED BY AN "EXECUTIONER"...
I CAN'T SEEM TO TIE THAT TO ELLIOT AND BLOOD.
RUMMAGE
I HAVEN'T EVEN SEEN THEM SINCE HALLOWEEN. ARE THEY OKAY?
FLOAT
HM? I SMELL... ROSES.
...

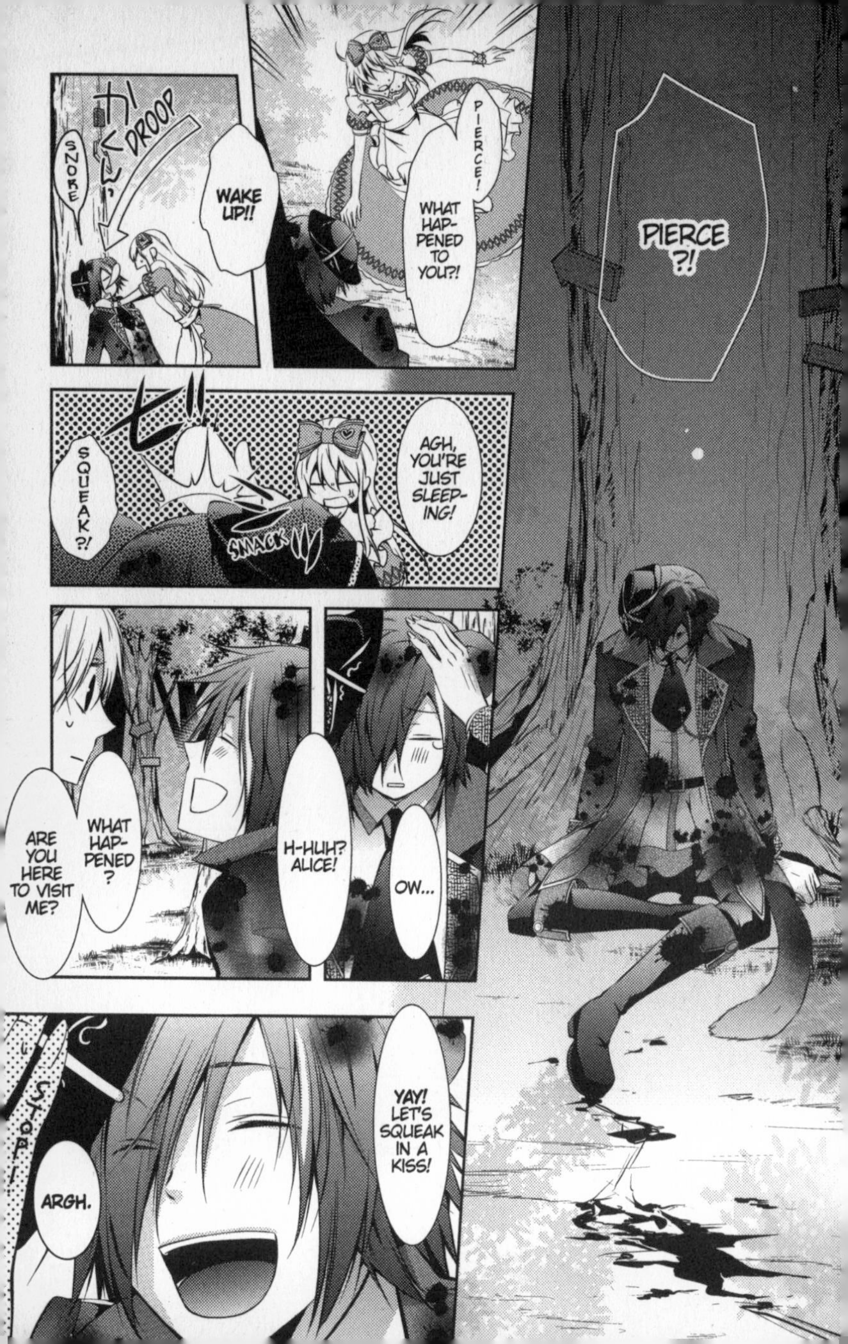
PIERCE ?!
PIERCE! WHAT HAPPENED TO YOU?!
WAKE UP!!
DROOP
SNORE
AGH, YOU'RE JUST SLEEPING!
SMACK
SQUEAK?!
OW...
H-HUH? ALICE!
WHAT HAPPENED?
ARE YOU HERE TO VISIT ME?
YAY! LET'S SQUEAK IN A KISS!
ARGH.
STOP!

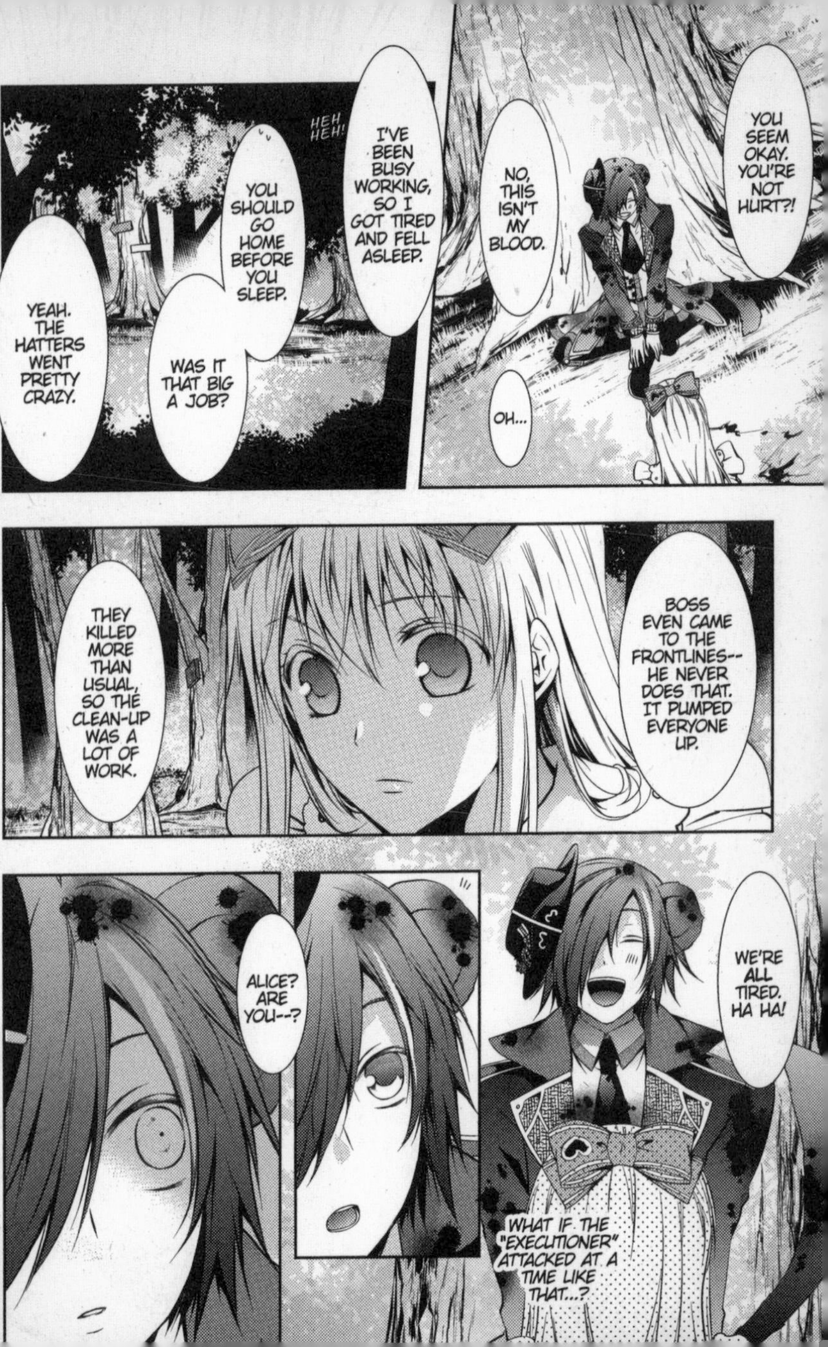
YOU SEEM OKAY. YOU'RE NOT HURT?!
NO, THIS ISN'T MY BLOOD.
OH...
I'VE BEEN BUSY WORKING, SO I GOT TIRED AND FELL ASLEEP.
HEH HEH!
YOU SHOULD GO HOME BEFORE YOU SLEEP.
WAS IT THAT BIG A JOB?
YEAH. THE HATTERS WENT PRETTY CRAZY.
BOSS EVEN CAME TO THE FRONTLINES-- HE NEVER DOES THAT. IT PUMPED EVERYONE UP.
THEY KILLED MORE THAN USUAL, SO THE CLEAN-UP WAS A LOT OF WORK.
WE'RE ALL TIRED. HA HA!
WHAT IF THE "EXECUTIONER" ATTACKED AT A TIME LIKE THAT...?
ALICE? ARE YOU--?

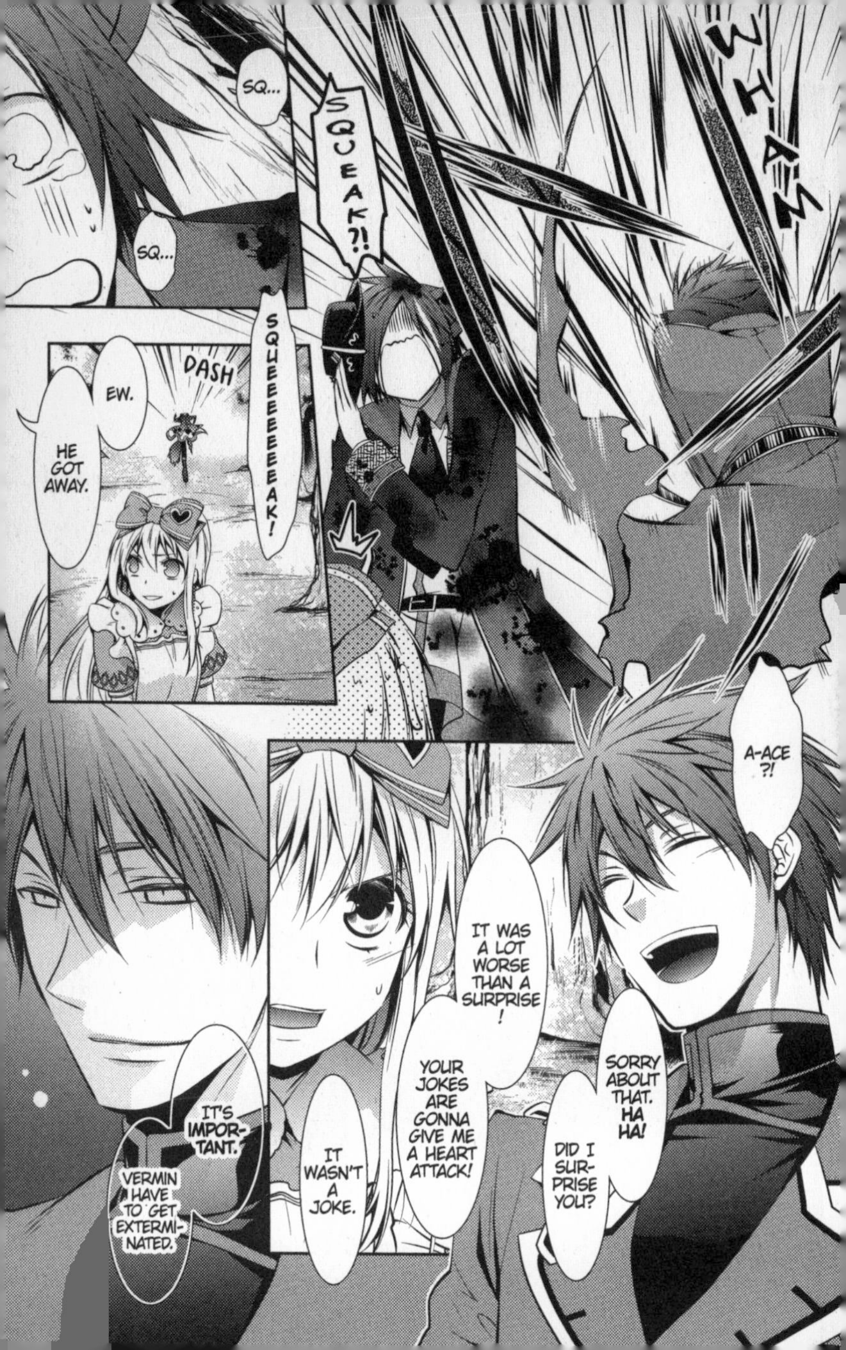
WHAM
SQUEAK?!
SQ...
SQ...
SQUEEEEEEEAK!
DASH
EW.
HE GOT AWAY.
A-ACE?!
DID I SURPRISE YOU?
IT WAS A LOT WORSE THAN A SURPRISE!
SORRY ABOUT THAT. HA HA!
YOUR JOKES ARE GONNA GIVE ME A HEART ATTACK!
IT WASN'T A JOKE.
IT'S IMPORTANT.
VERMIN HAVE TO GET EXTERMINATED.

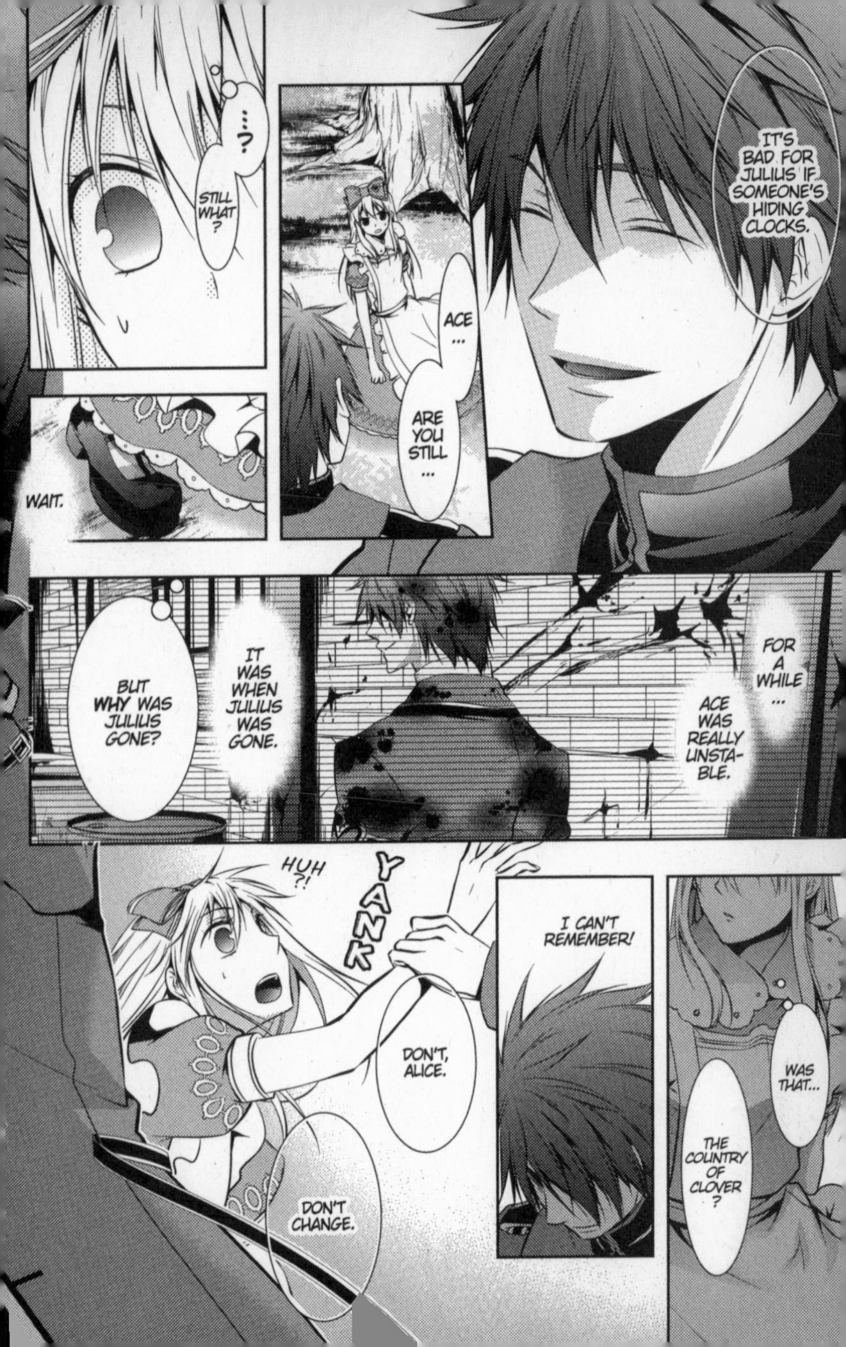

IT'S BAD FOR JULIUS IF SOMEONE'S HIDING CLOCKS.
ACE ...
ARE YOU STILL ...
...?
STILL WHAT?
WAIT.
FOR A WHILE ...
ACE WAS REALLY UNSTA-BLE.
IT WAS WHEN JULIUS WAS GONE.
BUT WHY WAS JULIUS GONE?
WAS THAT...
THE COUNTRY OF CLOVER?
I CAN'T REMEMBER!
HUH?!
YANK
DON'T, ALICE.
DON'T CHANGE.

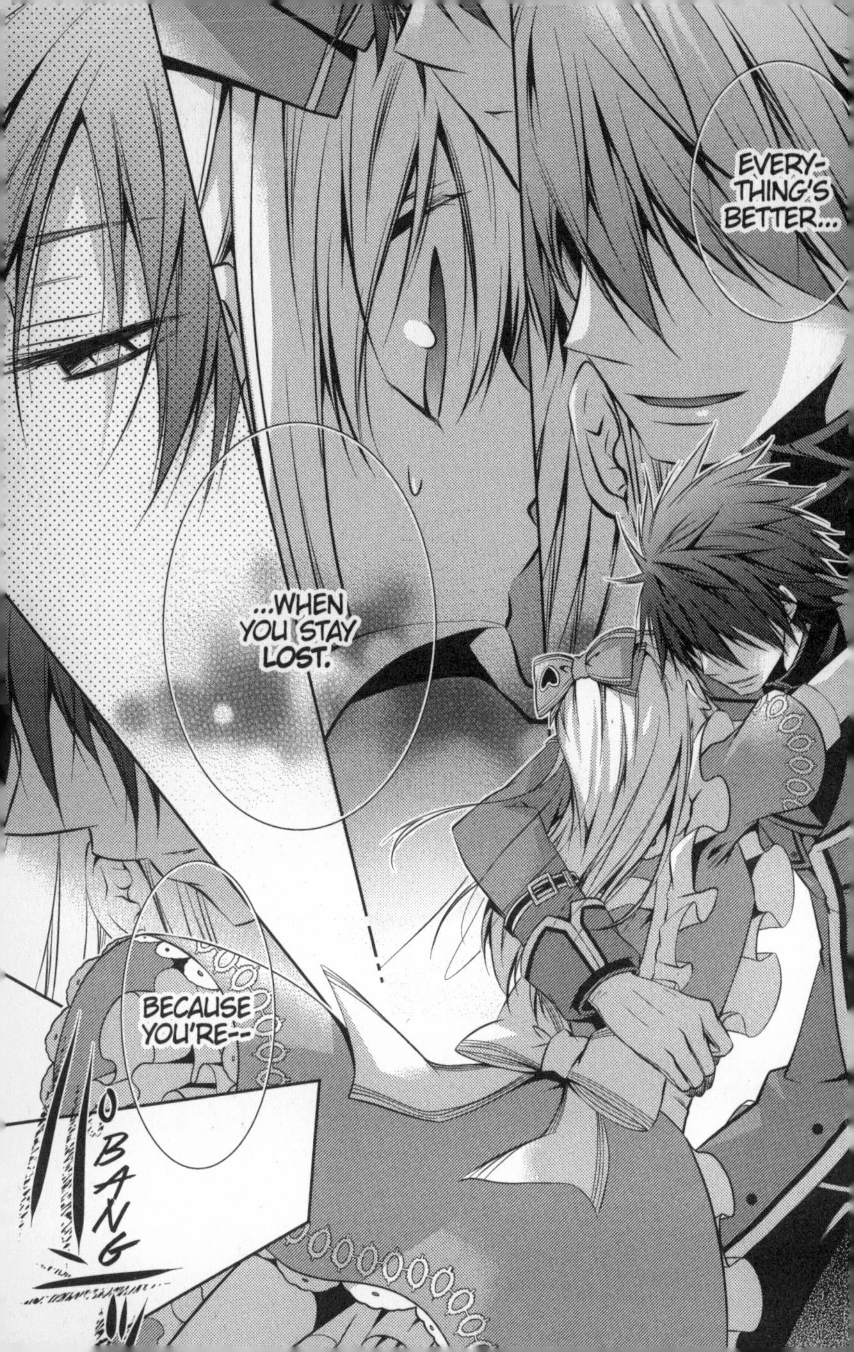
EVERY-THING'S BETTER...
...WHEN YOU STAY LOST.
BECAUSE YOU'RE--
BANG

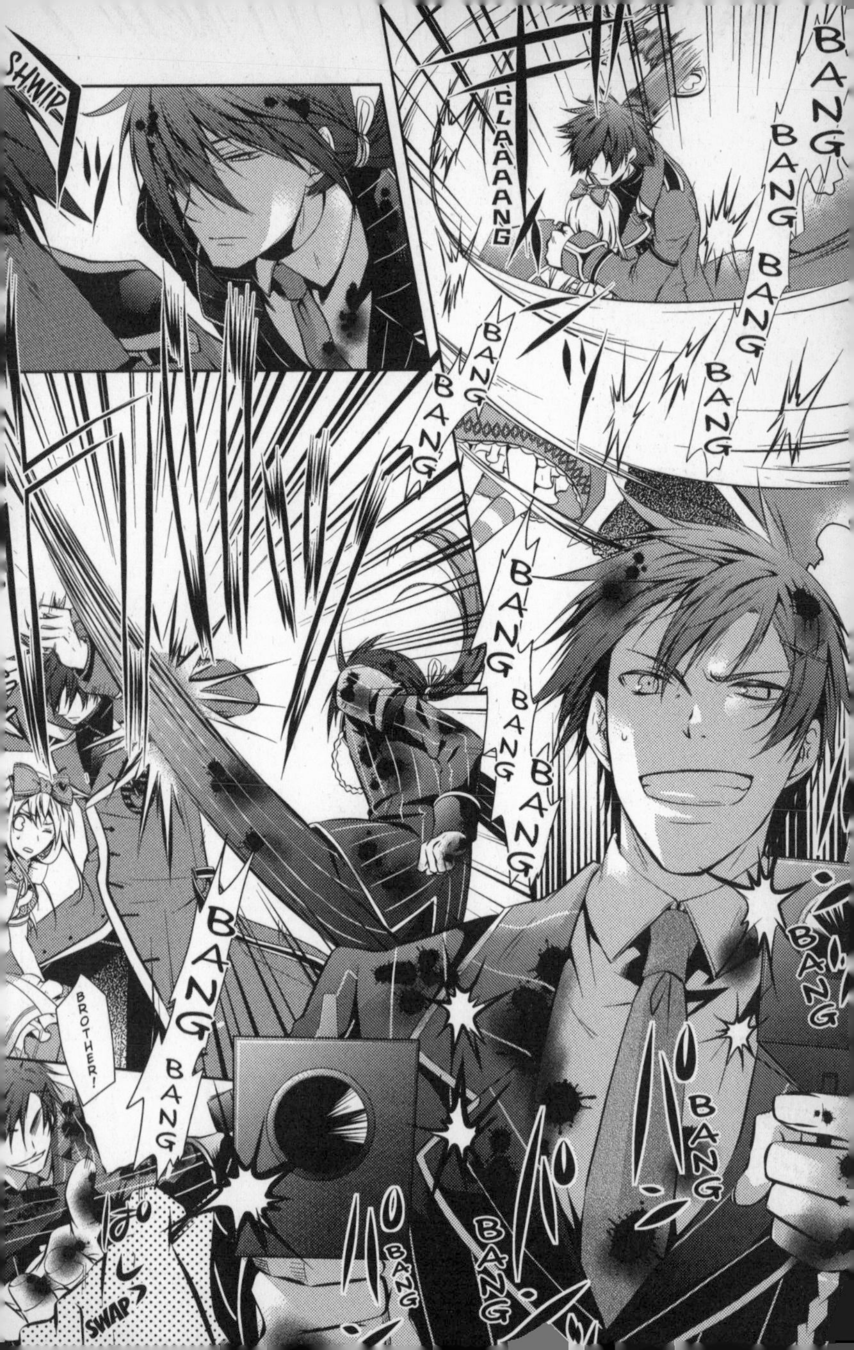
BANG
BANG
BANG
BANG
BANG
CLAAAANG
BANG
BANG
SHWIP
BANG
BANG
BANG
BANG
BANG
BANG
BANG
BANG
BANG
BROTHER!
SWAP

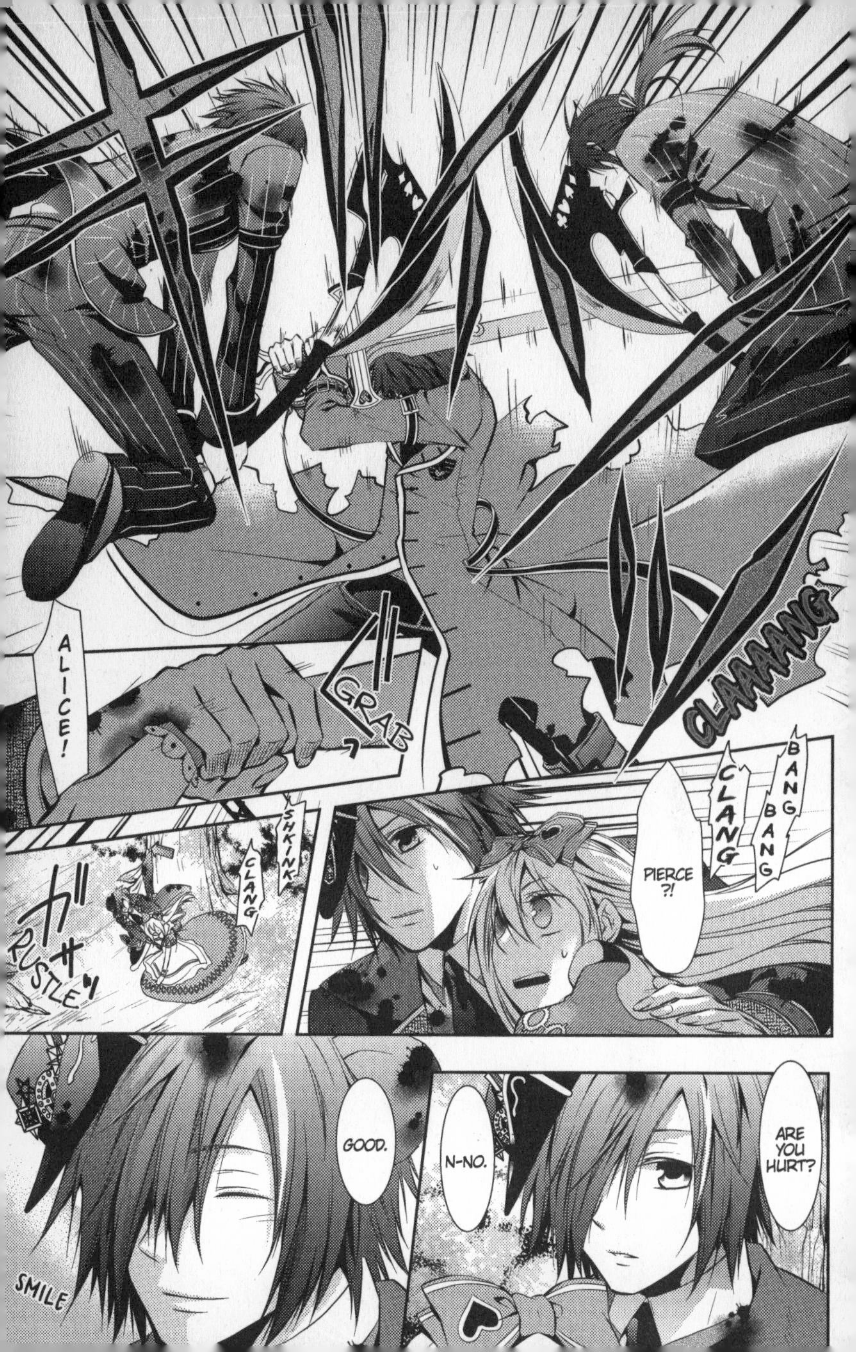
CLAAAANG
GRAB
ALICE!
BANG BANG BANG
CLANG CLANG
PIERCE?!
SHKINK
CLANG
RUSTLE
ARE YOU HURT?
N-NO.
GOOD.
SMILE

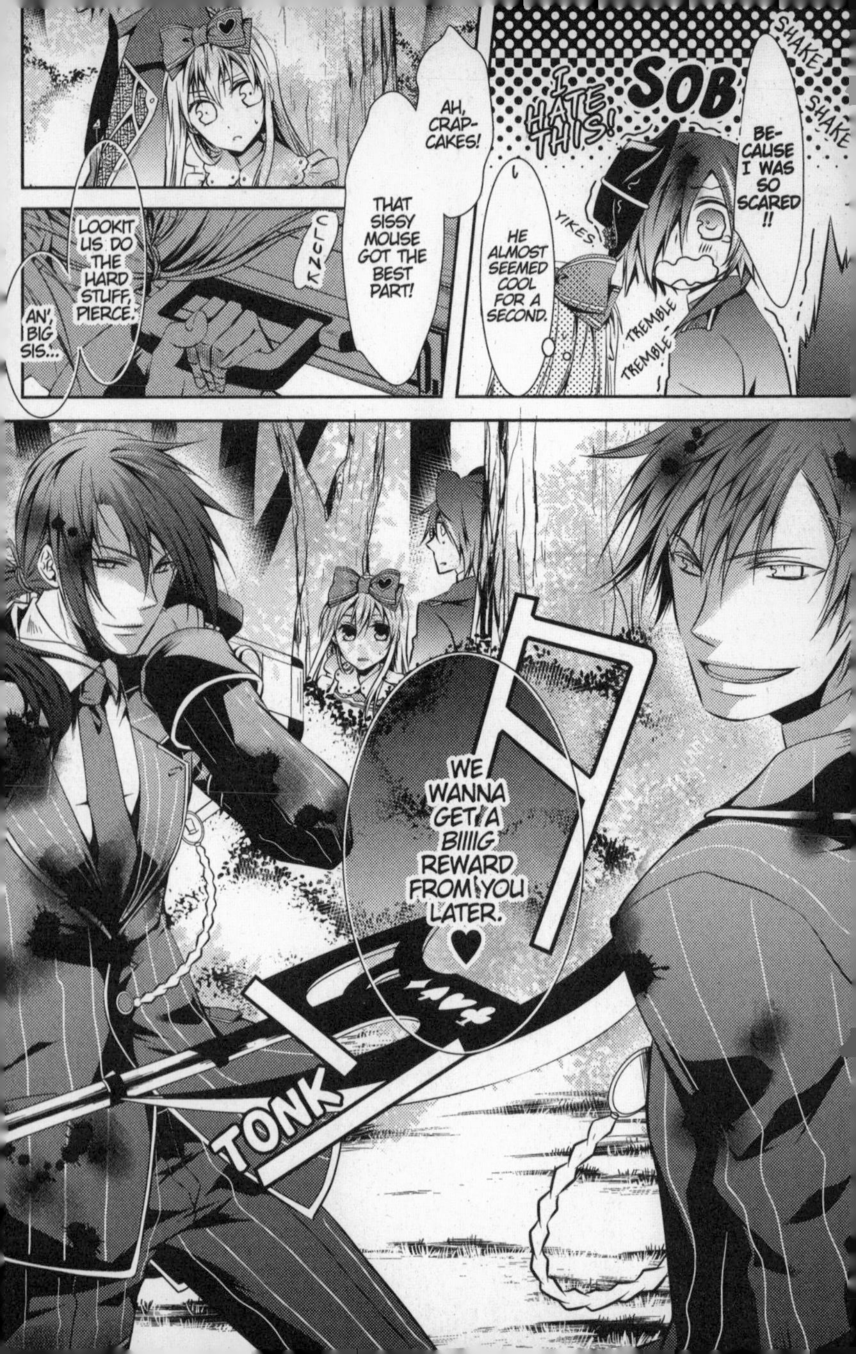
SHAKE SHAKE
SOB
I HATE THIS!
BECAUSE I WAS SO SCARED!!
YIKES
TREMBLE TREMBLE
HE ALMOST SEEMED COOL FOR A SECOND.
AH, CRAPCAKES!
THAT SISSY MOUSE GOT THE BEST PART!
CLUNK
LOOKIT US DO THE HARD STUFF, PIERCE.
AN' BIG SIS...
WE WANNA GET A BIIIIG REWARD FROM YOU LATER. ♥
TONK

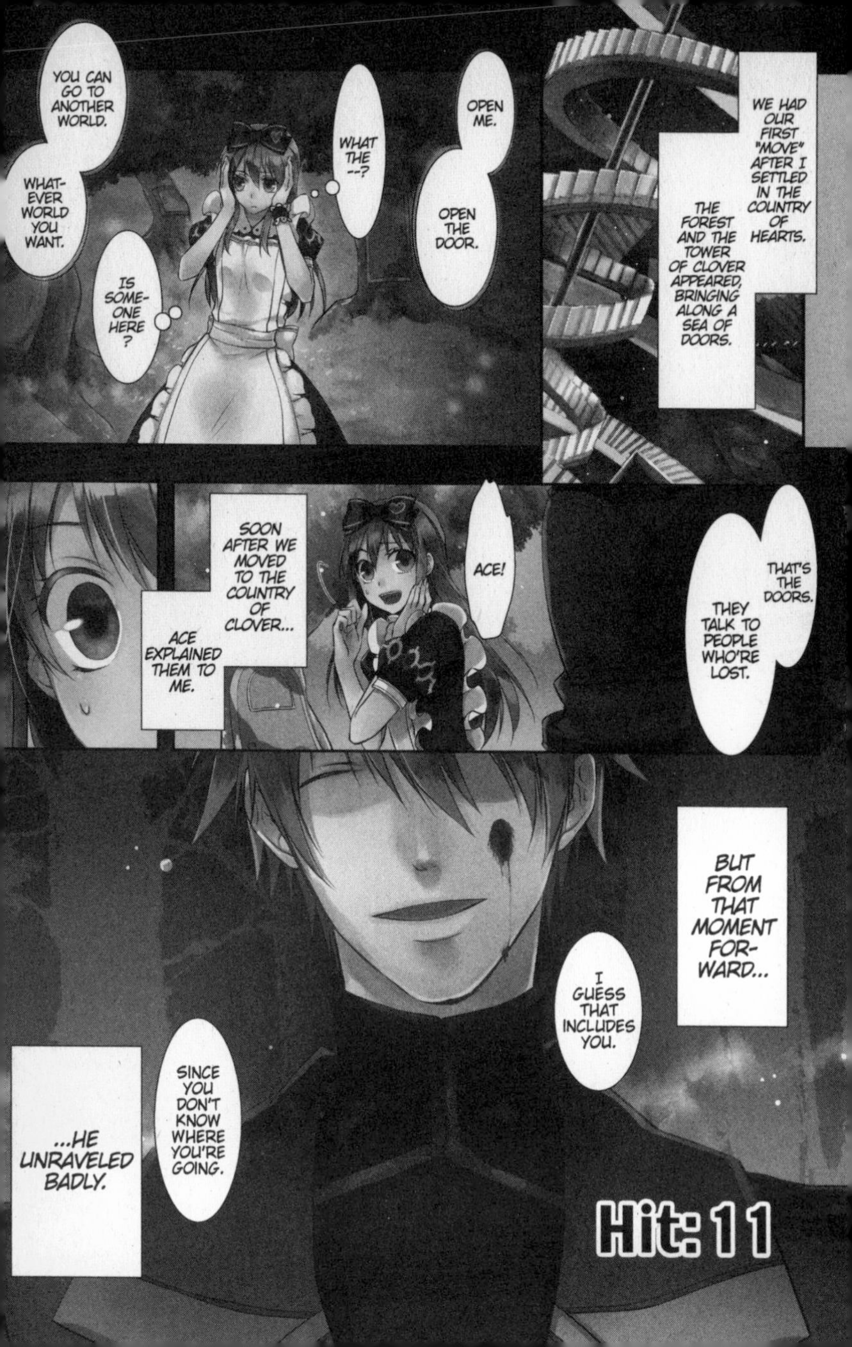
WE HAD OUR FIRST "MOVE" AFTER I SETTLED IN THE COUNTRY OF HEARTS.
THE FOREST AND THE TOWER OF CLOVER APPEARED, BRINGING ALONG A SEA OF DOORS.
OPEN ME.
WHAT THE --?
OPEN THE DOOR.
YOU CAN GO TO ANOTHER WORLD.
WHAT-EVER WORLD YOU WANT.
IS SOME-ONE HERE?
THAT'S THE DOORS.
THEY TALK TO PEOPLE WHO'RE LOST.
ACE!
SOON AFTER WE MOVED TO THE COUNTRY OF CLOVER...
ACE EXPLAINED THEM TO ME.
BUT FROM THAT MOMENT FOR-WARD...
I GUESS THAT INCLUDES YOU.
SINCE YOU DON'T KNOW WHERE YOU'RE GOING.
...HE UNRAVELED BADLY.
Hit: 11

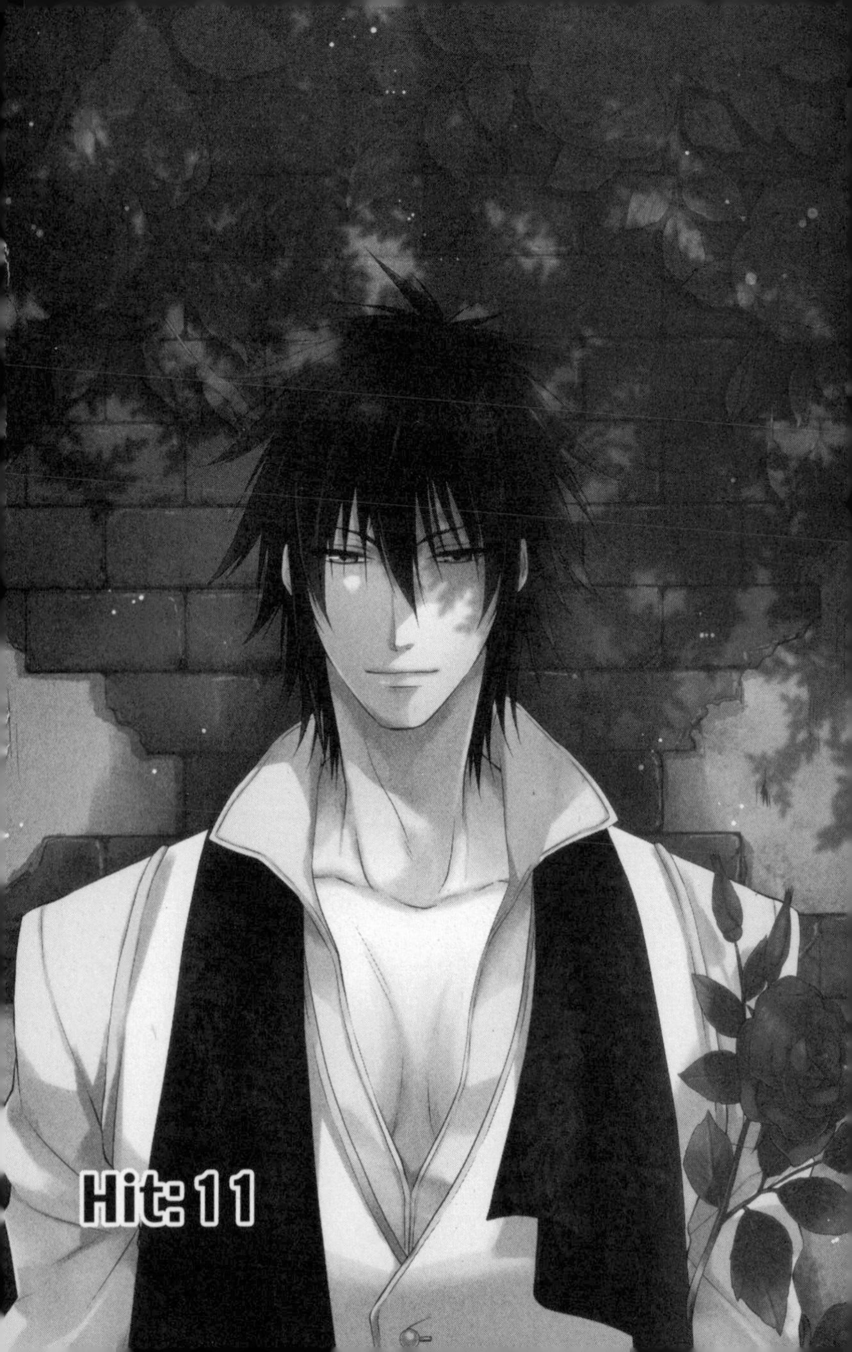
Hit: 11

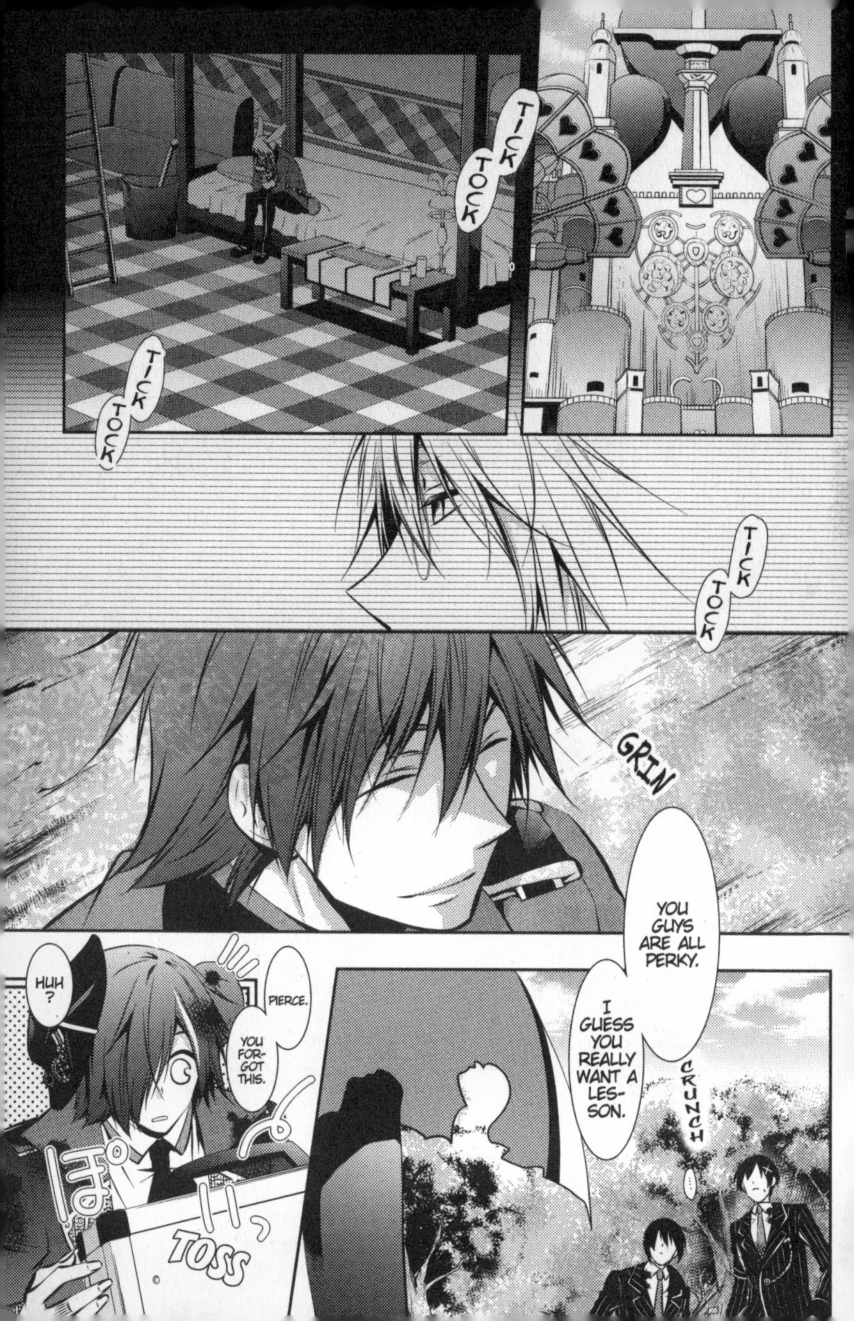
TICK TOCK
TICK TOCK
TICK TOCK
GRIN
YOU GUYS ARE ALL PERKY.
I GUESS YOU REALLY WANT A LES-SON.
CRUNCH
...
PIERCE.
YOU FOR-GOT THIS.
HUH?
ぽいっ
TOSS

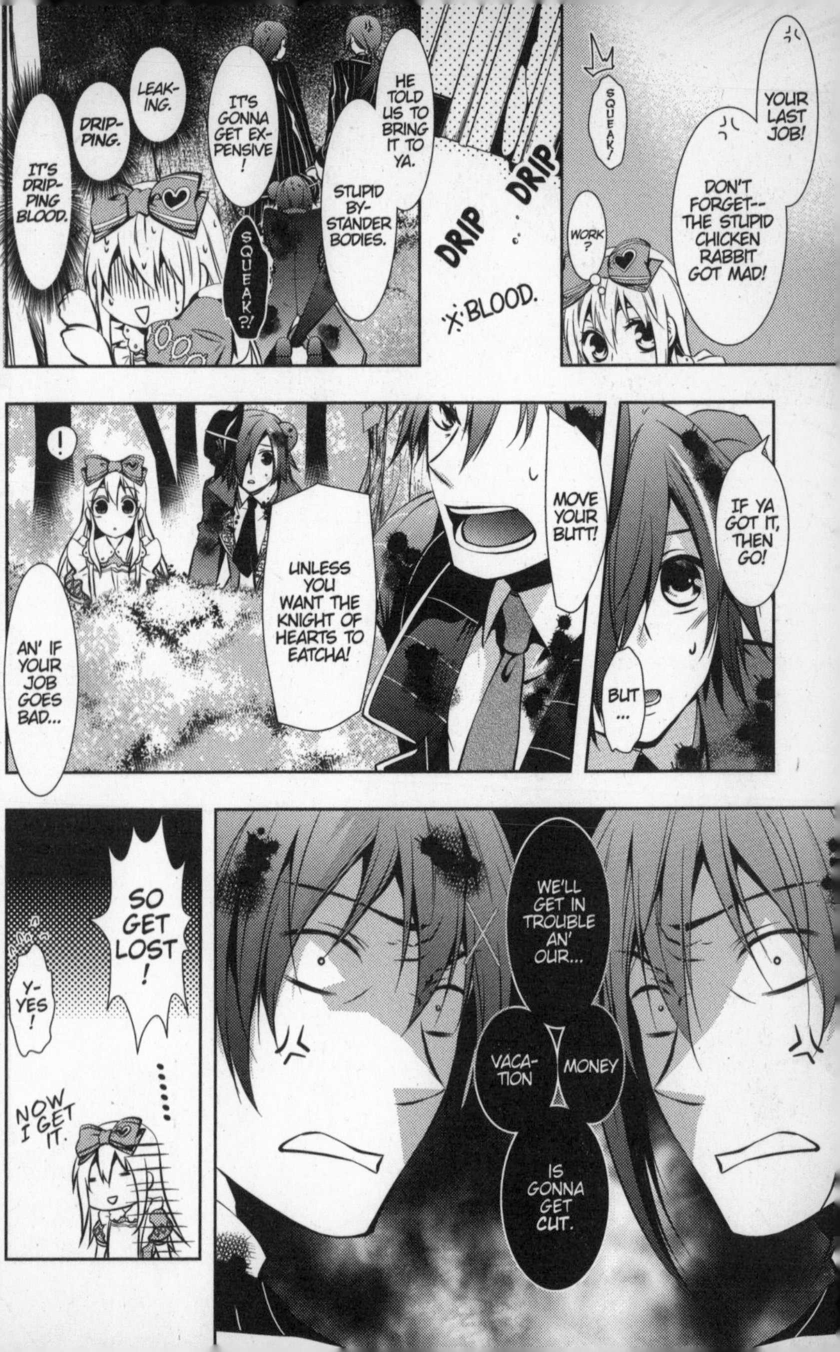
YOUR LAST JOB!
SQUEAK!
DON'T FORGET-- THE STUPID CHICKEN RABBIT GOT MAD!
WORK?
DRIP
DRIP
※BLOOD.
HE TOLD US TO BRING IT TO YA.
STUPID BYSTANDER BODIES.
IT'S GONNA GET EXPENSIVE!
LEAKING.
SQUEAK?!
DRIPPING.
IT'S DRIPPING BLOOD.
IF YA GOT IT, THEN GO!
BUT...
MOVE YOUR BUTT!
UNLESS YOU WANT THE KNIGHT OF HEARTS TO EATCHA!
!
AN' IF YOUR JOB GOES BAD...
WE'LL GET IN TROUBLE AN' OUR...
MONEY
VACATION
IS GONNA GET CUT.
SO GET LOST!
Y-YES!
......
NOW I GET IT.

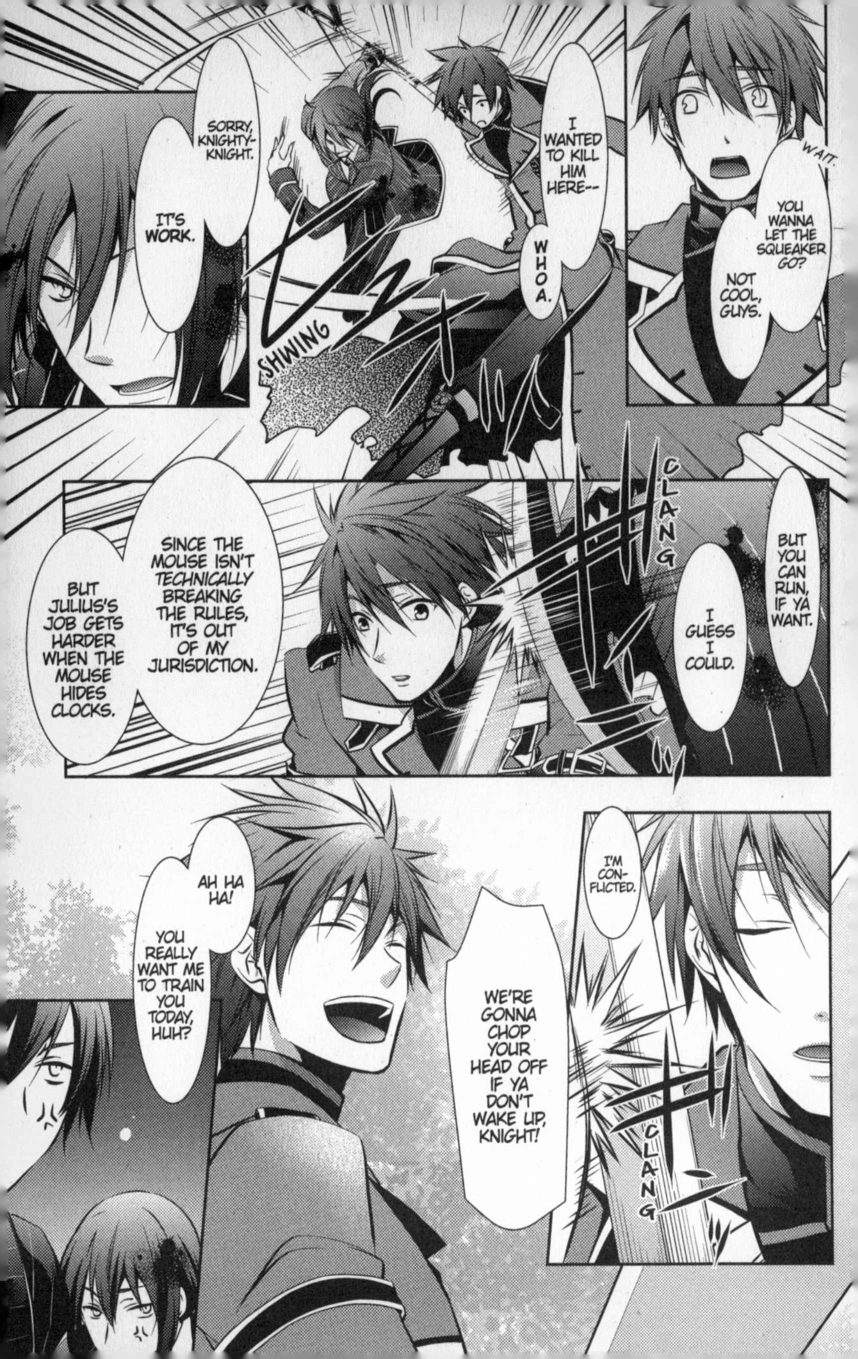
WAIT.
YOU WANNA LET THE SQUEAKER GO?
NOT COOL, GUYS.
I WANTED TO KILL HIM HERE--
WHOA.
SORRY, KNIGHTY-KNIGHT.
IT'S WORK.
SHWING
CLANG
BUT YOU CAN RUN, IF YA WANT.
I GUESS I COULD.
SINCE THE MOUSE ISN'T TECHNICALLY BREAKING THE RULES, IT'S OUT OF MY JURISDICTION.
BUT JULIUS'S JOB GETS HARDER WHEN THE MOUSE HIDES CLOCKS.
I'M CON-FLICTED.
CLANG
WE'RE GONNA CHOP YOUR HEAD OFF IF YA DON'T WAKE UP, KNIGHT!
AH HA HA!
YOU REALLY WANT ME TO TRAIN YOU TODAY, HUH?

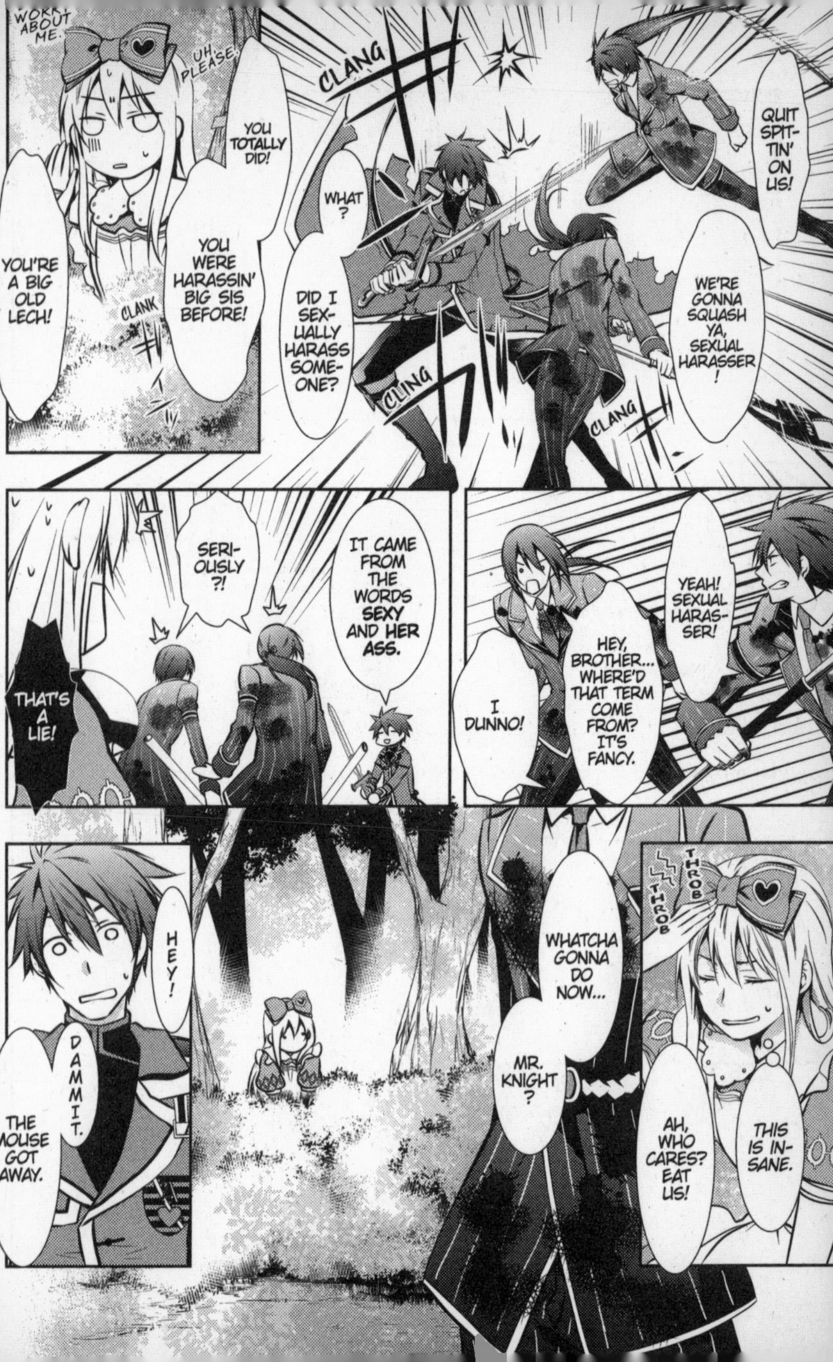
CLANG
QUIT SPITTIN' ON US!
WE'RE GONNA SQUASH YA, SEXUAL HARASSER!
CLING
CLANG
WHAT?
DID I SEXUALLY HARASS SOMEONE?
YOU TOTALLY DID!
YOU WERE HARASSIN' BIG SIS BEFORE!
UH PLEASE.
ABOUT ME.
YOU'RE A BIG OLD LECH!
CLANK
YEAH! SEXUAL HARASSER!
HEY, BROTHER... WHERE'D THAT TERM COME FROM? IT'S FANCY.
I DUNNO!
IT CAME FROM THE WORDS SEXY AND HER ASS.
SERIOUSLY?!
THAT'S A LIE!
THROB THROB
THIS IS INSANE.
AH, WHO CARES? EAT US!
WHATCHA GONNA DO NOW...
MR. KNIGHT?
HEY!
DAMMIT.
THE MOUSE GOT AWAY.

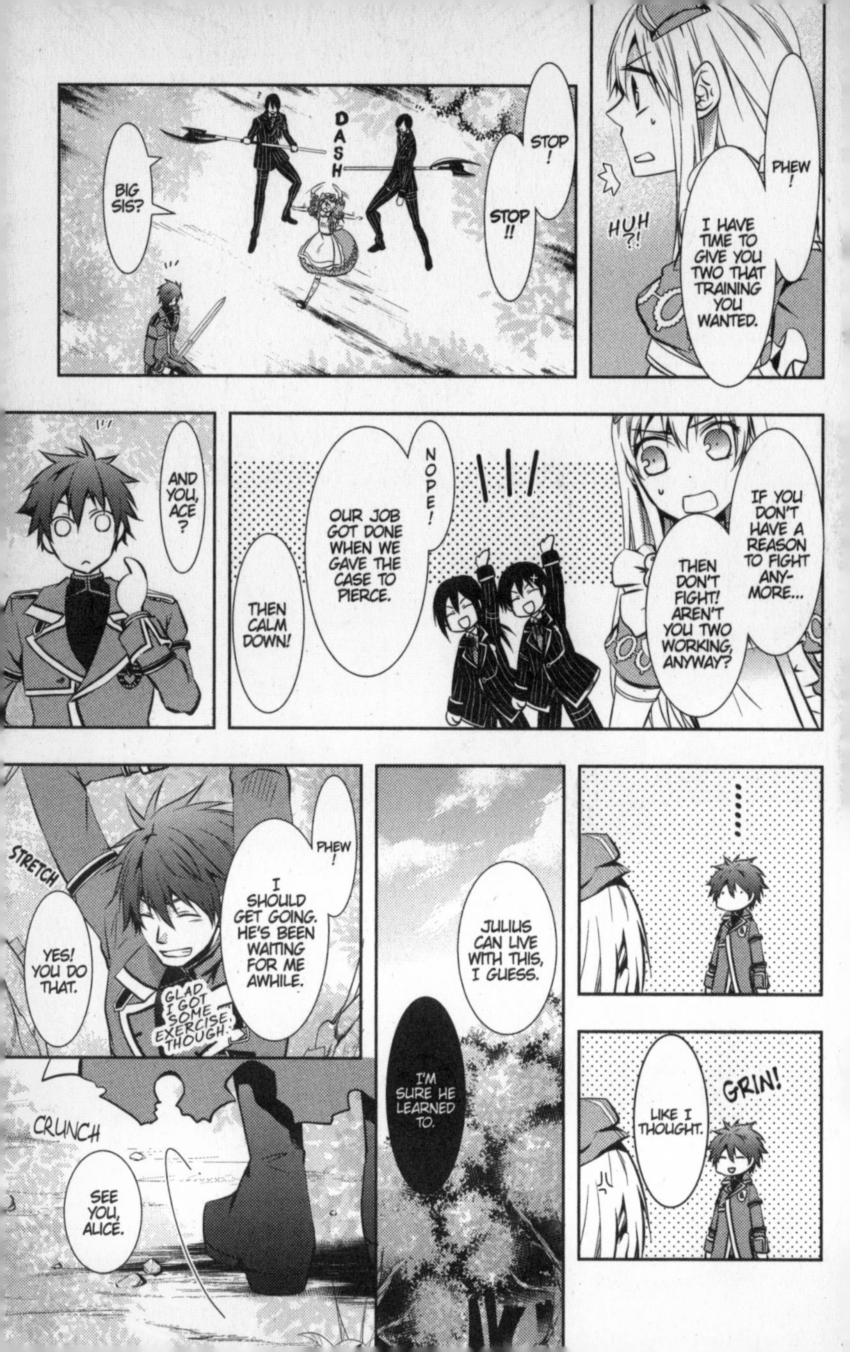
PHEW!
I HAVE TIME TO GIVE YOU TWO THAT TRAINING YOU WANTED.
HUH?!
STOP!
STOP!!
DASH
BIG SIS?
IF YOU DON'T HAVE A REASON TO FIGHT ANY-MORE...
THEN DON'T FIGHT! AREN'T YOU TWO WORKING, ANYWAY?
NOPE!
OUR JOB GOT DONE WHEN WE GAVE THE CASE TO PIERCE.
THEN CALM DOWN!
AND YOU, ACE?
......
GRIN!
LIKE I THOUGHT.
JULIUS CAN LIVE WITH THIS, I GUESS.
I'M SURE HE LEARNED TO.
PHEW!
I SHOULD GET GOING. HE'S BEEN WAITING FOR ME AWHILE.
GLAD I GOT SOME EXERCISE, THOUGH.
STRETCH
YES! YOU DO THAT.
CRUNCH
SEE YOU, ALICE.

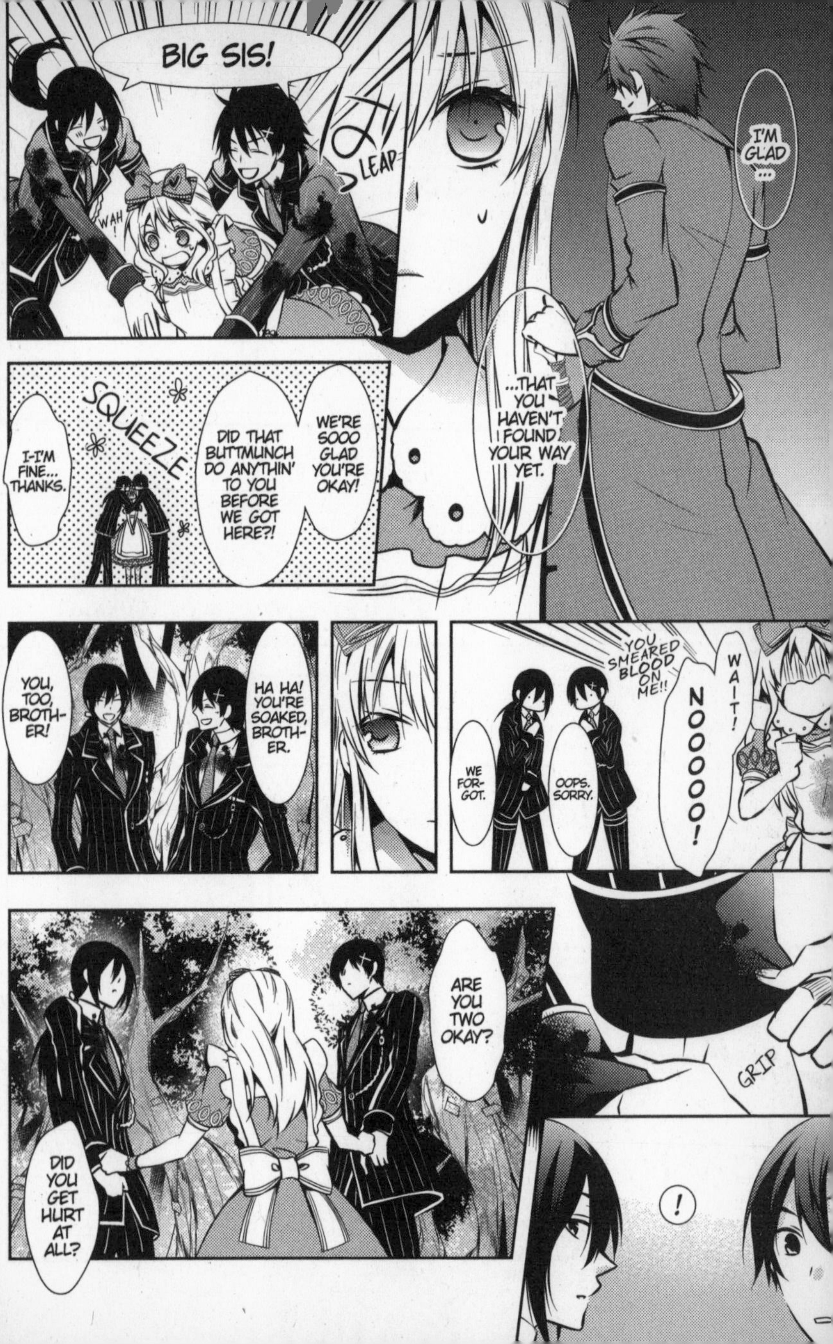
I'M GLAD...
...THAT YOU HAVEN'T FOUND YOUR WAY YET.
BIG SIS!
LEAP
WAH!
WE'RE SOOO GLAD YOU'RE OKAY!
DID THAT BUTTMUNCH DO ANYTHIN' TO YOU BEFORE WE GOT HERE?!
SQUEEZE
I-I'M FINE... THANKS.
WAIT!
NOOOOOO!
YOU SMEARED BLOOD ON ME!!
OOPS. SORRY.
WE FORGOT.
HA HA! YOU'RE SOAKED, BROTHER.
YOU, TOO, BROTHER!
GRIP
!
ARE YOU TWO OKAY?
DID YOU GET HURT AT ALL?

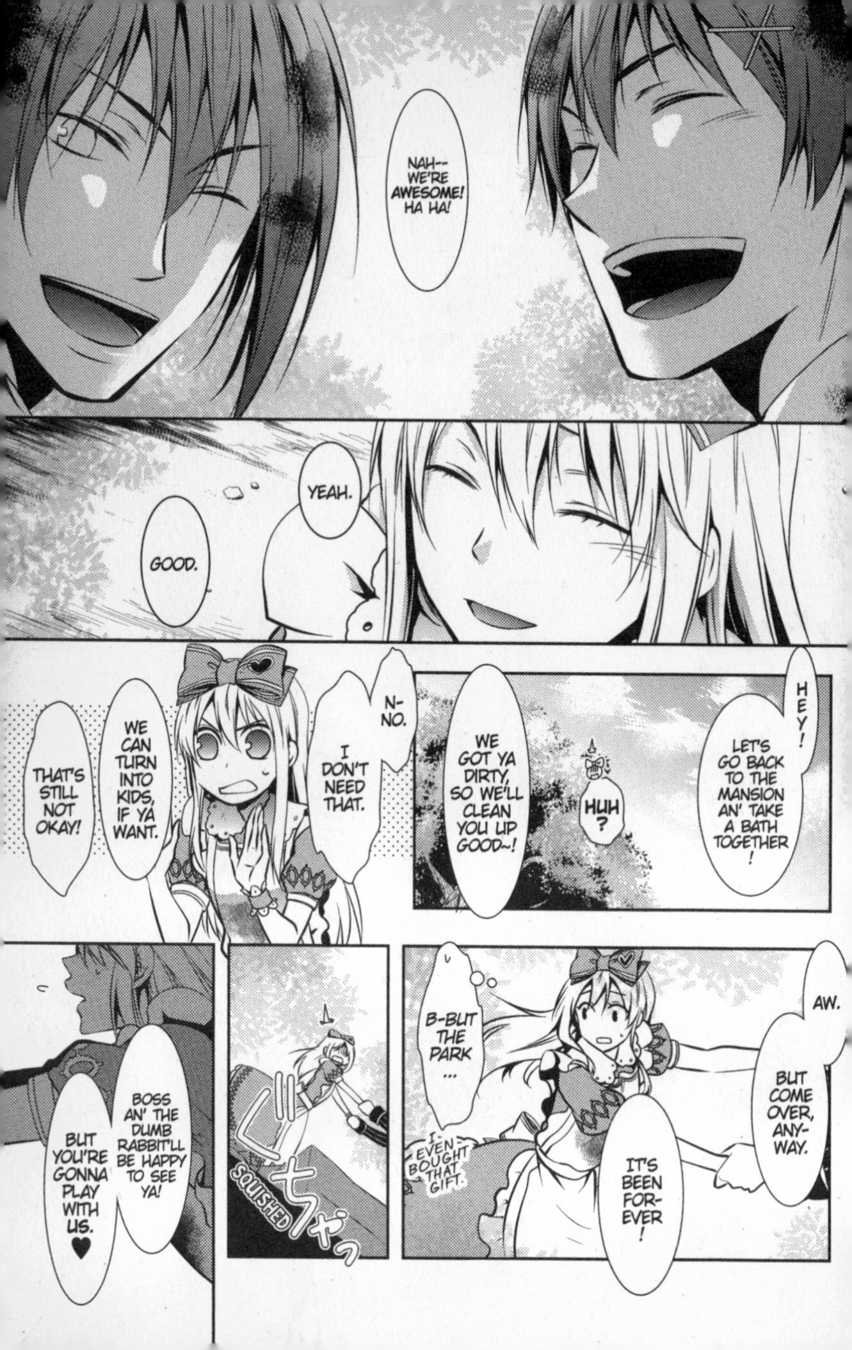
NAH-- WE'RE AWESOME! HA HA!
YEAH.
GOOD.
HEY! LET'S GO BACK TO THE MANSION AN' TAKE A BATH TOGETHER!
HUH?
WE GOT YA DIRTY, SO WE'LL CLEAN YOU UP GOOD~!
N-NO.
I DON'T NEED THAT.
WE CAN TURN INTO KIDS, IF YA WANT.
THAT'S STILL NOT OKAY!
AW.
BUT COME OVER, ANY-WAY.
IT'S BEEN FOR-EVER!
B-BUT THE PARK...
I-EVEN-BOUGHT THAT GIFT.
SQUISHED
BOSS AN' THE DUMB RABBIT'LL BE HAPPY TO SEE YA!
BUT YOU'RE GONNA PLAY WITH US. ♥

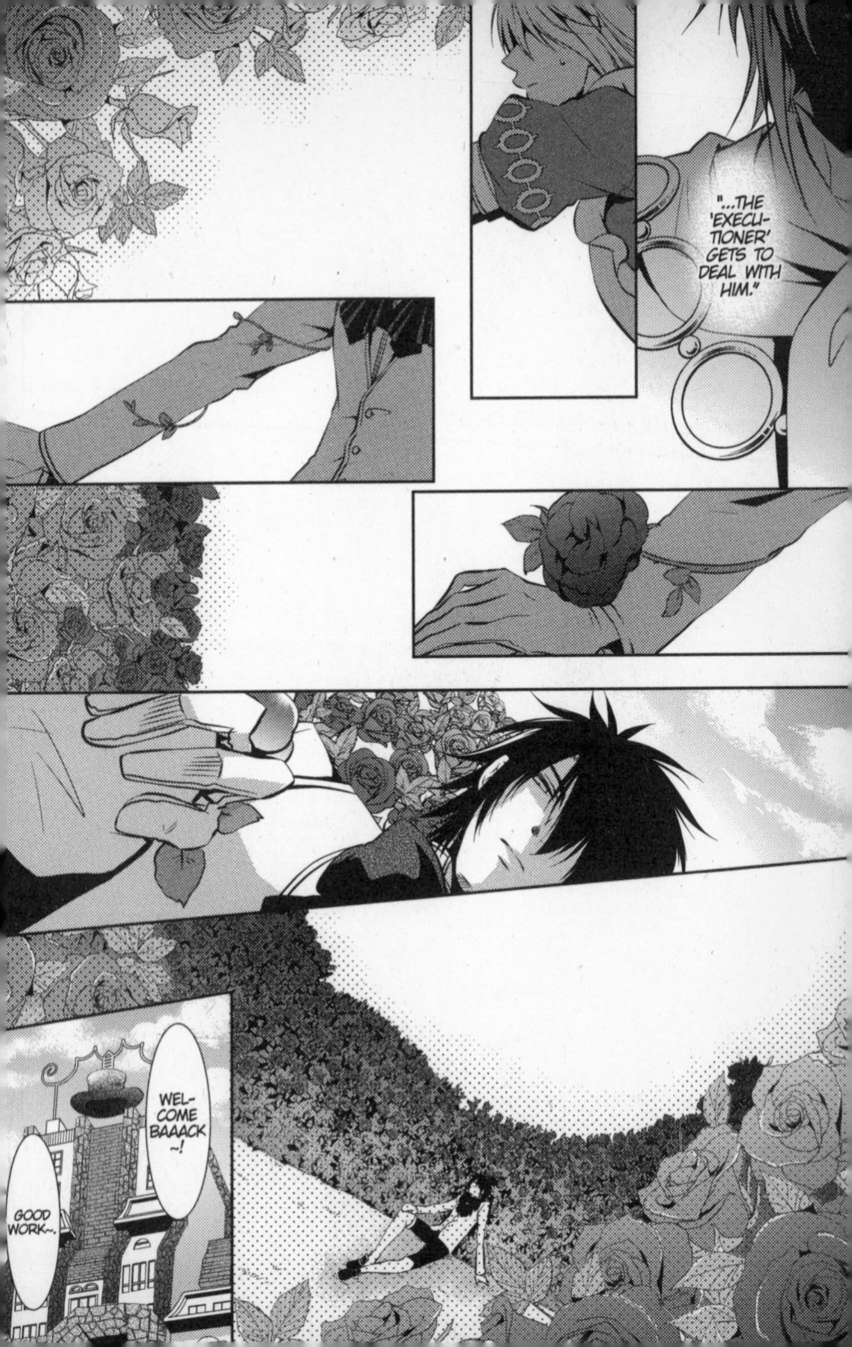
"...THE 'EXECUTIONER' GETS TO DEAL WITH HIM."
WEL-COME BAAACK~!
GOOD WORK~.

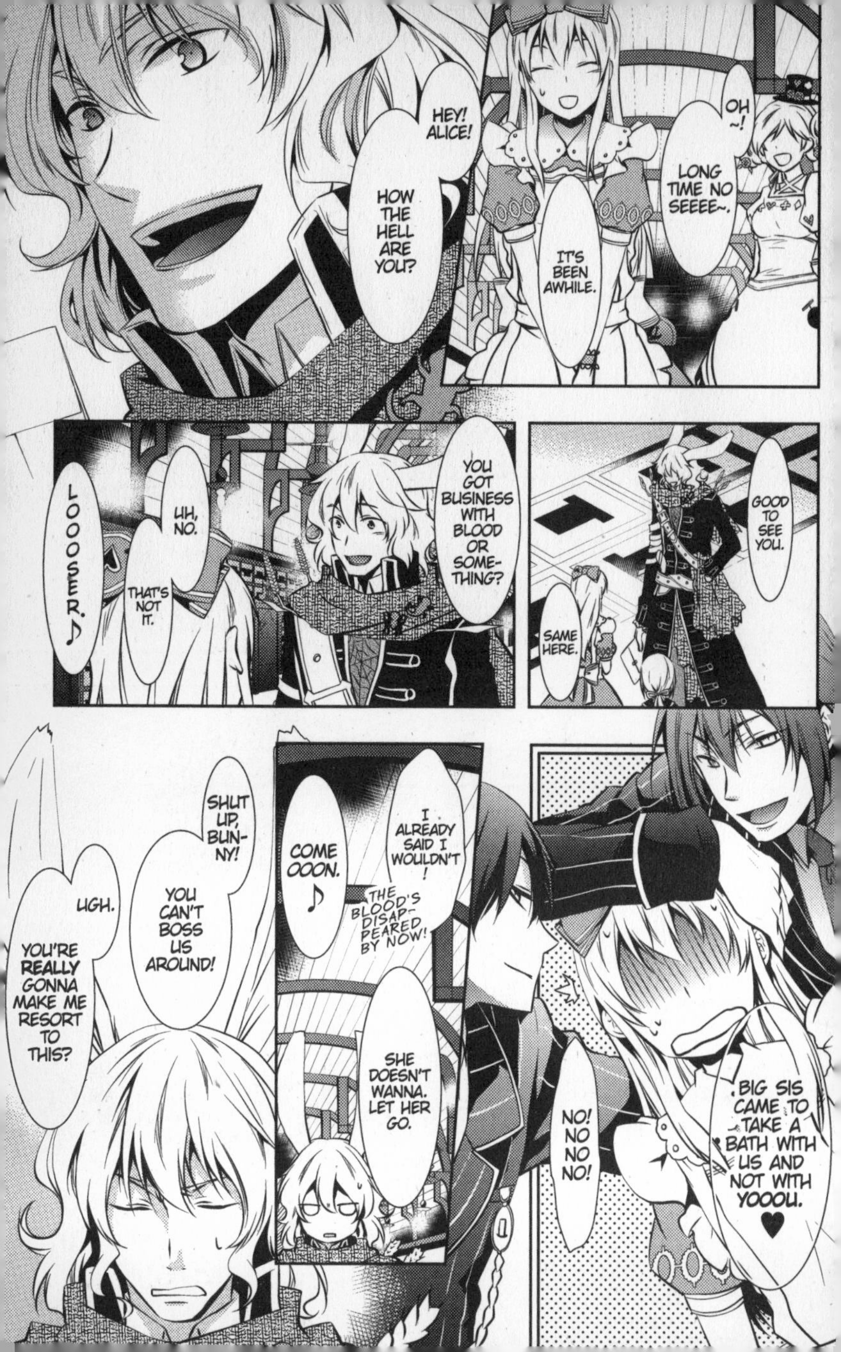
OH ~!
LONG TIME NO SEEEE~.
IT'S BEEN AWHILE.
HEY! ALICE!
HOW THE HELL ARE YOU?
GOOD TO SEE YOU.
SAME HERE.
YOU GOT BUSINESS WITH BLOOD OR SOMETHING?
UH, NO.
THAT'S NOT IT.
LOOOSER.♪
BIG SIS CAME TO TAKE A BATH WITH US AND NOT WITH YOOOU. ♥
NO! NO NO NO!
I ALREADY SAID I WOULDN'T!
COME OOON. ♪
THE BLOOD'S DISAPPEARED BY NOW!
SHE DOESN'T WANNA. LET HER GO.
SHUT UP, BUNNY!
YOU CAN'T BOSS US AROUND!
UGH.
YOU'RE REALLY GONNA MAKE ME RESORT TO THIS?

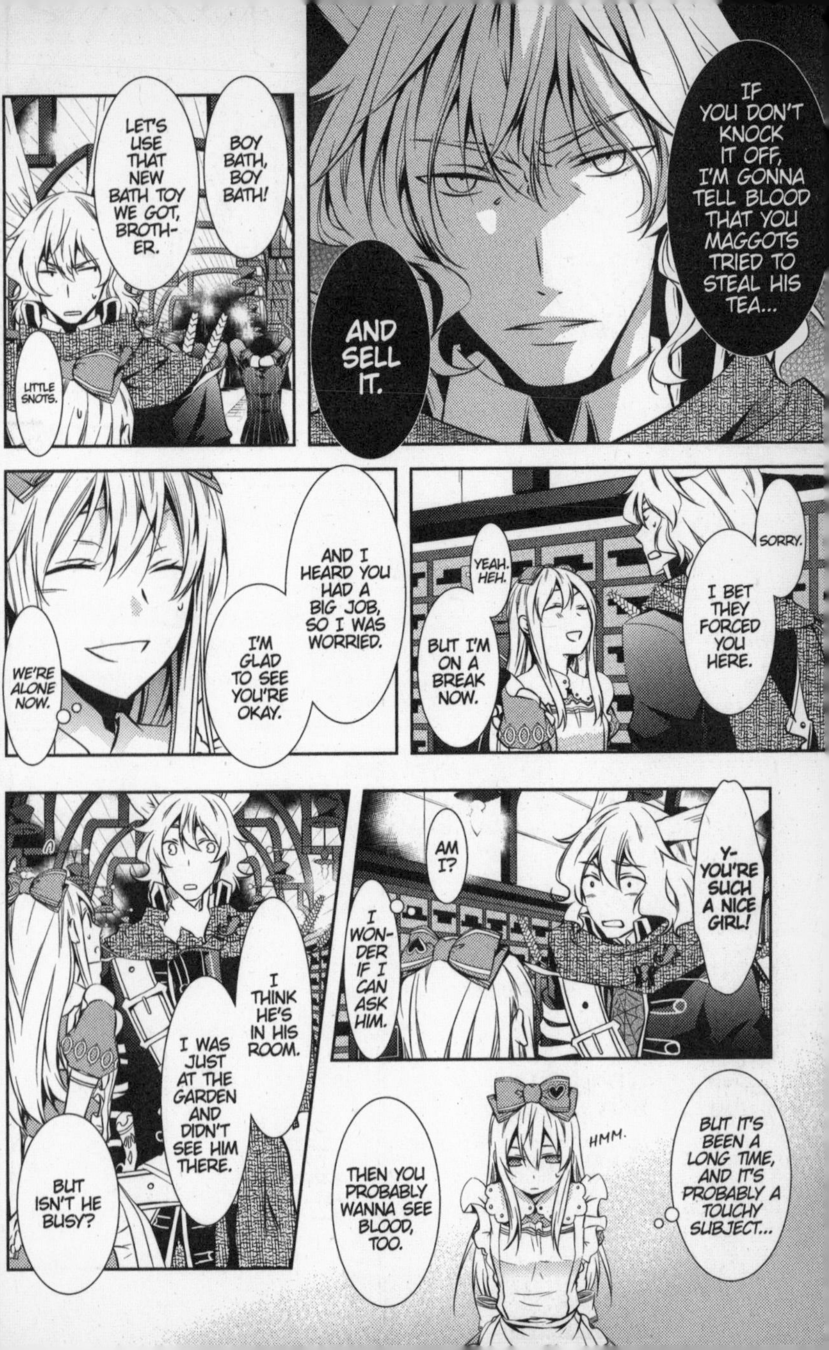
IF YOU DON'T KNOCK IT OFF, I'M GONNA TELL BLOOD THAT YOU MAGGOTS TRIED TO STEAL HIS TEA...
AND SELL IT.
BOY BATH, BOY BATH!
LET'S USE THAT NEW BATH TOY WE GOT, BROTHER.
LITTLE SNOTS.
SORRY.
I BET THEY FORCED YOU HERE.
YEAH. HEH.
BUT I'M ON A BREAK NOW.
AND I HEARD YOU HAD A BIG JOB, SO I WAS WORRIED.
I'M GLAD TO SEE YOU'RE OKAY.
WE'RE ALONE NOW.
Y-YOU'RE SUCH A NICE GIRL!
AM I?
I WONDER IF I CAN ASK HIM.
BUT IT'S BEEN A LONG TIME, AND IT'S PROBABLY A TOUCHY SUBJECT...
HMM.
THEN YOU PROBABLY WANNA SEE BLOOD, TOO.
I THINK HE'S IN HIS ROOM.
I WAS JUST AT THE GARDEN AND DIDN'T SEE HIM THERE.
BUT ISN'T HE BUSY?

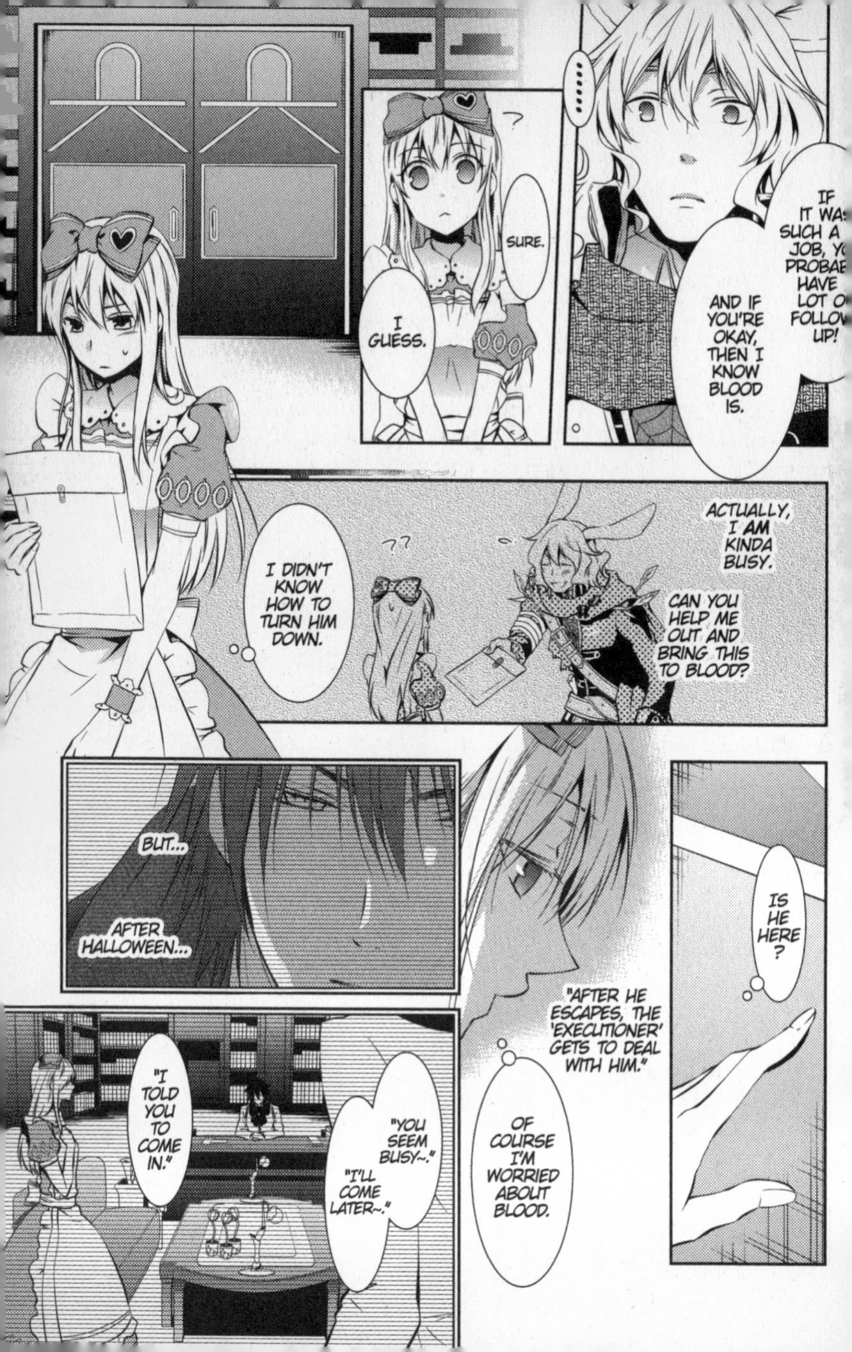
......
IF IT WAS SUCH A JOB, YO PROBAB HAVE LOT O FOLLOW UP!
AND IF YOU'RE OKAY, THEN I KNOW BLOOD IS.
?
SURE.
I GUESS.
ACTUALLY, I AM KINDA BUSY.
CAN YOU HELP ME OUT AND BRING THIS TO BLOOD?
??
I DIDN'T KNOW HOW TO TURN HIM DOWN.
IS HE HERE?
"AFTER HE ESCAPES, THE 'EXECUTIONER' GETS TO DEAL WITH HIM."
OF COURSE I'M WORRIED ABOUT BLOOD.
BUT...
AFTER HALLOWEEN...
"YOU SEEM BUSY~."
"I'LL COME LATER~."
"I TOLD YOU TO COME IN."

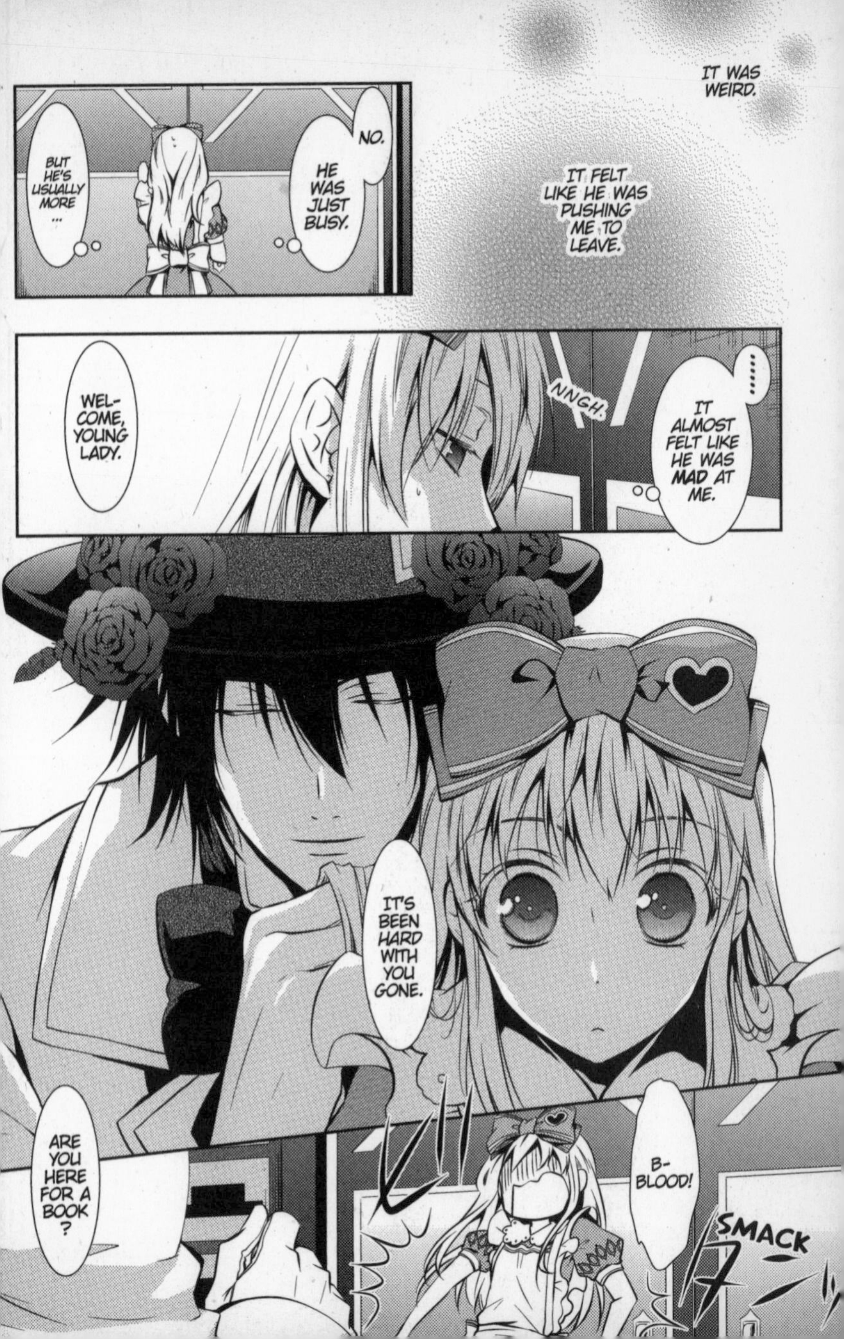
IT WAS WEIRD.
IT FELT LIKE HE WAS PUSHING ME TO LEAVE.
NO.
HE WAS JUST BUSY.
BUT HE'S USUALLY MORE ...
......
IT ALMOST FELT LIKE HE WAS MAD AT ME.
NNGH.
WEL-COME, YOUNG LADY.
IT'S BEEN HARD WITH YOU GONE.
SMACK
B-BLOOD!
ARE YOU HERE FOR A BOOK?

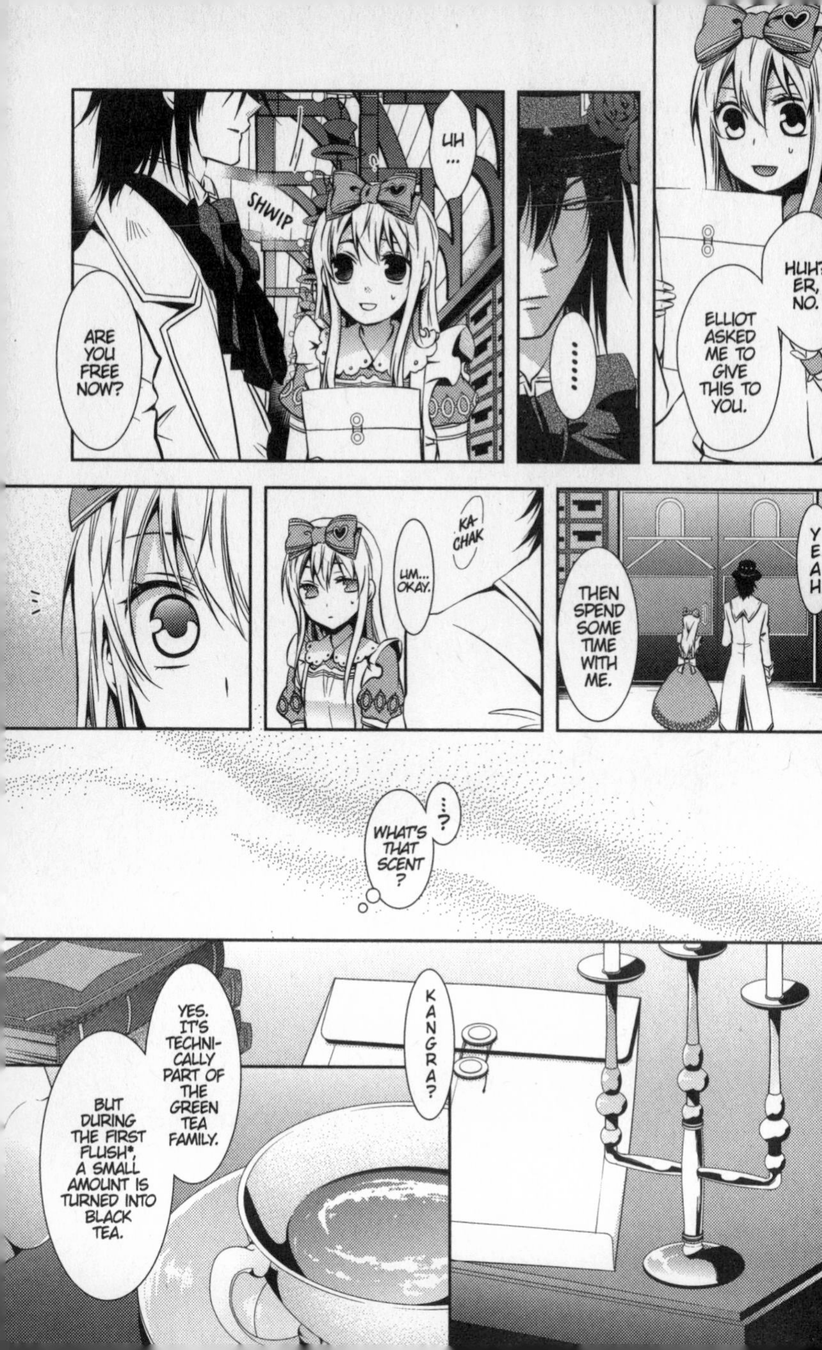
HUH? ER, NO.
ELLIOT ASKED ME TO GIVE THIS TO YOU.
......
UH ...
SHWIP
ARE YOU FREE NOW?
YEAH.
THEN SPEND SOME TIME WITH ME.
KA-CHAK
UM... OKAY.
...?
WHAT'S THAT SCENT?
KANGRA?
YES. IT'S TECHNICALLY PART OF THE GREEN TEA FAMILY.
BUT DURING THE FIRST FLUSH*, A SMALL AMOUNT IS TURNED INTO BLACK TEA.

*The first tea-picking season of the year.

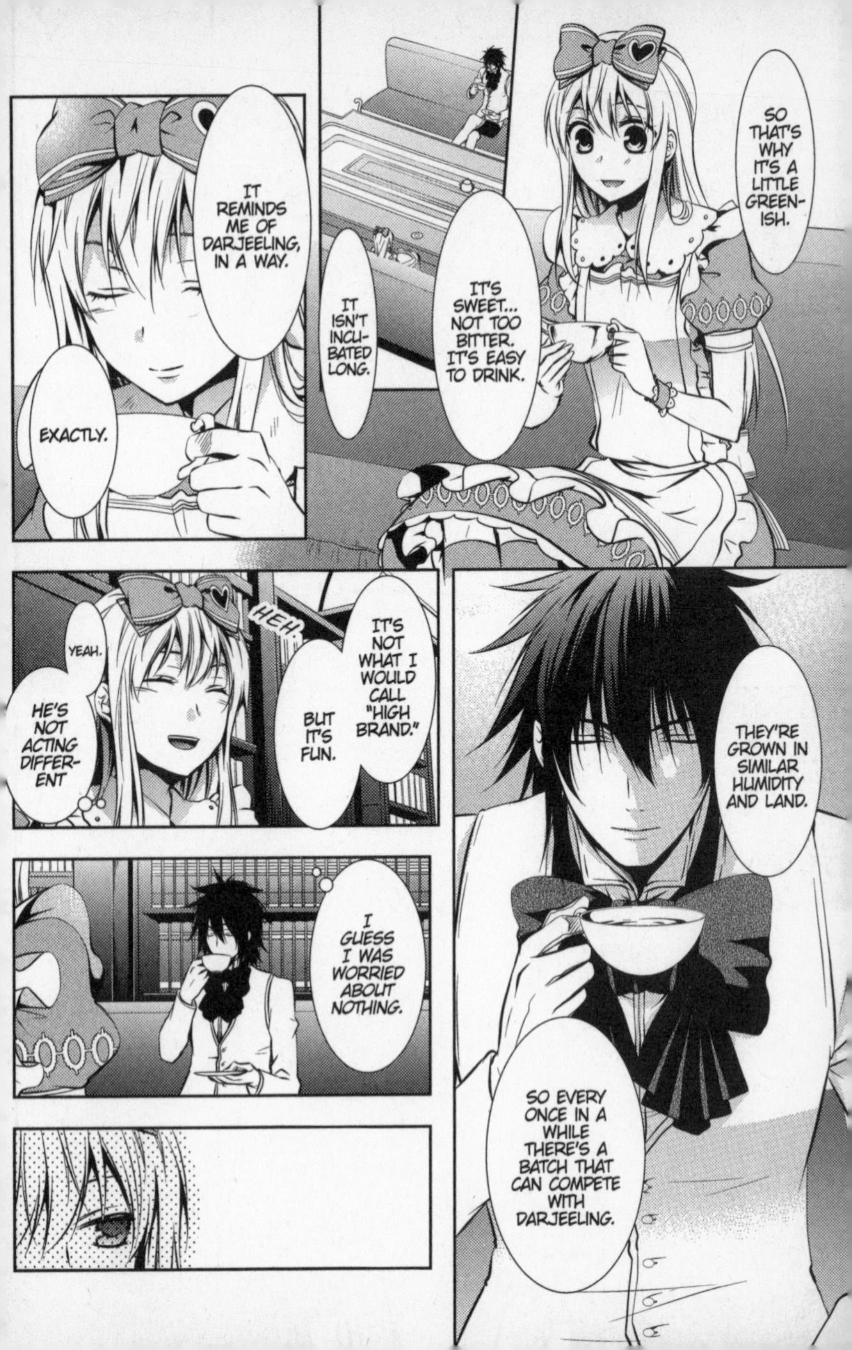
SO THAT'S WHY IT'S A LITTLE GREENISH.
IT'S SWEET... NOT TOO BITTER. IT'S EASY TO DRINK.
IT ISN'T INCUBATED LONG.
IT REMINDS ME OF DARJEELING, IN A WAY.
EXACTLY.
THEY'RE GROWN IN SIMILAR HUMIDITY AND LAND.
SO EVERY ONCE IN A WHILE THERE'S A BATCH THAT CAN COMPETE WITH DARJEELING.
IT'S NOT WHAT I WOULD CALL "HIGH BRAND."
HEH.
BUT IT'S FUN.
YEAH.
HE'S NOT ACTING DIFFERENT
I GUESS I WAS WORRIED ABOUT NOTHING.

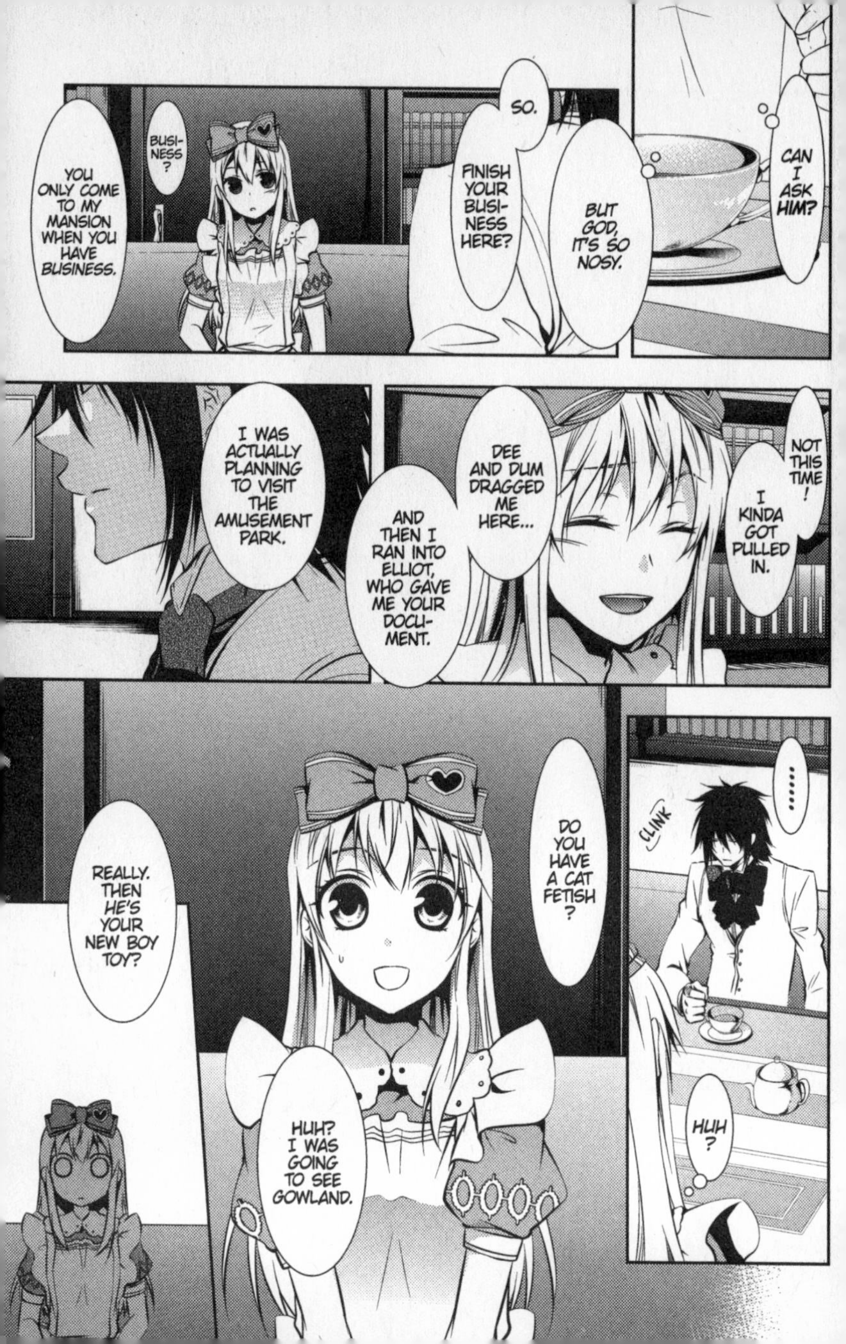
CAN I ASK HIM?
BUT GOD, IT'S SO NOSY.
SO.
FINISH YOUR BUSI-NESS HERE?
BUSI-NESS?
YOU ONLY COME TO MY MANSION WHEN YOU HAVE BUSINESS.
NOT THIS TIME!
I KINDA GOT PULLED IN.
DEE AND DUM DRAGGED ME HERE...
AND THEN I RAN INTO ELLIOT, WHO GAVE ME YOUR DOCU-MENT.
I WAS ACTUALLY PLANNING TO VISIT THE AMUSEMENT PARK.
......
CLINK
DO YOU HAVE A CAT FETISH?
HUH?
REALLY. THEN HE'S YOUR NEW BOY TOY?
HUH? I WAS GOING TO SEE GOWLAND.

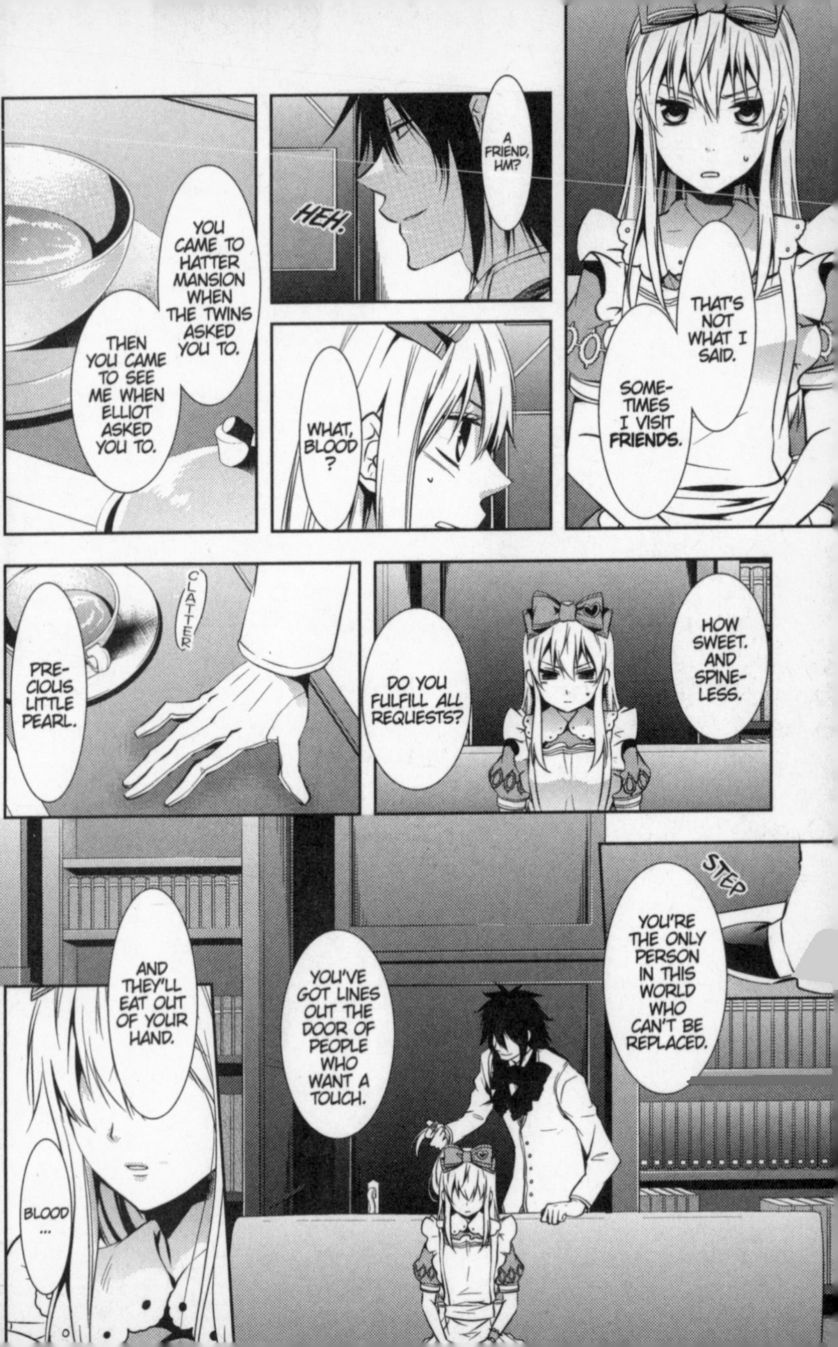
THAT'S NOT WHAT I SAID.
SOMETIMES I VISIT FRIENDS.
A FRIEND, HM?
HEH.
WHAT, BLOOD?
YOU CAME TO HATTER MANSION WHEN THE TWINS ASKED YOU TO.
THEN YOU CAME TO SEE ME WHEN ELLIOT ASKED YOU TO.
HOW SWEET. AND SPINELESS.
DO YOU FULFILL ALL REQUESTS?
CLATTER
PRECIOUS LITTLE PEARL.
STEP
YOU'RE THE ONLY PERSON IN THIS WORLD WHO CAN'T BE REPLACED.
YOU'VE GOT LINES OUT THE DOOR OF PEOPLE WHO WANT A TOUCH.
AND THEY'LL EAT OUT OF YOUR HAND.
BLOOD...

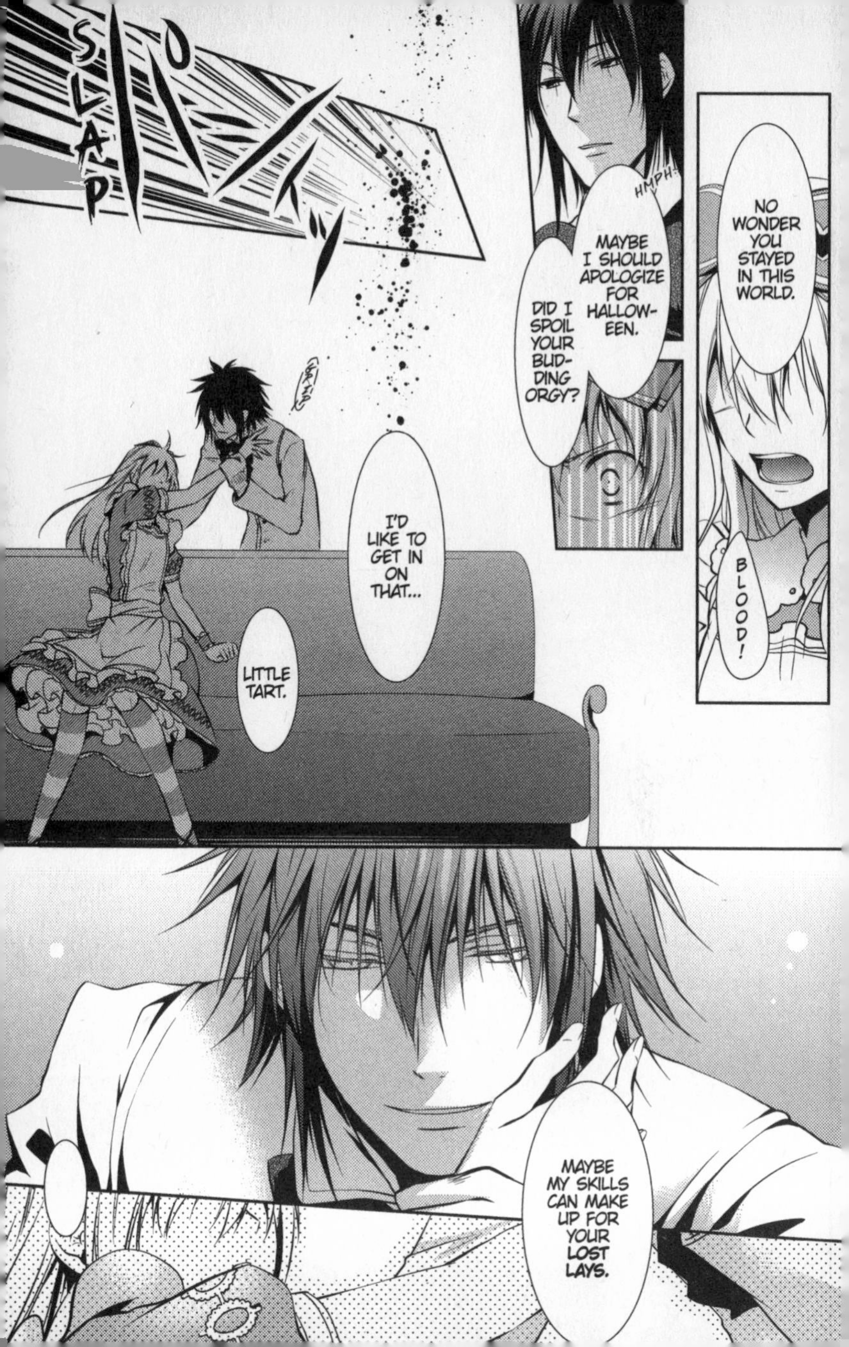
NO WONDER YOU STAYED IN THIS WORLD.
BLOOD!
HMPH!
MAYBE I SHOULD APOLOGIZE FOR HALLOWEEN.
DID I SPOIL YOUR BUDDING ORGY?
SLAP
I'D LIKE TO GET IN ON THAT...
LITTLE TART.
MAYBE MY SKILLS CAN MAKE UP FOR YOUR LOST LAYS.

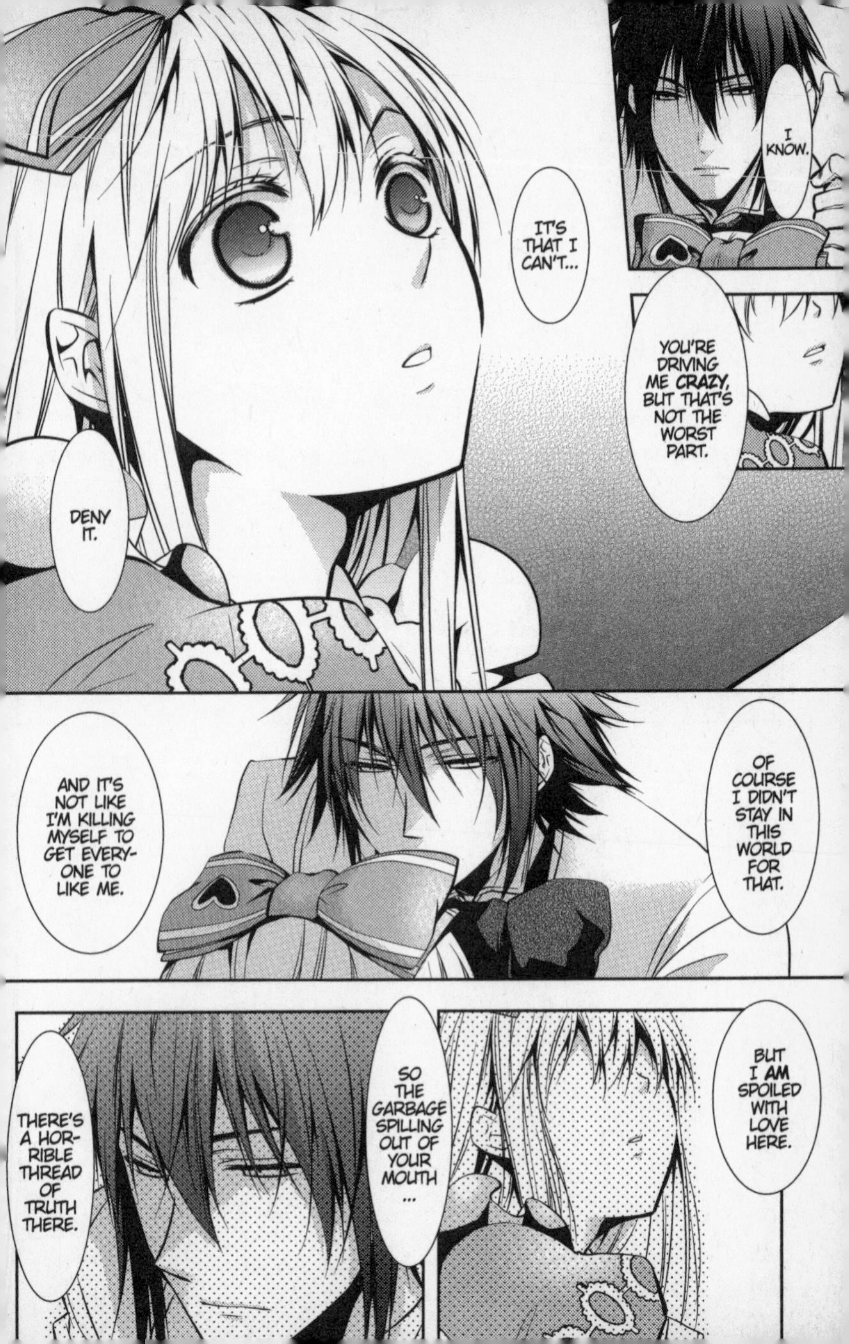
I KNOW.
YOU'RE DRIVING ME **CRAZY**, BUT THAT'S NOT THE WORST PART.
IT'S THAT I CAN'T...
DENY IT.
OF COURSE I DIDN'T STAY IN THIS WORLD FOR THAT.
AND IT'S NOT LIKE I'M KILLING MYSELF TO GET EVERY-ONE TO LIKE ME.
BUT I **AM** SPOILED WITH LOVE HERE.
SO THE GARBAGE SPILLING OUT OF YOUR MOUTH...
THERE'S A HOR-RIBLE THREAD OF TRUTH THERE.

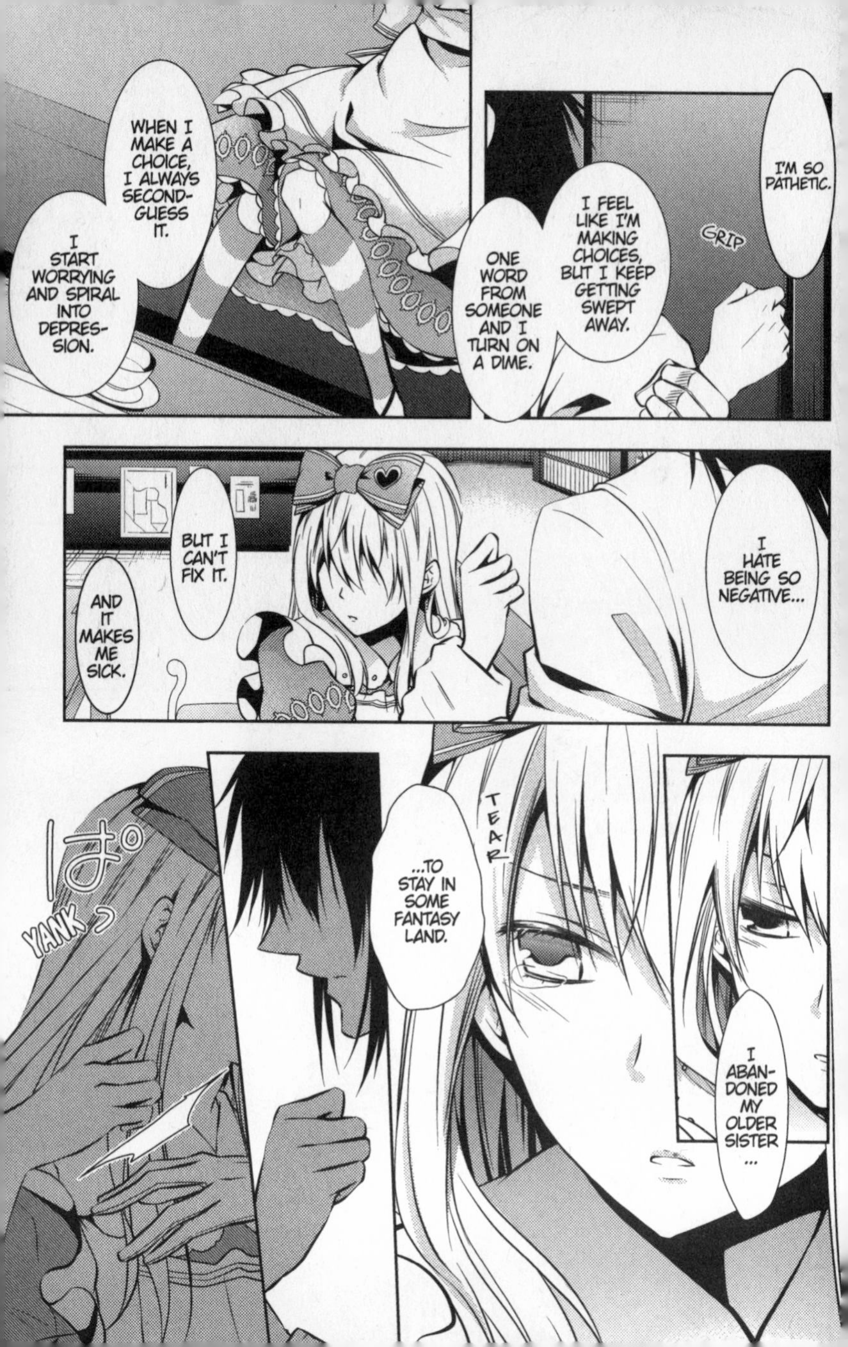
I'M SO PATHETIC.
GRIP
I FEEL LIKE I'M MAKING CHOICES, BUT I KEEP GETTING SWEPT AWAY.
ONE WORD FROM SOMEONE AND I TURN ON A DIME.
WHEN I MAKE A CHOICE, I ALWAYS SECOND-GUESS IT.
I START WORRYING AND SPIRAL INTO DEPRESSION.
I HATE BEING SO NEGATIVE...
BUT I CAN'T FIX IT.
AND IT MAKES ME SICK.
I ABANDONED MY OLDER SISTER...
TEAR
...TO STAY IN SOME FANTASY LAND.
ぱっ
YANK

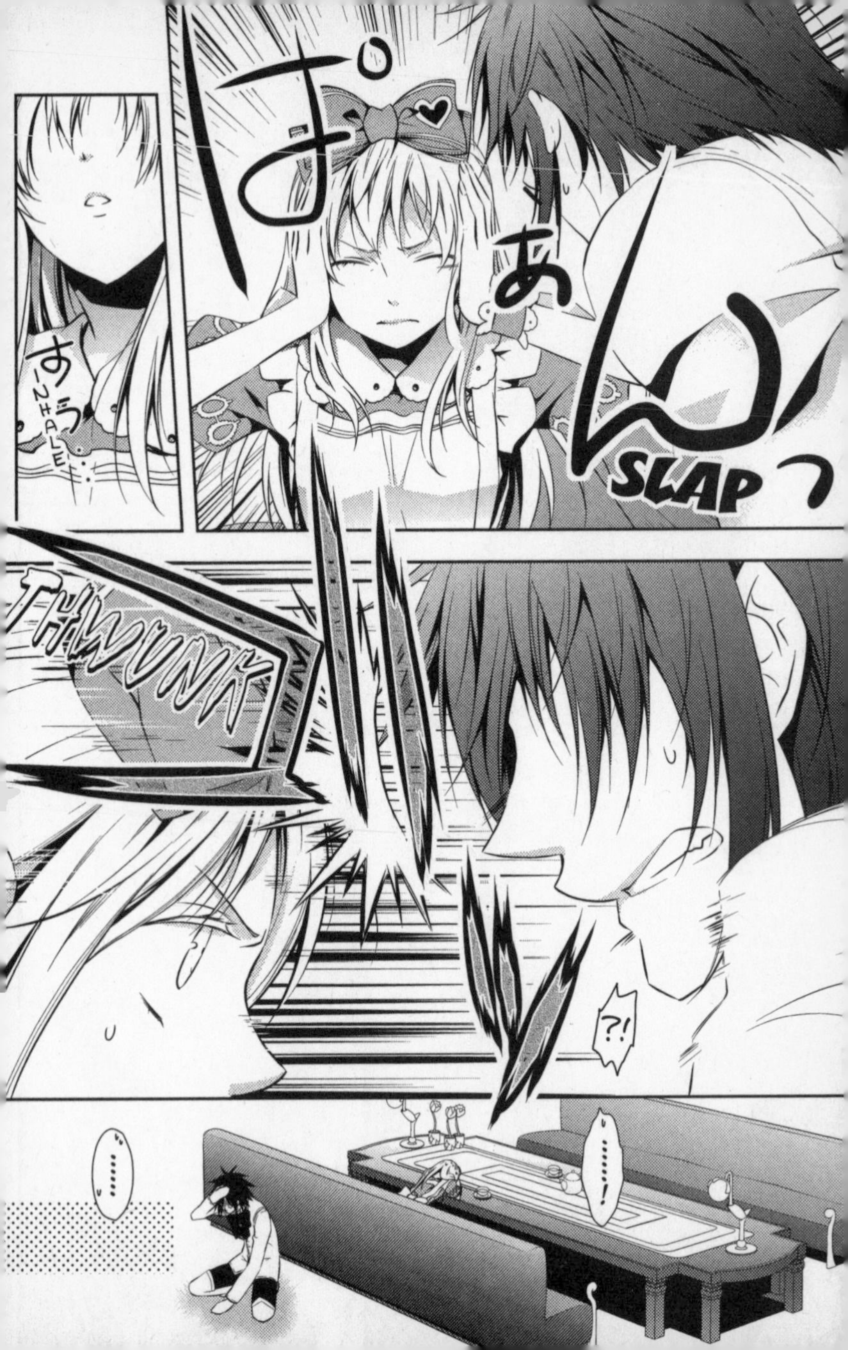
ぱあんっ
SLAP
すぅ
INHALE
THWUNK
?!
......!
......

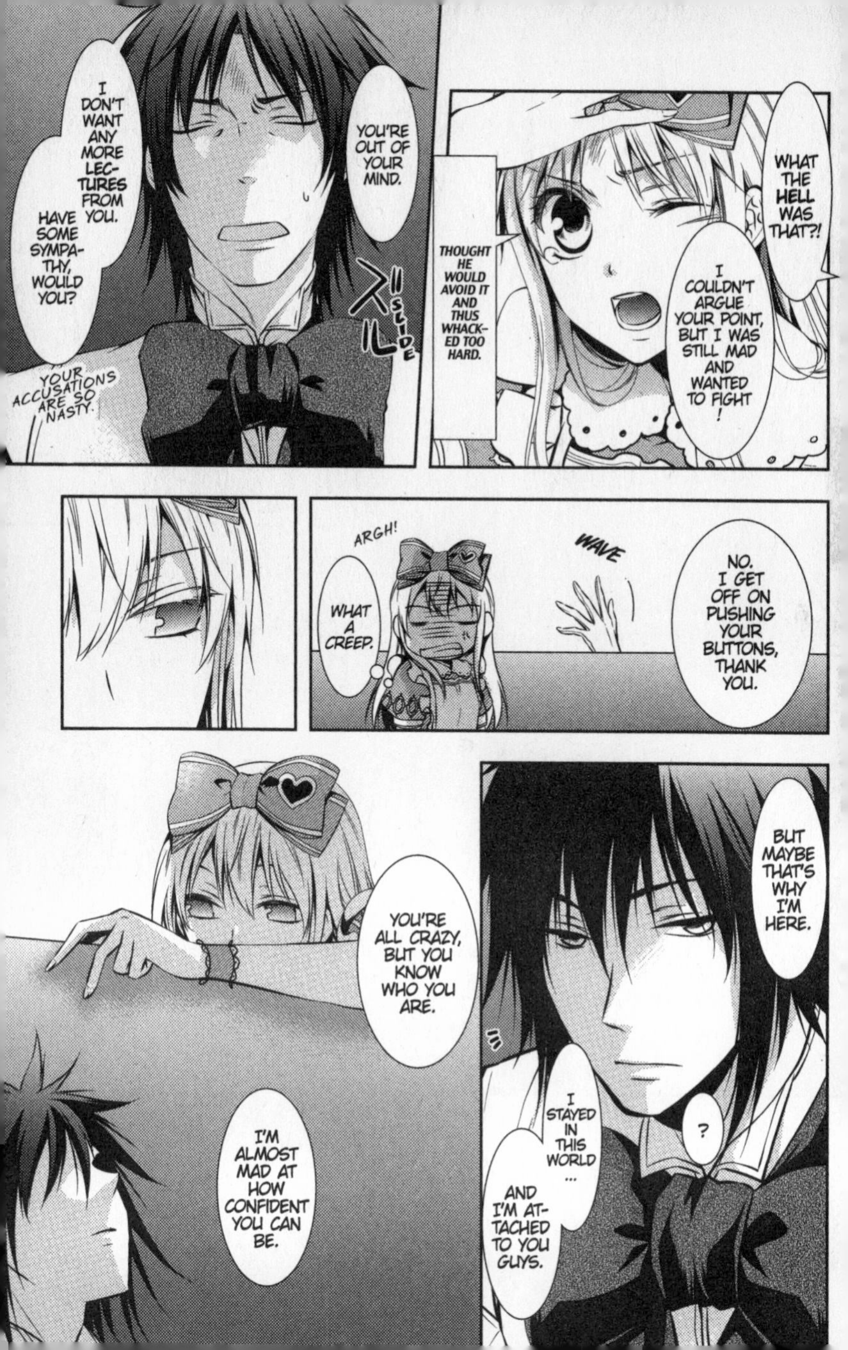
WHAT THE HELL WAS THAT?!
I COULDN'T ARGUE YOUR POINT, BUT I WAS STILL MAD AND WANTED TO FIGHT!
THOUGHT HE WOULD AVOID IT AND THUS WHACKED TOO HARD.
YOU'RE OUT OF YOUR MIND.
I DON'T WANT ANY MORE LECTURES FROM YOU.
HAVE SOME SYMPATHY, WOULD YOU?
SLIDE
YOUR ACCUSATIONS ARE SO NASTY.
WAVE
NO. I GET OFF ON PUSHING YOUR BUTTONS, THANK YOU.
ARGH!
WHAT A CREEP.
BUT MAYBE THAT'S WHY I'M HERE.
?
I STAYED IN THIS WORLD...
AND I'M ATTACHED TO YOU GUYS.
YOU'RE ALL CRAZY, BUT YOU KNOW WHO YOU ARE.
I'M ALMOST MAD AT HOW CONFIDENT YOU CAN BE.

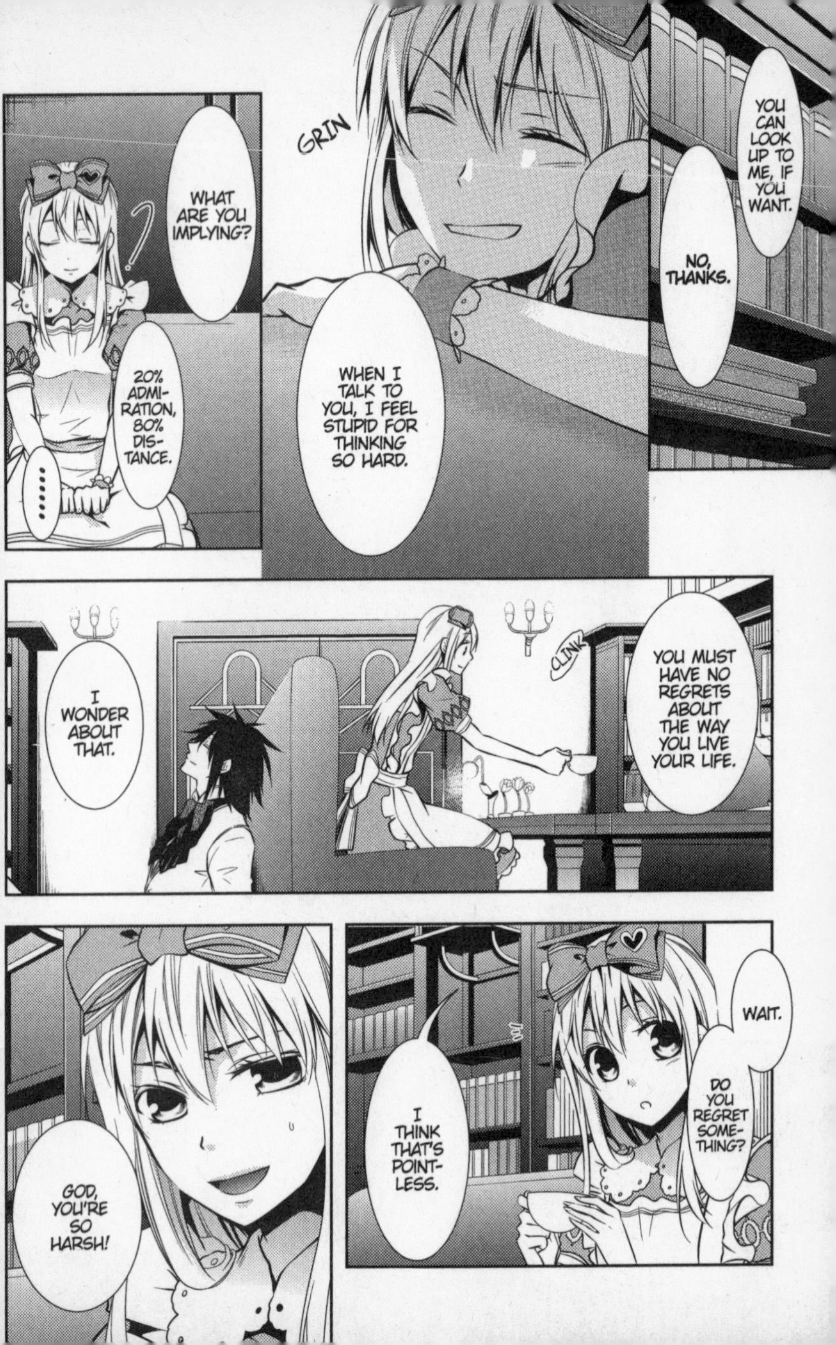
YOU CAN LOOK UP TO ME, IF YOU WANT.
NO, THANKS.
GRIN
WHEN I TALK TO YOU, I FEEL STUPID FOR THINKING SO HARD.
WHAT ARE YOU IMPLYING?
20% ADMIRATION, 80% DISTANCE.
......
CLINK
YOU MUST HAVE NO REGRETS ABOUT THE WAY YOU LIVE YOUR LIFE.
I WONDER ABOUT THAT.
WAIT.
DO YOU REGRET SOMETHING?
I THINK THAT'S POINTLESS.
GOD, YOU'RE SO HARSH!

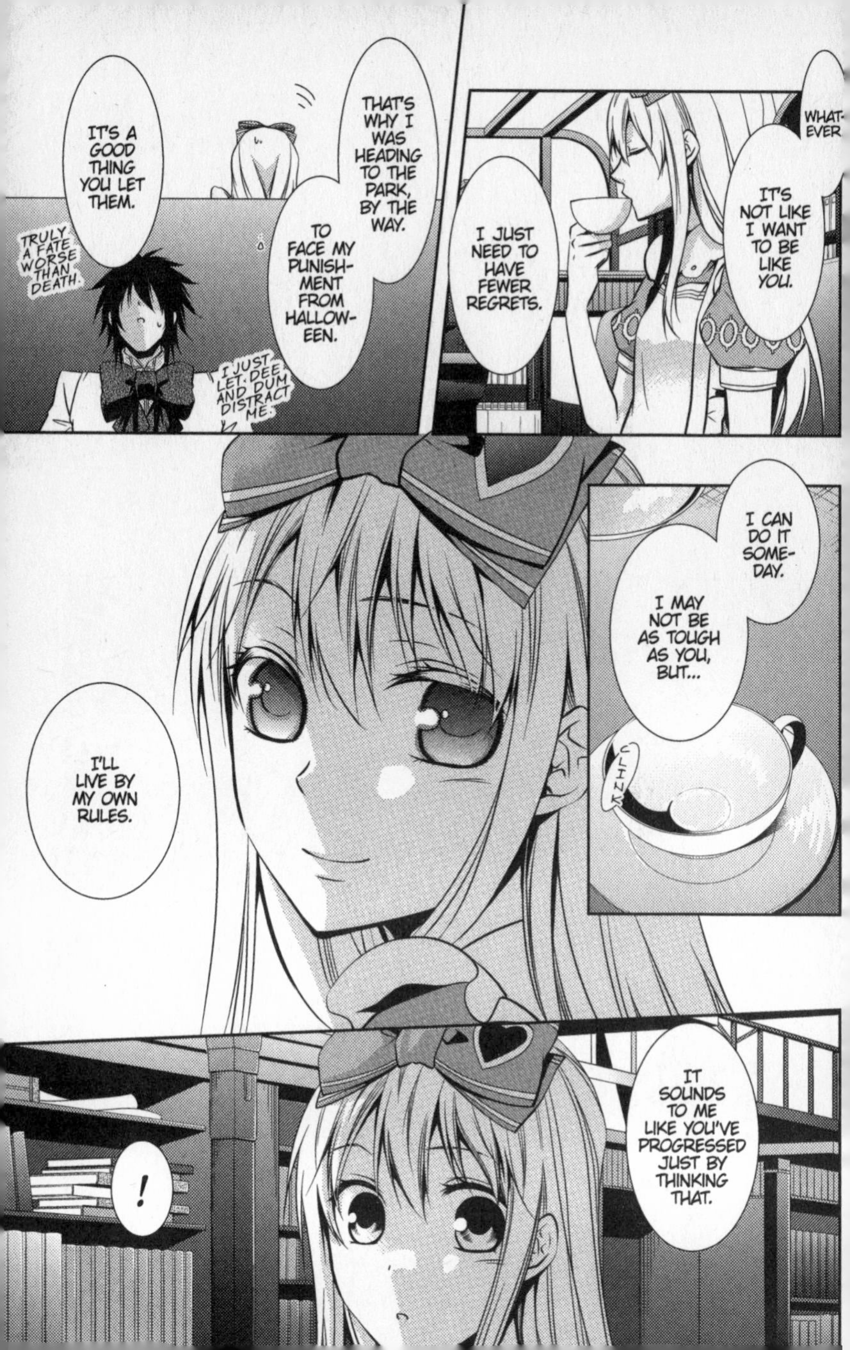
WHATEVER
IT'S NOT LIKE I WANT TO BE LIKE YOU.
I JUST NEED TO HAVE FEWER REGRETS.
THAT'S WHY I WAS HEADING TO THE PARK, BY THE WAY.
TO FACE MY PUNISHMENT FROM HALLOWEEN.
I JUST LET DEE AND DUM DISTRACT ME.
IT'S A GOOD THING YOU LET THEM.
TRULY A FATE WORSE THAN DEATH.
I CAN DO IT SOMEDAY.
I MAY NOT BE AS TOUGH AS YOU, BUT...
CLINK
I'LL LIVE BY MY OWN RULES.
IT SOUNDS TO ME LIKE YOU'VE PROGRESSED JUST BY THINKING THAT.
!

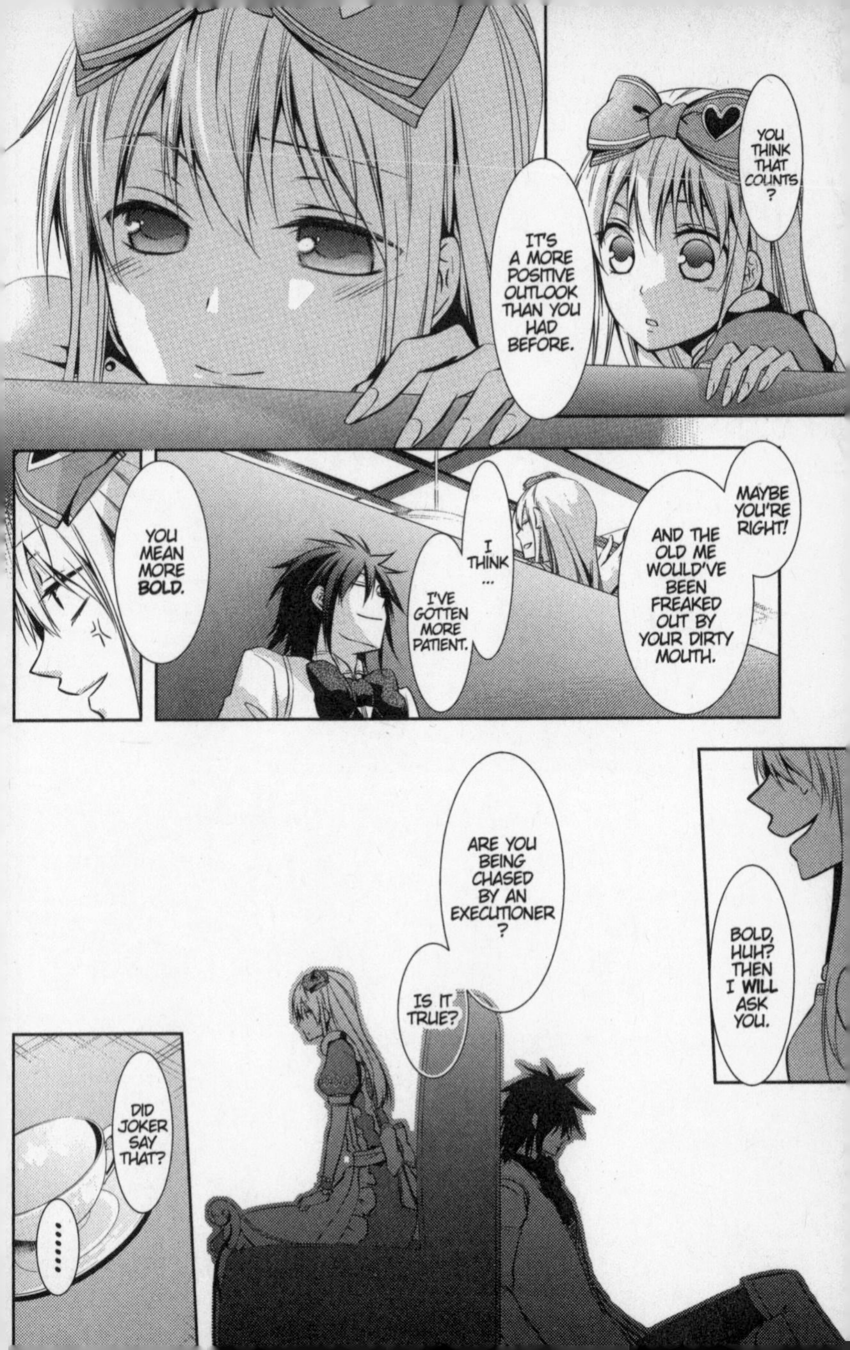
YOU THINK THAT COUNTS?
IT'S A MORE POSITIVE OUTLOOK THAN YOU HAD BEFORE.
MAYBE YOU'RE RIGHT!
AND THE OLD ME WOULD'VE BEEN FREAKED OUT BY YOUR DIRTY MOUTH.
I THINK...
I'VE GOTTEN MORE PATIENT.
YOU MEAN MORE BOLD.
BOLD, HUH? THEN I WILL ASK YOU.
ARE YOU BEING CHASED BY AN EXECUTIONER?
IS IT TRUE?
DID JOKER SAY THAT?
......

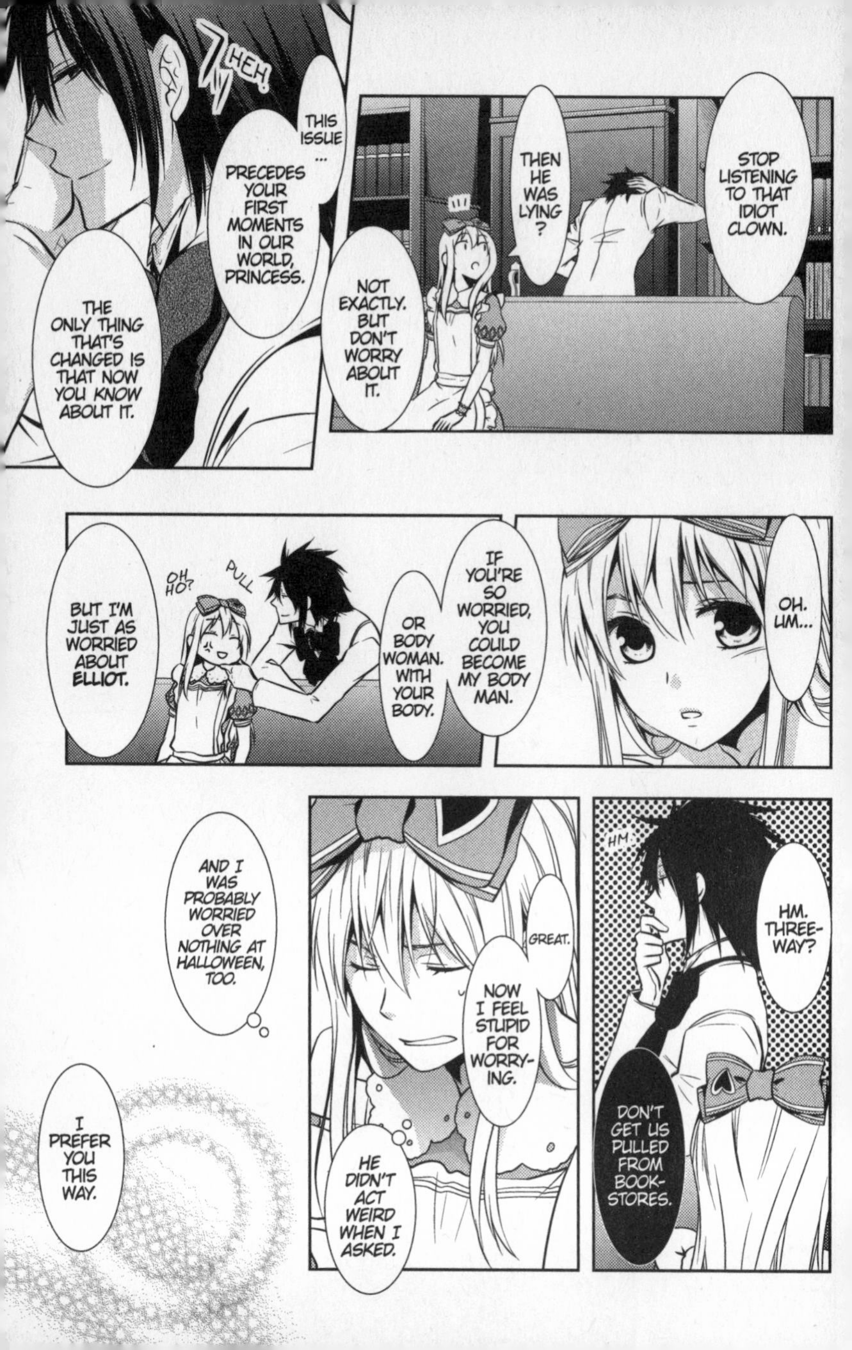
STOP LISTENING TO THAT IDIOT CLOWN.
THEN HE WAS LYING?
NOT EXACTLY. BUT DON'T WORRY ABOUT IT.
HEH
THIS ISSUE ...
PRECEDES YOUR FIRST MOMENTS IN OUR WORLD, PRINCESS.
THE ONLY THING THAT'S CHANGED IS THAT NOW YOU KNOW ABOUT IT.
OH. UM...
IF YOU'RE SO WORRIED, YOU COULD BECOME MY BODY MAN.
OR BODY WOMAN. WITH YOUR BODY.
PULL
OH HO?
BUT I'M JUST AS WORRIED ABOUT ELLIOT.
HM.
HM. THREE-WAY?
DON'T GET US PULLED FROM BOOK-STORES.
GREAT.
NOW I FEEL STUPID FOR WORRY-ING.
HE DIDN'T ACT WEIRD WHEN I ASKED.
AND I WAS PROBABLY WORRIED OVER NOTHING AT HALLOWEEN, TOO.
I PREFER YOU THIS WAY.

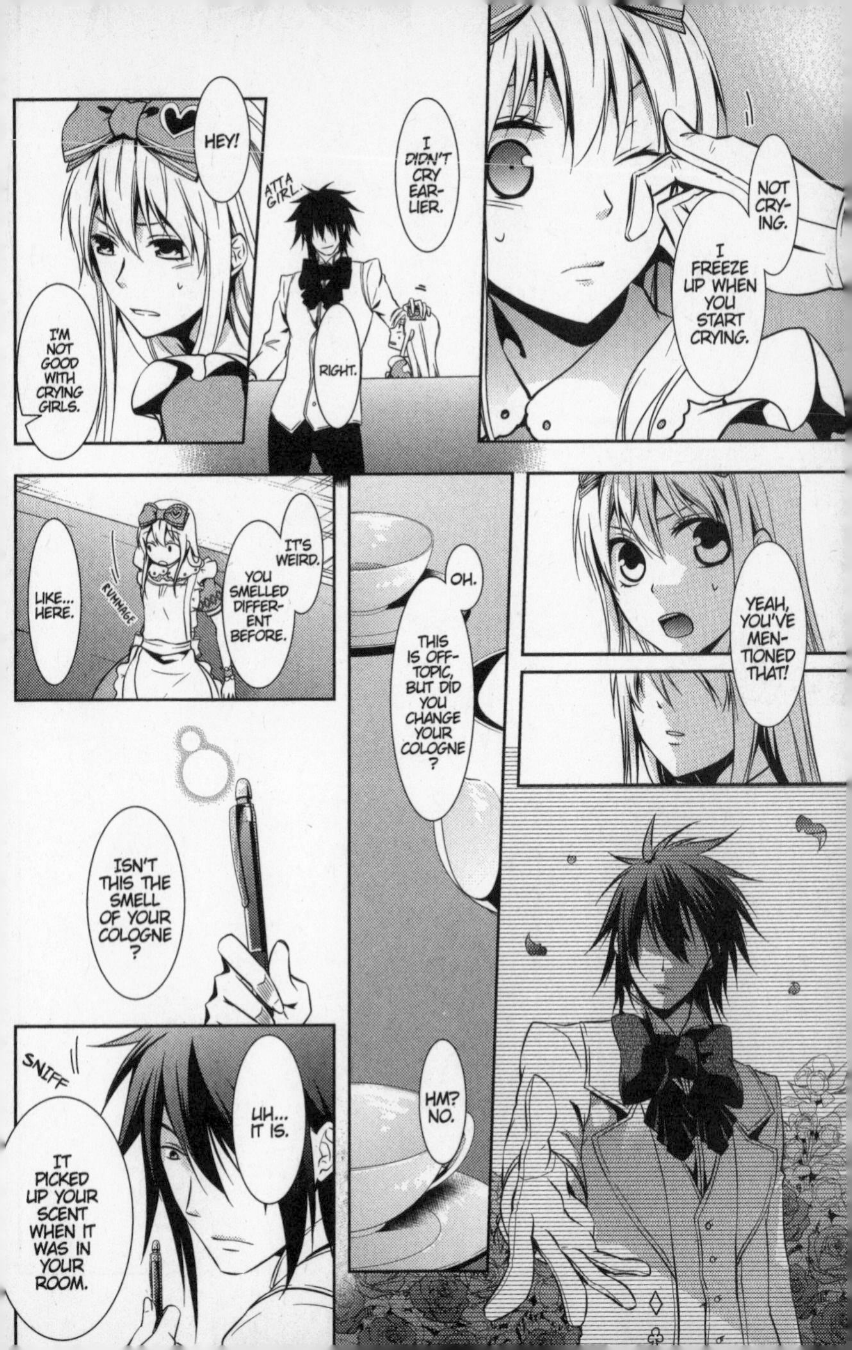
NOT CRYING.
I FREEZE UP WHEN YOU START CRYING.
I DIDN'T CRY EARLIER.
HEY!
ATTA GIRL.
I'M NOT GOOD WITH CRYING GIRLS.
RIGHT.
YEAH, YOU'VE MENTIONED THAT!
OH.
THIS IS OFF-TOPIC, BUT DID YOU CHANGE YOUR COLOGNE?
HM? NO.
IT'S WEIRD. YOU SMELLED DIFFERENT BEFORE.
RUMMAGE
LIKE... HERE.
ISN'T THIS THE SMELL OF YOUR COLOGNE?
UH... IT IS.
SNIFF
IT PICKED UP YOUR SCENT WHEN IT WAS IN YOUR ROOM.

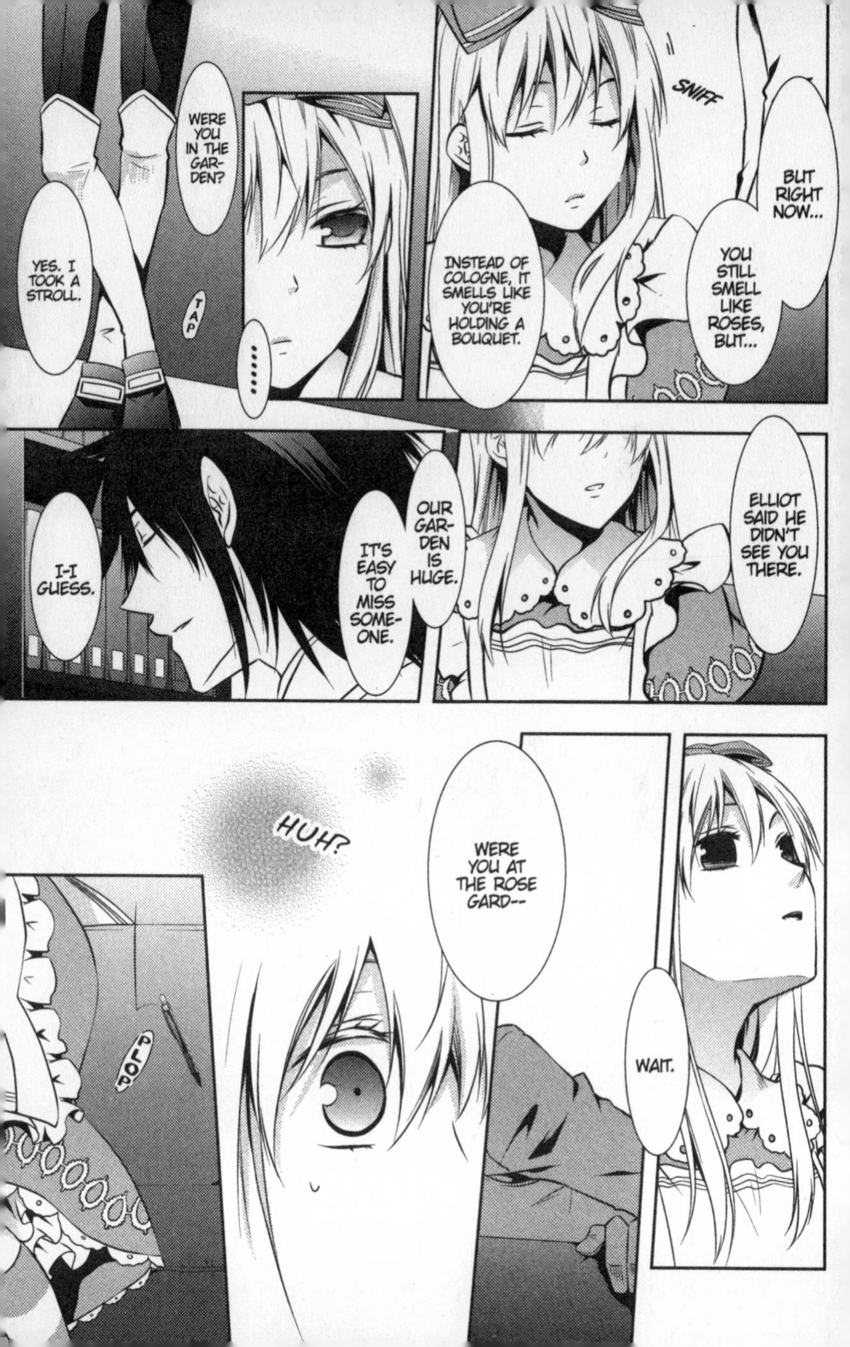
SNIFF
BUT RIGHT NOW...
YOU STILL SMELL LIKE ROSES, BUT...
INSTEAD OF COLOGNE, IT SMELLS LIKE YOU'RE HOLDING A BOUQUET.
WERE YOU IN THE GAR- DEN?
......
TAP
YES. I TOOK A STROLL.
ELLIOT SAID HE DIDN'T SEE YOU THERE.
OUR GAR- DEN IS HUGE.
IT'S EASY TO MISS SOME- ONE.
I-I GUESS.
WERE YOU AT THE ROSE GARD--
WAIT.
HUH?
PLOP

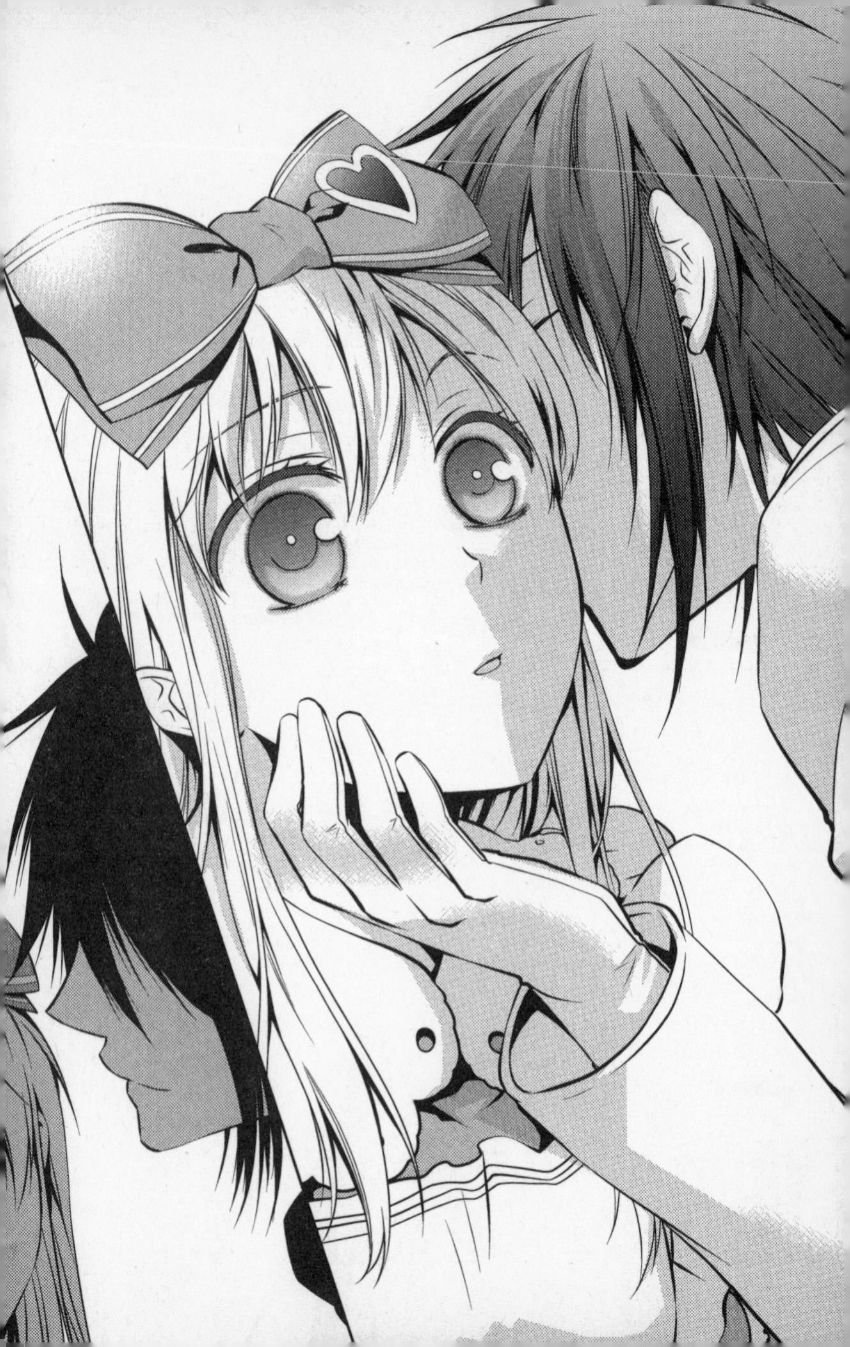

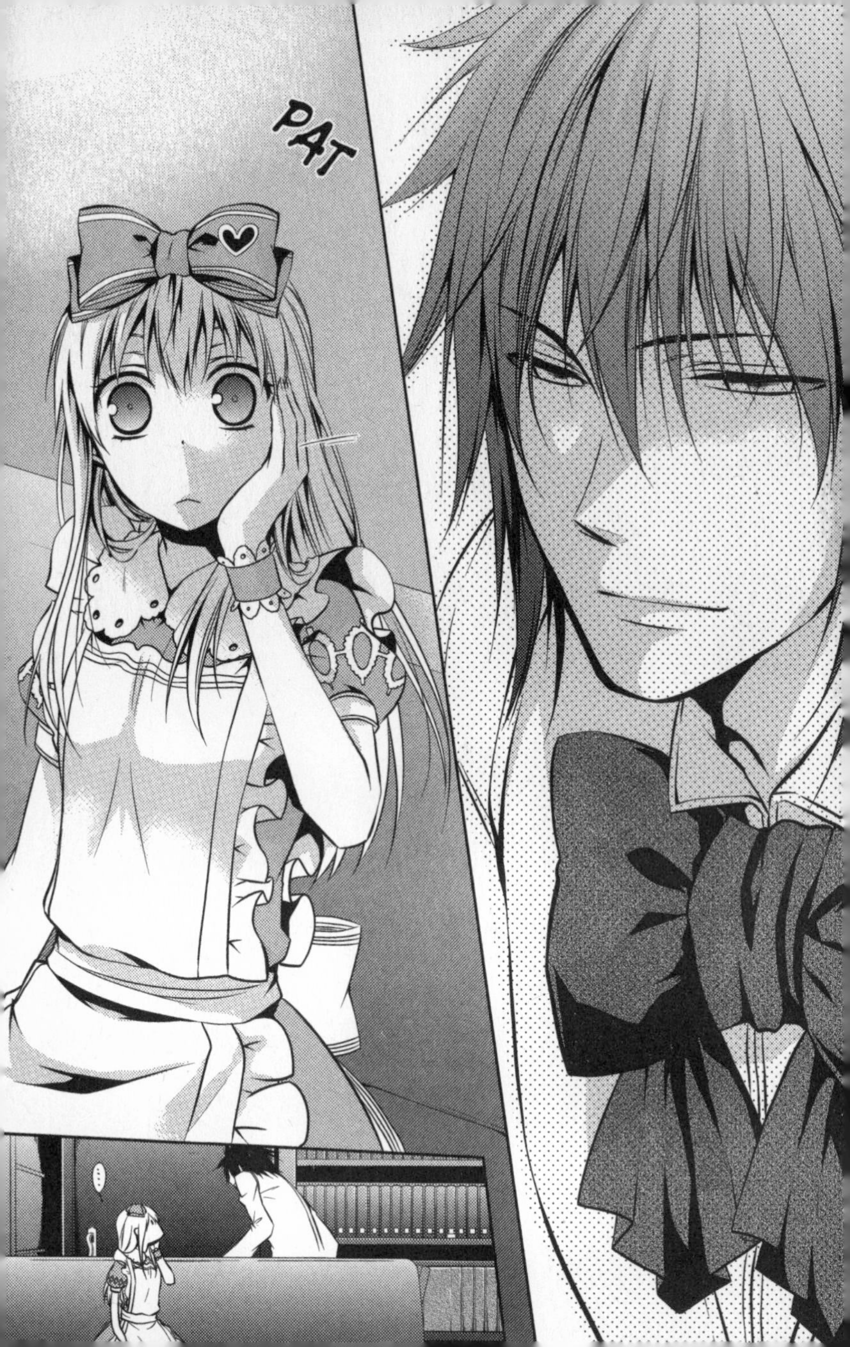
PAT
...

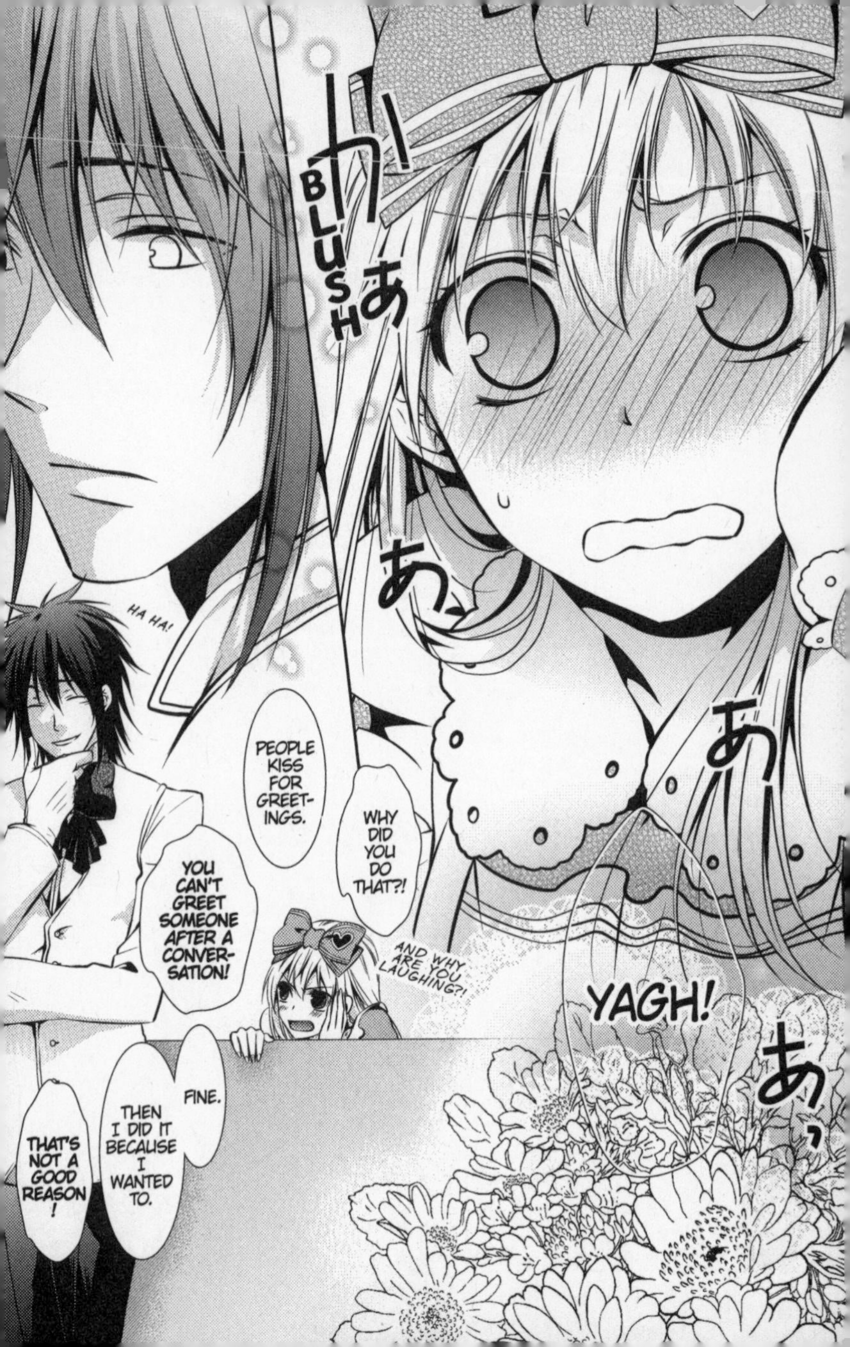
わー
BLUSH
あ
あ
あ
あ
YAGH!
WHY DID YOU DO THAT?!
PEOPLE KISS FOR GREETINGS.
HA HA!
AND WHY ARE YOU LAUGHING?!
YOU CAN'T GREET SOMEONE AFTER A CONVERSATION!
FINE.
THEN I DID IT BECAUSE I WANTED TO.
THAT'S NOT A GOOD REASON!

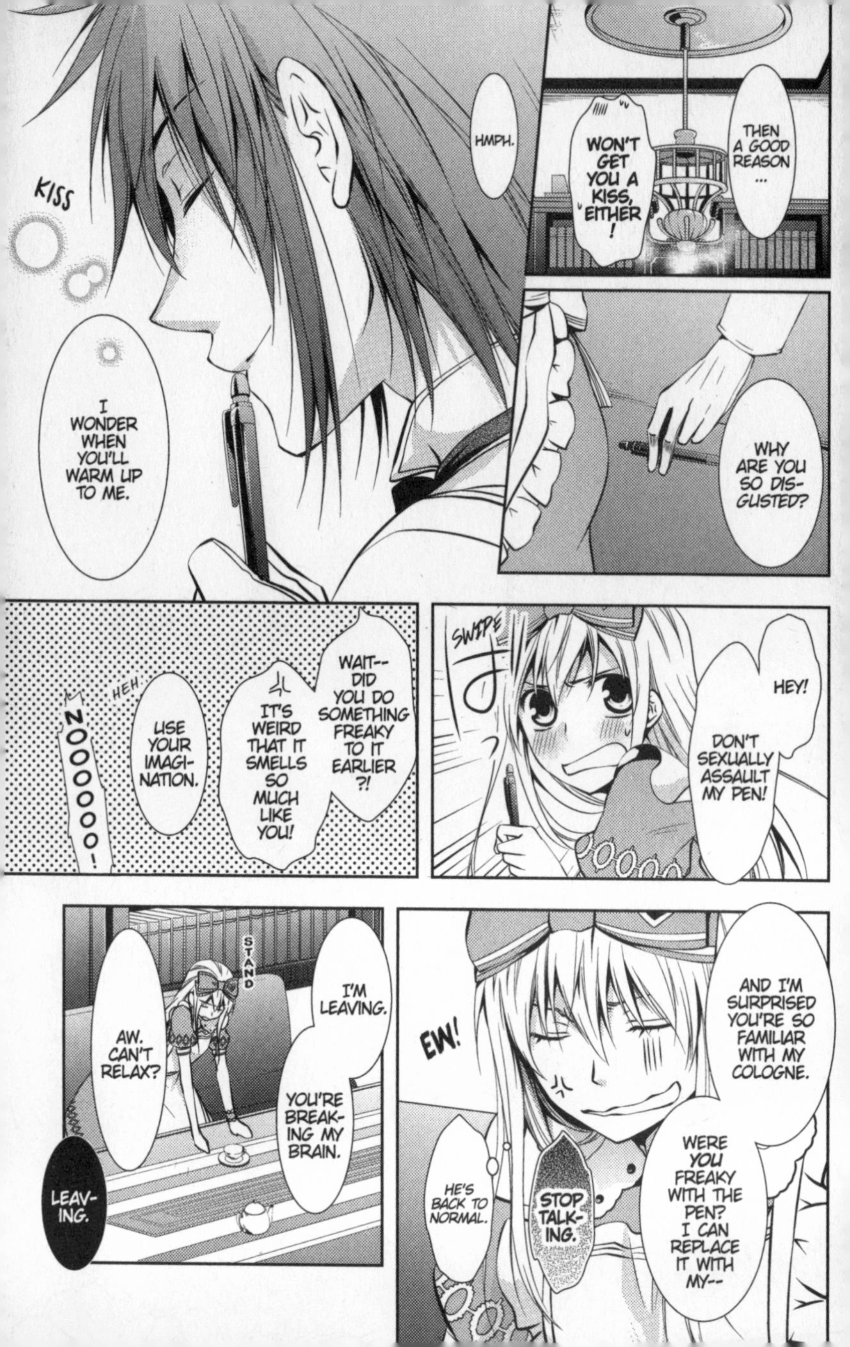
THEN A GOOD REASON ...
WON'T GET YOU A KISS, EITHER!
WHY ARE YOU SO DIS-GUSTED?
HMPH.
KISS
I WONDER WHEN YOU'LL WARM UP TO ME.
SWIPE
HEY!
DON'T SEXUALLY ASSAULT MY PEN!
WAIT--DID YOU DO SOMETHING FREAKY TO IT EARLIER?!
IT'S WEIRD THAT IT SMELLS SO MUCH LIKE YOU!
HEH.
USE YOUR IMAGI-NATION.
NOOOOOOO!
AND I'M SURPRISED YOU'RE SO FAMILIAR WITH MY COLOGNE.
EW!
WERE YOU FREAKY WITH THE PEN? I CAN REPLACE IT WITH MY--
STOP TALK-ING.
HE'S BACK TO NORMAL.
STAND
I'M LEAVING.
YOU'RE BREAK-ING MY BRAIN.
AW. CAN'T RELAX?
LEAV-ING.

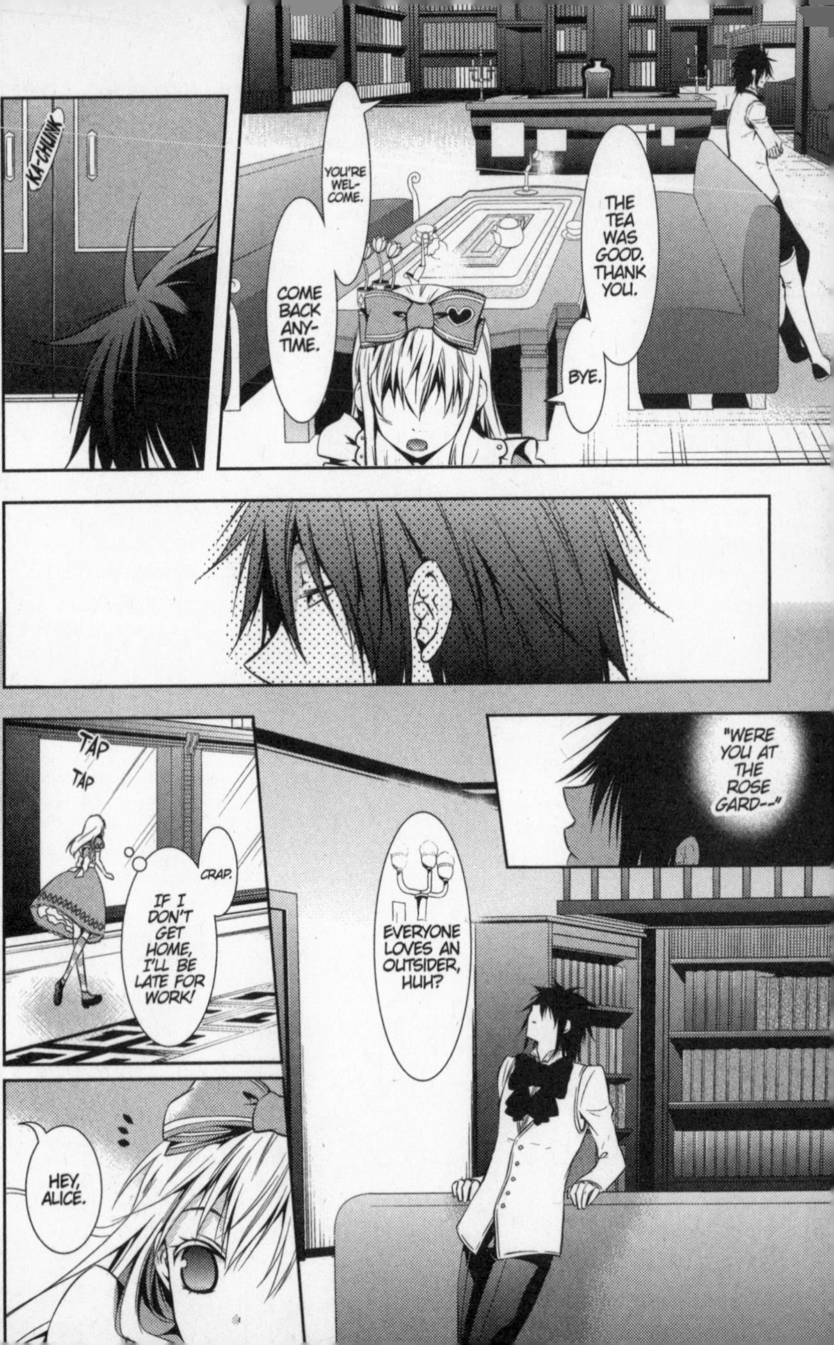
THE TEA WAS GOOD. THANK YOU.
YOU'RE WEL-COME.
BYE.
COME BACK ANY-TIME.
KA-CHUNK
"WERE YOU AT THE ROSE GARD--"
EVERYONE LOVES AN OUTSIDER, HUH?
TAP
TAP
CRAP.
IF I DON'T GET HOME, I'LL BE LATE FOR WORK!
HEY, ALICE.

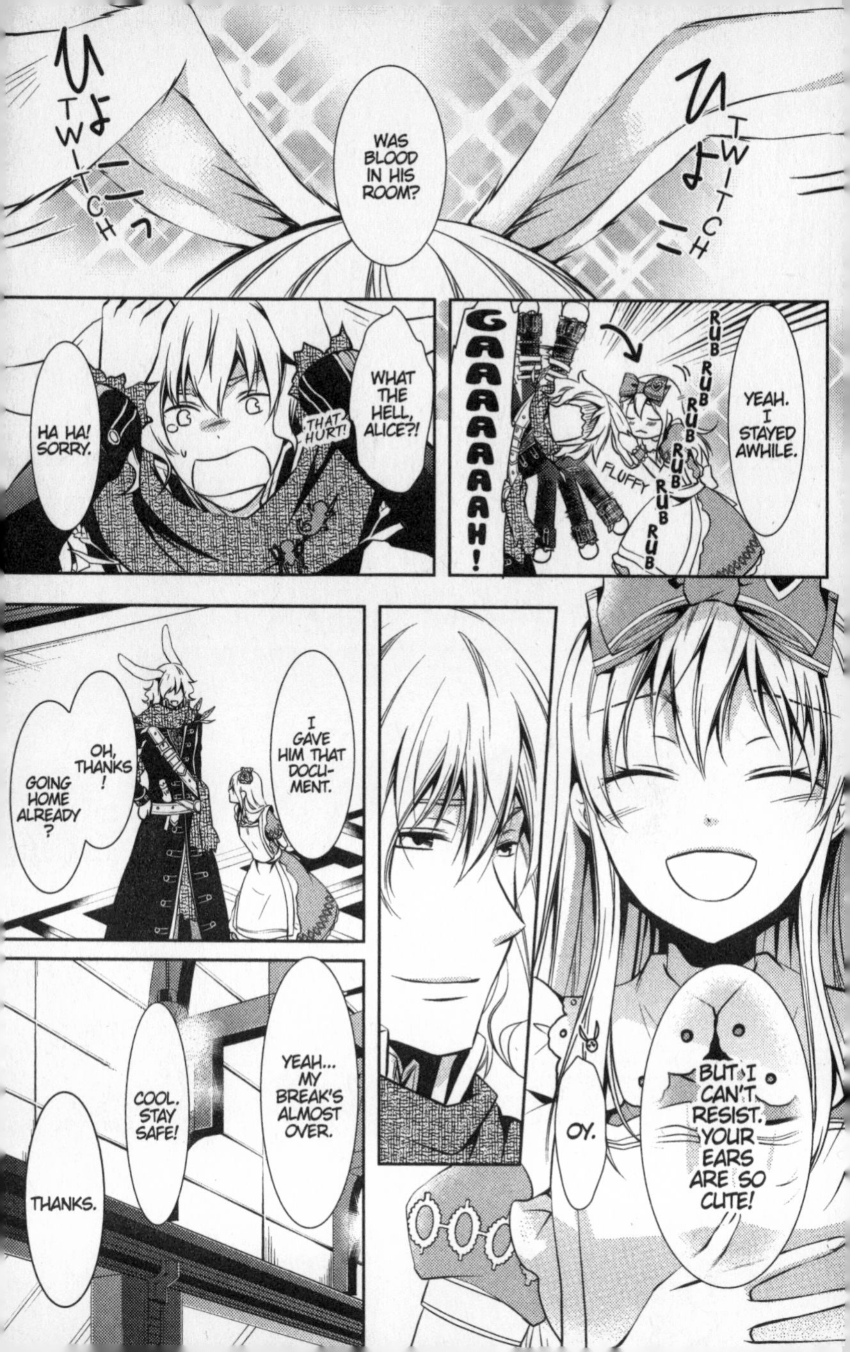
ぴょ
TWITCH
ぴょ
TWITCH
WAS BLOOD IN HIS ROOM?
YEAH. I STAYED AWHILE.
RUB RUB RUB RUB RUB RUB RUB RUB
FLUFFY
GAAAAAAAH!
WHAT THE HELL, ALICE?!
THAT HURT!
HA HA! SORRY.
BUT I CAN'T RESIST. YOUR EARS ARE SO CUTE!
OY.
I GAVE HIM THAT DOCUMENT.
OH, THANKS!
GOING HOME ALREADY?
YEAH... MY BREAK'S ALMOST OVER.
COOL. STAY SAFE!
THANKS.

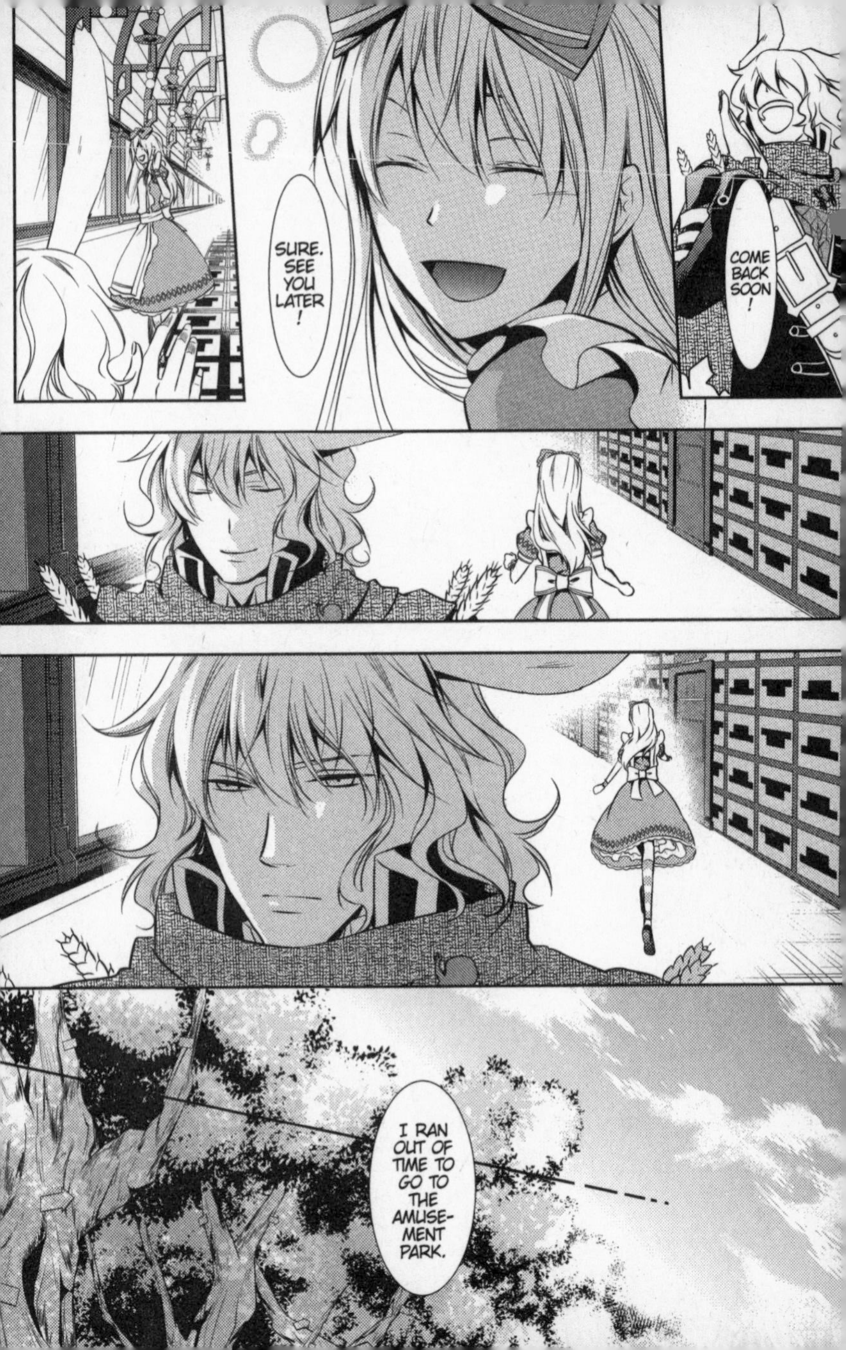
COME BACK SOON!
SURE. SEE YOU LATER!
I RAN OUT OF TIME TO GO TO THE AMUSEMENT PARK.

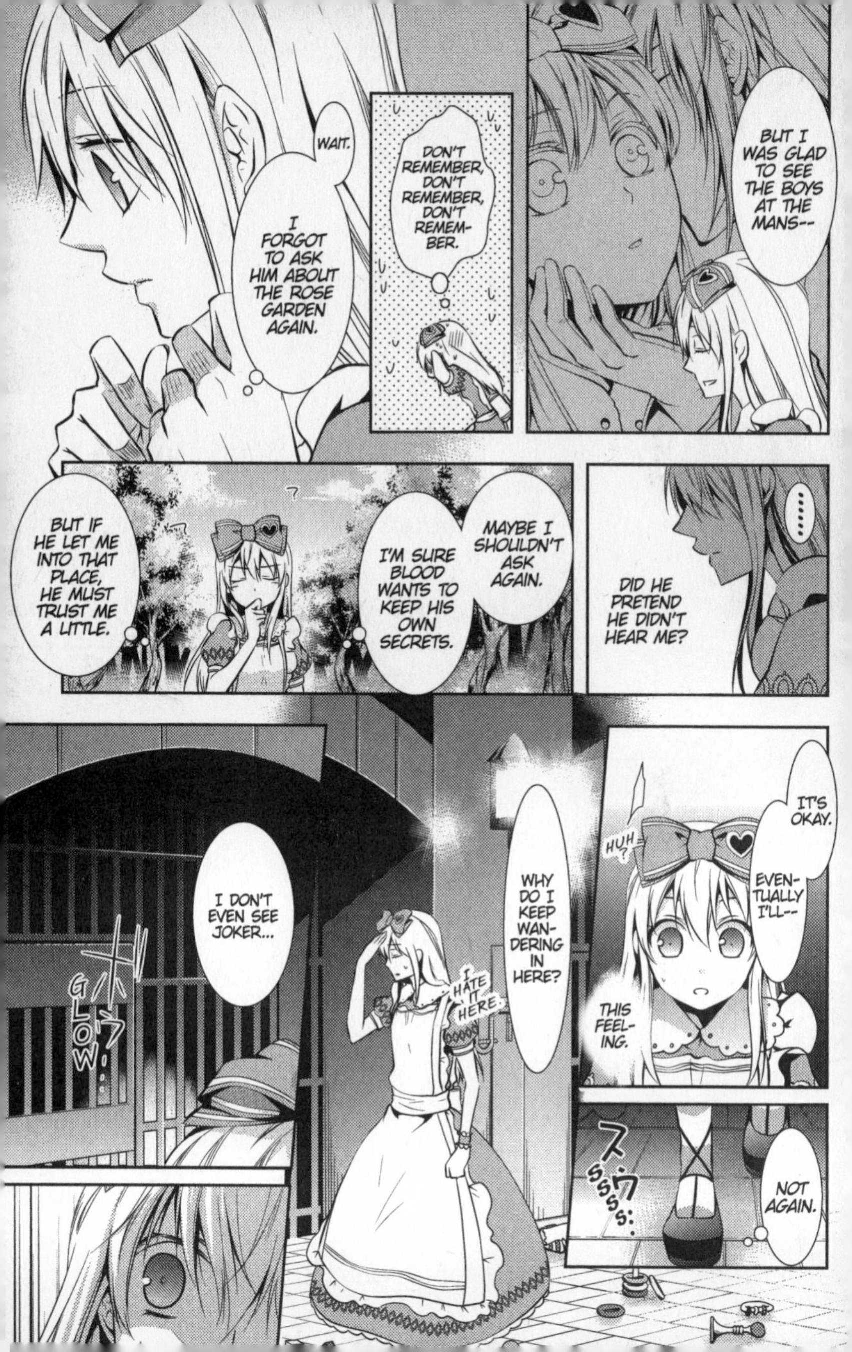
BUT I WAS GLAD TO SEE THE BOYS AT THE MANS--
DON'T REMEMBER, DON'T REMEMBER, DON'T REMEMBER.
WAIT.
I FORGOT TO ASK HIM ABOUT THE ROSE GARDEN AGAIN.
......
DID HE PRETEND HE DIDN'T HEAR ME?
MAYBE I SHOULDN'T ASK AGAIN.
I'M SURE BLOOD WANTS TO KEEP HIS OWN SECRETS.
BUT IF HE LET ME INTO THAT PLACE, HE MUST TRUST ME A LITTLE.
IT'S OKAY.
EVENTUALLY I'LL--
HUH?
THIS FEELING.
NOT AGAIN.
SSSS
WHY DO I KEEP WANDERING IN HERE?
I HATE IT HERE.
I DON'T EVEN SEE JOKER...
GLOW

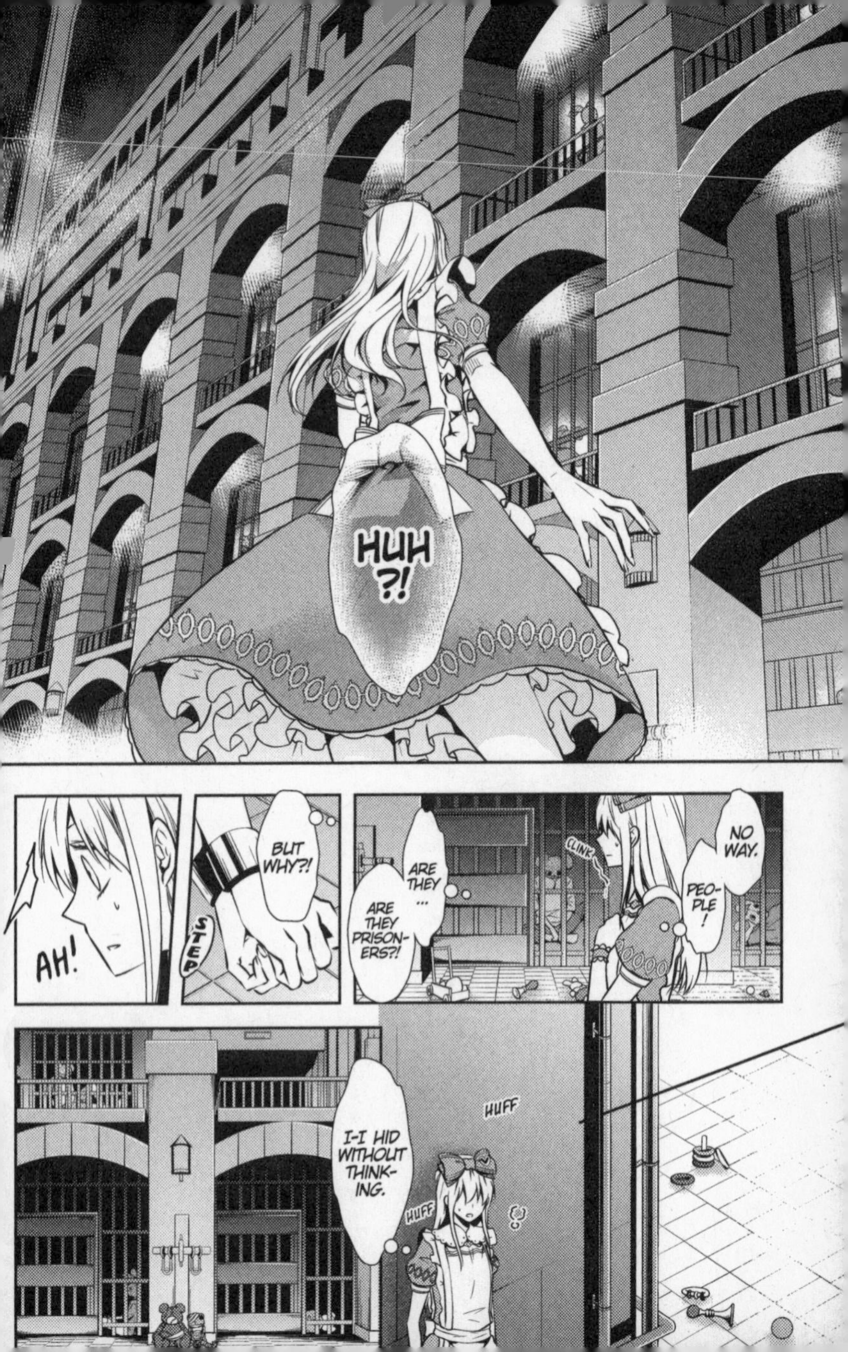
HUH ?!
NO WAY.
PEO-PLE!
CLINK
ARE THEY ...
ARE THEY PRISONERS?!
BUT WHY?!
STEP
AH!
HUFF
I-I HID WITHOUT THINK-ING.
HUFF

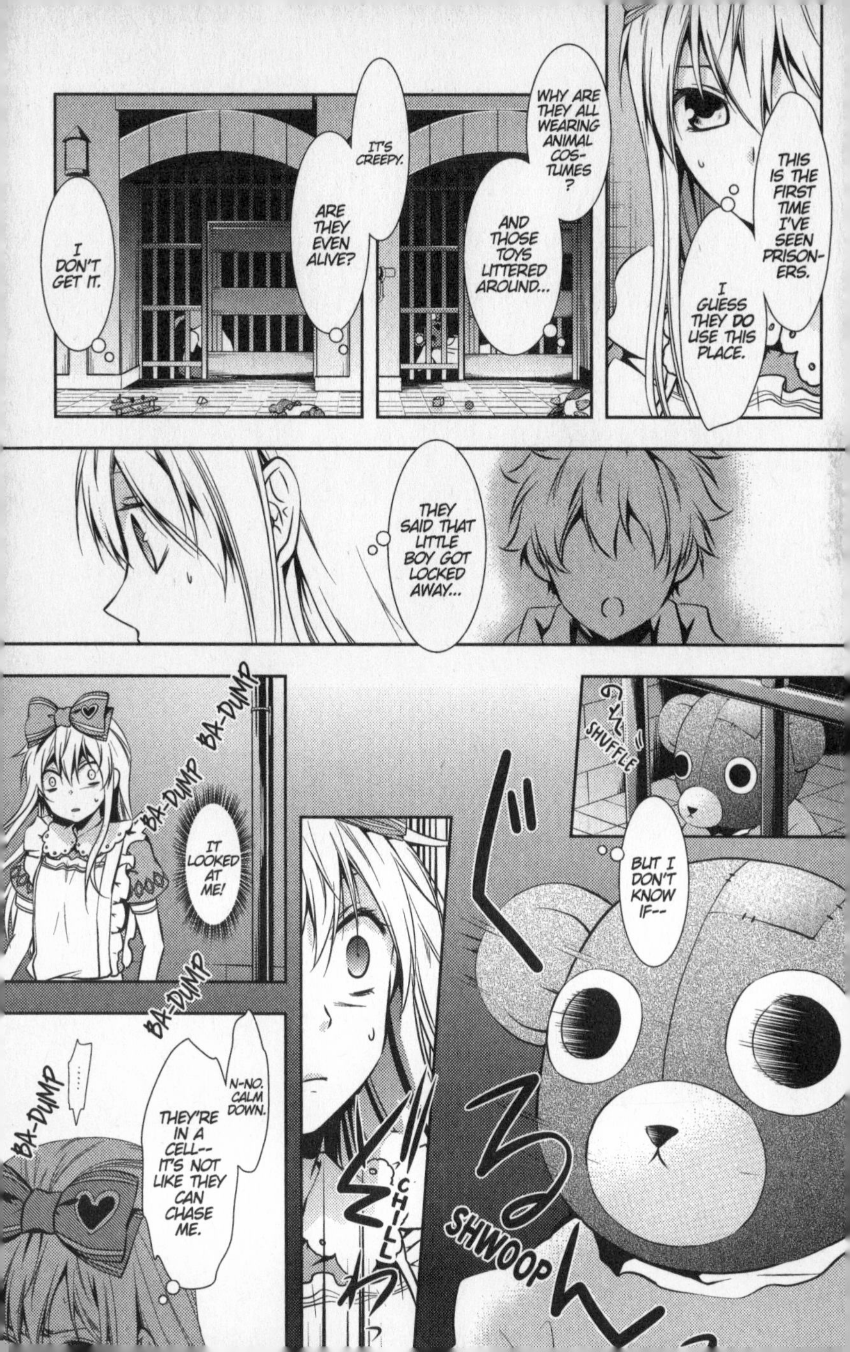
THIS IS THE FIRST TIME I'VE SEEN PRISONERS.
I GUESS THEY DO USE THIS PLACE.
WHY ARE THEY ALL WEARING ANIMAL COS-TUMES?
AND THOSE TOYS LITTERED AROUND...
IT'S CREEPY.
ARE THEY EVEN ALIVE?
I DON'T GET IT.
THEY SAID THAT LITTLE BOY GOT LOCKED AWAY...
SHUFFLE
BUT I DON'T KNOW IF--
SHWOOP
BA-DUMP
BA-DUMP
IT LOOKED AT ME!
BA-DUMP
CHILL
N-NO. CALM DOWN.
THEY'RE IN A CELL-- IT'S NOT LIKE THEY CAN CHASE ME.
BA-DUMP
......

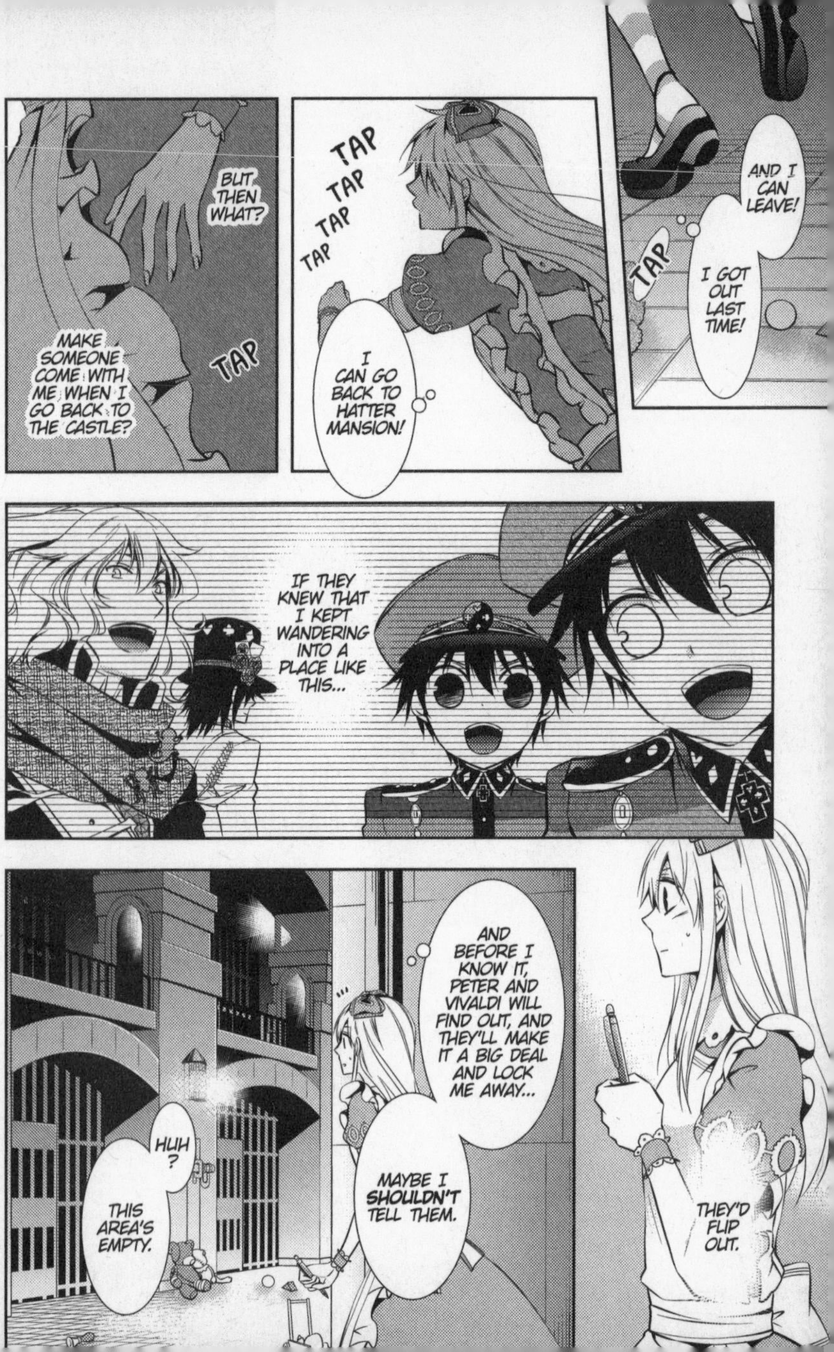
AND I CAN LEAVE!
I GOT OUT LAST TIME!
TAP
TAP
TAP
TAP
TAP
I CAN GO BACK TO HATTER MANSION!
BUT THEN WHAT?
TAP
MAKE SOMEONE COME WITH ME WHEN I GO BACK TO THE CASTLE?
IF THEY KNEW THAT I KEPT WANDERING INTO A PLACE LIKE THIS...
AND BEFORE I KNOW IT, PETER AND VIVALDI WILL FIND OUT, AND THEY'LL MAKE IT A BIG DEAL AND LOCK ME AWAY...
THEY'D FLIP OUT.
...
MAYBE I SHOULDN'T TELL THEM.
HUH?
THIS AREA'S EMPTY.

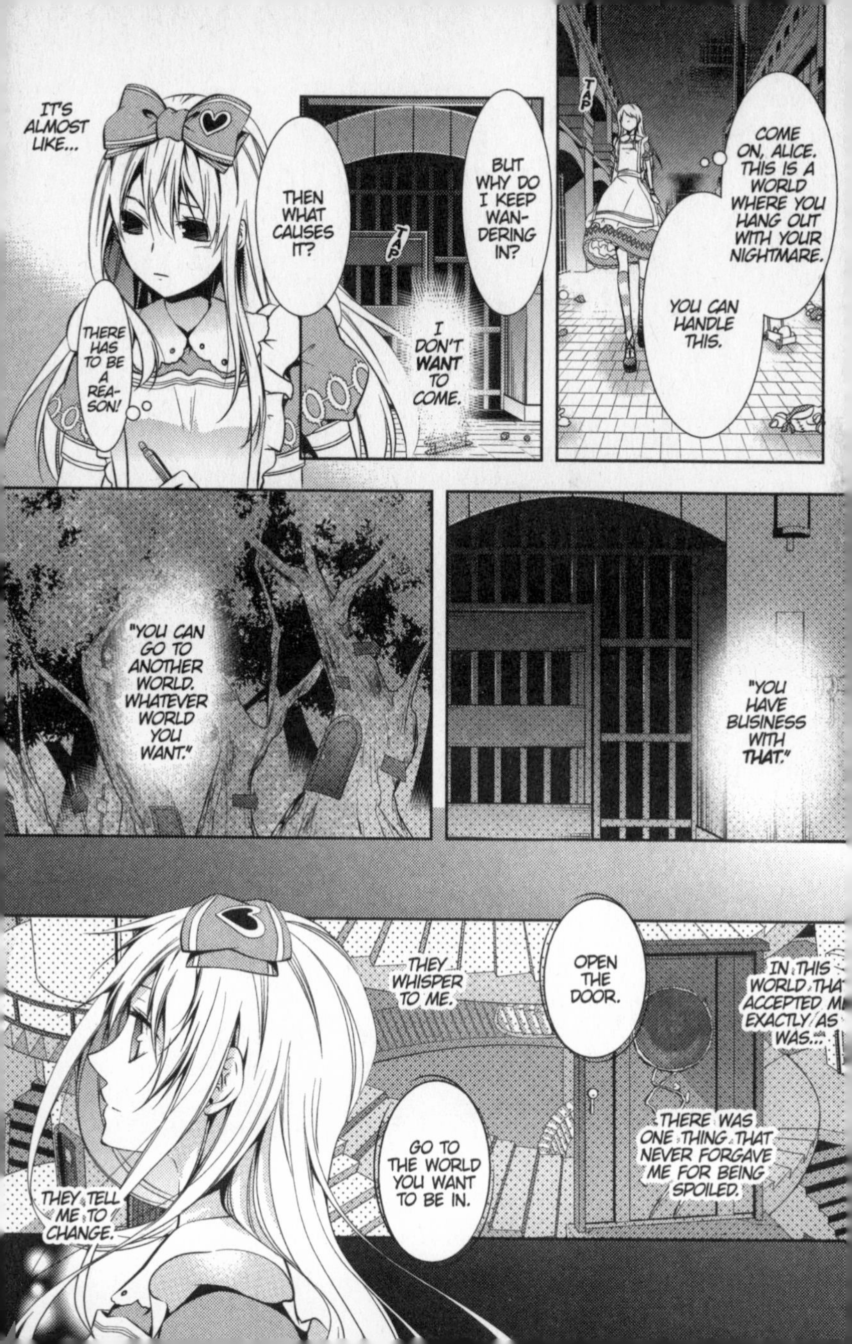
TAP
TAP
COME ON, ALICE. THIS IS A WORLD WHERE YOU HANG OUT WITH YOUR NIGHTMARE.
YOU CAN HANDLE THIS.
BUT WHY DO I KEEP WAN-DERING IN?
TAP
THEN WHAT CAUSES IT?
I DON'T WANT TO COME.
IT'S ALMOST LIKE...
THERE HAS TO BE A REA-SON!
"YOU HAVE BUSINESS WITH THAT."
"YOU CAN GO TO ANOTHER WORLD. WHATEVER WORLD YOU WANT."
IN THIS WORLD THAT ACCEPTED M EXACTLY AS WAS...
THERE WAS ONE THING THAT NEVER FORGAVE ME FOR BEING SPOILED.
OPEN THE DOOR.
GO TO THE WORLD YOU WANT TO BE IN.
THEY WHISPER TO ME.
THEY TELL ME TO CHANGE.

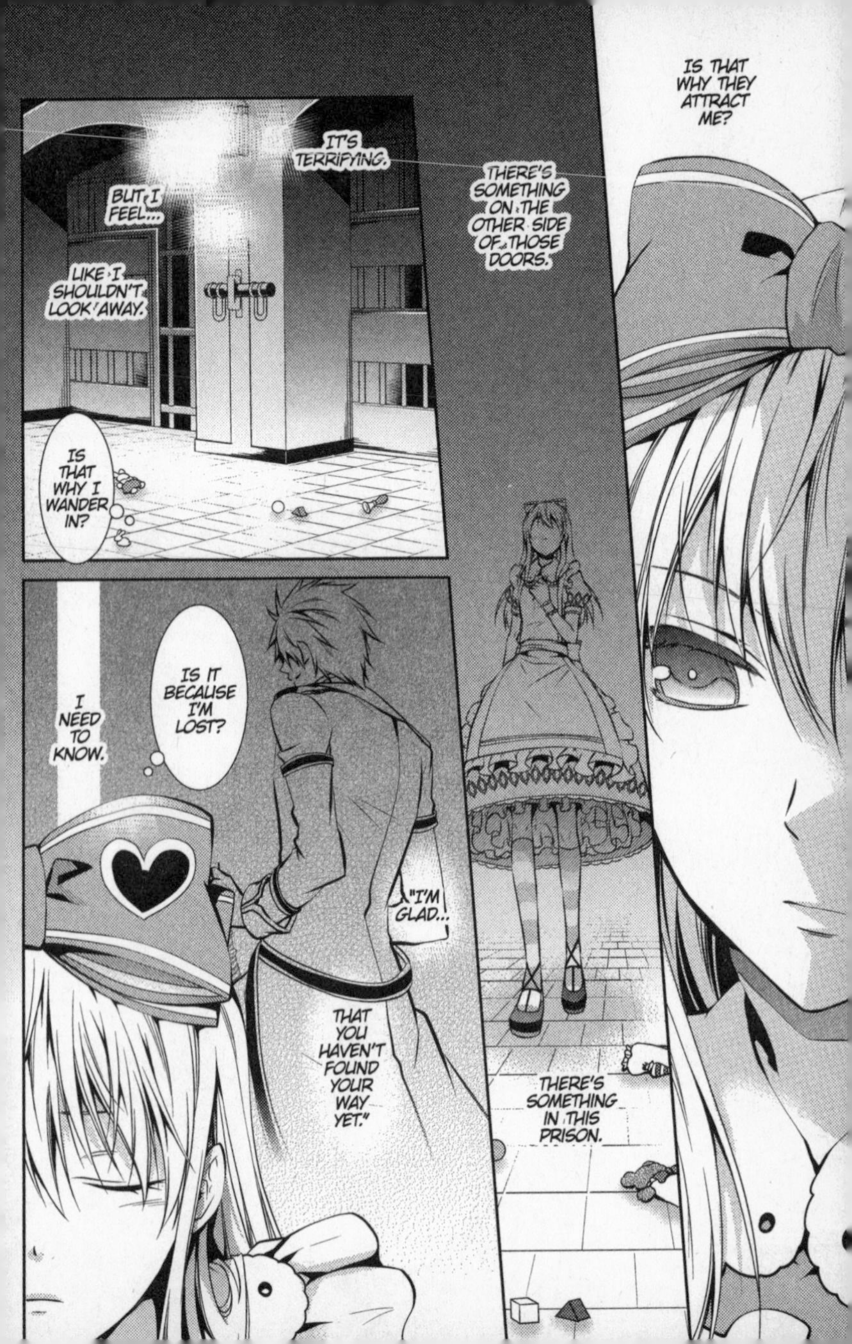
IS THAT WHY THEY ATTRACT ME?
THERE'S SOMETHING ON THE OTHER SIDE OF THOSE DOORS.
IT'S TERRIFYING.
BUT I FEEL...
LIKE I SHOULDN'T LOOK AWAY.
IS THAT WHY I WANDER IN?
THERE'S SOMETHING IN THIS PRISON.
"I'M GLAD...
THAT YOU HAVEN'T FOUND YOUR WAY YET."
IS IT BECAUSE I'M LOST?
I NEED TO KNOW.

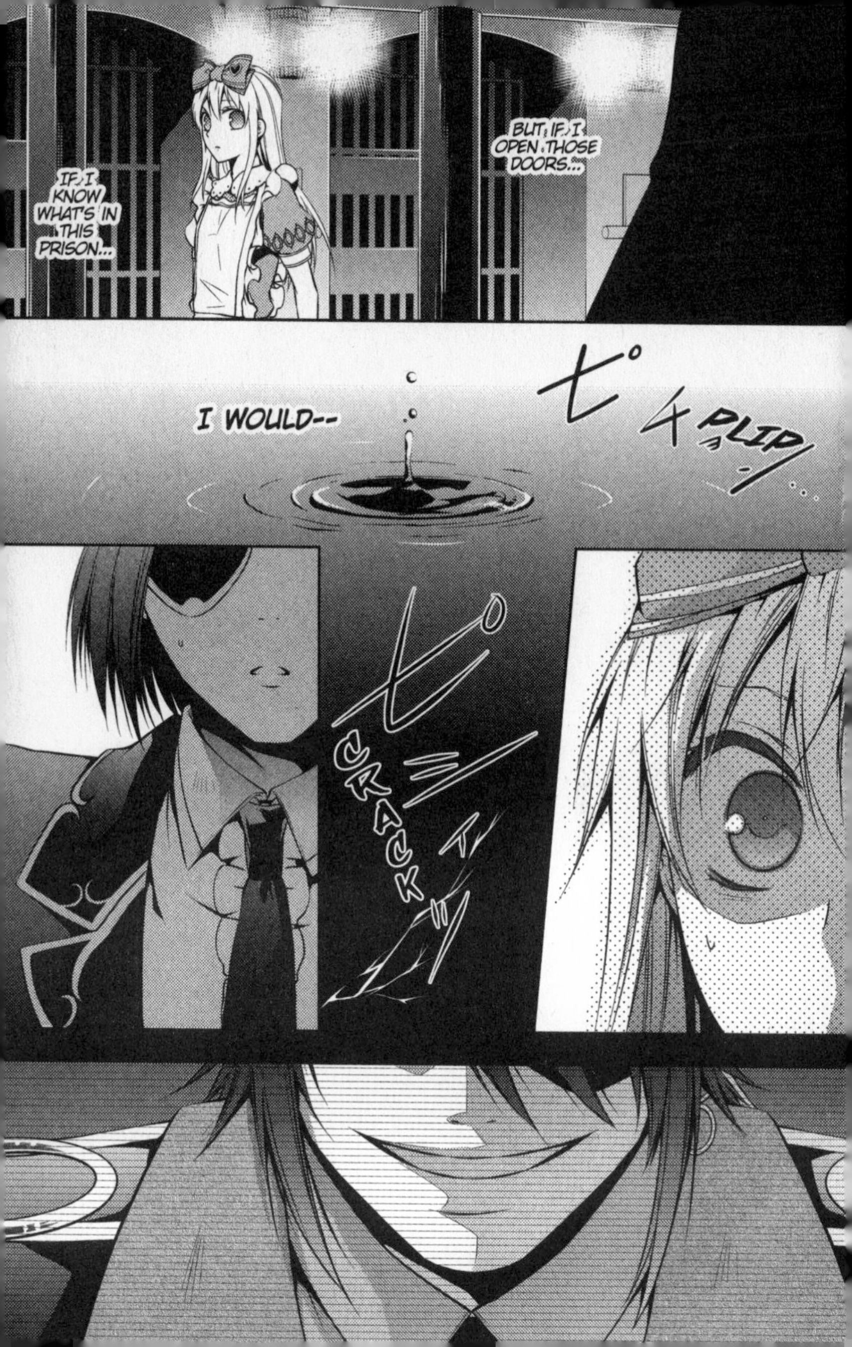
IF I KNOW WHAT'S IN THIS PRISON...
BUT IF I OPEN THOSE DOORS...
I WOULD--
PLIP...
CRACK!!

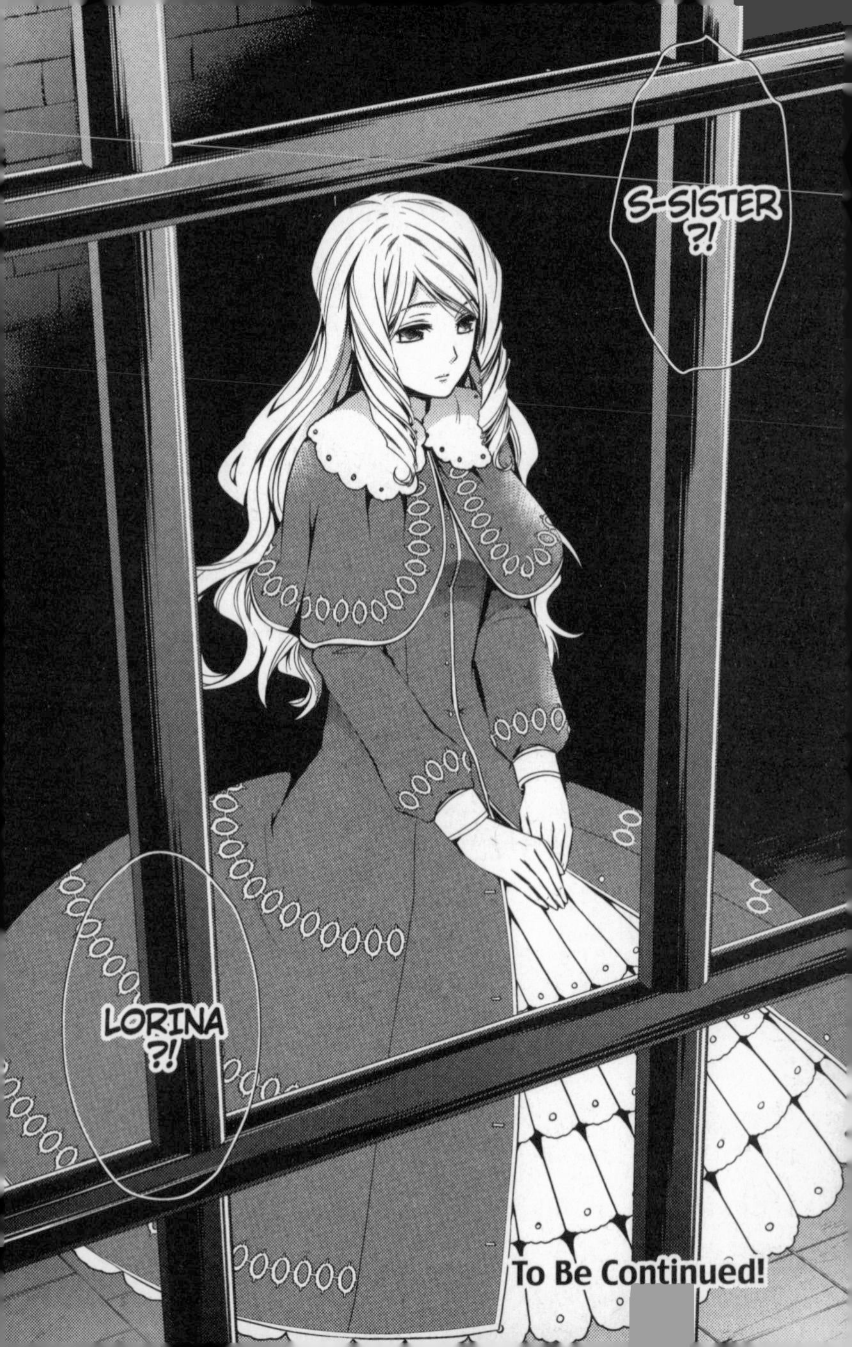
S-SISTER ?!
LORINA ?!
To Be Continued!

THANK YOU VERY MUCH!

Everyone who helped with the script:

My friends & family
QuinRose-sama
The publisher

And most importantly, the readers!

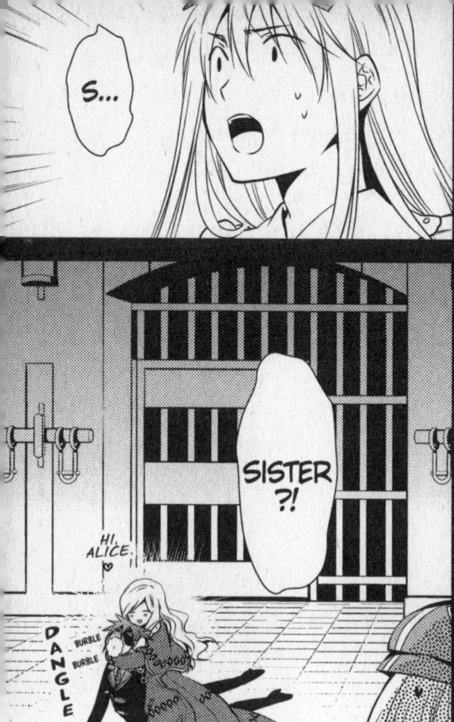
S...
SISTER ?!
HI, ALICE. ♡
DANGLE
BURBLE BURBLE

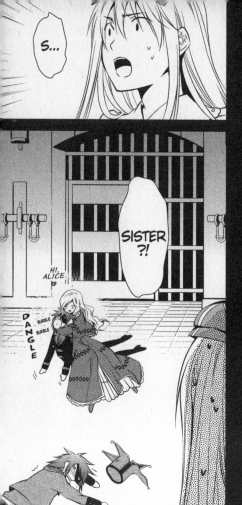

The Final Boss Has Appeared!

WHAT IF ALICE WAS SMALL? – THE SAGA CONTINUES!

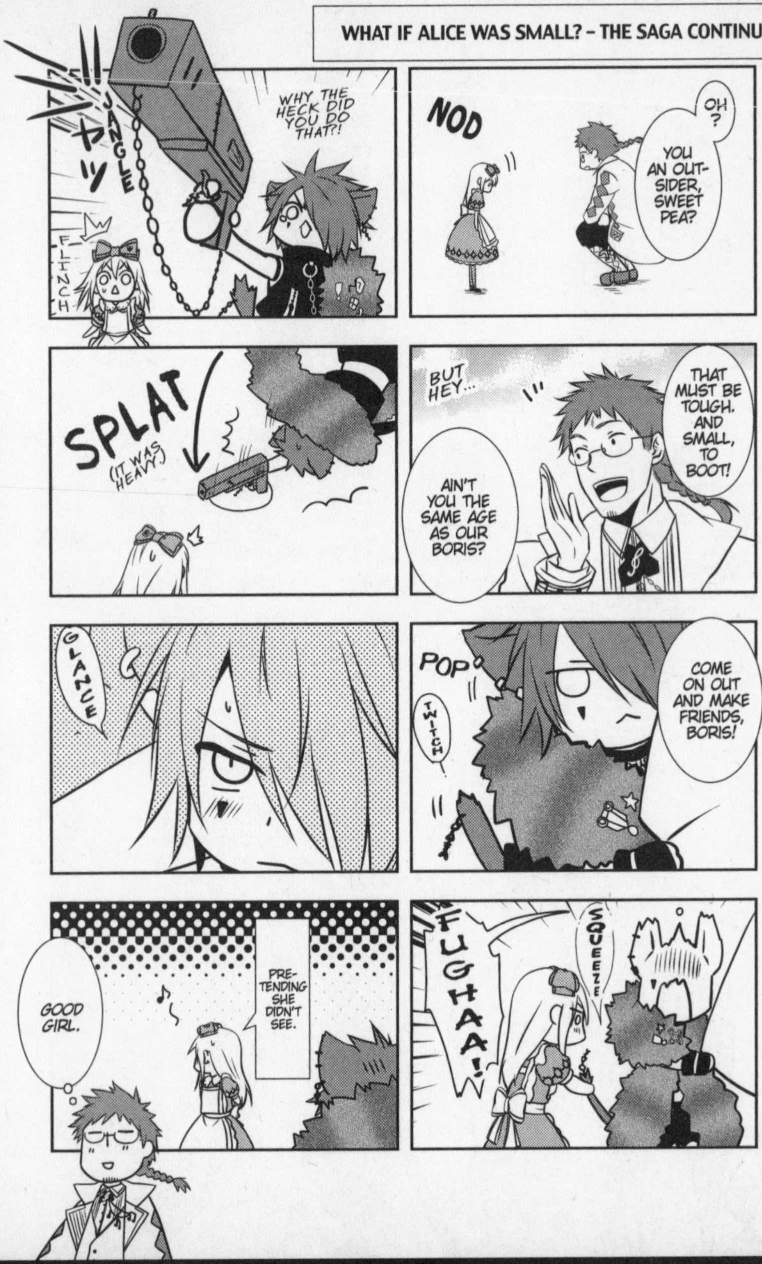
NOD
OH?
YOU AN OUT-SIDER, SWEET PEA?
ヤッ
JANGLE
WHY THE HECK DID YOU DO THAT?!
FLINCH
BUT HEY...
THAT MUST BE TOUGH. AND SMALL, TO BOOT!
AIN'T YOU THE SAME AGE AS OUR BORIS?
SPLAT
(IT WAS HEAVY.)
POP
COME ON OUT AND MAKE FRIENDS, BORIS!
TWITCH
GLANCE
FUGHAA!
SQUEEZE
PRE-TENDING SHE DIDN'T SEE.
GOOD GIRL.

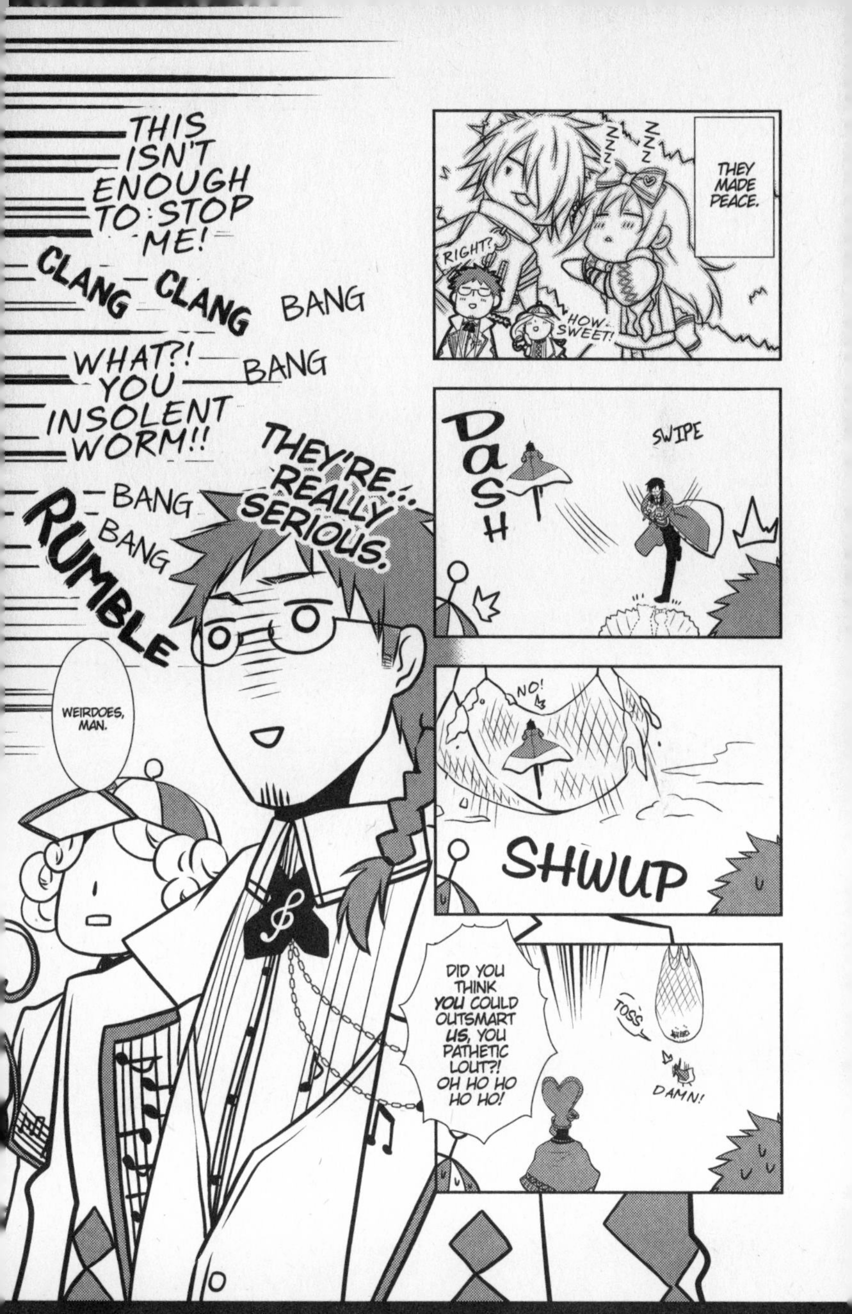
THEY MADE PEACE.
RIGHT?
HOW SWEET!
SWIPE
DASH
NO!
SHWUP
TOSS
DID YOU THINK YOU COULD OUTSMART US, YOU PATHETIC LOUT?! OH HO HO HO HO!
DAMN!
THIS ISN'T ENOUGH TO STOP ME!
BANG
CLANG CLANG
BANG
WHAT?! YOU INSOLENT WORM!!
THEY'RE... REALLY SERIOUS.
BANG
BANG
RUMBLE
WEIRDOES, MAN.

COMING SOON

NOVEMBER 2013
Alice in the Country of Clover:
Cheshire Cat Waltz Vol. 7

DECEMBER 2013
Alice Love Fables: Toy Box

Crimson Empire Vol. 3

JANUARY 2014
Alice in the Country of Hearts:
The Mad Hatter's Late Night
Tea Party Vol. 2

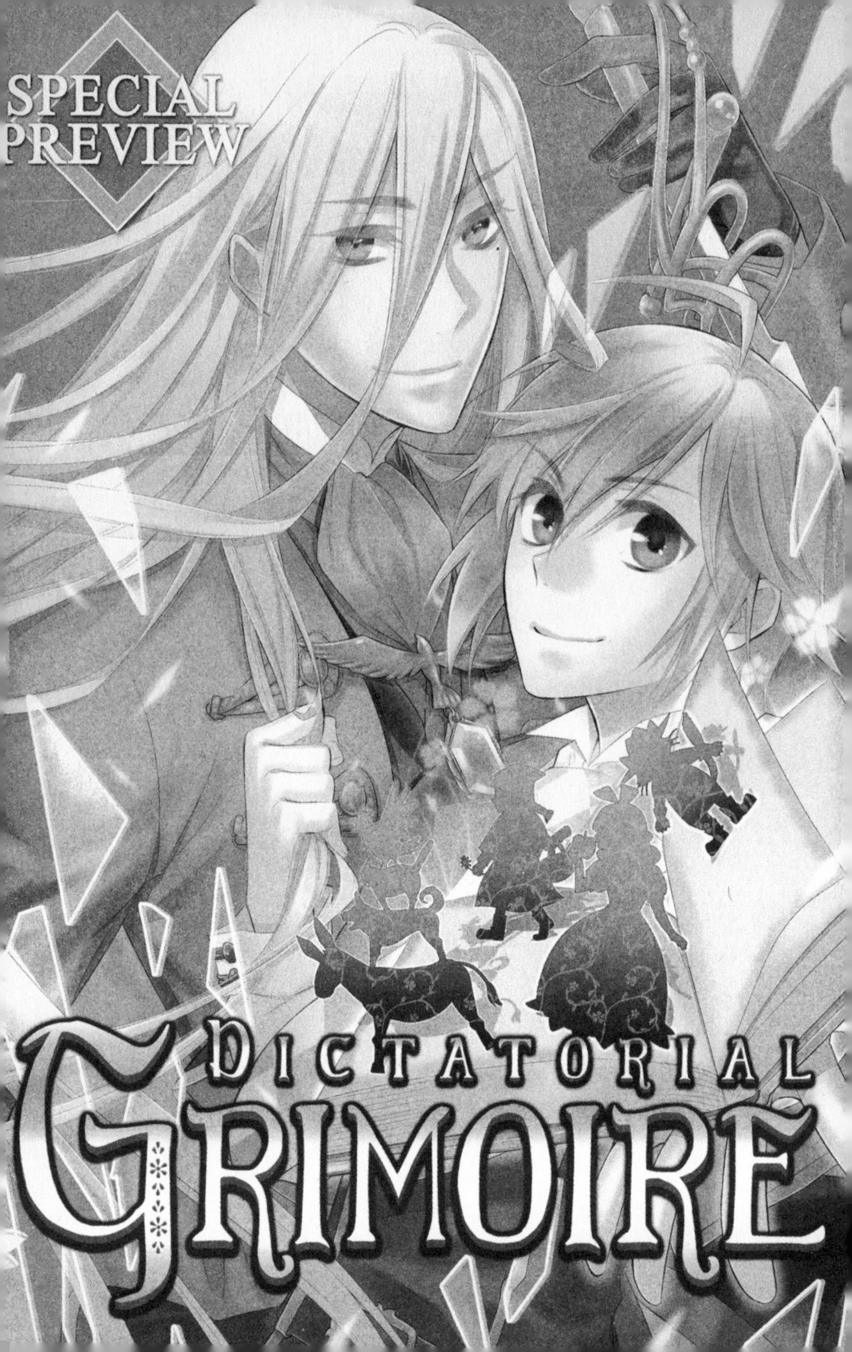
SPECIAL PREVIEW
DICTATORIAL GRIMOIRE

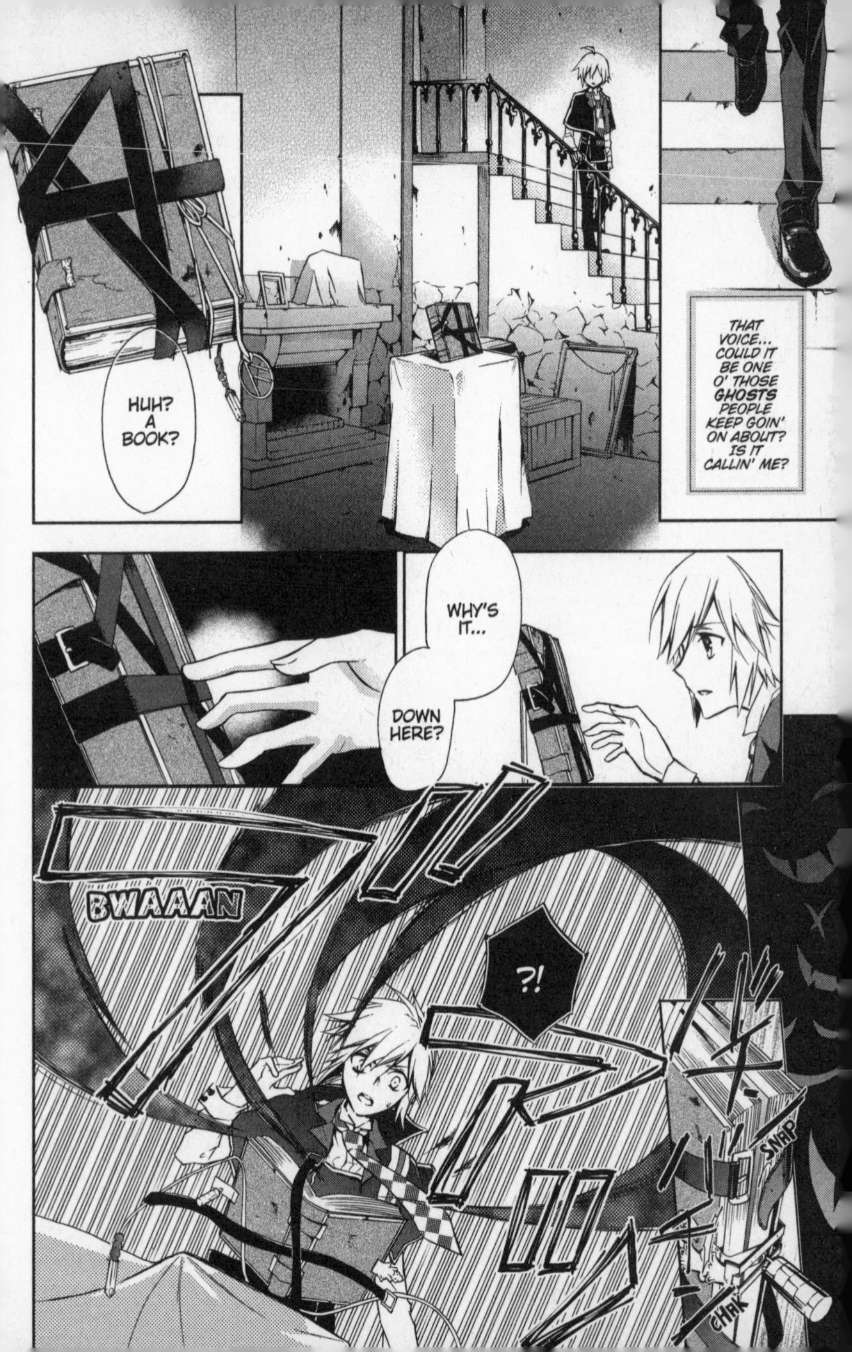
THAT VOICE... COULD IT BE ONE O' THOSE GHOSTS PEOPLE KEEP GOIN' ON ABOUT? IS IT CALLIN' ME?
HUH? A BOOK?
WHY'S IT...
DOWN HERE?
?!
BWAAAN
SNAP
CHAK

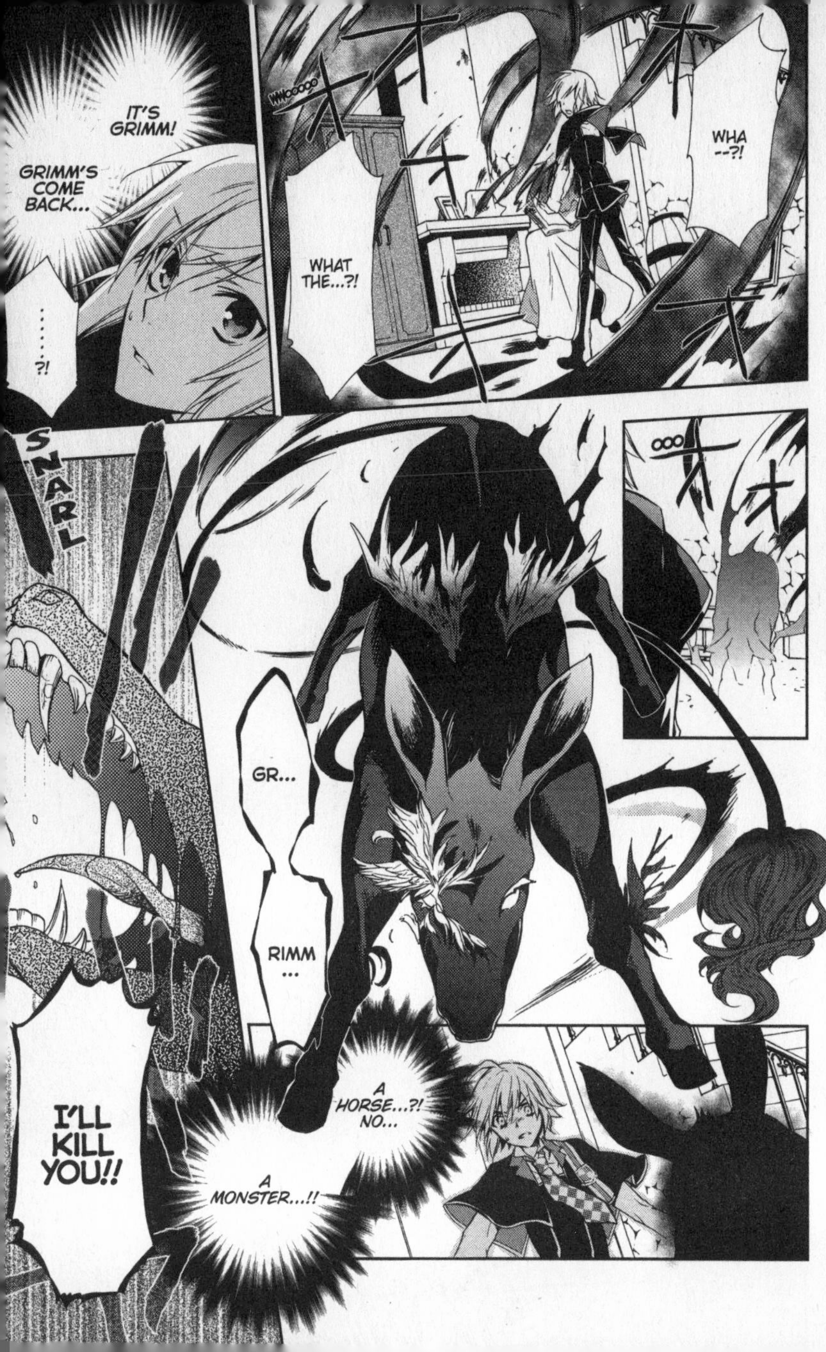
WHA --?!
WHOOOOO
WHAT THE...?!
IT'S GRIMM!
GRIMM'S COME BACK...
......?!
OOO
GR...
RIMM ...
A HORSE...?! NO...
A MONSTER...!!
SNARL
I'LL KILL YOU!!

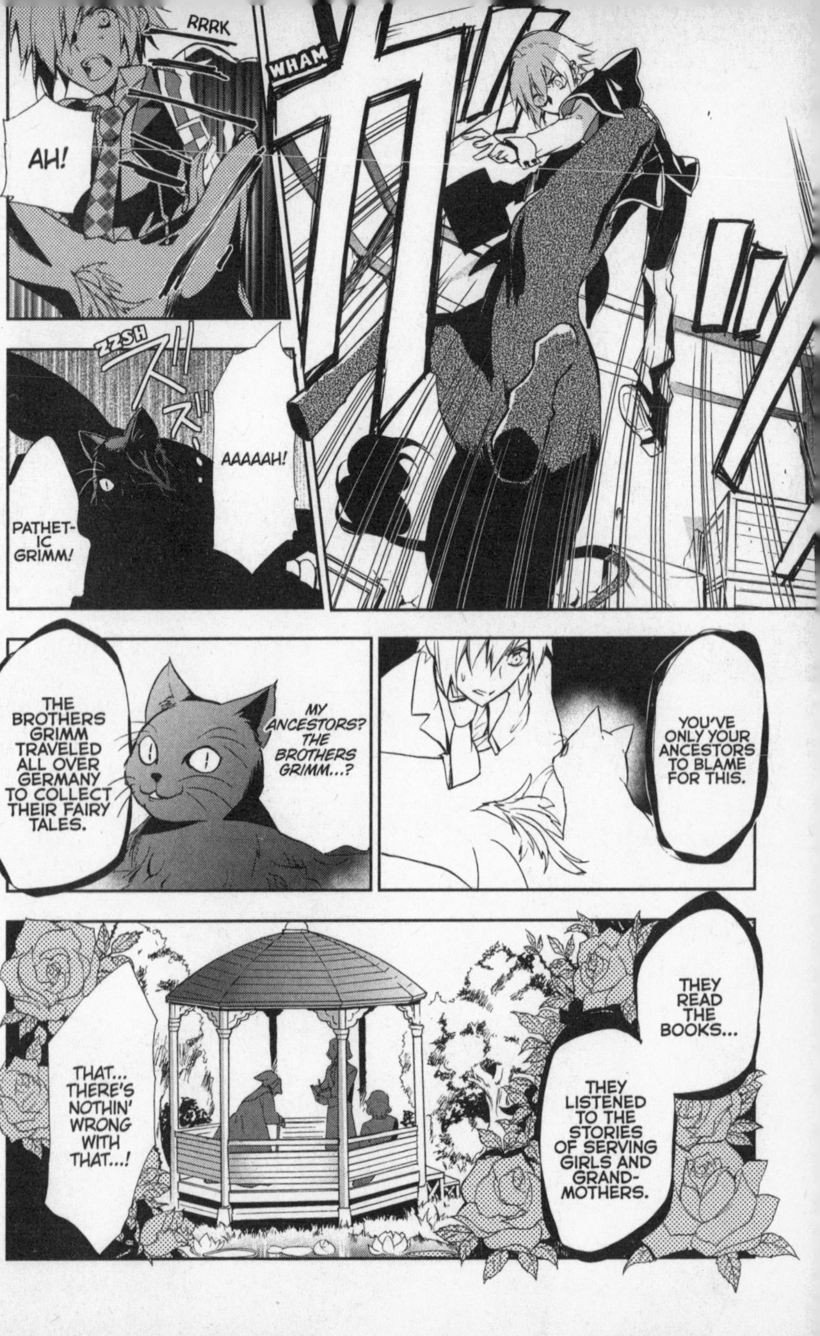
WHAM
RRRK
AH!
ZZSH
AAAAAH!
PATHETIC GRIMM!
YOU'VE ONLY YOUR ANCESTORS TO BLAME FOR THIS.
MY ANCESTORS? THE BROTHERS GRIMM...?
THE BROTHERS GRIMM TRAVELED ALL OVER GERMANY TO COLLECT THEIR FAIRY TALES.
THEY READ THE BOOKS...
THEY LISTENED TO THE STORIES OF SERVING GIRLS AND GRAND-MOTHERS.
THAT... THERE'S NOTHIN' WRONG WITH THAT...!

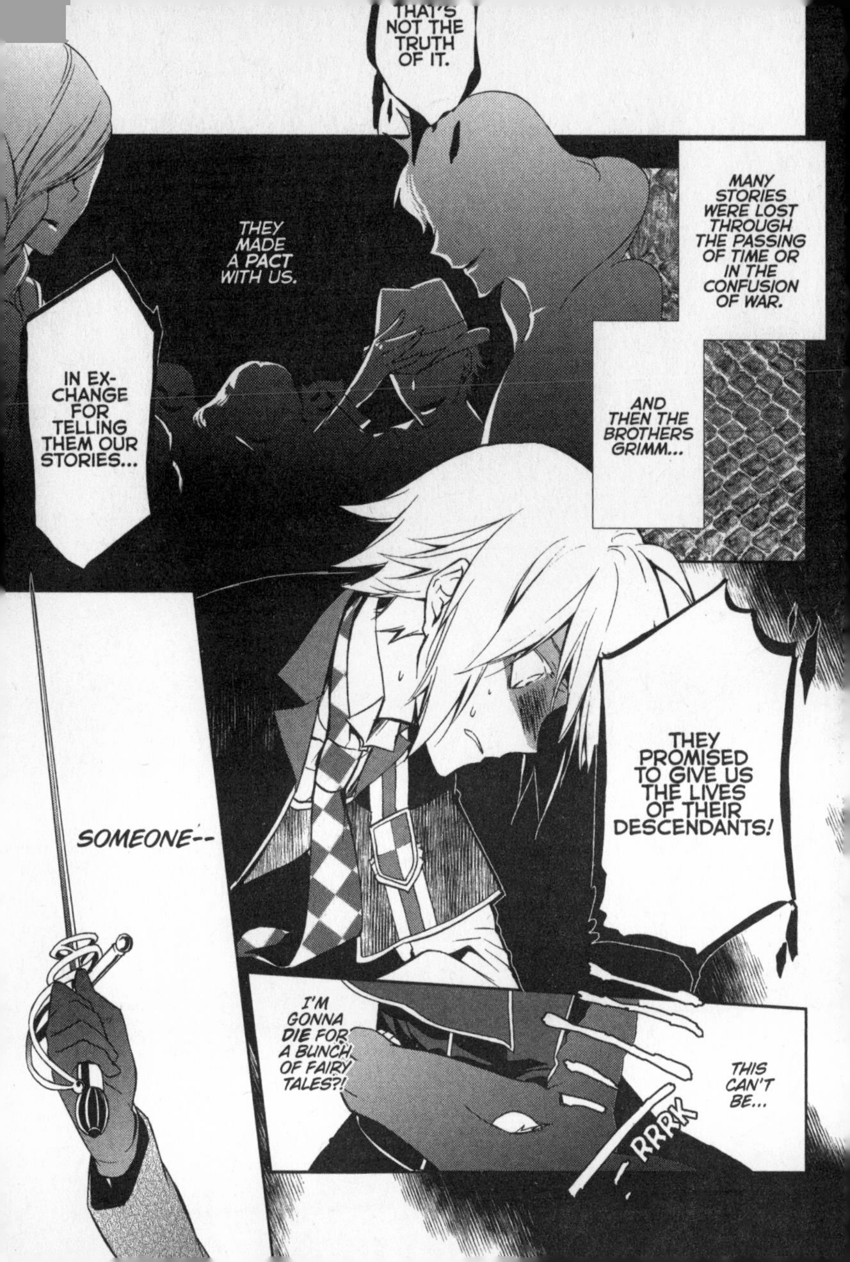
THAT'S NOT THE TRUTH OF IT.
MANY STORIES WERE LOST THROUGH THE PASSING OF TIME OR IN THE CONFUSION OF WAR.
AND THEN THE BROTHERS GRIMM...
THEY MADE A PACT WITH US.
IN EX-CHANGE FOR TELLING THEM OUR STORIES...
THEY PROMISED TO GIVE US THE LIVES OF THEIR DESCENDANTS!
THIS CAN'T BE...
I'M GONNA DIE FOR A BUNCH OF FAIRY TALES?!
RRRK
SOMEONE--

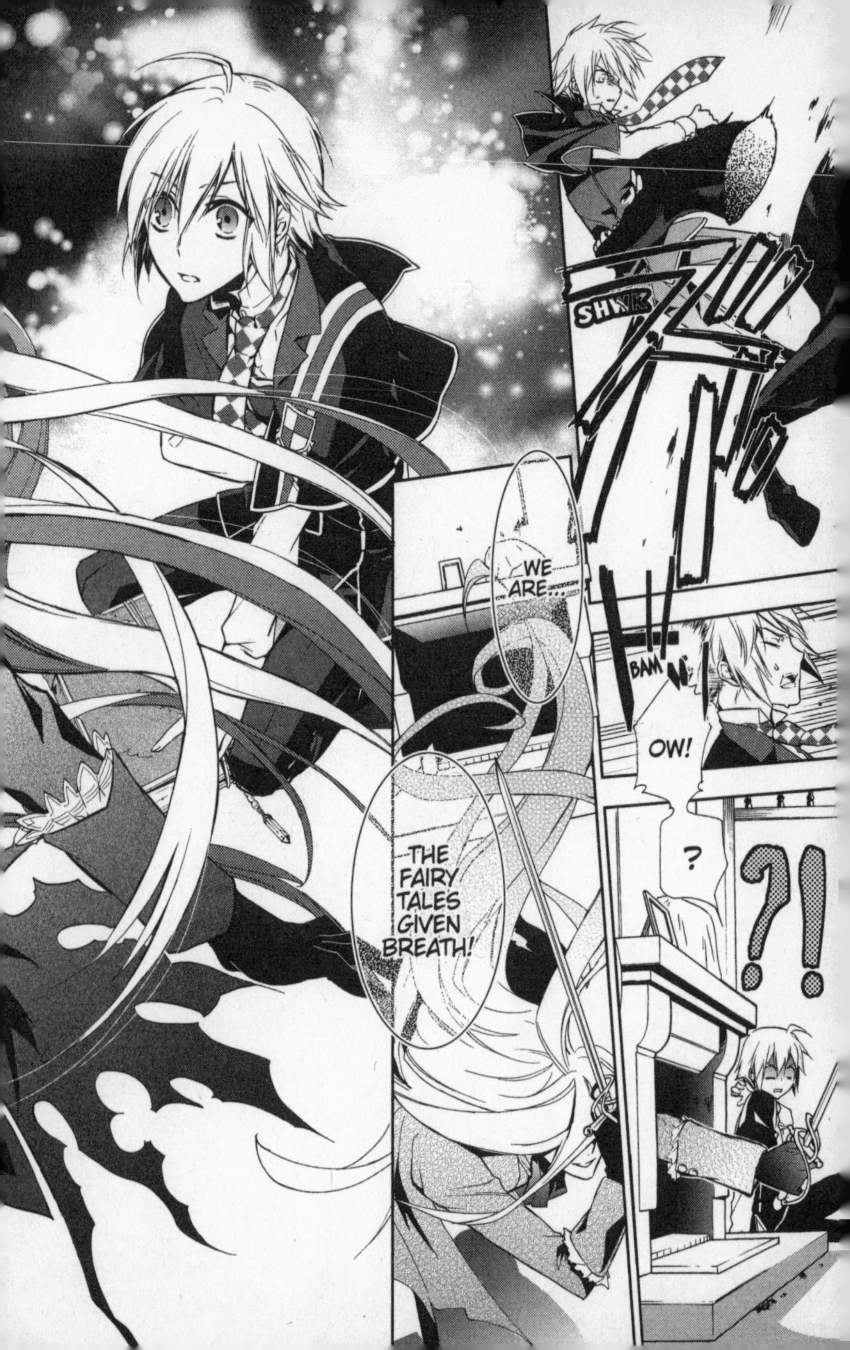
SHWK
BAM
OW!
?
?!
WE ARE...
THE FAIRY TALES GIVEN BREATH!

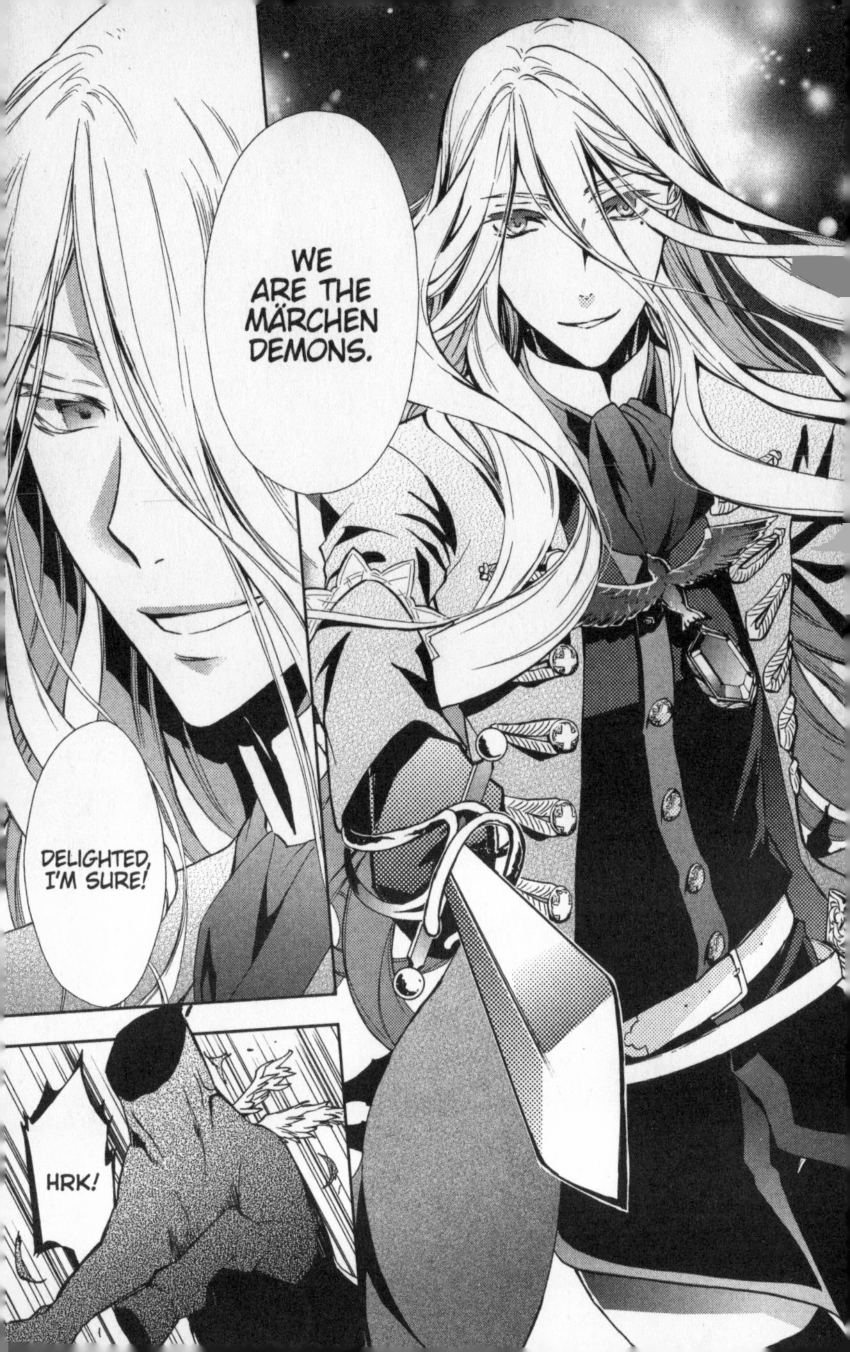
WE ARE THE MÄRCHEN DEMONS.
DELIGHTED, I'M SURE!
HRK!

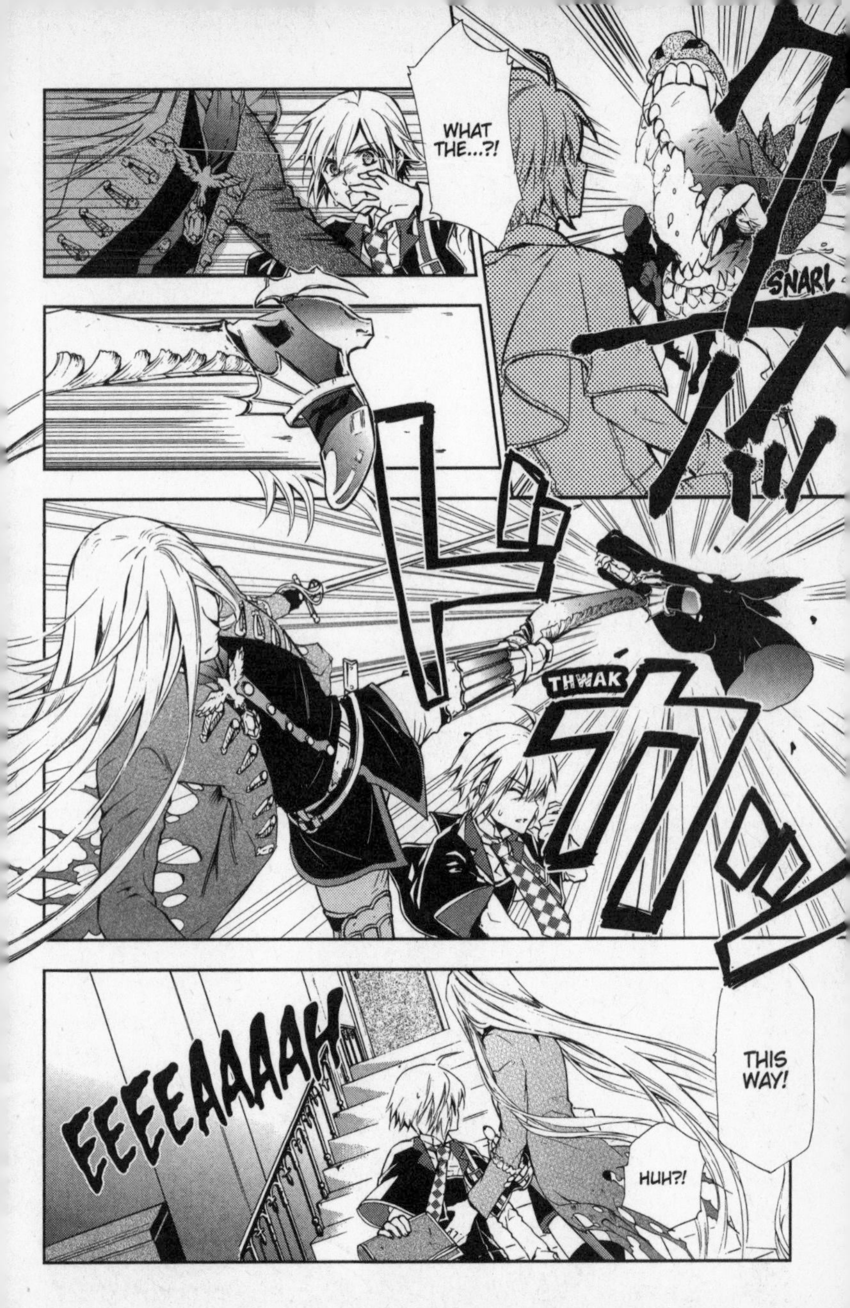
SNARL
WHAT THE...?!
THWAK
THIS WAY!
EEEEAAAAH
HUH?!

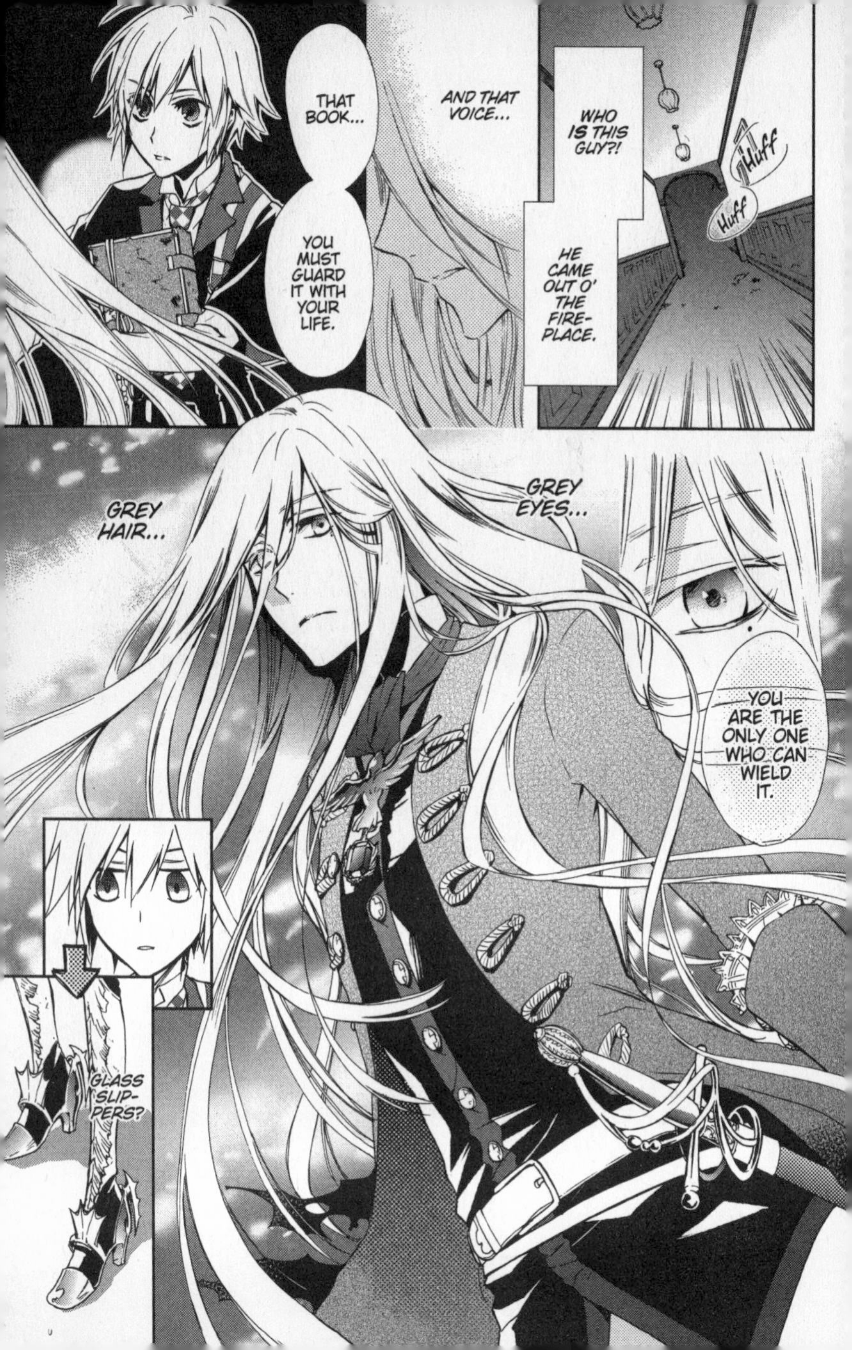
WHO IS THIS GUY?!
Huff
Huff
HE CAME OUT O' THE FIRE-PLACE.
AND THAT VOICE...
THAT BOOK...
YOU MUST GUARD IT WITH YOUR LIFE.
GREY EYES...
YOU ARE THE ONLY ONE WHO CAN WIELD IT.
GREY HAIR...
GLASS SLIPPERS?

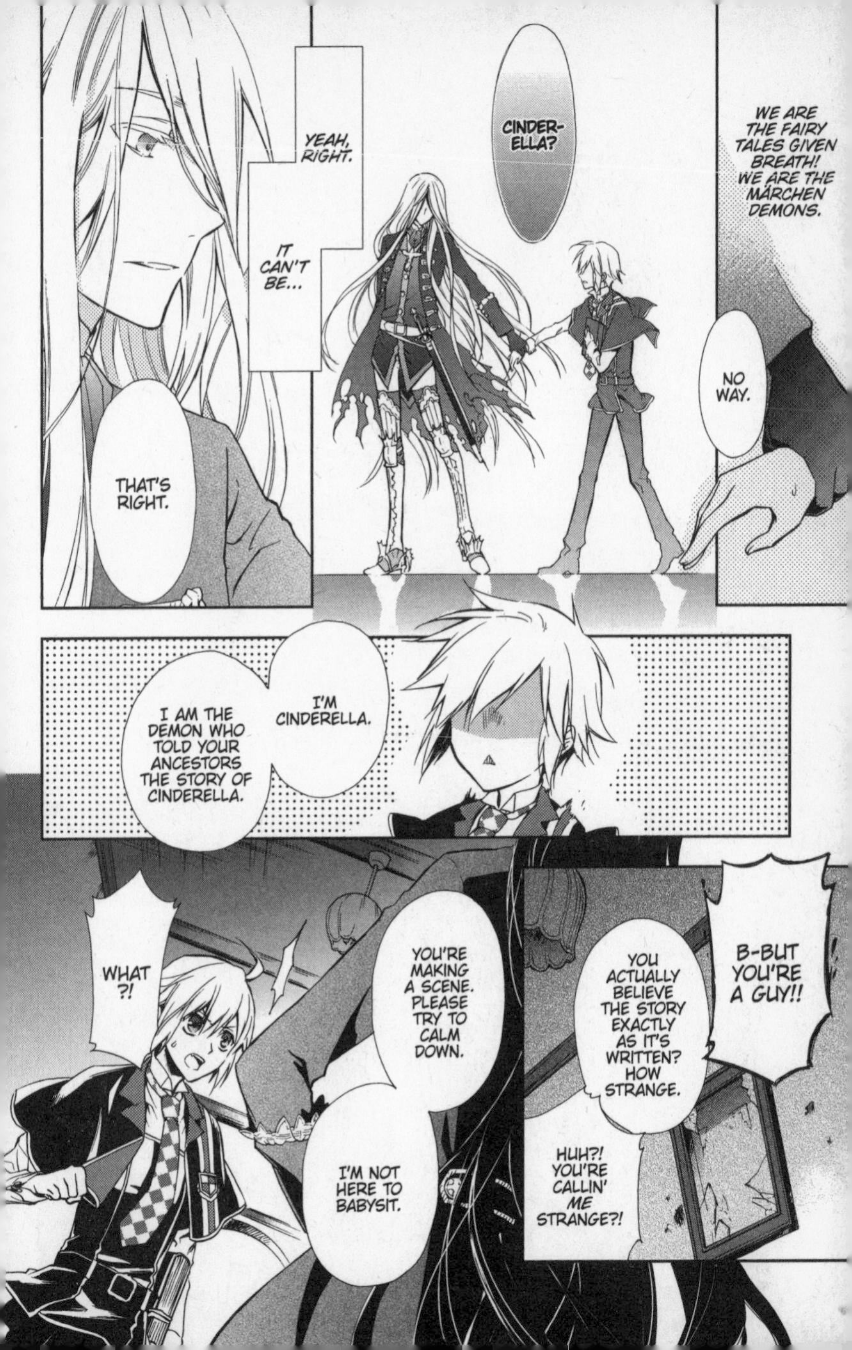
WE ARE THE FAIRY TALES GIVEN BREATH! WE ARE THE MÄRCHEN DEMONS.
NO WAY.
CINDER-ELLA?
YEAH, RIGHT.
IT CAN'T BE...
THAT'S RIGHT.
I'M CINDERELLA.
I AM THE DEMON WHO TOLD YOUR ANCESTORS THE STORY OF CINDERELLA.
B-BUT YOU'RE A GUY!!
YOU ACTUALLY BELIEVE THE STORY EXACTLY AS IT'S WRITTEN? HOW STRANGE.
HUH?! YOU'RE CALLIN' ME STRANGE?!
YOU'RE MAKING A SCENE. PLEASE TRY TO CALM DOWN.
WHAT?!
I'M NOT HERE TO BABYSIT.

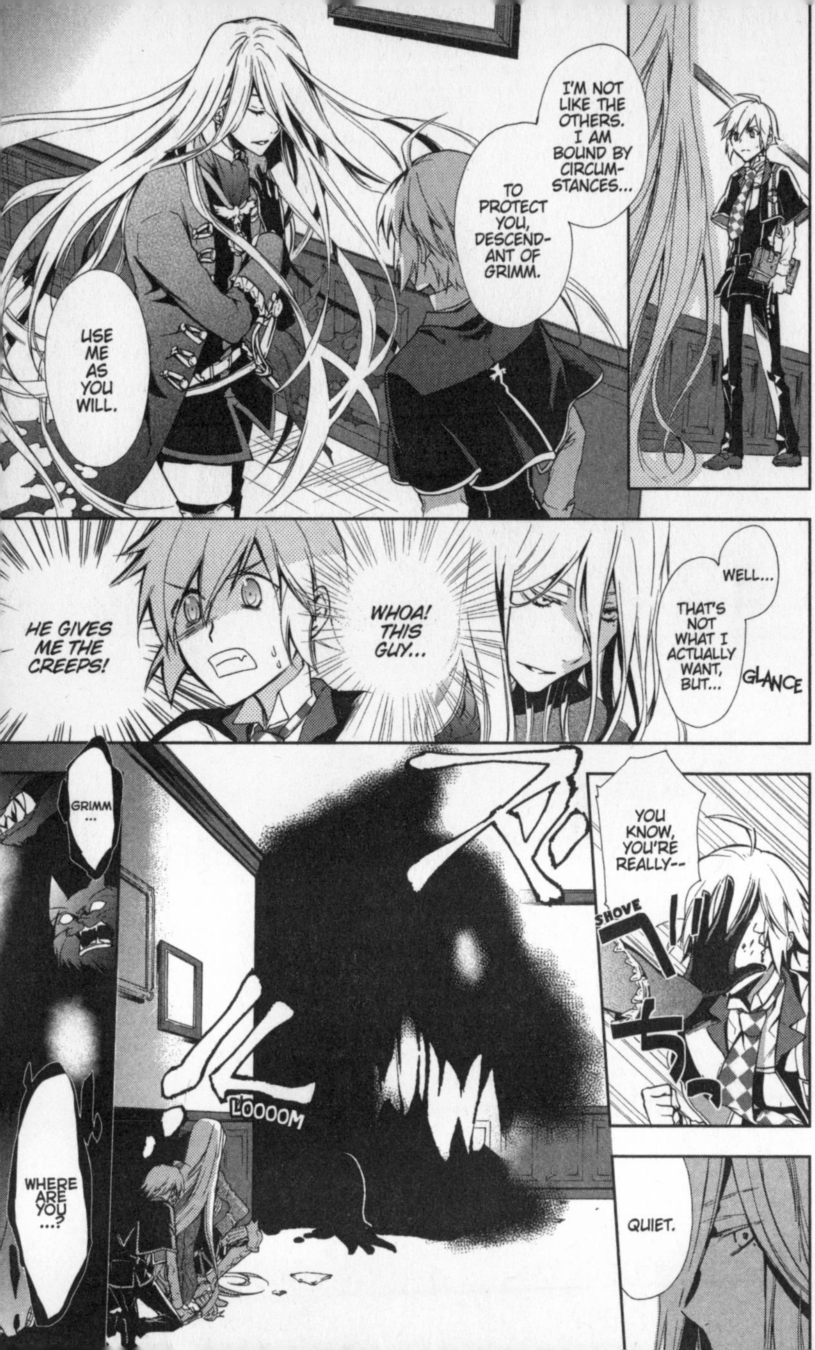
I'M NOT LIKE THE OTHERS. I AM BOUND BY CIRCUM-STANCES...
TO PROTECT YOU, DESCEND-ANT OF GRIMM.
USE ME AS YOU WILL.
WELL...
THAT'S NOT WHAT I ACTUALLY WANT, BUT...
GLANCE
WHOA! THIS GUY...
HE GIVES ME THE CREEPS!
YOU KNOW, YOU'RE REALLY--
SHOVE
QUIET.
LOOOOM
GRIMM...
WHERE ARE YOU...?

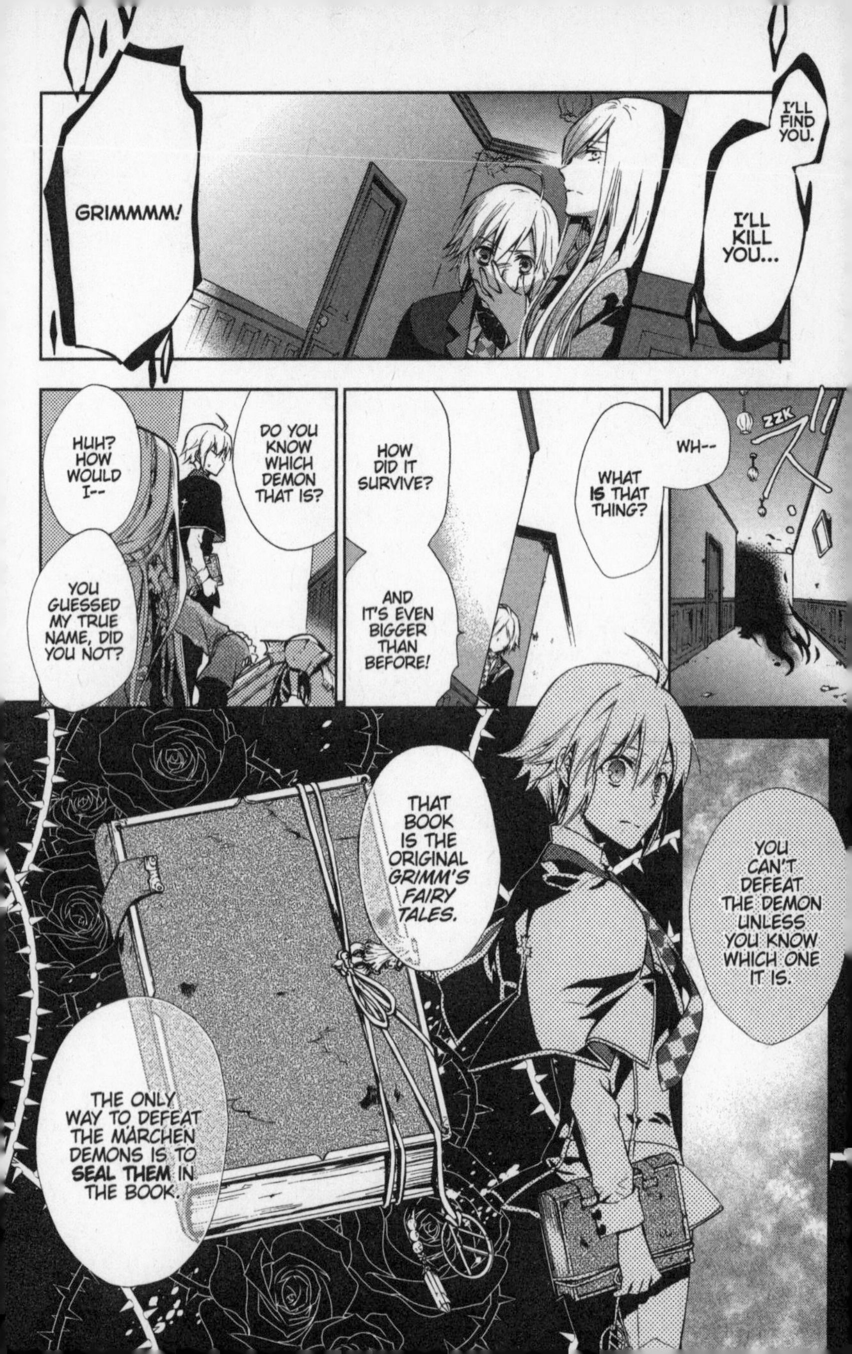
I'LL FIND YOU.
I'LL KILL YOU...
GRIMMMM!
ZZK
WH--
WHAT IS THAT THING?
HOW DID IT SURVIVE?
AND IT'S EVEN BIGGER THAN BEFORE!
DO YOU KNOW WHICH DEMON THAT IS?
HUH? HOW WOULD I--
YOU GUESSED MY TRUE NAME, DID YOU NOT?
YOU CAN'T DEFEAT THE DEMON UNLESS YOU KNOW WHICH ONE IT IS.
THAT BOOK IS THE ORIGINAL GRIMM'S FAIRY TALES.
THE ONLY WAY TO DEFEAT THE MÄRCHEN DEMONS IS TO SEAL THEM IN THE BOOK.